Critical Debates and Developments in Child Protection

Critical Debates and Developments in Child Protection

Editor

Nigel Parton

MDPI • Basel • Beijing • Wuhan • Barcelona • Belgrade • Manchester • Tokyo • Cluj • Tianjin

MDPI

Editor
Nigel Parton
University of Huddersfield
UK

Editorial Office
MDPI
St. Alban-Anlage 66
4052 Basel, Switzerland

This is a reprint of articles from the Special Issue published online in the open access journal *Social Sciences* (ISSN 2076-0760) (available at: https://www.mdpi.com/journal/socsci/special_issues/critical_debates_and_developments_in_child_protection).

For citation purposes, cite each article independently as indicated on the article page online and as indicated below:

LastName, A.A.; LastName, B.B.; LastName, C.C. Article Title. *Journal Name* **Year**, *Article Number*, Page Range.

ISBN 978-3-03936-601-9 (Hbk)
ISBN 978-3-03936-602-6 (PDF)

Contents

About the Editor

Nigel Parton, originally a social worker, he has been writing and researching about child protection for over forty years. He is the author, co-author and editor of 26 books and over 100 articles and book chapters on the subject.

social sciences

MDPI

Editorial

Critical Debates and Developments in Child Protection: Some Introductory Comments

Nigel Parton

School of Human and Health Sciences, University of Huddersfield, Huddersfield HD1 3DH, UK;
n.parton@hud.ac.uk

Received: 10 June 2020; Accepted: 10 June 2020; Published: 15 June 2020

I would like to begin by thanking all of the authors who have contributed to this *Social Sciences* Special on "critical debates and developments in child protection" for their hard work and timely dedication in responding so positively to the requests and timelines made of them. Additionally, I would like to thank the reviewers who work so tirelessly behind the scenes and who help insure that such high-quality articles are published. This Special Issue aimed to build on a previous Special Issue in *Social Sciences* in 2014—"Contemporary Developments in Child Protection".

The last 50 years have witnessed increasing public, political and media concern about the social problem of child maltreatment and what to do about it. This is now evident in most jurisdictions and is receiving serious attention from many international and transnational organisations. While the (re)discovery of the problem originally took place in the USA and was particularly associated with the "battered baby syndrome" (Kempe et al. 1962), the objects of concern have now expanded to include physical abuse, sexual abuse, neglect, emotional abuse, abuse on the internet, child trafficking, sexual exploitation, female genital mutilation, gang membership and radicalization and is seen to affect all children and young people and not just young babies. In the process, the focus of attention has widened from simply intra-familial abuse to abuse in a wide variety of extra-familial settings including schools, sports clubs, day care, the church and the wider community. There has also been a broadening of concern from not only protecting children from "serious harm" but also to preventing the impairment of their health and development and ensuring that they are able to grow up in circumstances that are consistent with the provision of effective care so that all children can achieve the best outcomes.

To reflect these changes, the laws, policies, practices and systems designed to identify and prevent child maltreatment have themselves become much more wide-ranging and complex and have been subject to regular review. Social workers, health and education workers, the police and other criminal justice workers, as well as members of the wider community, are now all seen to have key roles to play in both protecting children and young people and assessing and monitoring actual and potential perpetrators.

Increasingly, the efficacy and effectiveness of child protection policies, practices and systems have been subject to high-profile media and political scrutiny and critical social science analysis and research. It is clear that what we understand by child protection, together with the idea of child maltreatment itself, is shaped by a wide range of social, cultural and political factors and that this varies both over time and in different contexts (see, for example, Parton 1985, 2014, 2020).

The international nature of these challenges is reflected in the different countries represented in the papers published in this Special Issue, with authors based in Australia, Canada, England, Ireland, Kenya, New Zealand, Norway, South Africa, Spain and Switzerland.

The broad and diverse nature of the challenges for child protection are demonstrated by the range of topics addressed in these papers. Ben Matthews, Leah Bromfield and Kerryann Walsh compare official reports of child sexual and physical abuse in two Australian jurisdictions with different mandatory reporting laws, Victoria and Western Australia, paying particular attention to the impact of the introduction of a reporting duty for child sexual abuse in Western Australia. We have two papers concerned with child protection in sport: the paper by Daniel Rhind and Jamie McDermott reports on an investigation of a framework designed to safeguard children with a disability in Rugby Union called TACL (Trigger, Action Plan, Communicate, Learn), while Gretchen Kerr, Bruce Kidd and Peter Donnelly discuss the "struggle" to advance child protection in Canadian sport.

The article by Susan Young, Margaret McKenzie, Cecilie More, Liv Schjelderup and Shayne Walker reflects on the child rights and family inclusion provisions of the United Nations Convention on the Rights of the Child (UNCRoC) and the Aotearoa New Zealand Children, Young Persons and their Families Act (1989) as these apply to Aotearoa New Zealand, Norway and Western Australia. Sara Perez–Hernando and Nuria Fuentes–Pelaez provide a systematic review which analyses the conceptualisation of social support in order to create social support networks and the benefits of the intervention for families. The article by Eduard Vaquero, M Angels Balsells, Carmen Ponce, Aida Urrea and Alicia Navajas is also concerned with the benefits of social support but specifically for the biological family during the foster care process. The article by Caroline McGregor and Carmel Devaney discusses the challenges and possible obstacles of a framework which aims to inform "protective support and supportive protection" in child protection and welfare practice and supervision.

The article by Afrooz Kaviani and Julia Sloth–Nielson applies a child rights lens to safeguarding efforts in the aid sector with a focus on the least developed countries in Africa. It argues that child rights law can be leveraged to encourage the effective government oversight of NGOs in contact with children as part of national frameworks for child protection. Njeri Chege and Stephen Ucembe critically analyse what they call Kenya's "over-reliance" on institutionalisation as a childcare and child protection model for children deprived of parental care, which they argue requires a root-cause approach in order to provide alternative family-based care. Emily Keddell discusses the important justice implications of the increasing reliance on algorithmic tools in child protection decision-making, while Edgar Marthinsen, Graham Clifford, Halvor Fauske and Willy Lichtwarck argue that the increasing reliance on case management and overly rationalised procedures in child protection fails to take into account the needs of both families and children. The article reports on a piece of work to help practitioners challenge these developments and to enhance their knowledge of innovation in child protection. Lauren Elizabeth Wroe and Jenny Lloyd address a central tension at the core of social work in child protection—the need to develop relationships of trust and the practice of surveillance—in the context of extra-familial forms of harm. They discuss an analytic framework which they have developed in order to address these challenges and, in the light of applying this to two case studies, they identify the critical issues that should be considered in future work in this area.

Conflicts of Interest: The author declares no conflict of interest.

References

Kempe, Henry, Frederic Silverman, Brandt Steele, William Droegemueller, and Henry Silver. 1962. The Battered Child Syndrome. *Journal of the American Medical Association* 181: 17–24. [CrossRef] [PubMed]

Parton, Nigel. 1985. *The Politics of Child Abuse*. Basingstoke: Palgrave/Macmillan.

Parton, Nigel. 2014. *The Politics of Child Protection: Contemporary Issues and Future Directions*. Basingstoke: Palgrave/Macmillan.

Parton, Nigel. 2020. Addressing the Relatively Autonomous Relationship between Child Maltreatment and Child Protection Policies and Practices. *International Journal on Child Maltreatment: Research, Policy and Practice* 3: 19–34. [CrossRef]

social sciences

MDPI

Article

Comparing Reports of Child Sexual and Physical Abuse Using Child Welfare Agency Data in Two Jurisdictions with Different Mandatory Reporting Laws

Ben Mathews [1,2,*], Leah Bromfield [3] and Kerryann Walsh [4]

[1]   Faculty of Law, Queensland University of Technology, Brisbane City, QLD 4000, Australia
[2]   Bloomberg School of Public Health, Johns Hopkins University, Baltimore, MD 21205, USA
[3]   Australian Centre for Child Protection, University of South Australia, Adelaide, SA 5001, Australia;
      Leah.Bromfield@unisa.edu.au
[4]   Faculty of Education, Queensland University of Technology, Brisbane City, QLD 4000, Australia;
      k.walsh@qut.edu.au
*   Correspondence: b.mathews@qut.edu.au

Received: 6 April 2020; Accepted: 4 May 2020; Published: 11 May 2020

Abstract: Empirical analysis has found that mandatory reporting legislation has positive effects on case identification of child sexual abuse both initially and over the long term. However, there is little analysis of the initial and ongoing impact on child protection systems of the rate of reports that are made if a reporting duty for child sexual abuse is introduced, especially when compared with rates of reports for other kinds of child maltreatment. This research analysed government administrative data at the unique child level over a seven-year period to examine trends in reports of child sexual abuse, compared with child physical abuse, in two Australian states having different socio-legal dimensions. Data mining generated descriptive statistics and rates per 100,000 children involved in reports per annum, and time trend sequences in the seven-year period. The first state, Western Australia, introduced the legislative reporting duty in the middle of the seven-year period, and only for sexual abuse. The second state, Victoria, had possessed mandatory reporting duties for both sexual and physical abuse for over a decade. Our analysis identified substantial intra-state increases in the reporting of child sexual abuse attributable to the introduction of a new legislative reporting duty, and heightened public awareness resulting from major social events. Victoria experienced nearly three times as many reports of physical abuse as Western Australia. The relative burden on the child protection system was most clearly different in Victoria, where reports of physical abuse were relatively stable and two and a half times higher than for sexual abuse. Rates of children in reports, even at their single year peak, indicate sustainable levels of reporting for child welfare agencies. Substantial proportions of reports were made by both legislatively mandated reporters, and non-mandated community members, suggesting that government agencies would benefit from engaging with communities and professions to enhance a desirable reporting practice.

Keywords: child sexual abuse; child physical abuse; reports; child welfare systems; mandatory reporting laws; comparative analysis; cross-jurisdictional analysis; analysis over time; agency data; systems burden

---

1. Introduction

Child sexual abuse causes substantial psychological, behavioural and physical harms which often continue through adolescence and endure through adulthood (Chen et al. 2010; Gilbert et al. 2009; Paolucci et al. 2001; Putnam 2003; Spataro et al. 2004; Trickett et al. 2011). Sexual abuse involves contact and non-contact sexual acts, inflicted by any adult or child in a position of power over the victim, to seek or obtain physical or mental sexual gratification, when the child does not have capacity to provide consent, or has capacity, but does not provide consent (Mathews and Collin-Vézina 2019). It is widespread worldwide, with meta-analyses finding prevalence rates of approximately 15–20% for girls, and 7–10% for boys (Barth et al. 2013; Pereda et al. 2009; Stoltenborgh et al. 2011).

Rates of child sexual abuse in the UK and Ireland are similar to these global rates. In the UK, Radford et al. (2013) found that 24.1% of children experienced sexual abuse (2013), and May-Chahal and Cawson (2005) found that 19% of children experienced sexual abuse. In Ireland, a national study found that 30.4% of girls and 23.5% of boys experienced any kind of sexual abuse, and 12.8% of girls and 12% of boys experienced contact sexual abuse (McGee et al. 2011).

Child sexual abuse constitutes a massive and persistent public health problem (Mathews 2019a), and a recent long-term historical analysis in the UK concluded child maltreatment should remain a public health priority (Degli Espositi et al. 2019). Societies have vested interests in improving child maltreatment detection and responses, as they can reduce socio-economic costs attributable to out-of-home care, lost productivity from attenuated functional capacity, other costs to mental and physical health, and social welfare (Widom and Longterm Consequences of Child Maltreatment 2014; Currie and Widom 2010). The human costs attributable to pain and suffering from child sexual abuse are immense and preventable.

Governments have responsibilities to respond to facilitate the identification of cases of child sexual abuse, provide services and support to the child, and reduce the incidence. These responsibilities are embedded in international policies and instruments. The United Nations 2015 Agenda for Sustainable Development has set a program for global human development efforts from 2015 to 2030 (United Nations General Assembly 2015). The Sustainable Development Goals recognise that child abuse presents a fundamental obstacle to health, and demand concerted action with two specific targets for governments. Target 16.2 aims to end the abuse of children, and Target 5.2 aims to eliminate all forms of violence against women and girls, including sexual exploitation. Governments must report on their progress against these targets. Similarly, and preceding the UN SDGs by some 25 years, the United Nations Convention on the Rights of the Child 1989 article 19 requires states' parties to take all appropriate legislative, administrative, social and educational measures to protect children from all forms of abuse and exploitation. The prevention of and response to child maltreatment must clearly be also seen as an urgent matter of protecting and promoting children's rights (Reading et al. 2009).

In this respect, an enduring challenge for governments is to identify cases of child sexual abuse. As summarised later in this article, a substantial majority of cases of child sexual abuse do not come to the attention of child welfare agencies or other social welfare bodies such as criminal justice or health systems. Child sexual abuse, although prevalent, remains "hidden in plain sight" (Erooga et al. 2019). This concealment of criminal activity occurs for multiple reasons, including the clandestine environment in which sexual abuse occurs, and the child's inherent tendency not to disclose their experience, or to do so only many years later. A further concern is that a proportion of those child disclosures that are made are concealed by adults and are not conveyed to social welfare, health or justice systems (Australian Government Royal Commission into Institutional Responses to Child Sexual Abuse 2017).

Accordingly, governments often adopt policy measures in an attempt to identify more cases of sexual abuse, to enable child protection, interruption of offending, prevention of further offending, detection of offenders, and the provision of health and rehabilitation services to children. These can take many forms and be tailored to specific contexts of criminal offending against children (Mathews 2019b). In many countries, one such measure has been the adoption of a legislative mandatory reporting duty, requiring members of designated occupations who deal with children in the course of their work to report known and suspected cases of sexual abuse to child welfare agencies (Mathews and Kenny 2008; Mathews and Walsh 2014). These duties have been found to have positive effects on case identification, in studies using different methodologies including time trend analyses of effects of the introduction of a new duty (Mathews et al. 2016), long-term analysis over 20 years (Mathews et al. 2017), particularly vulnerable to physical abuse, and are susceptible to extreme physical injuries and fatality. This extreme vulnerability, together with the fact that, like sexual abuse, physical abuse occurs in private and is rarely witnessed, catalysed the development of the first mandatory reporting laws in the USA in the 1960s (Kempe et al. 1962; Paulsen et al. 1965).

2.2. The True Prevalence of Child Sexual Abuse and Physical Abuse, and the Problem of Secrecy and Non-Disclosure

It is widely accepted that the official rates of child abuse recorded by government child protection agencies are only a small proportion of its true prevalence (Stoltenborgh et al. 2011). Government child protection data only count the cases coming to official attention during the survivor's childhood, and that are substantiated after investigation. This is particularly evident for both sexual and physical abuse, since many survivors do not ever reveal their experience to anyone, or only do so after a substantial period of time. This phenomenon of non-disclosure and delayed disclosure has been studied in particular depth regarding sexual abuse. A substantial body of evidence shows that many survivors of child sexual abuse will not ever tell anyone about their experience, or will only do so years or decades later (Alaggia et al. 2019; Easton 2013; Easton et al. 2014; Lemaigre et al. 2017; McElvaney 2013; Smith et al. 2000). In a study of 487 men, for example, where the mean age of onset was 10.3 years, it took participants an average of 21 years to tell someone, and the mean age at the time of first telling was 32 (Easton 2013). A comprehensive review of studies found that 60–70% of adult survivors did not disclose during childhood (London et al. 2007). Rigorous research has illuminated a range of factors influencing non-disclosure and delayed disclosure, with these factors related to the child, to the offender, and to society (Collin-Vézina et al. 2015; Fontes and Plummer 2010). Abuse by relatives, trusted authority figures, and institutional authorities produce especially powerful silencing effects, due to the impact of individual, organisational and spiritual authority. Exemplifying this, the Australian Government Royal Commission into Institutional Responses to Child Sexual Abuse found that, for those survivors who were able to disclose their experience to the Commission, it took an average of 22 years from the events to do so (Australian Government Royal Commission into Institutional Responses to Child Sexual Abuse 2014). Most disclosures are to trusted individuals rather than social agencies. Disclosure is more likely where the child is older, the offender is unknown, and the child has a trusted confidante (Alaggia et al. 2019; Lemaigre et al. 2017; Collin-Vézina et al. 2015).

Non-disclosure and delayed disclosure of child physical abuse by survivors has not been the subject of as much investigation. However, it is plausible that the patterns are similar, perhaps for slightly different reasons. While it lacks the unique constellation of psychological, sexual and emotional dimensions of sexual abuse (Mathews 2019a), physical abuse is more normative than sexual abuse, and much of it occurs in earlier stages of child development, before the child would have a cognitive understanding of its wrongfulness. In addition, unlike sexual abuse, a considerable proportion of physical abuse, including in its most severe forms, as identified by Kempe et al. (1962), occur in the first three or four years of life, the developmental period in which children are least able to seek help or protect themselves. Data from the USA on the source of disclosures of physical abuse reports to child protective agencies indicates that very few come from the child (U.S. Department of Health and Human Services 2009), and data from multiple states in Australia also show this trend (Mathews 2018; Mathews et al. 2015a, 2015b).

Accordingly, the prevalence rates revealed by rigorous epidemiological studies using representative samples of the population provide a more reliable understanding of lived experience. Meta-analyses have suggested that self-report studies provide rates thirty times higher than those obtained by informant studies (Stoltenborgh et al. 2011), and it is well-established that only a fraction of cases are recorded by official government agencies. Those cases that are brought to the attention of these agencies are a result of reports made either by members of the public who are not under a legal duty to make such reports, or by individuals who have been entrusted with a legislative duty to report known and suspected cases.

2.3. Mandatory Reporting Laws: Nature and Purpose

The difficulty of identifying cases of child sexual abuse, and other forms of maltreatment including physical abuse, has led many nations to adopt a major socio-legal policy. Mandatory reporting laws, located in child protection legislation, require designated persons to report known and suspected cases of child sexual abuse by any person to government child protection agencies. As discussed elsewhere (Mathews and Kenny 2008; Mathews and Bross 2008; Mathews 2012), the laws are intended to bring otherwise hidden cases of sexual abuse to the attention of child welfare agencies. The laws provide these reporters with protections. They also expressly empower other persons to make reports. The first reporting laws were created in the 1960s in the USA for physical abuse, after Henry Kempe and his colleagues identified "The Battered-child Syndrome" (Kempe et al. 1962). They have since been adopted by scores of nations around the world, especially to respond to child sexual abuse and physical abuse (Mathews 2014b).

The laws aim primarily to enable the cessation of the child's abusive experience and to enable provision of protection and health support to the child. They are also intended to overcome the tendency for those who know of or suspect serious child abuse to do nothing. These legal reporting duties are intended to be one component of a systematic approach to child protection, involving education of mandated reporters, and the appropriate resourcing of child welfare and law enforcement agencies, to increase the identification of cases of sexual abuse which otherwise would remain hidden. The ultimate goal of the laws is not primary prevention, but to increase identification of cases and support children who need assistance, preventing further abuse of the child and possibly of other children, facilitating health and safety responses for the child, and enabling criminal justice responses to detect perpetrators.

As explained elsewhere (Mathews 2012, 2014a, 2015; Mathews et al. 2015a, 2015b), the laws are not uniform across jurisdictions, and there are broader and narrower models. The first main dimension of difference is in which types of abuse and neglect must be reported. An example of this is that in Australia, three of the eight jurisdictions—Victoria, Queensland, and the Australian Capital Territory—require reports of sexual abuse and physical abuse, but not of the other three kinds of maltreatment (emotional abuse, neglect, and exposure to domestic violence) (Mathews et al. 2015a, 2015b; Mathews 2014b). Other Australian jurisdictions require reports of only sexual abuse (Western Australia), or of all five types (for example, New South Wales). The second main dimension of difference is in which persons are required to report. Some jurisdictions—such as the Northern Territory—require all citizens to report; others, such as Queensland, Victoria and Western Australia, apply the duty only to members of a small range of occupations.

Due to the non-disclosure and secrecy of child sexual abuse, professional and public sentinels will always have a circumscribed capacity to detect cases. Physical abuse is often difficult to detect, due to the absence of clear physical indicators, concealment of injury under clothing, or consistency of injury with innocuous childhood incidents. However, identification of sexual abuse is arguably even more challenging, as behavioural indicators of sexual abuse are often consistent with innocent explanations or other childhood adversities, and most sexual abuse leaves no physical evidence (Anderst et al. 2009; Heger et al. 2002), meaning that even doctors who can conduct physical examinations might easily not detect an abusive situation. However, professionals often receive disclosures, and are well-placed, because of their frequent interaction with and knowledge of the children they serve, to notice changes in behaviour and other indicators that may suggest sexual abuse. Members of the public—family members, neighbours, and others who know a child, and who are aware of who interacts with the child—are also in a position where they can either come to know of a child's experience, or to suspect it through witnessing behaviour. Where child protection systems record the source of reports of child sexual abuse and their outcomes, it is consistently shown that reports of children's suspected abuse are made by both professionals and members of the public, many of which lead to the identification of cases of abuse.

3. Recent Analysis of Empirical Trends in Reporting of Child Sexual Abuse

Recent analyses of empirical trends in the reporting of child maltreatment over time have been conducted, with a focus on consideration of trends associated with legislative reporting duties, particularly for child sexual abuse. Six recent studies have explored different aspects of this context in Australia. First, a three-State study found that primary school teachers in a jurisdiction with mandatory reporting were more likely to have made a report of suspected child sexual abuse in their career, than their counterparts in jurisdictions without a duty, or with a restricted duty; in addition, teachers who knew school policy required them to report child sexual abuse were more likely to report it than those who did not (Mathews et al. 2009c; Walsh et al. 2012). Second, in 2014, a comparative analysis of two similar jurisdictions, only one of which had a legislative reporting duty for child sexual abuse, found the jurisdiction with mandatory reporting received twice the number of reports of sexual abuse (with 53% of these made by mandated reporters), and identified 4.73 times the number of sexually abused children (Mathews 2014a). It also found that confirmed cases identified as a result of mandated reports were 2.5 times the total identified by all reporters in the non-mandated jurisdiction (Mathews 2014a).

Third, in 2015, a national study in Australia over 10 years, which examined reporting trends in each of eight states and territories, found that reports of child sexual abuse comprised approximately 10–12% of the total amount of reports of all kinds of child maltreatment, and that mandated reporters made approximately half of these (Mathews et al. 2015a, 2015b). Fourth, similarly, an analysis of a single state's reporting data over the year 2017 found that reports of child sexual abuse and physical abuse constituted approximately 13.6% and 18.1% respectively of the total amount of reports of all kinds of child maltreatment (Mathews 2018).

Fifth, in 2016, an analysis of the impact of the introduction of a new legislative mandatory reporting duty for child sexual abuse in Western Australia compared reporting trends for a period before and after the new duty commenced operation (Mathews et al. 2016). It found that, on average per annum: the number of reports by mandated reporters of suspected child sexual abuse increased by a factor of 3.7; the number of investigated reports increased threefold; and the number of substantiated investigations doubled.

Finally, in 2017, a 20-year time trend analysis of reporting of child sexual abuse in Victoria found several trends, including: an increase for two years after introduction of mandatory reporting; a 12 year period of stability; and a rapid increase in the last five years, influenced by major social factors (including awareness raised through government inquiries), and political and agency-related factors, including extra investment (Mathews et al. 2017). Positive report outcomes (i.e. substantiations, findings of harm, and referral to services) increased twelve-fold for boys, and nearly five-fold for girls (Mathews et al. 2017).

A Gap in the Evidence Base

These recent analyses have, for good reason, focused mainly on the reporting practices of mandated reporters, and particular mandated occupations. Despite this growing body of evidence, however, less attention has been paid to trends in reports made by all persons, whether mandated or non-mandated, at the society-wide level, for child sexual abuse, over substantial time periods and under different conditions. For legislators and policy-makers, important questions arise about the systems needs associated with reporting duties for the child protection agency's intake and response system, the long-term trends in reporting child sexual abuse under different legislative models, and comparisons of systemic intake needs for child sexual abuse reports compared with different types of child maltreatment. Our primary focus of interest in this study was to consider these needs at the intake level.

In Australia, the eight states and territories form a natural laboratory in which we can consider many of these questions of substantial social, legal and public health significance. Most Australian jurisdictions have government child protection agencies which have well-developed data recording systems, each of which are collated into a national minimum data set and hence have a degree of data comparability. As well, the different socio-legal contexts, and particularly the different legislative frameworks for the reporting of child sexual and physical abuse, provide comparative settings enabling the analysis of the three policy-relevant research questions posed in this study for child protection agency intake systems:

1. What are the trends in reports of distinct children in suspected cases of child sexual abuse over the seven-year period 2006–2012 in the two different jurisdictions?
2. What are the trends in reports of distinct children in suspected cases of child physical abuse over the seven-year period 2006–2012 in the two different jurisdictions?
3. What are the relative systems impacts regarding the reporting of children in suspected cases of sexual abuse and physical abuse in the two different jurisdictions?

To explore the three research questions, we selected the two states of Western Australia and Victoria as comparators. Our chosen comparator maltreatment type was physical abuse, because it is generally the next least often reported type of child maltreatment (Mathews et al. 2015a, 2015b), was the progenitor maltreatment type inspiring the original mandatory reporting laws in both the USA and Australia (Mathews 2014b), and, like sexual abuse, is an act of commission. In Western Australia, during the seven-year time period 2006–2012 analysed in this study, there was no legislative duty to report child physical abuse, and a newly introduced duty to report child sexual abuse mid-way through the time period (Mathews et al. 2009a). The legislative framework set out by the Children and Community Services Act 2004 (WA) ss 124A-H created a system of mandatory reporting of child sexual abuse, but not physical abuse. This legislative framework was created only on 1 January 2009; before that, there were no mandatory reporting requirements (74). The groups of mandated reporters were doctors, nurses, midwives, teachers and police. The duty in s 124B(1) required a mandated reporter who believed on reasonable grounds that a child had been sexually abused, or was being sexually abused, to report it as soon as practicable after forming the belief. Unlike Victoria, the duty did not apply to belief about the likelihood of future sexual abuse, such as in cases of grooming or other clear risk. Additionally, unlike Victoria, the duty was not technically limited to situations where the child lacked a protective parent. Other non-mandated persons were empowered, but not required, to make such reports of child sexual abuse. The duty did not apply to suspected events occurring before 1 January 2009. In Western Australia, no person was required to report physical abuse, but all citizens were empowered to report it. The Children and Community Services Act 2004 (WA) s 3 defined a "child" as a person aged under 18. Accordingly, the mandatory reporting duty applied to situations of sexual abuse involving any child aged under 18 (0–17 inclusive).

In Victoria, during the seven-year time period 2006–2012 analysed in this study, the legislative framework was markedly different. The legislative framework set out in the Children, Youth and Families Act 2005 (Vic) ss 162, 182, 184 created a system of mandatory reporting of both child physical abuse and sexual abuse. This legislative framework had existed practically unchanged since 1993 (Mathews et al. 2015b). The groups of mandated reporters were doctors, nurses, midwives, teachers, school principals, and police. The duty was technically limited to situations where the reporter had a belief on reasonable grounds that a child has suffered, or is likely to suffer, significant harm as a result of physical injury or sexual abuse, and the child's parents have not protected, or are unlikely to protect, the child from harm of that type. It has been hypothesised that this second limb of the duty likely has little effect on limiting reports where the person suspects abuse, although this question has not been empirically studied. Like Western Australia, reports were required to be made as soon as practicable after forming the belief. Other non-mandated persons were empowered, but not required, to make reports of both child physical and sexual abuse. In Victoria, a "child" was defined in the Children, Youth and Families Act 2005 (Vic) s 3 as a person aged under 17. Accordingly, the mandatory reporting duty applied to situations of physical or sexual abuse involving any child aged under 17 (0–16 inclusive).

4. Analysing Trends in Reporting Suspected Cases of Child Sexual Abuse and Physical Abuse to Child Welfare Agencies

4.1. Method

This study's research design draws broadly on the principles of knowledge discovery and data mining (Kum et al. 2015), in which existing child welfare information systems can be used to generate evidence to inform practice evaluation and improvement. Data analysis involved accessing and collating administrative child protection data for the seven-year period 1 January 2006 to 31 December 2012, to generate descriptive statistics, calculating rates per 100,000 children.

4.2. Data

The research was approved by the Queensland University of Technology Human Research Ethics Committee. De-identified data from existing datasets were provided under an agreement between the Victorian Department of Health and Human Services, the Western Australia Department for Child Protection and Family Support and the researchers' institutions, as part of a broader study supported by the Victorian Government, and funded by the Commonwealth of Australia (Mathews et al. 2015a, 2015b). These Departments routinely collect and store data on reports of suspected child maltreatment. Data on reports (technically termed "notifications") of child sexual abuse and physical abuse were provided in electronic unit record form, giving disaggregated de-identified data at the unique child level. The data provided information about each distinct individual child who had been the subject of a report, and were provided in a form which allowed the removal of duplicate reports made about the same child. The data provided information on: the date of the report; the reporter's occupation or status (e.g., family member); the primary form of maltreatment reported; and the outcome of the report (including whether investigated by the department, whether substantiated, and whether referred for services). The data did not enable analysis based on demographic variables such as ethnicity, family income, or geographical location within the state (e.g., metropolitan, regional, remote). However, it can be noted that geographically, Western Australia (2,645,615 km^2) is much larger than Victoria (237,659 km^2). Western Australia also has a higher proportion of the population who identify as Indigenous Australians (3.1%) than Victoria (0.8%) (Australian Bureau of Statistics 2016).

Based on the definition of a "child" in the Western Australian and Victorian child protection legislation (Mathews et al. 2015a, 2015b), we analysed data in Victoria for children aged under 17 (that is, aged 0–16 inclusive), and in Western Australia for children aged under 18 (that is, aged 0–17 inclusive). Two data artefacts created limitations which required consideration in interpretation. First, in Western Australia, data for 2010 are from 10 months only (6 March to 31 December), due to a transition in its recording system. Second, in Victoria, data for 2007 are artificially low because of a transition in its recording system.

4.3. Procedures

For the analysis presented here, which examines reports for the years 2006–2012, we extracted relevant data from our existing dataset. The dataset had previously been cleaned, coded and collated by two researchers, and descriptive totals had been checked both independently and together for both Western Australia (Mathews et al. 2015a), and Victoria (Mathews et al. 2015b). Duplicate reports for the same child were removed, so that the aggregate counts of reports were calculated at the distinct child level.

For the purpose of this study, we analysed numbers of reports of sexual abuse and physical abuse, made by all persons combined, whether mandated reporters or non-mandated reporters. Descriptive statistics and associated data mining enabled the identification of aggregate numbers of reports, and identification of trends in reporting over time, in each jurisdiction for the two maltreatment subtypes. It also enabled rate calculations at the population level for within-state and inter-state comparisons, using rates standardised per 100,000 children, as is common practice in health research.

4.4. Statistical Methods

For each year in the seven-year period 2006–2012, we analysed the rate of reports per 100,000 children. Rates per 100,000 for each year of analysis were calculated using Australian Bureau of Statistics data regarding the population of children aged 0–17 years in Western Australia, and the population of children aged 0–16 in Victoria, respectively (Australian Bureau of Statistics 2007, 2009, 2010, 2011a, 2011b, 2012, 2013, 2014, 2015, 2020a, 2020b). To evaluate temporal changes, we compared rates of children, per 100,000 children, in reports of physical and sexual abuse over the seven-year period.

For both jurisdictions, we were able to consider the contextual influence of major legal change during this period on reporting trends for child physical and sexual abuse. Interpretation was informed by analysis of which individuals were made mandated reporters, for what types of child maltreatment, and when (Mathews et al. 2015a, 2015b). The major legal change was the introduction in Western Australia on 1 January 2009, of a new reporting duty for child sexual abuse only. In Victoria, the reporting duty, applied to both physical and sexual abuse, which had been in place since 4 November 1993, remained unchanged for the entire seven-year period (Mathews 2014b). We were also able to consider the influence of any major social or systemic changes during this period.

4.5. Results

4.5.1. Trends in Numbers and Rates of Reports of Suspected Child Sexual Abuse

For Western Australia, which in the time period, had a stable population of approximately 520,000 children aged 0–17, the number of children in reports of sexual abuse, annually, ranged from a low of 1502 to a high of 3580 (Table 1). This equated to rates per 100,000 children of a low of 303 to a high of 641. The mean was 468 per 100,000 children. At the single year peak of reporting, this equated to 1 in 156 children being the subject of a report of suspected sexual abuse. In the seven-year period, there were three identifiable time trend sequences (Table 1). First, there was stability from 2006–2008, in which the rate was around 310 per 100,000 children. Second, there was a marked increase from in 2009–2010 to around 540 per 100,000 children. Third, there was a further increase in 2011–2012, when the rate was around 630 per 100,000 children.

Table 1. Number and rate of children in reports of child sexual abuse: Western Australia 2006–2012.

Year [1]	Number of Distinct Children Aged 0–17 Who Were the Subject of Reports of Suspected Sexual Abuse	Population of Children Aged 0–17 in Western Australia	Rate of Distinct Children/100,000 in Reports of Suspected Sexual Abuse	Proportion of Distinct Children in Reports of Suspected Sexual Abuse
2006	1502	495,615	303 per 100,000	1 out of 330
2007	1627	505,216	322 per 100,000	1 out of 310
2008	1609	515,898	312 per 100,000	1 out of 321
2009	2898	527,182	550 per 100,000	1 out of 182
2010 [2]	2886	535,085	530 per 100,000	1 out of 185
2011	3383	544,776	621 per 100,000	1 out of 161
2012	3580	558,451	641 per 100,000	1 out of 156

[1] Bold years indicate those in which mandatory reporting legislation existed. [2] Data for 2010 are from 6 March to 31 December, due to a transition in Western Australia's recording system.

For Victoria, which in the time period, had a stable population of approximately 1.1 million children aged 0–16, the number of children in reports of sexual abuse, annually, ranged from a low of 2932 to a high of 6775 (Table 2). This equated to rates per 100,000 children of a low of 262 to a high of 580. The mean was 406 per 100,000 children. At the single year peak of reporting, this equated to

1 in 172 children being the subject of a report of suspected sexual abuse. In the seven-year period, there were three identifiable time trend sequences (Table 2). First, there was stability from 2006–2009, with the rate stable, at approximately 335 per 100,000 children. Second, there was a marked increase in 2010–2011, where the rate increased to 478 and 493 per 100,000 children, respectively. Third, in 2012, there was a further notable increase to 580 per 100,000 children.

Table 2. Number and rate of children in reports of child sexual abuse: Victoria 2006–2012.

Year [1]	Number of Distinct Children Aged 0–16 Who Were the Subject of Reports of Suspected Sexual Abuse	Population of Children Aged 0–16 in Victoria	Rate of Distinct Children/100,000 in Reports of Suspected Sexual Abuse	Proportion of Distinct Children in Reports of Suspected Sexual Abuse
2006	4083	1,112,123	367 per 100,000	1 out of 272
2007 [2]	2932	1,119,696	262 per 100,000	1 out of 382
2008	3777	1,133,638	333 per 100,000	1 out of 300
2009	3832	1,147,242	334 per 100,000	1 out of 299
2010	5445	1,139,649	478 per 100,000	1 out of 209
2011	5682	1,152,251	493 per 100,000	1 out of 203
2012	6775	1,168,144	580 per 100,000	1 out of 172

[1] Bold years indicate those in which mandatory reporting legislation existed. [2] Data are limited due to a transition in the recording system for Victoria in 2007.

A comparison of the impact of these rates for the two states' child protection agency intake systems can be shown by graphically depicting the respective rates per 100,000 children in reports over the seven-year period (Figure 1).

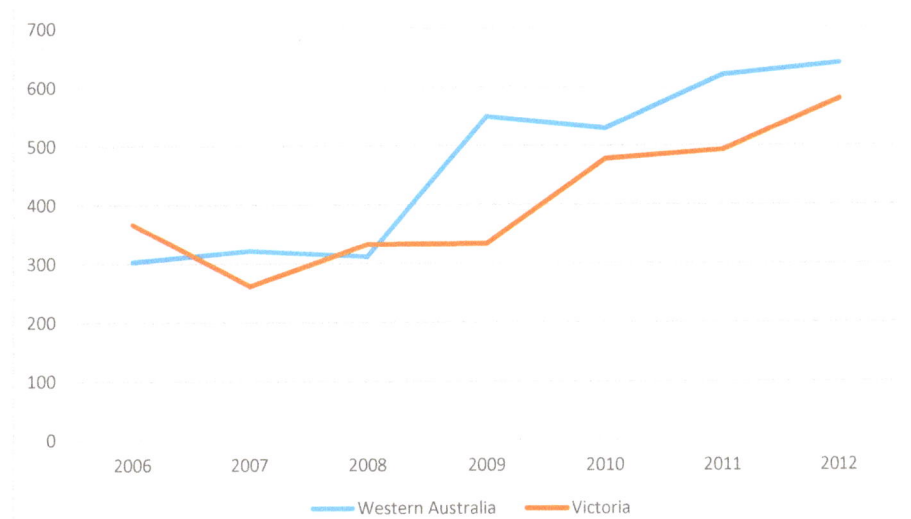

Figure 1. Sexual abuse reports: Western Australia and Victoria 2006–2012 (rate/100,000 children).

4.5.2. Trends in Numbers and Rates of Reports of Suspected Child Physical Abuse

For Western Australia, the number of children in reports of physical abuse, annually, ranged from a low of 1603 to a high of 2559 (Table 3). This equated to rates per 100,000 children of a low of 299 to a high of 485. The mean was 376 per 100,000 children. At the single year peak of reporting, this equated to 1 in 206 children being the subject of a report of physical abuse. In the seven-year period, there were three identifiable time trend sequences. First, there was stability from 2006–2008, in which the rate was stable, at around 350 per 100,000 children. Second, there was a marked increase in 2009 to 485 per 100,000 children (which we theorise below was likely due to the introduction of mandatory reporting for sexual abuse and associated community sensitisation to child maltreatment generally). Third, there was a relatively stable period in 2011–2012 where rates returned to levels similar to prior years, at around 380–400 per 100,000.

Table 3. Number and rate of children in reports of child physical abuse: Western Australia 2006–2012.

Year [1]	Number of Distinct Children Aged 0–17 Who Were the Subject of Reports of Suspected Physical Abuse	Population of Children Aged 0–17 in Western Australia	Rate of Distinct Children/100,000 in Reports of Suspected Physical Abuse	Proportion of Distinct Children in Reports of Suspected Physical Abuse
2006	1626	495,615	328 per 100,000	1 out of 305
2007	1786	505,216	353 per 100,000	1 out of 283
2008	1956	515,898	379 per 100,000	1 out of 264
2009	2559	527,182	485 per 100,000	1 out of 206
2010 [2]	1603	535,085	299 per 100,000	1 out of 334
2011	2081	544,776	382 per 100,000	1 out of 262
2012	2284	558,451	409 per 100,000	1 out of 244

[1] Bold years indicate those in which mandatory reporting legislation existed. [2] Data for 2010 are from 6 March to 31 December due to a transition in Western Australia's recording system.

For Victoria, the number of children in reports of physical abuse, annually, ranged from a low of 9340 to a high of 13,604 (Table 4). This equated to rates per 100,000 children of a low of 834 to a high of 1192. The mean was 1048 per 100,000 children. At the single year peak of reporting, this equated to 1 in 84 children being the subject of a report of suspected physical abuse. In the seven-year period, there were three identifiable time trend sequences (Table 4). First, there was relative stability from 2006–2007, with a rate of 840 per 100,000 children. Second, there was a marked increase in 2008 to 1034 per 100,000 children, and another more moderate increase in 2009 to 1165 per 100,000 children. Third, from 2009–2012, rates remained stable, at around 1160 per 100,000 children.

Table 4. Number and rate of children in reports of child physical abuse: Victoria 2006–2012.

Year [1]	Number of Distinct Children Aged 0–16 Who Were the Subject of Reports of Suspected Physical Abuse	Population of Children Aged 0–16 in Victoria	Rate of Distinct Children/100,000 in Reports of Suspected Physical Abuse	Proportion of Distinct Children in Reports of Suspected Physical Abuse
2006	9402	1,112,123	845 per 100,000	1 out of 118
2007 [2]	9340	1,119,696	834 per 100,000	1 out of 120
2008	11,724	1,133,638	1034 per 100,000	1 out of 97
2009	13,364	1,147,242	1165 per 100,000	1 out of 86
2010	13,595	1,139,649	1192 per 100,000	1 out of 84
2011	12,720	1,152,251	1104 per 100,000	1 out of 90
2012	13,604	1,168,144	1164 per 100,000	1 out of 86

[1] Bold years indicate those in which mandatory reporting legislation existed. [2] Data are limited due to a transition in the recording system for Victoria in 2007.

A comparison of the impact of these rates for the two states' child protection agency intake systems can be shown by graphically depicting the respective rates per 100,000 children in reports over the seven-year period for physical abuse (Figure 2).

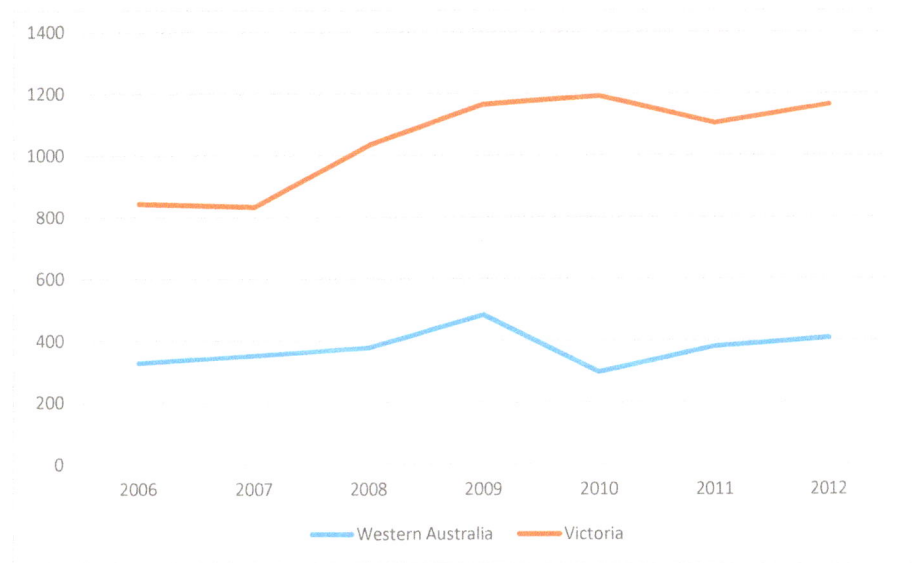

Figure 2. Physical abuse reports: Western Australia and Victoria 2006–2012 (rate/100,000 children).

5. Discussion

This analysis considered three research questions regarding trends in reports of children over time, for child physical abuse and sexual abuse, in two jurisdictions with different legislative frameworks. We considered trends over time within each state, for each of the two types of child abuse. We also considered comparative trends over time between the two states, for each of the two types of child abuse. For each state, we analysed numbers and rates of distinct children in reports. The analysis by rate per 100,000 children enabled comparison across states, which was further warranted by the two jurisdictions having different child populations, with Victoria having slightly more than double the relevant child population. The broad social context in the two states was similar, with no existing evidence of substantially different underlying rates of child sexual abuse or physical abuse in the communities. However, Western Australia, with a much lower population density, had a higher proportion of children who likely encounter professionals less frequently, which may have influenced reporting rates. In addition, we can note that there is no evidence that ethnicity is associated in Australia with higher incidence of child abuse. However, Western Australia had a higher proportion of Indigenous Australians than Victoria, and Indigenous children are known to be over-represented in the child protection system. This may indicate a higher underlying incidence of some types of maltreatment in Western Australia, or, it may indicate a differential application of child protection responses.

The data sources were comparable, with three notable artefacts. First, the data for Western Australia for 2010 contained information from only 10 months, likely under-representing the true figures by approximately one-sixth; we proceeded on this basis. Second, the data for Victoria in 2007 substantially under-represented the true figures, due to a change in the state's recording system; we accounted for this in our interpretation. Third, because of the different statutory definitions of a "child" in the Western Australian and Victorian child protection legislation, the data for Western Australia included reports of 17-year-olds, and the data for Victoria did not. In general, we took this into account, but also proceeded on the basis that this was unlikely to substantially affect our interpretation, since relatively few 17 year olds are the subjects of reports, particularly for physical abuse.

5.1. Child Sexual Abuse

The first research question asked: What are the trends in reports of distinct children in suspected cases of child sexual abuse over the seven-year period 2006–2012 in the two different jurisdictions? We identified significant findings within each jurisdiction, and across the two jurisdictions.

In Western Australia, the mean rate of reports over the entire seven-year period was 468 per 100,000 children. Here, it is notable that the pre-mandatory reporting law reporting rate in Western Australia (around 310/100,000 children) was only slightly lower than that in Victoria during the same years 2006–2008 (around 350/100,000 children, discounting the artefact year 2007). Victoria by then was in a very stable pattern of reporting, long after its reporting duty had commenced more than a decade previously, and before its increase in 2010–2012. As shown elsewhere, over the long-term, reports of sexual abuse stabilise after an initial increase after the introduction of mandatory reporting, rather than continuing upwards (Mathews et al. 2017).

The post-law rates in Western Australia are higher than the rates in Victoria, even at a time when Victoria was witnessing a higher than normal rate, which coincided with renewed sensitisation to child sexual abuse in the wake of multiple government inquiries (Mathews et al. 2017). This included the announcement on 31 January 2011 of the Protecting Victoria's Vulnerable Children Inquiry (Cummins et al. 2012), the Betrayal of Trust—Inquiry into the Handling of Child Abuse by Religious and other Non-Government Organisations (Victorian Family and Community Development Committee 2013), and the 2012 announcement of the Australian Government Royal Commission Into Institutional Responses to Child Sexual Abuse, all of which were accompanied by widespread media coverage. In Western Australia, at the peak of reporting in 2012, this equated to 1 in 156 children being the subject of a report of suspected sexual abuse. These findings regarding rates of reports by all members of the community in Western Australia extend the earlier finding about the increase in reports by mandated groups only (Mathews et al. 2016).

In Victoria, the mean rate of reports over the entire seven-year period was 406 per 100,000 children. Overall, Victoria experienced less variation over time, but did experience an increase, despite no change in legislative reporting duties. As explained elsewhere (Mathews et al. 2017), this is likely attributable to the increased sensitisation through social developments referred to above.

Importantly, we can also note that substantial proportions of reports were made by members of specific occupational groups, and by members of the public. As detailed elsewhere, in Victoria 2006–2012, mandated reporters made 36–56% of reports of sexual abuse, and non-mandated reporters made 44–63% (Mathews et al. 2015b, Table 2.5). Similar proportions were evident in Western Australia over 2006–2012. Those in the mandated occupations made 49–71% of reports of sexual abuse, and other reporters made 29–51% (Mathews et al. 2015a, Table 2.5).

Overall, the rates of reports of child sexual abuse made in these two states suggest that over a selected seven-year period, jurisdictions with similar socio-legal contexts may receive a rate of reports of approximately 300–640 per 100,000 children. Within these ranges, increases in these rates will occur if a new legislative reporting duty is introduced, as occurred in Western Australia, and when significant social contextual awareness is heightened, as occurred in Victoria. In each jurisdiction, substantial proportions of these reports are made by those in mandated reporter groups, and non-mandated groups.

5.2. Child Physical Abuse

The second research question asked: What are the trends in reports of distinct children in suspected cases of child physical abuse over the seven-year period 2006–2012 in the two different jurisdictions?

In Western Australia, the mean rate of reports over the seven-year period was 376 per 100,000 children. The increase in 2009 was likely associated with an increased sensitisation towards child abuse of all forms, accompanying the introduction of the legislative reporting duty, even though it did not apply to physical abuse. Accordingly, jurisdictions without any form of legislative reporting duty may reasonably assume that the introduction of a duty, even if restricted to one type of maltreatment, may have a short-term impact on increasing reports of other forms of child maltreatment. This appears to be of short duration, however, since the rate soon returned to the rates near those existing in the years 2006–2008. We can also note that, as explained elsewhere, there had been sustained media and policy attention in Western Australia to encourage reports of sexual abuse before the introduction of the legislative duty, as well as professional education and awareness-building (Mathews et al. 2009a, 2009c). This likely did not extend to physical abuse in the same way, as there were no comparable events that elevated the awareness of physical abuse among reporter groups. There had also been policy support to report sexual abuse, following government inquiries in 2002 (Gordon et al. 2020) and especially in 2007 (Ford 2007), which did not extend in the same way to physical abuse.

In Victoria, by contrast, the mean rate of reports over the seven-year period was 1048 per 100,000 children. This marked difference in rates of reports of physical abuse is possibly the most notable finding of this study. Victoria, which had a legislative reporting duty, had an annual mean rate of reports 2.78 times as high as Western Australia (1048:376). On the face of it, this indicates a substantially lower intake system burden for a jurisdiction not having a legislative reporting duty for child physical abuse. However, it may indicate a level of underreporting. Comparing the two states' substantially different reporting rates for physical abuse, it is plausible that Victoria's relatively long history of the duty with associated cultural development in child protection may have had a greater impact on sensitising both professionals and public alike to be alert to signs of physical abuse and to be more likely to make reports. Despite some small differences in trends in the seven-year period, the rates of reporting of physical abuse did not differ substantially over time in Victoria, indicating that this difference in mean level was stable and not attributable to an outlier in any one year.

Here, again, we can note that substantial proportions of reports are made by members of specific occupational groups, and by members of the public. In Victoria 2006–2012, mandated reporters made 37–55% of reports of physical abuse, and non-mandated reporters made 44–62% (Mathews et al. 2015b, Table 2.4). Similar proportions were evident in Western Australia over 2006–2012. Those in the mandated occupations for sexual abuse made 40–57% of reports of physical abuse (even though not required by the legal duty to report physical abuse), and non-mandated reporters made 43–60% (Mathews et al. 2015a, Table 2.4).

Overall, the rates of reports of child physical abuse made in the two states suggest that over a selected seven-year period, jurisdictions with similar socio-legal contexts may receive a rate of reports of approximately 330–1200 per 100,000 children. Within these ranges, lower rates appear to be associated with the absence of a legislative mandatory reporting duty and the lack of any other strong social contextual factor stimulating reports, as in Western Australia. Higher rates may be attributable to the long-term embedding of legislative reporting of physical abuse in Victoria, likely together with ongoing professional education about that duty, and possibly a general community-wide awareness of child physical abuse.

5.3. Relative Systems Impacts: Reports of Sexual Abuse Compared to Physical Abuse

The third research question asked: What are the relative systems impacts regarding the reporting of children in suspected cases of sexual abuse and physical abuse in the two different jurisdictions? Our analysis identified several major findings.

First, the differential rates of reporting of each type of abuse are notable. In Victoria, the rates for physical abuse compared with sexual abuse are 1048:406 per 100,000 children, despite the exact same legislative duty to report. At the population level, both kinds of abuse are widespread, although physical abuse may be more readily identifiable and or suspected, due to its greater tendency to have physically observable signs. In addition, physical abuse may be somewhat less likely to be subject to non-disclosure by children. The higher rate of reporting of physical abuse relative to sexual abuse by a factor of 2.5 may well be explained by inherent differences between the two types of abuse, their different presentations, and different capacity to detect cases. As well, it is possible that physical abuse is more common in the community, because parental corporal punishment is lawful when "reasonable" (R v Hughes 2015), and since a substantial proportion of physical abuse occurs through the escalation of parental discipline into abusive acts (Gershoff and Bitensky 2007).

Second, in Western Australia, where the reporting duty was introduced for sexual abuse but not for physical abuse, the rates of reports of physical vs. sexual abuse are 376:468 per 100,000 children. This pattern, where reports of physical abuse are lower than those for sexual abuse, inverts the trend found in Victoria, where reports of physical abuse are two and a half times those for sexual abuse, at 1048:406 per 100,000 children. These substantially different ratios suggest both that the presence of the new duty to report sexual abuse (together with associated education and general public sensitisation towards sexual abuse) had a distinct impact on reporting, and the absence of an equivalent duty to report for physical abuse (together with the absence of equivalent education and public sensitisation towards it). However, an associated finding is that the overall rate of reports of sexual abuse in Western Australia for this time period surpassed that of Victoria. This outcome is not unexpected, given that the experience of other jurisdictions shows that it can reasonably be anticipated that the introduction of a reporting duty for the first time will produce a sharp rise in reports in the next several years, which will then plateau (26).

Third, significantly, we can also note that substantial proportions of reports are made both by members of specific occupational groups, and by members of the public. In Victoria 2006–2012, mandated reporters made 36–56% of reports of sexual abuse, and non-mandated reporters made 44–63% (Mathews et al. 2015b, Table 2.5). Similarly, in Victoria, mandated reporters made 37–55% of reports of physical abuse, and non-mandated reporters made 44–62% (Mathews et al. 2015b, Table 2.4). Similar proportions were evident in Western Australia over 2006–2012. Those in the mandated occupations made 49–71% of reports of sexual abuse, and other reporters made 29–51% (Mathews et al. 2015a, Table 2.5). Those in the mandated occupations made 40–57% of reports of physical abuse (even though not required by the legal duty to report physical abuse), and non-mandated reporters made 43–60% (Mathews et al. 2015a, Table 2.4). This suggests that both members of the public and professionals who deal regularly with children are key parts of an entire child welfare apparatus, reflecting an appropriate whole-of-community response to child maltreatment, as befitting a public health approach (Mercy et al. 1993; Hammond et al. 2006; Daro 2016). This, in turn, means that support from government agencies needs to be provided to both these groups, to ensure that when reports are made, they are made about the kinds of circumstances intended by public policy, and that they contain the specific details needed by child welfare agencies to respond in the best possible way.

Fourth, while this article has the purpose of being exploratory and descriptive, we can note the overall systems burden in contextual terms, and draw tentative conclusions about sustainability, or at least provide useful factual findings about the extent to which the different reporting trends involve children in child welfare systems to any extent. For both types of abuse, the levels of report, even at their peak, involved quite low numbers of children. For sexual abuse, the single year peak of reporting in Western Australia (2012) equated to 1 in 156 children being the subject of a report: for context, in a school of 400 children, two to three per year. In Victoria, the single year peak in 2012 equated to 1 in 172 children being the subject of a report: a similar contextual proportion for a school of 400 children involving two to three per year. For physical abuse, the single year peak of reporting in Western Australia (2009) equated to 1 in 206 children being the subject of a report: for context, in a school of 400 children, two per year. In Victoria, the single year peak in 2010 equated to 1 in 84 children being the subject of a report: a similar contextual proportion for a school of 400 students children involving five per year. This rate in Victoria was consistent over several years.

5.4. Limitations

This study has several limitations. First, it was subject to the three data inconsistences that were artefacts of the two states' child protection data systems and beyond the control of the researchers.

However, despite this, the data systems are broadly comparable, and this was one reason justifying the selection of these two jurisdictions for comparison. Moreover, the choice of a seven-year period provides scope for longitudinal analysis, in which it is possible to detect trends. Second, the data were analysed at the distinct child level, rather than as the raw sum of all reports, including multiple reports for the same child. It could be argued that an assessment of the burden on child protection intake systems should be to consider all reports, without excluding multiple reports of the same child. However, our justification for analysing data at the distinct child level is that multiple reports of the same child can be screened out, or simply added to an existing file. The proportion of children with additional reports within the study period was relatively similar in each state. In Victoria, over the decade in which this seven-year period occurred, 55% of all children involved in reports were the subject of only one report, and a further 19% were the subject of two reports (Mathews et al. 2015b, Table 3.1). In Western Australia, 66% of all children involved in reports were the subject of only one report, and a further 19% were the subject of two reports (Mathews et al. 2015a, Table 3.1). These figures were for all forms of child maltreatment combined, and were not disaggregated. Re-reporting of this level in the study period was assessed as unlikely to significantly affect findings.

Third, the data are taken from 2006–2012 and have been analysed retrospectively for the purpose of considering our research questions. It may be argued that the information is dated, but alternatively, these data hold unique historical significance in providing information, frozen in time, that can be used to examine reporting rates and trends in two jurisdictions at a time when the differences in their two different legislative frameworks were perhaps the most salient. Fourth, for reasons of feasibility, our analysis here was limited to considering systems burden for agency intake data, and did not consider the systems burden associated with subsequent levels of agency disposition of reports, such as investigations. Further analysis exploring this question would be useful. Fifth, we did not consider other outcome measures, including case identification, service provision, child outcomes, and family outcomes. Such multi-level research with knowledge discovery and data mining, while beyond the scope of this paper, would substantially advance the field in the future.

6. Conclusions

This analysis of child welfare agency data found different trends in reports of child sexual abuse and physical abuse over the seven-year period 2006–2012. The two states had not dissimilar levels of reporting of child sexual abuse, with intra-State increases attributable to the introduction of a new legislative reporting duty, and heightened public awareness resulting from major social events. Arguably, the single most notable finding was the substantially different level of reporting of physical abuse between the two states. Victoria experienced nearly three times as many reports of physical abuse as Western Australia. While further research would be required to confirm the reasons for this, the presence in Victoria of a legislative mandatory reporting duty for physical abuse since 1993 may have strongly contributed to this difference.

The analysis found that the relative burden on the child protection system in terms of intake of reports for sexual abuse and physical abuse respectively was different in each of the two states, with the clearest difference evident in Victoria, where reports of physical abuse were two and a half times higher than for sexual abuse. Overall consideration of the rates of children involved in reports for these two types of abuse even at their single year peak suggest that levels of reporting were at a sustainable level. Finally, the analysis found that substantial proportions of reports were made by both legislatively mandated reporters, and non-mandated community members. This indicates that these sectors of society each play an important part in child protection from sexual and physical abuse, and that as part of a systematic public health approach to child protection, government agencies will benefit by engaging with communities and professions to enhance a desirable reporting practice.

Author Contributions: B.M. led acquisition of grant funding, supervised data curation and team administration, conceived the article, and wrote the first draft of the manuscript; L.B. collaborated on acquisition of grant funding, interpreted data and provided critical analysis and revision of the manuscript; K.W. interpreted data and provided

Soc. Sci. **2020**, *9*, 75

critical analysis and revision of the manuscript. All authors have read and agreed to the published version of the manuscript.

Funding: De-identified data from existing datasets were provided under an agreement between the Victorian Department of Health and Human Services, the Western Australia Department for Child Protection and Family Support and the researchers' institutions, as part of a broader study supported by the Victorian Government, and funded by the Australian Government Department of Social Services.

Acknowledgments: The authors would like to thank Sandra Coe and Stephanie Jowett for initial research assistance on the datasets. We gratefully acknowledge Andrea Boskovic for research assistance to support these analyses.

Conflicts of Interest: The authors declare no conflicts of interest.

References

Alaggia, Ramona, Delphine Collin-Vézina, and Rusan Lateef. 2019. Facilitators and Barriers to Child Sexual Abuse (CSA) Disclosures: A Research Update (2000–2016). *Trauma, Violence and Abuse* 20: 260–83. [CrossRef] [PubMed]

Anderst, Jim, Nancy Kellogg, and Inkyung Jung. 2009. Reports of repetitive penile-genital penetration often have no definitive evidence of penetration. *Pediatrics* 124: 403–9. [CrossRef] [PubMed]

Australian Bureau of Statistics. 2007. *3201.0: Australian Demographic Statistics, Table 6: Estimated Resident Population, by Age and Sex-at 30 June 2006*. Canberra: Commonwealth of Australia.

Australian Bureau of Statistics. 2009. *31010DO002: Australian Demographic Statistics, Table 6: Estimated Resident Population, by Age and Sex-at 30 June 2007*. Canberra: Commonwealth of Australia.

Australian Bureau of Statistics. 2010. *31010DO002: Australian Demographic Statistics, Table 7: Estimated Resident Population, by Age and Sex-at 30 June 2008*. Canberra: Commonwealth of Australia.

Australian Bureau of Statistics. 2011a. *31010DO002: Australian Demographic Statistics, Table 7: Estimated Resident Population, by Age and Sex-at 30 June 2009*. Canberra: Commonwealth of Australia.

Australian Bureau of Statistics. 2011b. *Census 2011b*. Canberra: Commonwealth of Australia.

Australian Bureau of Statistics. 2012. *31010DO002: Australian Demographic Statistics, Table 7: Estimated Resident Population, by Age and Sex-at 30 June 2010*. Canberra: Commonwealth of Australia.

Australian Bureau of Statistics. 2013. *31010DO002: Australian Demographic Statistics, Table 7: Estimated Resident Population, by Age and Sex-at 30 June 2011*. Canberra: Commonwealth of Australia.

Australian Bureau of Statistics. 2014. *31010DO002: Australian Demographic Statistics, Table 7: Estimated Resident Population, by Age and Sex-at 30 June 2012*. Canberra: Commonwealth of Australia.

Australian Bureau of Statistics. 2015. *31010DO002 Australian Demographic Statistics (Table 7: Estimated Resident Population, by Age and Sex at 30 June 2013)*. Canberra: Commonwealth of Australia.

Australian Bureau of Statistics. 2016. *2016 Census of Population and Housing: General Community Profile. Cat 2001.0*; Canberra: Commonwealth of Australia. Available online: https://www.abs.gov.au/ausstats/abs@.nsf/Lookup/by%20Subject/2071.0~{}2016~{}Main%20Features~{}Ageing%20Population~{}14 (accessed on 3 May 2020).

Australian Bureau of Statistics. 2020a. *3101.0 Australian Demographic Statistics (Table 52: Estimated Resident Population, by Single Year of Age, Victoria*. Canberra: Commonwealth of Australia.

Australian Bureau of Statistics. 2020b. *3101.0 Australian Demographic Statistics (Table 55: Estimated Resident Population, by Single Year of Age, Western Australia*. Canberra: Commonwealth of Australia.

Australian Government Royal Commission into Institutional Responses to Child Sexual Abuse. 2017. *Final Report*; Sydney: Commonwealth of Australia. Available online: https://www.childabuseroyalcommission.gov.au/final-report (accessed on 25 March 2020).

Australian Government Royal Commission into Institutional Responses to Child Sexual Abuse. 2014. Sydney: Commonwealth of Australia. Available online: https://www.childabuseroyalcommission.gov.au/other-reports (accessed on 25 March 2020).

Barth, Jule, Lilian Bermetz, Eva Heim, Sven Trelle, and Thomy Tonia. 2013. The current prevalence of child sexual abuse worldwide: A systematic review and meta-analysis. *International Journal of Public Health* 58: 469–83. [CrossRef] [PubMed]

Chen, Laura, M. Hassan Murad, Molly Paras, Kristina Colbenson, Amelia Sattler, Erin Goranson, Mohamed Elamin, Richard Seime, Gen Shinozaki, Larry Prokop, and et al. 2010. Sexual Abuse and Lifetime Diagnosis of Psychiatric Disorders: Systematic Review and Meta-Analysis. *Mayo Clinic Proceedings* 85: 618–29. [CrossRef]

Collin-Vézina, Delphine, Mireille De La Sablonniere-Griffin, Andrea Palmer, and Lise Milne. 2015. A preliminary mapping of individual, relational and social factors that impede disclosure of childhood sexual abuse. *Child Abuse & Neglect* 43: 123–34.

Cummins, Philip, Dorothy Scott, and Bill Scales. 2012. *Report of the Protecting Victoria's Vulnerable Children Inquiry*. Melbourne: State of Victoria Department of Premier and Cabinet.

Currie, Janet, and Cathy Spatz Widom. 2010. Long-term Consequences of Child Abuse and Neglect on Adult Economic Well-Being. *Child Maltreatment* 15: 111–20. [CrossRef]

Cutajar, Margaret, Paul Mullen, James Ogloff, Stuart Thomas, David Wells, and Josie Spataro. 2010a. Psychopathology in a large cohort of sexually abused children followed up to 43 years. *Child Abuse & Neglect* 34: 813–22.

Cutajar, Margaret, Paul Mullen, James Ogloff, Stuart Thomas, David Wells, and Josie Spataro. 2010b. Suicide and fatal drug overdose in child sexual abuse victims: A historical cohort study. *Medical Journal of Australia* 192: 184–87. [CrossRef]

Daignault, Isabelle, and Martine Hebert. 2009. Profiles of school adaptation: Social, behavioural and academic functioning in sexually abused girls. *Child Abuse & Neglect* 33: 102–15.

Danese, Andrea, Terrie Moffitt, Louise Arseneault, Ben Bleiberg, Perry Dinardo, Stephanie Gandelman, Renate Houts, Anthony Ambler, Helen Fisher, Richie Poulton, and et al. 2016. The origins of cognitive deficits in victimized children: implications for neuroscientists and clinicians. *American Journal of Psychiatry* 174: 349–61. [CrossRef]

Daro, Deborah. 2016. A public health approach to prevention: What will it take? *Trauma, Violence & Abuse* 17: 420–21.

Degli Esposti, Michelle, David K. Humphreys, Benjamin M. Jenkins, Antonio Gasparrini, Siân Pooley, Manuel Eisner, and Lucy Bowes. 2019. Long-term trends in child maltreatment in England and Wales, 1858–2016: An observational, time-series analysis. *Lancet Public Health* 4: e148–e158. [CrossRef]

Dube, Shanta, Jacqueline Miller, David Brown, Wayne Giles, Vincent Felitti, Maxia Dong, and Robert Anda. 2006. Adverse childhood experiences and the association with ever using alcohol and initiating alcohol use during adolescence. *Journal of Adolescent Health* 38: 444.e1–444.e10. [CrossRef]

Easton, Scott. 2013. Disclosure of Child Sexual Abuse among Adult Male Survivors. *Clinical Social Work Journal* 41: 344–55. [CrossRef]

Easton, Scott, Leia Y. Saltzman, and Danny G. Willis. 2014. 'Would You Tell Under Circumstances Like That?' Barriers to Disclosure of Child Sexual Abuse for Men. *Psychology of Men and Masculinity* 15: 460–69. [CrossRef]

Edwards, Valerie, Jennifer Freyd, Shanta Dube, Robert Anda, and Vincent Felitti. 2012. Health outcomes by closeness of sexual abuse perpetrator: A test of betrayal trauma theory. *Journal of Aggression, Maltreatment, and Trauma* 21: 133–48. [CrossRef]

Erooga, Marcus, Keith Kaufman, and Judith G. Zatkin. 2019. Powerful perpetrators, hidden in plain sight: An international analysis of organizational child sexual abuse cases. *Journal of Sexual Aggression* 26: 62–90. [CrossRef]

Fang, Xiangming, Derek Brown, Curtis Florence, and James Mercy. 2012. The economic burden of child maltreatment in the United States and implications for prevention. *Child Abuse & Neglect* 36: 156–65.

Fang, Xiangming, Deborah Fry, Derek Brown, James Mercy, Michael Dunne, Alexander Butchart, Phaedar Corso, Kateryna Maynzyuk, Yuriy Dzhygyr, Amalee McCoy, and et al. 2015. The burden of child maltreatment in the East Asia and Pacific region. *Child Abuse & Neglect* 42: 146–62.

Feldman, Kenneth, Ross Bethel, Richard Shugeman, David Grossman, M. Sean Grady, and Richard Ellenbogen. 2001. The cause of infant and toddler subdural hemorrhage: a prospective study. *Pediatrics* 108: 636–46. [CrossRef]

Flaherty, Emalee, Jeannette M. Perez-Rossello, Michael A. Levine, William L. Hennrikus, and The American Academy of Pediatrics Committee on Child Abuse and Neglect. 2014. Evaluating Children with Fractures for Child Physical Abuse. *Pediatrics* 133: e477–e489. [CrossRef] [PubMed]

Fontes, Lisa Aronson, and Carol Plummer. 2010. Cultural Issues in Disclosures of Child Sexual Abuse. *Journal of Child Sexual Abuse* 19: 491–518. [CrossRef] [PubMed]

Ford, Prudence. 2007. *Review of the Department for Community Development*. Perth: Department for Community Development.

Gershoff, Elizabeth T., and Susan H. Bitensky. 2007. The Case against Corporal Punishment of Children: Converging Evidence from Social Science Research and International Human Rights Law and Implications for U.S. Policy. *Psychology, Public Policy, and Law* 13: 231–72. [CrossRef]

Gilbert, Ruth, Cathy Widom, Kevin Browne, David Fergusson, Elspeth Webb, and Staffan Janson. 2009. Burden and consequences of child maltreatment in high-income countries. *Lancet* 373: 68–81. [CrossRef]

Gordon, Sue, Kay Hallahan, and Darrell Henry. 2020. *Putting the Picture Together: Inquiry into Response by Government Agencies to Complaints of Family Violence and Child Abuse in Aboriginal Communities*; Melbourne: Department of Premier and Cabinet. Available online: https://ww.slp.wa.gov/au/publications/ (accessed on 5 April 2020).

Hammond, W. Rodney, Daniel Whitaker, John Lutzker, James Mercy, and Pamela Chin. 2006. Setting a violence prevention agenda at the centers for disease control and prevention. *Aggression and Violent Behavior* 11: 112–19. [CrossRef]

Heger, Astrid, Lynne Ticson, Oralia Velasquez, and Raphael Bernier. 2002. Children referred for possible sexual abuse: Medical findings in 2384 children. *Child Abuse & Neglect* 26: 645–59.

Independent Inquiry Into Child Sexual Abuse. 2015. Terms of Reference. Available online: https://www.iicsa.org.uk/terms-reference (accessed on 29 March 2020).

Kemp, Alison, Frank Dunstan, Sara Harrison, Susan Morris, Mala Mann, Kim Rolfe, Shalini Datta, D. Phillip Thomas, Jonathan Sibert, and Sabine Maguire. 2008. Patterns of skeletal fractures in child abuse: Systematic review. *British Medical Journal* 337: a1518. [CrossRef]

Kempe, Charles H., Frederic Silverman, Brandt Steele, William Droegemueller, and Henry Silver. 1962. The Battered-Child Syndrome. *Journal of the American Medical Association* 181: 17–24. [CrossRef]

Kolko, David. 1992. Characteristics of child victims of physical violence: research findings and clinical implications. *Journal of Interpersonal Violence* 7: 244–76. [CrossRef]

Kum, Hye-Chung, Stewart C. Joy, Roderick A. Rose, and Dean F. Duncan. 2015. Using big data for evidence based governance in child welfare. *Children and Youth Services Review* 58: 127–36. [CrossRef]

Lansford, Jennifer, Kenneth Dodge, Gregory Pettit, John Bates, Joseph Crozier, and Julie Kaplow. 2002. A 12 year prospective study of the long-term effects of early child physical maltreatment. *Archives of Pediatric and Adolescent Medicine* 156: 824–30. [CrossRef] [PubMed]

Lemaigre, Charlotte, Emily Taylor, and Claire Gittoes. 2017. Barriers and facilitators to disclosing sexual abuse in childhood and adolescence: A systematic review. *Child Abuse & Neglect* 70: 39–52.

Letourneau, Elizabeth, Derek Brown, Xiangming Fang, Ahmed Hassan, and James Mercy. 2018. The economic burden of child sexual abuse in the United States. *Child Abuse & Neglect* 79: 413–22.

Liley, William, Anne Stephens, Melissa Kaltner, Sarah Larkins, Richard C. Franklin, Komla Tsey, Rebecca Stewart, and Simon Stewart. 2012. Infant abusive head trauma. *Australian Family Physician* 41: 823–32.

London, Kamala, Maggie Bruck, Stephen Ceci, and Daniel Shuman. 2007. Disclosure of Child Sexual Abuse: A Review of the Contemporary Empirical Literature. In *Child Sexual Abuse: Disclosure, Delay, and Denial*. Edited by Margaret-Ellen Pipe, Michael Lamb, Yael Orbach and Ann-Christin Cederborg. New York: Routledge, pp. 11–47.

Mathews, Ben. 2012. Exploring the contested role of mandatory reporting laws in the identification of severe child abuse and neglect. In *Current Legal Issues Volume 14: Law and Childhood Studies*. Edited by Michael Freeman. Oxford: Oxford University Press, pp. 302–38.

Mathews, Ben. 2014a. Mandatory Reporting Laws and Identification of Child Abuse and Neglect: Consideration of Differential Maltreatment Types, and a Cross-Jurisdictional Analysis of Child Sexual Abuse Reports. *Social Sciences* 3: 460–82. [CrossRef]

Mathews, Ben. 2014b. *Mandatory Reporting Laws for Child Sexual Abuse in Australia—A Legislative History: Report for the Royal Commission into Institutional Responses to Child Sexual Abuse*. Sydney: Commonwealth of Australia.

Mathews, Ben. 2015. Mandatory reporting laws: Their origin, nature and development over time. In *Mandatory Reporting Laws and the Identification of Severe Child Abuse and Neglect*. Edited by Ben Mathews and Donald Bross. Dordrecht: Springer, pp. 3–27.

Mathews, Ben. 2018. *Research on Reporting of Child Maltreatment: Report for the New South Wales Department of Family and Community Services*. Brisbane: Queensland University of Technology.

Mathews, Ben. 2019a. *New International Frontiers in Child Sexual Abuse: Theory, Problems and Progress*. Dordrecht: Springer.

Mathews, Ben. 2019b. A taxonomy of duties to report child sexual abuse: Legal developments offer new ways to facilitate disclosure. *Child Abuse & Neglect* 88: 337–47.

Mathews, Ben, and Donald Bross. 2008. Mandated reporting is still a policy with reason: Empirical evidence and philosophical grounds. *Child Abuse and Neglect* 32: 511–16. [CrossRef]

Mathews, Ben, and Delphine Collin-Vézina. 2019. Child Sexual Abuse: Towards a conceptual model and definition. *Trauma, Violence & Abuse* 20: 131–48.

Mathews, Ben, and Maureen Kenny. 2008. Mandatory reporting legislation in the USA, Canada and Australia: A cross-jurisdictional review of key features, differences and issues. *Child Maltreatment* 13: 50–63. [CrossRef]

Mathews, Ben, and Kerryann Walsh. 2014. Mandatory reporting laws. In *Families, Policy and the Law: Selected Essays on Contemporary Issues for Australia*. Edited by Alan Hayes and Daryl Higgins. Melbourne: Australian Institute for Family Studies, pp. 131–42.

Mathews, Ben, Chris Goddard, Robert Lonne, Stephanie Short, and Freda Briggs. 2009a. Developments in Australian laws requiring the reporting of suspected child sexual abuse. *Children Australia* 34: 18–23. [CrossRef]

Mathews, Ben, Heather Payne, Catherine Bonnet, and David Chadwick. 2009b. A way to restore British paediatricians' engagement with child protection. *Archives of Disease in Childhood* 94: 329–32. [CrossRef]

Mathews, Ben, Kerryann Walsh, Mehdi Rassafiani, Des Butler, and Ann Farrell. 2009c. Teachers reporting suspected child sexual abuse: results of a three-State study. *University of New South Wales Law Journal* 32: 772–813.

Mathews, Ben, Bromfield Leah, Walsh Kerryann, and Vimpani Graham. 2015a. *Child Abuse and Neglect: A Socio-Legal Study of Mandatory Reporting in Australia—Report for the Western Australian Government*; Brisbane: Queensland University of Technology. Available online: https://www.dss.gov.au/sites/default/files/documents/03_2016/child-abuse-and-neglect-v9-wa.pdf (accessed on 25 March 2020).

Mathews, Ben, Bromfield Leah, Walsh Kerryann, and Vimpani Graham. 2015b. *Child Abuse and Neglect: A Socio-Legal Study of Mandatory Reporting in Australia—Report for the Victorian Government*; Brisbane: Queensland University of Technology. Available online: https://www.dss.gov.au/sites/default/files/documents/03_2016/child-abuse-and-neglect-v8-vic.pdf (accessed on 25 March 2020).

Mathews, Ben, Xing Ju Lee, and Rosana Norman. 2016. Impact of a new mandatory reporting law on reporting and identification of child sexual abuse: A seven-year time trend analysis. *Child Abuse & Neglect* 56: 62–79.

Mathews, Ben, Leah Bromfield, Kerryann Walsh, Qinglu Cheng, and Rosana Norman. 2017. Reports of child sexual abuse of boys and girls: Longitudinal trends over a 20-year period in Victoria, Australia. *Child Abuse & Neglect* 66: 9–22.

May-Chahal, Corinne, and Patricia Cawson. 2005. Measuring child maltreatment in the United Kingdom: A study of the prevalence of child abuse and neglect. *Child Abuse & Neglect* 29: 969–84.

McElvaney, Rosaleen. 2013. Disclosure of child sexual abuse: Delays, non-disclosure and partial disclosure. *Child Abuse Review* 24: 159–69. [CrossRef]

McGee, Hannah, Rebecca Garavan, Joanne Byrne, Madeleine O'Higgins, and Ronan Conroy. 2011. Secular trends in child and adult sexual violence—One decreasing and the other increasing: A population survey in Ireland. *European Journal of Public Health* 21: 98–103. [CrossRef]

Mercy, James, Mark Rosenberg, Kenneth Powell, Claire Broome, and William Roper. 1993. Public health policy for preventing violence. *Health Affairs* 12: 7–29. [CrossRef]

Norman, Rosana, Munkhtsetseg Byambaa, Rumna De, Alexander Butchart, James Scott, and Theo Vos. 2012. The long-term health consequences of child physical abuse, emotional abuse, and neglect: a systematic review and meta-analysis. *PLoS Medicine* 9: e1001349. [CrossRef] [PubMed]

Paolucci, Elizabeth Oddone, Mark Genuis, and Claudio Violato. 2001. A meta-analysis of the published research on the effects of child sexual abuse. *The Journal of Psychology* 135: 17–36. [CrossRef]

Paulsen, Monrad, Graham Parker, and Lynn Adelman. 1965. Child Abuse Reporting Laws: Some Legislative History. *The George Washington Law Review* 34: 482–506.

Pereda, Noemi, Georgina Guilera, Maria Forns, and Juana Gomez-Benito. 2009. The prevalence of child sexual abuse in community and student samples: A meta-analysis. *Clinical Psychology Review* 29: 328–38. [CrossRef]

Putnam, Frank. 2003. Ten-year research update review: Child sexual abuse. *Journal of the American Academy of Child & Adolescent Psychiatry* 42: 269–78.

R v Hughes. 2015. VSC 312. Available online: https://jade.io/j/?a=outline&id=399903 (accessed on 25 March 2020).

Radford, Lorraine, Susana Corral, Christine Bradley, and Helen Fisher. 2013. The prevalence and impact of child maltreatment and other types of victimization in the UK: findings from a population survey of caregivers, children and young people and young adults. *Child Abuse & Neglect* 37: 801–13.

Reading, Richard, Susan Bissell, Jeffrey Goldhagen, Judith Harwin, Judith Masson, Sian Moynihan, Nigel Parton, Marta Santos Pais, June Thoburn, and Elspeth Webb. 2009. Promotion of children's rights and prevention of child maltreatment. *Lancet* 373: 332–43. [CrossRef]

Simpson, Tracy, and William R. Miller. 2002. Concomitance between childhood sexual and physical abuse and substance abuse problems: A review. *Clinical Psychological Review* 22: 27–77. [CrossRef]

Smith, Carly Parnitzke, and Jennifer Freyd. 2013. Dangerous Safe Havens: Institutional Betrayal Exacerbates Sexual Trauma. *Journal of Traumatic Stress* 26: 119–24. [CrossRef]

Smith, Daniel, Elizabeth Letourneau, Benjamin Saunders, Dean Kilpatrick, Heidi Resnick, and Connie Best. 2000. Delay in Disclosure of Childhood Rape: Results from a National Survey. *Child Abuse and Neglect* 24: 273–87. [CrossRef]

Spataro, Josie, Paul Mullen, Philip Burgess, David Wells, and Simon Moss. 2004. Impact of child sexual abuse on mental health: Prospective study in males and females. *British Journal of Psychiatry* 184: 416–21. [CrossRef]

Stoltenborgh, Marije, Marinus H. van Ijzendoorn, Eveline M. Euser, and Marian J. Bakermans-Kranenburg. 2011. A global perspective on child sexual abuse: Meta-analysis of prevalence around the world. *Child Maltreatment* 16: 79–101. [CrossRef] [PubMed]

Teicher, Martin, and Jacqueline Samson. 2016. Annual research review: enduring neurobiological effects of childhood abuse and neglect. *Journal of Child Psychology and Psychiatry* 57: 241–66. [CrossRef] [PubMed]

Trickett, Penelope, Jennie Noll, and Frank Putnam. 2011. The impact of sexual abuse on female development: Lessons from a multigenerational, longitudinal research study. *Developmental Psychopathology* 23: 453–76. [CrossRef] [PubMed]

U.S. Department of Health and Human Services. 2009. *Child Maltreatment 2007*. Available online: http://www.acf.hhs.gov/programs/cb/resource/childmaltreatment-2007 (accessed on 25 March 2020).

United Nations General Assembly. 2015. *Sustainable Development Goals 2015*. Available online: https://sustainabledevelopment.un.org/ (accessed on 25 March 2020).

Victorian Family and Community Development Committee. 2013. *Betrayal of Trust: Inquiry into the Handling of Child Abuse by Religious and Other Nongovernment Organisations*; Melbourne: Family and Community Development Committee. Available online: http://www.parliament.vic.gov.au/component/content/article/340-inquiry-into-thehandling-of-child-abuse-by-religious-and-other-organisations/1788-reportVictorianGovernment (accessed on 25 March 2020).

Walsh, Kerryann, Ben Mathews, Mehdi Rassafiani, Ann Farrell, and Des Butler. 2012. Understanding teachers' reporting of child sexual abuse: Measurement methods matter. *Children and Youth Services Review* 34: 1937–46. [CrossRef]

Widom, Cathy Spatz, and Longterm Consequences of Child Maltreatment. 2014. *Handbook of Child Maltreatment*. Edited by Jill Korbin and Richard Krugman. Dordrecht: Springer Scientific, pp. 225–50.

World Health Organization and International Society for Prevention of Child Abuse and Neglect. 2006. *Preventing Child Maltreatment: A Guide to Taking Action and Generating Evidence*. Available online: http://www.who.int/iris/handle/10665/43499 (accessed on 25 March 2020).

1.3. Safeguarding Children with a Disability

Children who have a disability have been said to be one of the most vulnerable groups in our society (Jones et al. 2012; National Society for the Prevention of Cruelty to Children 2003; Oosterhoorn and Kendrick 2001; Sanghera 2007). In a scoping review of the literature, Stalker and McArthur (2012) stated that "Several studies have revealed a strong association between disability and child maltreatment indicating that disabled children are significantly more likely to experience abuse than their non-disabled peers" (p. 24).

There is some evidence which suggests that children with a disability are at greater risk of abuse in sport. For example, Vertommen et al. (2016) found that 50% of survey respondents with a disability reported experiencing psychological violence as a child within sport, compared to 38% of people without a disability. In terms of physical violence, the prevalence was 32% for those with a disability compared to 11% for those without a disability. Finally, 34% of people with a disability reported experiencing sexual violence in sport compared to 14% of those without a disability. These findings emphasize that, whilst it is important for all children, safeguarding takes on additional significance when considering children with a disability because of the higher rates of abuse in this population.

1.4. Rugby Union

In the English Rugby Football Union (RFU), Club Safeguarding Officers (CSOs) and Constituent Body Safeguarding Managers (CBSMs) are volunteers with a specialist duty to safeguard children who participate within their club or county respectively. As described in the RFU safeguarding policy, CSOs are " ... the first point of contact for safeguarding and welfare concerns", and are " ... member[s] of, or attends the appropriate club committees making safeguarding issues a priority at the proper level" (Rugby Football Union 2011, p. 9). Moreover, CBSMs ensure " ... all safeguarding incidents or issues are reported to the RFU Safeguarding team and manages disciplinary cases referred back to the CB by the RFU" (Rugby Football Union 2011, p. 8).

1.5. Research Aims

There is a growing acknowledgement that sports organizations have a duty of care (Grey-Thompson 2017). It is important that such strategic efforts are informed by empirical evidence. The perceptions and experiences of people with a safeguarding role in Rugby Union were explored in the present research because of the central role they play in safeguarding children with a disability. A mixed-methods design was used for the research, which was divided into two studies.

2. Study 1—Materials and Methods

2.1. Participants

In study 1, all (N = 2219) Club Safeguarding Officers (CSOs) and all (N = 62) Constituate Body Safeguarding Managers (CBSMs) that represented the different regions were contacted via email with a link to the online questionnaire. A sample (N = 389: 51.7% male and 48.3% female) was achieved which represented a response rate of 17%.

2.2. Instruments and Procedures

Ethical approval was gained for this study from the first author's university prior to data collection. An online questionnaire was created on SmartSurvey™ (www.smartsurvey.co.uk). Owing to the exploratory nature of the research, the questionnaire was developed by the researchers and further developed in consultation with the RFU Safeguarding team. The questionnaire consisted of a series of quantitative questions grouped within three categories. The first section focused on demographics (i.e., gender, occupation, duration in their role, if they had any other roles in the sport and the training they had received). Secondly, they were asked about their experiences of working with a child with a disability in Rugby Union.

We developed the categories of disability based on the Equality Act 2010 and resources developed by the Child Protection in Sport Unit (National Society for the Prevention of Cruelty to Children 2015). As such, we asked about experiences of working with children who have a behavioral, neurological, physical or sensory disability, whilst also providing an 'other' category. The third section explored the extent to which they feel that children with a disability had been successfully safeguarded as well as the extent to which their club was ready to effectively safeguard these children in the future.

2.3. Data Analysis

The quantitative data were analyzed using basic descriptive statistics.

3. Study 1—Results

The following sections summarize the findings with respect to study 1.

3.1. Experiences of the Participants

Table 1 summarizes the experiences of the participants with respect to the length of time in the role and any relevant training that they had received. Overall, these data demonstrate the variety of experience, ranging from less than a year through to more than 10 years. The majority of participants had been in their role for less than 3 years.

Table 1. Time in role and related training.

Time in Role (Years)	% (N)	Training	Contact	% (N)
<1	22.6% (88)	Outside	36.2%	14.9% (58)
1–3	35.2% (137)	None	32.4%	43.7% (170)
4 or 5	21.3% (83)	Both	19%	4.1% (16)
6–9 years	12.3% (46)	Inside	10.3%	26.5% (103)
10+	8.5% (33)	Not provided	2.1%	1.5% (6)
Not provided	0.5% (2)		Not provided	9.3% (36)

The participants were asked whether they had received safeguarding training in relation to children with a disability. Respondents had received training outside of Rugby Union (36.2%), inside Rugby Union (10.3%) or both (19%). The data thus revealed that almost two-thirds of participants had received a form of relevant safeguarding training. Interestingly, this also means that almost one-third of respondents (32.4%) reported that they had received no relevant training.

Participants also reported having multiple roles within the club such as being a parent (42.9%), coach (25.2%) or committee member (24.7%). Furthermore, 31.4% (N = 122) currently work or had worked in a role with relevance to child protection (e.g., in education, health care, Police). This highlights the variety of skills which people may well bring to their role from outside sport which could inform the effective safeguarding of children with a disability.

3.2. Types of Disability and How these Were Identified

The participants were asked about the different types of disability which they had worked with in their role (see Table 2). The most frequent category was behavioral disabilities, and this was reported by over 50% of this sample. This was followed by physical (20.6%), neurological (14%) and sensory (9.6%) disabilities. Interestingly, 5.6% of respondents selected the 'other' category with the majority of related examples concerning poverty. One participant explained "Some children can be financially vulnerable through teasing for not being able to afford the correct kit". This suggests that these participants adopt a broad conceptualization of disability to include a range of factors which may render a child more vulnerable. The principles outlined in the rest of the findings may well be applicable to these broader categories. However, the focus was on children with a behavioral, neurological, physical or sensory disability.

Table 2. Working with children who have a disability.

Category	%	How Identified?	%	Contact	%
Behavioral	50.2%	Parent/Guardian	46.7%	Never	14.9%
Physical	20.6%	Coach	23.6%	Rarely	43.7%
Neurological	14%	Induction	14.8%	Monthly	4.1%
Sensory	9.6%	Own observations	12.3%	Weekly	26.5%
Other	5.6%	Child	2.6%	Daily	1.5%

Table 2 also summarizes the various ways in which a child with a disability was identified. These included the parent/guardian, coach, induction process, the respondent's own observation or the child themselves. This range of methods emphasizes that a variety of stakeholders may be the first to identify a child's disability. Overall, 75.8% of respondents said that they had worked with at least one child with a disability within Rugby Union. Table 2 displays the different frequencies of interactions. A total of 32.1% worked with a child who has a disability at least on a monthly basis. These statistics serve to emphasize the significance of this research topic within Rugby Union and sport more generally.

3.3. Inclusion and Exclusion Related to Safeguarding

Participants were asked about their perceptions and experiences regarding how children with a disability had been included or excluded from a safeguarding perspective. In total, 54.0% (N = 210) felt that a child with a disability had been safely included within their club. However, 15.2% (N = 59) of this sample felt that a child with a disability was participating but that they had not been safely included in their club. Overall, 15.9% (N = 62) of participants had experienced a child being excluded due to their disability. Looking forward, 59.7% (N = 232) agreed that their club was now ready to safely include a child with a disability.

Overall, study 1 highlighted that the majority of participants had interacted with a child who had a disability. Furthermore, not all participants had received appropriate training to support this aspect of their role and many people felt that their club was not ready to effectively safeguard these children. As a result, a second study was conducted to help develop a framework to guide the safeguarding of children with a disability.

4. Study 2—Material and Methods

4.1. Participants

A follow-up survey was sent to the 389 respondents from study 1. This survey invited the respondents to write about their experiences with respect to any challenges or examples of promising practice. Participants were also asked to indicate whether they would be happy to be interviewed regarding their experiences. A total of 329 completed the written responses (response rate = 85%) and 172 offered an interview (44%). The examples provided through this qualitative survey data were shared with the 62 Safeguarding Managers at their annual conference. Group discussions highlighted the need for promising practices to consider the key stages of identifying children with a disability, understanding how they can be safeguarded and then informing everyone who needs to know. Potential interviewees were then identified through consultations with staff at the Rugby Football Union based on ensuring that these topics were covered and that a geographical spread was achieved. Three participants were identified who gave promising practice examples in relation to each of the three topics. A further five participants were identified who provided examples across all of these topics. In order to capture experiences from across England, participants were identified such that there were 2 from each of the following seven regions: North West, North East, West Midlands,

East Midlands, South West, South East and London. All of the 14 identified participants agreed to be interviewed. It was felt that data saturation had been achieved at this point, and hence data collection was concluded.

4.2. Instruments and Procedures

Ethical approval was gained for this study from the first author's university prior to data collection. The 14 participants were e-mailed to make arrangements for the interview. A mutually convenient time was identified. The voluntary nature of participation, as well as assurances of anonymity and confidentiality, were reiterated prior to the interview. The interview began by reviewing the participant's responses to both the quantitative survey in study 1 as well as the qualitative survey in study 2. Any identified issues were discussed. The remainder of the interview adopted a temporal approach and focused on the three key topics of how children with a disability should be identified, how the safeguards can be identified and how stakeholders can appropriately be informed. The interviews were recorded using a Dictaphone and transcribed verbatim.

4.3. Data Analysis

The qualitative responses from the online survey as well as the interviews were analyzed using the stages of thematic analysis outlined by Braun and Clarke (2006). An inductive approach was adopted to identify the strategies which promote effective safeguarding. The first stage of this analytical process was familiarization. In order to do this, we read through the qualitative data several times. At this stage, notes were taken to be considered in more detail at a later stage. The second stage involved generating initial codes. We manually worked through the data to determine both semantic and latent features which described the challenges being experienced. The third stage began once all data had been coded and codes had been collated. We sorted through each of the codes attempting to place them into groups with codes which represented a particular strategy. This involved the researchers going to and from unsorted groups of codes, attempting to find the best groupings. We followed Braun and Clarke's suggestion that themes that do not fit anywhere may be temporarily categorized as miscellaneous (Braun and Clarke 2006). Stage 4 involved the review and refinement of the identified themes. In stage 5, the researchers defined each theme. Braun and Clarke describe this as "identifying the essence of what each theme is about" (Braun and Clarke 2006, p. 92). This required the researchers to interpret the codes, rather than merely paraphrase the data, and they relied upon the made when the codes were initially developed.

5. Study 2—Results

Study 1 highlighted that the safeguarding of children with a disability in Rugby Union was a significant issue. From analyzing the qualitative data collected through the survey and interviews, a four-stage model was developed to guide the safeguarding of children with a disability.

- Trigger—identification of the child;
- Action Plan—identifying the safeguards;
- Communication—communicating the plan and safeguards;
- Learning—disseminating good practice.

This approach was labelled the TACL model (pronounced tackle) such that it had relevance to the language of Rugby Union. Each of these four stages are now explained and illustrated with quotes from participants.

5.1. Trigger

The Trigger phase relates to how a child with a disability is identified. As every child's circumstances will vary, it is important that each club identify children in a sensitive way, such that parents and children feel able to disclose a disability. Parents may feel wary until they believe that their child could be included and safeguarded within the club setting. On the other hand, it was perceived that coaches may identify the need for a child to be assessed regarding a possible disability. It is, therefore, in the interests of all parties that the disability is identified sensitively.

Through analysis of the qualitative responses, participants perceived that children, who have a disability which was disclosed at the child's induction, were more likely to have a positive experience. Collaborative discussions with the parent/guardian were viewed as an important step towards safeguarding the child. However, the parent/guardian needs to have confidence in the system for this to be effective. The issue of confidentiality raises interesting questions, particularly when a child has a disability which may impact other children, but the parent/carer does not want other people to be made aware of the disability.

Participants reported particular challenges with respect to hidden disabilities. Often such disabilities were only identified as a result of an incident. Examples included a child being unhappy with the way in which they had been treated by the coach, a violent attack by a child, concerns of bullying and disruptive behavior. All of these cases were attributed to a lack of understanding of the child's disability which simply resulted from the coach or club not being aware of the disability.

One participant reported believing that a child was exhibiting challenging behavior that may be associated with a disability. However, the child's parents were reportedly unaware of the severity of their child's challenging behaviors, and the impact of the behavior on the coach and other children. The child assaulted an opposition player during a match and was sent off—something uncommon in that respective age group. What occurred afterwards was described below and explicates that the need for safeguarding pertains to more than just the individual child:

> "That then went to an informal disciplinary, we didn't call it a disciplinary, we called it a chat. I was there and the parents of course were invited to come along with the child and just have a chat about what had happened and why etcetera and during that talk we realized the parents didn't really fully realize how bad the child's behavior was. We decided we were actually going to issue a ban for half-a-season and this was actually called 'time out'. We called it 'time out' because his teammates were starting to reject him, they didn't want him to play with them."

The disclosure of a child's disability is not just to help to safeguard the individual child, but all children and coaches. Many interviewees identified the need for a standardized template for all clubs to use during induction. At present, when a child begins rugby at a club, a Young Player Registration Form (YPRF) has to be completed, which does not highlight all forms of disability. A form kept within the club, as suggested by some participants, could help the parent in disclosing their child's disability. Disclosing a disability from the outset could lead to a more proactive approach to dealing with any incidents that could occur. Participants reported that effective communication was important from the outset:

> "If you improve communication, training and publicize that the RFU actively promote children with additional vulnerabilities that would help."

It should be emphasized to the parent that their child having a disability will not necessarily preclude them from joining a club, but that their participation in certain areas of the sport might be limited. This is because of the physicality of Rugby Union. The first phase of effective safeguarding thus begins with disclosure. Once the trigger has taken place, there is then a need to develop an action plan.

5.2. Action Plan

After a child's disability has been disclosed through a trigger it could be appropriate for an action plan to be created through discussion with the child, parents, coaches and Safeguarding Officer. A participant suggested:

"Clubs need a support mechanism/group to guide individual training and implementation plans for specific children."

An example of how this had worked well is provided by the following quote:

"One of our kids has a neurological disability in our team and his Mum has just started to coach down the club … he can have quite challenging behavior, so when they joined we sat down and said look you know we want him to come … if your son is presenting this behavior, you're the expert, what works? What works for him? What doesn't work? What should we do? What's the first line he responds to?"

Through creating a plan and asking the parent for their advice as "the expert" regarding her child's needs, the child was successfully included in the sport. Consequently, it could be interpreted that it may be appropriate to discuss each child's needs and how the club has the best chance of successfully safeguarding a child on an on-going basis. As suggested by a participant, positioning the parent as the expert may help to facilitate their engagement in the process.

An action plan could also outline the use of different coaching methods, such as using visual aids, as used by one interviewee. Although one interviewee stated that:

"An action plan might become too formal because, you know … you don't want to take the fun out of it that's supposed to be there … you just want your child to take part … I think the only way I could see something, it has to be very individualized, depending on how the child would respond."

The action plan should be designed to help promote the protection of the child and to aid their involvement within the sport, whilst keeping their health and well-being at the center. Indeed, when a trigger has been identified but an action plan is not implemented then the following can occur:

"I know the child has a diagnosis of a disability, very, very hyperactive. There were constant issues, but Mum wasn't acknowledging that her child, at that point, had difficulties and was blaming everything on the coaches, you know, it's your fault because you're not talking to him in a way in which I do."

Safeguarding Officers explained that coaches may feel under pressure to create and facilitate a coaching environment which is inclusive for all children, without having the training for this to be achieved successfully.

"Challenging behavior puts more responsibility on coaches and greater expectation from some parents".

As a result, a conversation between all parties and the development of an action plan may facilitate more positive experiences. It was also highlighted that parents can play a critical support role:

"I think the other important part is that if the parents want their kids to succeed, they will support the coaches."

The action plan would provide a mechanism through which this support could be channeled. However, simply developing a plan is not the end of the process. It clearly needs to be effectively communicated to all relevant stakeholders.

5.3. Communication

Communicating the action plan to key stakeholders (e.g., coaches and parents) to promote the safeguarding of the child in Rugby Union was viewed as a key third stage. This communication stage was epitomized by one interviewee who outlined the following response after issues had arisen related to a child's behavioral disability:

"He had a diagnosis of what the boy's problems were. The Dad then came back and wrote out a letter for the coaches and circulated it to me. It explained how to manage his son's behavior, you know, the best way for the coaches to communicate with him. So, as a result of that the boy was integrated back into the game and we also asked the Dad if we could circulate it to the whole minis section. The Dad is always there on the touchline, he's very supportive. All the coaches know the way he [the child] is and this young lad is very much into the game."

This stage was viewed as being particularly important for coaches who may not have the knowledge, skills or experience of working with someone who has the given disability. For example:

"The coaches are volunteers, they're not trained to deal with psychological aspects, they're not trained particularly with children with vulnerabilities; they need to be aware of the vulnerabilities, but they're not actually trained."

"If we think about people on the Autism Spectrum, the people who are coaching them need specific skills in understanding their responses and then dealing with them appropriately, because it's no good well-meaning coaches who don't have any experience in working with young people with Autism."

It was this relationship with the parent that was seen as playing a critical role not only in the previous trigger and action plan stages but also in this communication stage. This should help to ensure that all stakeholders are kept aware of the action plan. An effective safeguarding system will adopt a reflective approach through continually reviewing and sharing good practice. This can help to promote learning throughout the organization.

5.4. Learning

The final stage was labelled Learning and this was focused on promoting a reflective approach in which good practice was identified, shared and utilized. This was not originally a key focus of the interview but emerged as a key theme through the data analysis process. Interviewees highlighted a number of ways through which this may be achieved.

The first recommendation was an online resource. Participants would welcome this as a useful starting point for understanding and safeguarding children with a disability. Participants felt that it would be beneficial to have clear summaries regarding a range of different disabilities which outlined the nature of the disability, the ways in which this may be manifested, along with case studies as to how safeguarding had previously been achieved in Rugby Union. It is recognized that a tailored approach is required but such resources would provide a foundation upon which these individualized strategies could be developed. One participant explained an existing resource which they had developed as part of their primary job working with local schools:

"The question they put to me was, 'how can teachers know better how to deal with young people with mental health problems.' Now, I've got many high schools in my area. I thought I can't get round and train every single high school. So, I've done exactly that, put an online resource together. It's freely available. It's about working with young people who self-harm, with mental health problems and eating disorders. There's a series of films and downloadable PDFs."

The use of a newsletter was also suggested. An issue that was raised by one interviewee was that some children, parents or coaches do not have access to a computer or the internet. It was suggested that a newsletter could be distributed to clubs to ensure that the information was widely accessible. Such an initiative is already planned by one club as follows:

"We're going to put out a newsletter with a SEN [Special Education Needs] kind of feel to it ... just looking at you know, what is Autism Spectrum and how does it look on the pitch? What do you need to do? What do you need to consider?"

Peer support and knowledge sharing were also identified as helpful. It was identified that an online forum could be used to share information and provide sounding boards for all parties to ask others for their opinions or share good practices. There would also be scope to share good practice and people's experiences through existing events, such as meetings or conferences. This would clearly have to be subject to data protection regulations.

The need to collect on-going data to explore the effectiveness of any strategies from a range of perspectives was also recommended. One participant suggested:

> "I'd suggest that research like this could provide some indication of the requirement, but I'd have concerns that some clubs/areas may not take the safeguarding role responsibly and as such would turn their back on individuals with additional vulnerabilities. Hence some form of auditing clubs and research into the charity/organizations with children that have the various additional vulnerabilities to get their feedback is required."

6. Discussion

The present research had two over-arching aims—firstly, to understand the experiences of people within Rugby Union who have safeguarding roles with respect to working with children who have a disability. The data revealed that the majority of respondents had worked with at least one child with a disability, with 28% doing so on a weekly basis. As almost one-third of respondents had not received any relevant training, these findings highlight that this is an important issue in Rugby Union and presumably in sport more generally. Children with a disability are encouraged to participate in sport by a range of stakeholders including policy makers, health professionals and practitioners (Kristén et al. 2002; Murphy and Carbone 2008; Wilhite and Shank 2009; Wilson and Clayton 2010). Organizations in sport must therefore be ready to effectively safeguard these children and to facilitate the range of potential physical and psychosocial benefits which can be achieved through sport (Janssen and LeBlanc 2010; Landry and Driscoll 2012; Findlay and Coplan 2008).

The second research aim was to identify how children with a disability can be effectively safeguarded within Rugby Union. The TACL model was developed: Trigger (creating a system that sensitively identifies children with a disability), Action Plan (creating an individualized approach such that the child is effectively included and protected), Communicate (ensuring that all key stakeholders are informed about the plan) and Learn (ensuring that cases of good practice are identified and disseminated).

The development of the TACL model builds on pillars of good practice identified in the literature when creating a safeguarding system (Rhind and Owusu-Sekyere 2018; Rhind et al. 2017; Wessells 2009). Specifically, Rhind et al. (2017) CHILDREN pillars (i.e., Cultural sensitivity, Holistic, Incentives, Leadership, Dynamic, Resources, Engaging stakeholders and Networks) highlight the importance of an approach which is holistic, provides supporting resources and engages stakeholders. The TACL model is holistic through incorporating all stages of a child's interaction with Rugby Union, from their first interaction with a club through to their transition either within the sport (e.g., to the adult game) or out of the sport. The TACL model suggests the provision of resources. In particular, this includes being embedded in the induction form, the provision of an action plan template and the dissemination of guidance and case studies through online resources, newsletters and peer-sharing opportunities. The model also promotes appropriate and effective engagement with stakeholders throughout all stages (e.g., the child, parent/guardian, coach and the wider club membership).

It is clear that sport is a context in which all children are vulnerable to abuse (Alexander et al. 2011; Rhind et al. 2014). Whilst it is important for all children, safeguarding takes on additional significance when considering children with a disability in sport. This is because research indicates that there are higher rates of abuse involving children with a disability relative to other children in contexts beyond sport (Stalker and McArthur 2012). One can therefore assume that children with a disability may also be at greater risk of abuse in the context of sport, and there is some evidence to support this assumption (Vertommen et al. 2016). There is a growing awareness of the need to safeguard participants in sport

(Grey-Thompson 2017). However, there is a need to move from awareness to action and this can be facilitated by this research which offers a clear framework to guide practice in this regard.

The implementation of the TACL model can be supported by recent research related to the International Safeguards for Children in Sport (Rhind and Owusu-Sekyere 2018, 2019). The associated research found that safeguarding is effective when the environmental, personal and behavioral factors are addressed. It is only through targeting this range of factors that a comprehensive approach will be adopted, which can influence the fundamental values, assumptions and behaviors related to safeguarding in an organization. This approach adopts a learning perspective to the study of safeguarding culture and is fundamentally grounded in Bandura (1986) Social Cognitive Theory (SCT). SCT has been applied to a range of contexts and concepts including education, the mass media and promoting healthy behaviors. SCT suggests that behavioral change can occur through the reciprocal interactions between the person, the behavior and the environment.

The application of the TACL model based on SCT can be illustrated using the example of a coach in Rugby Union. In terms of the 'person', this focuses on the level of self-efficacy that a given individual has towards a given behavior. In this case, it may relate to a coach and their perceptions regarding their ability to safeguard a child with a disability. The TACL model can help to facilitate self-efficacy through identifying a child with a disability (Trigger), clearly outlining any adjustments which are required (Action Plan), ensuring that these are communicated to the coach effectively (Communicate) and then reviewing and revising the practices over time (Learn). Vicarious learning can be promoted through the sharing of examples from other coaches in Rugby Union regarding the effective safeguarding of a child with a disability and this, in turn, can help to enhance the self-efficacy of a coach. In terms of 'behavior', this concerns the response experienced by a coach to a given action. The Communication and Learning aspects will be important in providing feedback to a coach with respect to recognizing and rewarding promising practice as well as identifying and supporting coaches in areas in which there is potential for improvement. In terms of 'environment', this concerns the extent to which the context is designed to promote the required behaviors. Examples include embedding mechanisms to identify children with a disability during induction, providing templates for Action Plans and promoting Learning through case studies, newsletters and peer learning opportunities.

This raises important questions for organizations in sport. In relation to the people within an organization, do they know what they need to do in relation to safeguarding? In terms of the behavior, what response do they experience when performing safe or unsafe behaviors when working with a child with a disability? Are unsafe behaviors consciously or unconsciously promoted, such as concerns not being acted upon when disclosures are made? Are there opportunities for successful learning and are safe behaviors reinforced? In relation to the environment, does the organization create conditions in which safe behaviors are conducive? Are policies, procedures and guidance readily available? Through addressing such questions, an organization can work to develop and maintain an effective safety culture which includes children with a disability whilst safeguarding all stakeholders (Rhind and Owusu-Sekyere 2019).

It is important to acknowledge that there are limitations associated with the approach adopted in this research. It is generally held that a level of engagement within the contexts that one wishes to study is useful in enhancing the researchers understanding. The authors made conscious efforts to build rapport with the participants. However, the relationships with these participants may have introduced bias into the data. For instance, at the start of the process, participants may have had concerns regarding the intentions of the research. Participants may have been apprehensive in terms of whether any information would be shared with their colleagues within the governing body. Funding agencies or the media. Efforts were made to allay these fears through written and verbal agreements, but these concerns still had the potential to impact the data. It is also important to acknowledge that only the perspective of people within safeguarding roles was captured in this research. This was purely due to what was feasible given the resources and timeframe available to this project. This ensures that there are a range of potential avenues for future studies.

Future research is now merited with respect to the antecedents, further development and outcomes of the TACL model. In terms of antecedents, research is required into how key stakeholders in sport can be encouraged to adopt the TACL model (e.g., Governing Bodies, Major Sports Events). Research can also explore the factors which influence the effective adaptation of the TACL model to a given context (e.g., the size, purpose and location of an organization). The present study only focused on a single sport. Their remains great scope for the experiences of people working towards safeguarding children with a disability in diverse settings across sport to be investigated. Finally, it is important to investigate the outcomes of the TACL model at various levels. This concerns children (e.g., well-being, participation and performance), the experiences of those around the children (e.g., parents and coaches) as well as the club/sport as a whole (e.g., organizational reputation and performance). The findings of this research should help to strengthen the rationale for safeguarding and ultimately enhance the experiences of children with a disability in sport as well as all other stakeholders.

The development and implementation of future safeguarding strategies should adopt a child-centered approach, where the children are at the focus of all decisions. Where possible, the child should be included in all phases of the TACL process, adhering to the adage "nothing about us without us". Adopting this philosophy, and using the TACL model, should help to tackle what is a significant issue within the growing area of safeguarding in sport.

Author Contributions: Conceptualization, D.J.A.R.; methodology, D.J.A.R.; formal analysis, D.J.A.R. and J.M.; data curation, J.M.; writing—original draft preparation, D.J.A.R. and J.M.; writing—review and editing, D.J.A.R. and J.M.; supervision, D.J.A.R. All authors have read and agreed to the published version of the manuscript.

Funding: This research was funded by the Rugby Football Union.

Acknowledgments: We would like to take this opportunity to thank all participants for their engagement with this project.

Conflicts of Interest: The funders facilitated access to participants, informed the interpretation of data and the dissemination of the findings.

References

Alexander, K., A. Stafford, and R. Lewis. 2011. *The Experiences of Children Participating in Organized Sport in the UK.* London: NSPCC.

Bandura, A. 1986. *Social Foundations of Thought and Action: A Social Cognitive Theory.* Englewood Cliffs: Prentice-Hall, Inc.

Brackenridge, Celia H. 2001. *Spoilsports: Understanding and Preventing Sexual Exploitation in Sport.* London: Routledge.

Brackenridge, Celia H., and Daniel Rhind. 2014. Institutional responses to child abuse in sport: Reflections on 30 years of science and activism. *Social Sciences* 3: 326–40. [CrossRef]

Brackenridge, Celia H., Tess Kay, and Daniel Rhind. 2012. *Sport, Children's Rights and Violence Prevention: A Source Book on Global Issues and Local Programmes.* London: Brunel University Press.

Braun, Virginia, and Victoria Clarke. 2006. Using thematic analysis in psychology. *Qualitative Research in Psychology* 3: 77–101. [CrossRef]

Child Protection in Sport Unit. 2013. What Is Safeguarding? Available online: https://thecpsu.org.uk/help-advice/introduction-to-safeguarding/what-is-safeguarding/ (accessed on 30 January 2020).

Fasting, Kari, Stiliani Chroni, Stein Egil Hervik, and Nada Knorre. 2011. Sexual harassment in sport toward females in three European countries. *International Review for the Sociology of Sport* 46: 76–89. [CrossRef]

Findlay, Leanne C., and Robert J. Coplan. 2008. Come out and play: Shyness in childhood and the benefits of organized sports participation. *Canadian Journal of Behavioral Science* 40: 153–61. [CrossRef]

Grey-Thompson, Tanni. 2017. Duty of Care in Sport Review. Available online: https://www.gov.uk/government/publications/duty-of-care-in-sport-review (accessed on 30 January 2020).

Her Majesty's Government. 2013. *Working Together to Safeguard Children: A Guide to Inter-Agency Working to Safeguard and Promote the Welfare of Children.* London: Department for Education.

Janssen, Ian, and Allana G. LeBlanc. 2010. Systematic review of the health benefits of physical activity and fitness in school-aged children and youth. *International Journal of Behavioral Nutrition and Physical Activity* 7: 1–16. [CrossRef] [PubMed]

Jones, Lisa, Mark A. Bellis, Sara Wood, Karen Hughes, Ellie McCoy, Lindsay Eckley, Geoff Bates, Christopher Mikton, Tom Shakespeare, and Alana Officer. 2012. Prevalence and risk of violence against children with disabilities: A systematic review and meta-analysis of observational studies. *Lancet* 380: 899–907. [CrossRef]

Kirby, Sandra Louise, Lorraine Greaves, and Olena Hankivsky. 2000. *The Dome of Silence: Sexual Harassment and Abuse in Sport.* Halifax: Fernwood Publishing.

Kristén, Lars, Göran Patriksson, and Bengt Fridlund. 2002. Conceptions of children and adolescents with physical disabilities about their participation in a sports programme. *European Physical Education Review* 8: 139–56. [CrossRef]

Landry, Bradford W., and Sherilyn Whateley Driscoll. 2012. Physical activity in children and adolescents. *Physical Medicine and Rehabilitation* 4: 826–32. [CrossRef]

Leahy, Trisha, Grace Pretty, and Gershon Tenenbaum. 2002. Prevalence of sexual abuse in organised competitive sport in Australia. *Journal of Sexual Aggression* 8: 16–36. [CrossRef]

Mountjoy, M., D. J. A. Rhind, A. Tiivas, and M. Leglise. 2016. Safeguarding the child athlete in sport: A review, a framework and recommendations for the IOC youth athlete development model. *British Journal of Sports Medicine* 49: 883–86. [CrossRef]

Murphy, Nancy A., and Paul S. Carbone. 2008. Promoting the participation of children with disabilities in sports, recreation, and physical activities. *Pediatrics* 121: 1057–61. [CrossRef] [PubMed]

National Society for the Prevention of Cruelty to Children. 2003. *It Doesn't Happen to Disabled Children': Child Protection and Disabled Children.* London: NSPCC.

National Society for the Prevention of Cruelty to Children. 2015. *Safeguarding Deaf and Disabled Children.* London: NSPCC, Available online: https://learning.nspcc.org.uk/safeguarding-child-protection/deaf-and-disabled-children/ (accessed on 30 January 2020).

Oosterhoorn, Rebecca, and Andrew Kendrick. 2001. No sign of harm: Issues for disabled children communicating about abuse. *Child Abuse Review* 10: 243–53. [CrossRef]

Papaefstathiou, Maria, Daniel Rhind, and Celia Brackenridge. 2012. Child protection in ballet: Experiences and views of teachers, administrators and ballet students. *Child Abuse Review* 22: 127–41. [CrossRef]

Rhind, Daniel, and Frank Owusu-Sekyere. 2018. *International Safeguards for Children in Sport: Developing and Embedding a Safeguarding Culture.* London: Routledge.

Rhind, Daniel J. A., and Frank Owusu-Sekyere. 2019. Evaluating the impacts of working towards the International Safeguards for Children in Sport. *Sport Management Review* 23: 104–16. [CrossRef]

Rhind, Daniel, Jamie McDermott, Emma Lambert, and Irena Koleva. 2014. A review of safeguarding cases in sport. *Child Abuse Review.* [CrossRef]

Rhind, Daniel J. A., Frank Owusu-Sekyere, Tess Kay, and Laura Hills. 2017. Building a system to safeguard children in sport: The 8 CHILDREN pillars. *Journal of Sport and Social Issues* 41: 151–71. [CrossRef]

Rugby Football Union. 2011. *Safeguarding Children and Vulnerable Adults in Rugby Union Policy and Guidance: Creating Safe Environments.* Twickenham: Rugby Football Union.

Sanghera, Pargan. 2007. Abuse of children with disabilities in hospital: Issues and implications. *Pediatric Nursing* 19: 29–32. [CrossRef]

Stalker, Kirsten, and Katherine McArthur. 2012. Child abuse, child protection and disabled children: A review of recent research. *Child Abuse Review* 21: 24–40. [CrossRef]

Vertommen, T., N. Schipper-Van Veldhoven, K. Wouters, J. K. Kampen, C. Brackenridge, Daniel J. A. Rhind, Karel Neels, and Filip Van Den Eede. 2016. Interpersonal violence against children in sport in the Netherlands and Belgium. *Child Abuse and Neglect* 51: 223–36. [CrossRef]

Soc. Sci. **2020**, *9*, 48

Wessells, Mike G. 2009. *What Are We Learning about Protecting Children in the Community: An Inter-Agency Review of the Evidence on Community-Based Child Protection Mechanisms in Humanitarian and Development Settings.* London: Save the Children.

Wilhite, Barbara, and John Shank. 2009. In praise of sport: Promoting sport participation as a mechanism of health among persons with a disability. *Disability and Health Journal* 2: 116–27. [CrossRef]

Wilson, Pamela E., and Gerald H. Clayton. 2010. Sports and disability. *Physical Medicine and Rehabilitation* 2: S46–S54. [CrossRef] [PubMed]

social sciences

MDPI

Review

One Step Forward, Two Steps Back: The Struggle for Child Protection in Canadian Sport

Gretchen Kerr *, Bruce Kidd and Peter Donnelly

Faculty of Kinesiology and Physical Education, University of Toronto, Toronto, ON M5S 2W6, Canada; bruce.kidd@utoronto.ca (B.K.); peter.donnelly@utoronto.ca (P.D.)
* Correspondence: gretchen.kerr@utoronto.ca

Received: 4 April 2020; Accepted: 27 April 2020; Published: 2 May 2020

Abstract: Millions of children and adolescents around the world participate in organized sport for holistic health and developmental benefits. However, for some, sport participation is characterized by experiences of maltreatment, including forms of abuse and neglect. In Canada, efforts to address and prevent maltreatment in sport have been characterized by recurring cycles of crisis, public attention, policy response, sluggish implementation, and active resistance, with very little observable change. These cycles continue to this day. Achieving progress in child protection in Canadian sport has been hindered by the self-regulating nature of sport, funding models that prioritize performance outcomes, structures that deter athletes from reporting experiences of maltreatment, and inadequate attention to athletes' recommendations and preventative initiatives. The culture of control that characterizes organized sport underpins these challenges to advancing child protection in sport. We propose that the establishment of a national independent body to provide safeguards against maltreatment in Canadian sport and to address this culture of control.

Keywords: sport; child; athlete; protection; Canadian; safe sport

---

1. Introduction

Concerns about the safety of young athletes in sport are as old as modern sports themselves. In the early 19th century, as teachers, social reformers, and players transformed the rough and ready games of the late medieval period into the rule-bound sports we know today, they sought to reduce the amount of unnecessary violence and injury, as well as to introduce the concept and rules of fairness to ensure that all participants could benefit from the experience (Elias 2000; Mangan 2012).

With the rapid growth of youth sport in post-WW2 Canada, efforts to make sport safer intensified. We have seen concerted campaigns to prohibit fighting and other forms of violence in hockey, eliminate boxing from schools and universities, teach coaches about injury prevention and fair play, discourage early specialization, mandate protective equipment, establish post-concussion return-to-play guidelines, outlaw doping, and recognize children's rights. However, none of these efforts has enjoyed complete success. When information about the injury or abuse of a young athlete is publicized, it results in an immediate flurry of media attention and public outrage. Sport organizations respond with changes to policies and practices, but attention often wanes; eventually, so does adherence to the new practices and policy changes, at least until the next case emerges. For decades, the Canadian sport landscape has been characterized by these recurring cycles of crisis, policy response, lethargic implementation, and resistance, with very little ultimate change. They continue to this day.

Until the past three years, there has never been a concerted effort to combat the full spectrum of maltreatment in Canadian sport—the subject of this paper. Here, we review the cycles of concern, response, and indifference that have characterized the struggle for the protection of young athletes in the Canadian sport system from physical, psychological and sexual abuse, and neglect. We argue that one major obstacle to reform is the concerted attempt by some leaders in sport to resist independent oversight in favour of self-regulation. We also suggest that the funding model for sport has been a contributing factor to maltreatment, and we highlight the struggles by Canadian athletes to have their experiences and recommendations included in the policies that affect them.

2. The Canadian Context

In the Olympic sector, Canadian sport is directed, financed, and monitored by Sport Canada, a federal agency with legislative authority from the Physical Activity and Sport Act (Government of Canada 2003). The mission of Sport Canada is to enhance opportunities for all Canadians to participate in and excel at sport. Sport Canada supports the National Sport Organizations (NSOs) and Multi-Sport Organizations (MSOs, e.g., Canadian Olympic Committee, Canadian Paralympic Committee), provides financial assistance to high-performance athletes, and helps Canadian organizations to host sport events that create opportunities for Canadian athletes to compete at the national and international levels (Government of Canada n.d.). The Physical Activity and Sport Act states that:

> "The Government of Canada's policy regarding sport is founded on the highest ethical standards and values, including doping-free sport, the treatment of all persons with fairness and respect, the full and fair participation of all persons in sport, and the fair, equitable, transparent and timely resolution of disputes."

Sport Canada policies and programs are coordinated with those of the provincial and territorial governments through the Canadian Sport Policy, an agreement between federal, provincial, and territorial governments. The provincial and territorial governments support provincial and territorial sports organizations in much the same way Sport Canada supports the national bodies.

In response to the public concern expressed during previous crises, Sport Canada has created or assisted the development of a number of new organizations for the purpose of protecting and strengthening the values and fairness of Canadian sport. These include the Coaching Association of Canada (established in 1970), Canadian Women and Sport (formerly the Canadian Association for the Advancement of Women and Sport or CAAWS, 1981), the Canadian Centre for Ethics in Sports (established in 1992), and the Sport Dispute Resolution Centre of Canada (established in 2003). Athletes' struggles to have representation on decision-making bodies in Canadian sport resulted in the 1992 establishment of the Canadian Athletes Association, which later changed its name to AthletesCAN. AthletesCAN is an independent association of national team athletes that seeks to provide a collective athlete voice in major decision-making and to bring about an athlete centred sport system (https://athletescan.com/en/about). The masculinist, capitalist, continentalist sports sector (e.g., National Hockey League, National Basketball Association, Major League Baseball, and Canadian Football League) operates outside this framework.

With respect to child protection, sport is the only child-populated domain in Canada that is completely autonomous and self-regulating. Unlike other domains in which children engage, such as day care and educational settings, sport lacks a regulatory body to oversee the health and well-being of children, which ensures persons in positions of authority and trust over young people are sufficiently trained and adhere to scope of practice, and apply sanctions to those who violate codes of conduct. Instead, sport organizations regulate themselves.

3. A Note about Terminology

The first policies developed to address the maltreatment of athletes focused exclusively on sexual maltreatment using the terms 'sexual harassment' and 'sexual abuse,' which were often used interchangeably. Many researchers have conceptualized harassment and abuse as existing on a continuum of harmful behaviours, with harassment referring to what may be considered less severe behaviours such as sexist comments or remarks and abuse used for more severe behaviours such as sexual assault (Brackenridge 2001). In practice however, distinguishing harassment and abuse on the basis of severity is very difficult. For example, when does harassing behaviour become abusive? Do less severe harassing behaviours become abusive if cumulative or repeated over time? How do we account for individuals' interpretations of severity? Furthermore, researchers and athletes have advocated for a perspective on harassment and abuse that extends beyond sexual misconduct to include other forms of harmful experiences such as psychological misconduct, physical misconduct, and neglect (Crooks and Wolfe 2007; Miller-Perrin and Perrin 2012). Canada has responded to these calls by using the term 'maltreatment.' Maltreatment has been defined by the World Health Organization (2016) as "(...) the abuse and neglect that occurs to children under 18 years of age. It includes all types of physical and/or emotional ill-treatment, sexual abuse, neglect, negligence, and commercial or other exploitation which results in actual or potential harm to the child's health, survival, development, or dignity in the context of a relationship of responsibility, trust, or power." In this way, maltreatment is an all-encompassing term that includes sexual, physical, and psychological abuse; neglect; bullying; harassment; and discrimination.

Safe Sport is a term that has recently emerged to encompass approaches aimed at promoting the holistic health and well-being of sport participants. Though a consensus on a universal definition is lacking, Safe Sport is typically used to refer to the prevention of harassment and abuse, as well as the promotion of the physical and psychological welfare of athletes (e.g., https://www.olympic.org/athlete365/library/safe-sport/). The U.S. Center for Safe Sport describes Safe Sport as "safeguard[ing] athletes from bullying, harassment, hazing, physical abuse, emotional abuse, sexual abuse, and sexual misconduct." This term is also used in Canada despite of the absence of a generally agreed upon definition.

4. Theorizing Safe Sport

In theoretical terms, it is important to understand two related themes: the characteristics that render sport unsafe in terms of athlete maltreatment and the characteristics that sport shares with other institutions where child maltreatment has been found. As Bruyninckx (2011) pointed out, "Sports (...) take place in a sort of separate [autonomous] sphere, detached from normal rules and regulations in society." Organizations at all levels of sport, from the international to the local, professional and non-professional, have consistently asserted their autonomy, a right of self-governance and exemption from oversight by governments and judiciaries. Gruneau (2017) argued that the claim to autonomy in sports emerged alongside similar claims in the visual arts in the midst of the turbulent class and ideological conflicts of 19th century Britain. They are thus historically contingent and open to change. Nevertheless, despite the intervening transformations to sports, especially the worldwide assumption by publicly accountable governments for their financing at the highest levels of performance, sports bodies continue to assert their claims to autonomy. Such claims increase the risk of maltreatment to the athletes involved.

Several researchers (e.g., Donnelly and Young 2004; Atkinson and Young 2008) have described organized sport as sharing many characteristics with total institutions (Goffman 1961) and greedy institutions (Coser 1974) with their implicit and explicit cultures of control (Donnelly and Young 2004; Garland 2001). The culture of control exists mainly in prolympic sports, high performance and professional sports, but it also exists in the youth/developmental levels of many sports[1] (Donnelly 1996). Prolympic sports are defined by: an increasing emphasis on outcome (success, victory, excellence, etc.), an increasing emphasis on control (grounded in the paternal notion that athletes would not be as committed to outcomes without some external controls), and a decreasing ability on the part of athletes to determine the form, circumstances, and meanings of their participation.

Control has become a central organizing principle for prolympic sports and provides a context in which sports-related violence (Young 2012) and the threat of violence may come to be approved,

---

[1] Youth/developmental levels of sport are frequently linked to prolympic sport by means of the widely-used Long-Term Athlete Development system. Available online: https://sportforlife.ca/long-term-development/ (accessed on 29 April 2020).

normalized, routine, and/or rewarded. This is not to argue that the culture of control causes sports-related violence; rather, certain forms of violence are employed to maintain the culture of control, and, in turn, the culture of control creates a climate in which certain forms of violence are facilitated, expected, and accepted. Thus, the outcomes of power relations in this culture of control are sometimes violent, abusive, exploitive, and otherwise dehumanizing. In the culture of control of modern prolympic sports, sports-related violence and the threat of sports-related violence is routine. It includes various forms of self-abuse, as well as abuse imposed by authority figures (psychological, physical, occasionally sexual) that is disturbingly out of step with most modern western educational and work places (e.g., worker and student rights, workplace health and safety regulations, principles of due process).

Control is justified in various ways. For example, there is a paternalistic aspect of control (e.g., athletes cannot be trusted, so control stands in contrast to trust); Howe (2003) asked, for example, "... whether the athlete or the administrator has more control over the body of the sportsperson." Control techniques are sometimes used and justified in total institutions such as prisons, the military, and sport to establish an overall climate of control, as well as to assert rank and authority. Additionally, control techniques are also used and justified to sanction behaviours that are defined, sometimes arbitrarily, as not contributing to 'success.' The increasingly high-handed treatment of athletes is sometimes paired with increasing rewards for success.

As a result of this climate of control, many sports are quite regimented, authority is clearly delineated, and athletes are motivated by fear and punishment (e.g., being benched, traded, demoted, dropped, ridiculed, and losing pay or funding). Thus, athletes are manipulatable in this climate; they are controlled by fear of ostracism, disrepute, stigma, identity loss, career loss, isolation, and so on. The exploitation often persists because athletes are expendable as a result of the "reserve army of athletes attempting to play at the elite level" (Connor 2009, p. 1369). Michael Robidoux (2001) exemplified this with his literal description of the American Hockey League as a 'farm system' for the National Hockey League (NHL): "[t]he players are literally cultivated on the farm; only those with suitable qualities are 'picked' to be used in the NHL market. The cultivation period, moreover, is limited, and those who do not develop sufficiently are eventually replaced with new 'stock'" (p. 190).

Thus, in the ideologically isolated, autonomous, conservative, and control culture of modern sport:

- Sport maintained its conservative nature throughout the liberation movements of the 1960s in North America and elsewhere, despite some athlete resistance.
- Sport has remained a bastion of masculinity when patriarchy faces serious challenge in many other areas of social and cultural life.
- Sport has maintained its 'right' to employ violent and abusive behaviours when such behaviours are now more severely controlled in other parts of society.
- Athletes submit to treatment by coaches, administrators, clinicians, and others that they would never dream of tolerating from authority figures in other areas of their lives.

The human rights of athletes are routinely violated, albeit at times with their consent. Much more egregiously, as Donnelly and Petherick (2004) and others have pointed out, up to half of the articles in the UN Convention on the Rights of the Child are occasionally or routinely violated in elite organized sports for children (those under 18 years of age in the UN definition). During discussions of recent years, we have regularly heard that punishments we defined as 'maltreatment' were considered 'just sport' by many of the coaches and officials in attendance. The autonomous and self-governing nature of sport raises the question of why sport organizations themselves, rather than organizations mandated to ensure child welfare and protection (such as the Children's Aid Societies in Canada and National

Society for the Prevention of Cruelty to Children (NSPCC) in the UK[2]) or the police, deal with cases of illegal and inappropriate behaviour (maltreatment) in children's and adult sport, respectively.

Given these characteristics, it is unsurprising that the maltreatment of children continues to occur in sport and that—according to many sources—it is rarely reported because the only means available to report maltreatment is to the organization within which the maltreatment was perpetrated. Additionally, in terms of the culture of control, it is evident that sport shares that characteristic with other institutions (e.g., the Catholic church and boarding/residential schools) that are frequently identified for their involvement in child maltreatment.

The remainder of this paper addresses the struggle for Safe Sport in Canada with a particular focus on child protection in sport. This struggle is characterized by recurring cycles of resistance by athletes and others to the prevailing culture of control on the one hand and reinforcement of this control by sport leaders on the other. In support of athletes' calls, we propose changes to the sport context that reflect congruence with the standards, norms, and approaches seen in other child-dominated contexts.

5. One Step Forward, Two Steps Back

In the 1990s, several international, high-profile cases emerged detailing experiences of sexual abuse of athletes at the hands of their coaches—persons in positions of authority who are entrusted with responsibility for athlete safety. In 1995, a British Olympic Swimming coach was charged with 15 counts of sexual assault and the rape of two teenaged swimmers (Reid 2012). Two-time Olympic rower Heather Clarke alleged that her long-time coach had sexually abused her, her sister, and two other rowers for many years. Additionally, at that time, Sheldon Kennedy, a player in the National Hockey League, revealed that he had been groomed and sexually victimized by his coach, Graham James, beginning when Kennedy was just 13 years of age (Kennedy and Grainger 2006; The Canadian Press 2015). In subsequent years, other hockey players coached by James also disclosed sexual victimization (e.g., Fleury and Day 2010). The 1997 arrest of former Maple Leaf Gardens (Toronto) equipment manager, Gordon Stuckless, preceded the announcement that a 'pedophile ring' had been operating at the Gardens between the mid-1970s and the early 1980s (Vine and Challen 2002).

In response to these revelations, there was an outbreak of public concern by Canadians. How could sport, an endeavour assumed to be healthy and growth-enhancing for young people, become a place where such harm could occur? The government at the time responded by engaging in a consultation process that led to new policies and systems of compliance that represented one of the most progressive examples in the world at that time to deal with harassment and abuse in sport. Specifically, in 1996, all National Sport Organizations that received public funding were mandated to: (i) develop and disseminate a publicly accessible harassment policy (the term used at the time), (ii) to designate arm's length trained Harassment Officers (one male and one female) with whom athletes and/or their parents and others could raise queries and to whom they could address complaints without fear of reprisal from coaches or other sport officials, and (iii) to annually report to Sport Canada on their compliance with these directives as a condition of continued funding (Christie 1997). These federal initiatives began to spread to provincial ministries responsible for sport and to Provincial Sport Organizations (PSOs), and they also began to be considered internationally. A progressive policy guide was produced by Canadian Association for the Advancement of Women and Sport (CAAWS) (1994) that assisted sport organizations through the development and implementation of mandated harassment policies. This guide continues to form the basis of policies used today in Canada and internationally.

---

[2]   The National Society for the Prevention of Cruelty to Children (NSPCC) established, with Sport England and others, the Child Protection in Sport Unit in 2001. However, that unit has advisory and educational functions, and it does not violate the autonomy of sports to carry out their own investigations and impose discipline in cases of child maltreatment.

5.1. A Failed Policy

Twenty years after these advances, Donnelly et al. (2016) conducted a study to assess the extent to which Canadian sport organizations complied with these requirements. By reviewing sport organizations' websites and contacting the heads of these organizations, they found that 86% and 71% of the NSOs and PSOs, respectively, had harassment policies. Of these, less than half were publicly accessible as required. The existing policies focused primarily or exclusively on sexual maltreatment, with far less content on psychological and physical maltreatment, neglect, bullying, harassment, and hazing. Only 33% of PSOs and 17% of NSOs addressed the inappropriateness of sexual relations between a coach and an of-age athlete. Only 27% of PSO and 39% of NSO policies mentioned a harassment officer, and far fewer stated that these positions included one male and one female who were trained, as recommended in the original CAAWS (1994) document. Of particular note is that none of the PSO and NSO policies identified the harassment officer as being at 'arm's-length' to the sport organization; instead, the CEO or another staff member of the sport organization was identified as a recipient of harassment/abuse concerns, contrary to the policy directives to have neutral, third party individuals receive concerns. We are not aware of a single sport organization that was denied funding for a lack of compliance with the Sport Canada mandates. Clearly, the 1996 policy to advance safety for athletes was not implemented effectively; sport organizations did not meet the requirements for funding, and Sport Canada did not ensure compliance. What had emerged since the 1996 policy was a system of self-regulation riddled with conflicts of interests.

In attempting to account for their failure to meet Sport Canada's requirements, sports organizations cite their lack of capacity—not their lack of will. They told us that they found it next to impossible to recruit, train and retain willing and qualified individuals to address complex cases of maltreatment. Potential investigators and adjudicators were discouraged by the difficult issues involved and the likelihood of costly legal proceedings. Given these difficulties and the lack of oversight by Sport Canada, sport organizations quietly ignored the requirements, with many regressing to a pre-1996 state without harassment policies or systems in place to address complaints.

At the same time, the emphasis on performance outcomes, reinforced by the existing system of funding of sport organizations in Canada, has been a significant barrier to addressing and preventing harassment and abuse. Sport organizations are funded primarily based upon the results (international medals, records, top-10 performances, and so on) attained by their athletes. As such, sports in which athletes earn high international standings are funded to a greater extent than those sports in which athletes do not perform as well; in fact, teams that drop in international rankings may experience funding cuts. For example, significant funding comes from a Sport Canada-funded organization, Own the Podium, which "(…) drive(s) Canada's high-performance sport system forward in a quest to help more athletes and coaches win more medals in future Olympic and Paralympic Games" (https://www.ownthepodium.org/en-CA/About-OTP/Vision,-Mission,-Mandate-Goals). Since the 2010 Winter Olympic and Paralympic Games in Vancouver/Whistler, Canada, the pressure for medals has intensified. We suggest that Own the Podium, driven by the relentless expectations of international success, pays inadequate attention to the means by which medals are earned and thus may enable athlete development methods that are inconsistent with athletes' rights and welfare. A vast body of literature in sport addresses the potential consequences of such a win-at-all-costs approach to sport, including overuse injuries, sport withdrawal, eating disorders, and maltreatment (Coakley 2015; Donnelly 1993; Stirling and Kerr 2015).

5.2. The Next Wave

A series of international and high-profile cases between 2010 and 2019 stimulated another flurry of activity and policy directives. In the United States, the 2011 Penn State University child sex abuse scandal emerged; this involved offences committed by a football coach, Jerry Sandusky, over a period of 15 years (Smith 2016). In 2018, Larry Nassar, a USA gymnastics team doctor was charged and convicted of sexually assaulting more than 150 minors over a period of two decades; he was subsequently sentenced to up to 125 years in prison (Levinson 2018). At around the same time, Barry Bennell, a football (soccer) coach in the U.K. was convicted of sexual abuse of numerous boys from the 1970s to the 1990s. Bennell was sentenced to a prison term of 30 years. He was found to be part of a pedophile ring in U.K. football that victimized over 800 boys at 340 different football clubs (BBC News 2018). Between 2016 and 2018, Canadian sport was also shaken by cases of sexual abuse of athletes in the sports of alpine skiing, gymnastics, wrestling, speed skating, and swimming, amongst others (Heroux 2019; Heroux et al. 2018).

5.3. Recognizing the Role of Bystanders

These cases, in contrast to those in the 1990s, drew attention to and consideration of the role of bystanders. Specifically, they highlighted the complicity of adults in positions of power and authority who are entrusted with the care and safety of athletes. We find it hard to countenance that perpetrators can harm so many individuals over such an extended period of time without someone knowing about the abuse or, at a minimum, suspecting abuse may be occurring. In fact, in the 2011 Penn State University child sex abuse case, evidence indicated that at least four other adults in positions of authority at the University were aware of the allegations and had "total and consistent disregard...for the safety and welfare of Sandusky's child victims" and "empowered" Sandusky to continue his acts of abuse by failing to disclose them (Freeh Sporkin and Sullivan 2012). Similarly, in the Larry Nassar case, the athletes did in fact disclose their abusive experiences to others, but their disclosures were ignored or dismissed based upon the prestige and reputation held by Nassar and the performance success of the U.S. women's gymnastics team (Raisman 2018a; 2018b). Their complicity enabled Nassar to continue with his abuses.

The critical role of bystanders in abuse cases was poignantly summarized by Mitch Garabedian[3], a lawyer for some of the survivors of abuses by Catholic priests in Boston, who stated, "If it takes a village to raise a child, it takes a village to abuse one." The focus of sexual abuse cases had clearly shifted from a sole focus on the perpetrator to inclusion of the critical role of bystanders, as well as the failure of adults in positions of responsibility for the care of young people to enact their duty to act when knowledge or suspicions of child abuse emerge.

As a consequence of their failure to act on their responsibilities to care for these young people, the President, Athletic Director, and executive Director of Alumni Relations of Michigan State University where Nassar was employed either resigned or were required to leave. The University also agreed to a settlement of $500 million (Jesse 2019). As a result of the Nassar case and associated legal costs, USA Gymnastics—a powerhouse of a sport organization—declared bankruptcy (Axon et al. 2018). In contrast to cases that emerged in earlier years, the trial of Nassar included seven days of testimonies from athletes who were survivors of Nassar's abuses (Raisman 2018b). This represented a shift in sexual abuse cases, with survivors having an opportunity to tell their stories and call for changes— a shift that was inevitably influenced by the broader #MeToo movement.

5.4. Renewing a Failed Policy

At the same time, Canada was dealing with cases of sexual abuse of female teenage alpine skiers by the national coach Bertrand Charest, who was sentenced to 10 years imprisonment upon appeal (The Canadian Press 2019); infractions within wrestling (Bennett 2018); and the allegations of sexual misconduct by the 2016 Olympic Women's Artistic Gymnastics Coach, David Brubaker. In response to the Nassar case in the U.S. and the Charest and Brubaker cases in Canada, there was, again, a flurry of public and scholarly attention paid to the abuse of athletes. The federal Minister of Science and Sport at

---

3   'Mitch' Garabedian is a Boston lawyer who represented a number of victims of Catholic church sexual abuse. The words in this quote, referring to the code of silence in the Catholic church, were spoken by actor Stanley Tucci, who played Garabedian in the 2015 film *Spotlight*.

the time, Kirsty Duncan, herself a former athlete, drew additional attention to the abuse of athletes by declaring that addressing abuse of athletes was a priority of her office. She announced that: "national sporting organizations will lose their federal funding if they don't immediately disclose to her office any allegations of abuse or harassment that occur within their ranks" and "Effective immediately, funding agreements also require sporting associations to establish an independent third party to investigate all allegations of abuse and have mandatory prevention training in place as soon as possible and no later than 1 April 2020" (Rabson 2018). Though these mandates caused a flurry of activity in sport organizations, the Minister's requirement to report cases and to establish an independent third party to investigate allegations of abuse or harassment were hardly new. On the contrary, these requirements had been in place since 1996 and had simply not been implemented or enforced. Despite the stirring words of priority, these mandates represented a retreat to a 20-year old policy that neither the sports bodies nor Sport Canada had been able to implement; this was two steps back.

The commitment to address abuse, harassment, bullying, and discrimination in sport was explicitly reinforced by the Red Deer Declaration for the Prevention of Harassment, Abuse and Discrimination in Sport (Sport Information Resource Centre 2019). Led by the Federal Minister, the group of Federal, Provincial, and Territorial Ministers responsible for Sport, Physical Activity and Recreation, met to endorse the Declaration. Specifically, they agreed to work together to reinforce and build on the existing work and commitments to activate the values of the Canadian Sport Policy; to foster a collaborative and coordinated relationship with sport organizations, participants, and stakeholders; and to engage relevant experts to identify effective approaches to prevent and respond to incidents of harassment, abuse, and discrimination.

The Minister also directed the development of a Universal Code of Conduct for stakeholders in sport. The Code was written to identify prohibited behaviours and be applicable to all members of the National Sport community. As part of the process of developing this Code, a series of Safe Sport Summits were held across the country in 2019. These summits gave stakeholders the opportunity to contribute to the definition of prohibited conduct and potential sanctions for egregious behaviour. Disturbingly, the summits, which were led by the Coaching Association of Canada, were framed by the assumption that sexually abusive behaviours were the most egregious behaviours, ignoring the compelling evidence from the vast body of research on child maltreatment indicating that all forms of maltreatment are deleterious to a child's health and wellbeing (Glaser 2002; Matthews 2004; McCoy and Keen 2014). In spite of the evidence that psychological abuse, physical abuse, and neglect are just as, or in some cases, more damaging than sexual abuse to a child in the short- and long-term (Horwath 2013), many in the sport community insisted on limiting the scope of their responsibility to sexual abuse.

It could be said that the preoccupation with sexual abuse was justified given the media focus at the time. In addition to a long history of media attention on sexual abuse in sport, a 2019 study by the Canadian Broadcasting Corporation indicated that at least 222 coaches involved in amateur sports in Canada were convicted of sexual offences in the previous 20 years, involving more than 600 victims under the age of 18 years. Cases involving another 34 accused coaches were before the courts at that time (Ward and Strashin 2019). The focus on sexual misconduct at the National Summit was reflected in the heated discussions and a lack of consensus on whether or not sexual relations between athletes over the age of 18 years and a person in a position of authority should be prohibited. Regarding this specific scenario, athletes were clear in their responses that the power differential was so great between athletes and persons such as coaches, sport administrators, and sport science personnel that consent was not possible, and sexual relations should therefore be prohibited. The views of other stakeholders were not as consistent. At the time of writing this paper, we have yet to see whether the athletes' recommendations will be implemented.

5.5. Expanding the Focus Beyond Sexual Abuse

The exclusive focus on sexual abuse by many in the sport community was challenged by the 2019 release of a prevalence study of maltreatment among Canadian national team athletes that highlighted the frequency of experiences of various forms of maltreatment (Kerr et al. 2019). These findings provided a new understanding of the experiences of athletes. Specifically, they broadened the focus on sexual abuse to include the psychological abuse and neglect of athletes. Of 1001 athletes, 17% of current athletes and 23% of retired athletes reported repeated experiences of psychologically harmful behaviours, and 15% of current athletes and 22% of retired athletes reported repeated experiences of neglect. These were followed by sexual harm (4% of current athletes and 7% of retired athletes) and physical abuse (3% of current athletes and 5% of retired athletes).

Despite the preoccupation of the media and sport organizations with cases of sexual abuse of athletes, these findings signaled that other forms of maltreatment are far more prevalent and may be just as damaging to athletes' health and well-being. The preponderance of psychological abuse has been supported by other prevalence studies conducted in the UK (Alexander et al. 2011) and the Netherlands and Belgium (Vertommen et al. 2016). More recently, the prevalence and impact of psychological abuse has been highlighted by several male, high-profile National Hockey League players who have described training in psychologically toxic environments (Prewitt 2019). The findings of the Canadian study also indicated that statistically significant relationships existed between all forms of maltreatment—psychological abuse, physical abuse, sexual abuse, and neglect—and disordered eating/eating disorders, depression, and suicide ideation. As causality cannot be ascertained from this analysis, the short and long-term effects of maltreatment on athletes remain a direction for future research.

5.6. The Athletes' Voices

A particularly disturbing finding from the Canadian prevalence study was that fewer than 15% of the responding athletes who had experienced maltreatment submitted a formal report of their experiences; furthermore, less than half of the current and retired athletes ever told anyone about the harmful experiences. The athletes shared that they did not report because they did not know who to report to, they did not have a safe and confidential place to report their concerns without fear of negative repercussions for their athletic careers, and they did not have confidence in their sport organizations to address their concerns in a fair and transparent manner. In the words of some of these athletes: "I would never feel comfortable going to my National Sport Organization if I were harassed in any way and would 100% need an independent body to report the harassment to. I would be far too scared to say anything to my coach or my HPD [high performance director]" and, "Asking sport organizations to deal with abuse in their ranks is like asking them to incriminate themselves."

The athletes' widespread fear of reprisal makes 'self-regulation' an inadequate policy response. Canadian women wrestlers were very public in their concerns about the self-regulating nature of sport: "(...) at times it doesn't feel safe or comfortable for an athlete to come forward because we don't want to put our goal, our lifelong dream of making an Olympic Games, in jeopardy. Sometimes it's this fear of keeping the status quo, because there's been no independent body that we can go to and feel safe;" "We want the minister to know that athletes support an independent body to handle safe sport issues," Jasmine Mian, a 2016 Olympian and chair of Wrestling Canada's athlete council, said in a press release. "It's not only in the best interest of athletes but also in the best interest of the NSO. What constitutes safe sport should be consistent across Canada" (Ewing 2018).

The findings of the national prevalence study, together with discussions at the Safe Sport Summits held across the country, culminated in a National Safe Sport Summit in 2019, which was led by the Coaching Association of Canada (Coaching Association of Canada 2019) and included over 300 stakeholders in sport. Informed by the individual Summits and the National Prevalence Study data, recommendations were presented for all egregious conduct to be included in the Universal Code of Conduct. The most powerful moment of the National Summit came in response to the athletes' presentation of their recommendations to advance Safe Sport, a presentation that was met with a standing ovation. The athletes clearly and courageously argued for the Canadian sport community to:

1. Address all forms of maltreatment.
2. Implement mandatory education for all stakeholders.
3. Prohibit sexual relations and forced intimacy between athletes and persons in positions of authority.
4. Enhance the focus on athletes' holistic wellbeing.
5. Strengthen accountability measures.
6. Ensure that supports and resources are available for victims of maltreatment.
7. Implement an independent body to receive, investigate, and adjudicate complaints, as well as to apply sanctions.

The peer solidarity demonstrated by the athletes in communicating a common message to the Canadian sport community was a display of resistance against the dominant culture. Athletes exerted agency in voicing their demands for healthier sport experiences and more opportunities to contribute to the decisions that affect them. Their unified call for an independent Safe Sport agency was a public challenge to the existing culture of control.

5.7. Development of the Universal Code of Conduct for Addressing and Preventing Maltreatment

After the National Summit, work began on a Universal Code of Conduct designed to be applicable to all stakeholders in sport—athletes, coaches, sport administrators, officials, sport science personnel, and volunteers. Progress was achieved in expanding the focus to include all forms of maltreatment, as the athletes had insisted. Additionally, advances were realized in terms of holding adults in positions of authority and trust over young people accountable for reporting knowledge or suspicions of maltreatment. In addition to reinforcing the legal duty to report any suspicions of child maltreatment, the Code also makes persons in positions of authority responsible for reporting inappropriate conduct that may not reach the threshold of a criminal offence. This latter addition was important for prevention given the known trajectory from inappropriate conduct to all forms of maltreatment (Canadian Centre for Child Protection n.d.).

The development of the Universal Code of Conduct to Prevent and Address Maltreatment in Sport was not without its challenges. Some members of the sport community insisted that the following clause be included in the Code:

> "Conduct and coaching methods that are acceptable to Canadian standards for skill enhancement, physical conditioning, team building, rule enforcement, or improved athletic performance [would be exempt from descriptions of maltreatment.]"

Given the research evidence illustrating the normalization of harmful practices such as the use of degrading, threatening, or humiliating comments, as well as the use of exercise as punishment, this clause was viewed by both athletes and researchers as problematic and indicative of efforts to maintain a punitive culture of control.

More than 20 experts were consulted; they represented a broad range of organizations and areas of expertise, including child protection, criminal law, police, under-represented groups, gender equity and gender-based violence, LGBTQ+ (Lesbian/Gay/Bisexual/Trangender/Queer/Plus), parasport and persons with disabilities, athletes and coaches, human rights advocates, and academics with expertise in child maltreatment and intimate partner violence. The goal of the consultation was to leverage extensive and diverse knowledge from independent experts and researchers to create an evidence-informed code that could protect all participants in sport in Canada from maltreatment. In response to the clause above, one researcher of child abuse stated, "The biggest risk factor to experiences of abuse in sport are that the practices are normalized as standard professionally-accepted methods for athlete development. I strongly suggest deleting this sentence as it completely undermines the purpose of the code of conduct and the expectation that this code will serve to safeguard athletes from these harmful experiences." The normalization of some harmful practices, especially with respect to psychological abuse, have been well-documented in the academic literature (Jacobs et al. 2017; Stafford et al. 2015). Another reviewer stated, "Often, longstanding customs demonstrate the failure of a profession or class of defendants to keep up with modern developments. The tainted blood cases in Canada illustrate this well. The Red Cross' customary practices were found to be out-of-date in comparison to standards in the US. I would not rely on accepted practice in coaching/training methods to defend allegations of misconduct without making sure the conduct is a best practice." An athlete added, "As long as this clause remains, abuse will continue unchecked." The Code was released in 2019 without the inclusion of the contentious clause (Sport Information Resource Centre 2019).

5.8. Establishment of a Helpline and Offering Independent Investigators

In 2019, the Minister of Science and Sport also established a Canadian Sport Helpline at http://abuse-free-sport.ca/en/. This was intended to provide a triage service, guiding people with concerns to either the police and child protection services or to their sport organization. While this initiative may have the appearance of representing progress in child protection, the fact that most complaints fall under the criminal threshold means that most complaints are directed back to the sport organization for resolution. Again, this leaves the complainant facing a system that is ill-equipped to address complaints, in addition to athletes' complaints being forwarded to persons who are in conflicts of interest. The value of the helpline is thus questionable.

In 2019, the Minister at the time also contracted an existing body, the Sport Dispute Resolution Centre of Canada, to provide independent investigators to assist sport organizations in addressing complaints. Some of the larger, better-funded National Sport Organizations appointed their own 'independent' investigators. While incorporating independent investigators was undoubtedly a step forward, the complaint system remains riddled with conflicts of interest. Employees of sport organizations, in most cases the CEO or the 'independent' Safe Sport Officer, make the initial decision about whether or not a complaint warrants an investigation. Furthermore, the report completed by the independent investigator is typically submitted to the sport organization itself for implementation and the application of sanctions. If the independent investigator recommends that the complaint proceeds to a hearing, the sport organization is responsible for selecting the members of the hearing panel, again representing a conflict of interest. Finally, if sanctions are recommended, the sport organization bears responsibility for their implementation—or not. In the words of one CEO of a large sport organization that has been through this process, 'the lawyer for [the respondent] is claiming conflict of interest as the independent investigator was paid for by [sport organization] and the hearing panel itself is not independent because [the sport organization] pays those bills as well!' (Kerr 2020).

Numerous problems exist in the current system of complaint management in addition to the conflicts of interests identified above. Most importantly, the current system fails to address the athletes' concerns and recommendations for a truly independent system that exists outside of and without the involvement of the sport organization. In our view, no new mechanism for realizing safe sport in Canada should be developed without the direct involvement of athletes in each stage of the process, nor should one be approved without the full support of elected athlete representatives, as represented by AthletesCAN. It is instructive that the Canadian anti-doping policy implemented in the wake of the Ben Johnson scandal in the early 1990s was only implemented after it was approved by a special meeting of elected athlete representatives convened by AthletesCAN.

6. The Next Steps

Currently, a coalition of athletes, researchers, sports bodies, and other organizations is pushing for a truly independent body, one that ensures due process for all parties involved and involves four fundamental components. First, in an independent system, a complaint would be filed with a body that is completely separate from the sport organization and Sport Canada. There would be no conflicts of interest between the recipient of the complaint and the sport organization. This independent body would serve a triage function, determining whether the complaint should be directed to the police or child protection services, to an independent investigator, or to another body if the complaint is not relevant to maltreatment. Second, an independent investigative process would be created. Any complaint that is identified as a potential violation of the Universal Code of Conduct would be directed by the independent body to an independent investigator to initiate an investigation. The independent investigator would have no relationship with the sport organization or any other conflicts of interest, perceived or otherwise, in relation to the complainant, respondent, or any other member of the sport organization. Third, independent adjudication processes would be created. If the independent investigator concludes that a complaint should be examined through a hearing or adjudication process, members of the hearing panel must have no relationship with the sport organization or any conflicts of interest, perceived or otherwise, in relation to the complainant, respondent, or any other member of the sport organization. The adjudication of sanctions appropriate for findings of a breach of the Universal Code must occur without input or involvement from the sport organization. Fourth, anyone affected by experiences of maltreatment should have access to educational, legal, and psychological supports and resources, including clear information about the expectations of the Universal Code of Conduct and the process of reporting a complaint (Kerr et al. 2020).

It should be noted that the Canadian government, through Sport Canada, has already established two independent agencies where athletes and sport organizations are able to realize due process: the Sport Dispute Resolution Centre of Canada, which functions as a national version of the International Court of Arbitration for Sport, and the Canadian Centre for Ethics in Sport, which manages Canada's anti-doping system. In our view, and those of the athletes, the safety and protection of children in sport warrants a similar independent agency (Donnelly et al. 2019). A single, independent, pan-Canadian body for Safe Sport would investigate, adjudicate, and ensure compliance with and consistency in the application of the Universal Code of Conduct to Address and Prevent Maltreatment in Sport. Fair, transparent, independent, and accessible processes would be assured to all athletes, regardless of sport, geographical location in the country, or the availability of external supports and resources. Furthermore, such a body would provide consistent, equitable support and expertise to sport organizations, both large and small, thus freeing capacity and resources within sport organizations to pursue their primary endeavours. Finally, it would have and deserve the trust of all participants in sport and be able to deliver on the promise of Safe Sport in Canada.

To advance Safe Sport, we also need to address sport leaders' concerns about the challenges to their leadership presented by an independent body to address complaints. Funding will be required to establish such a body, and sport leaders are concerned that this funding will be extracted from funding otherwise allocated to performance enhancement—which remains their primary mandate. Finally, we will need to address the 'issue fatigue' that many sport leaders experience. Over recent years, sport leaders have been challenged to, in addition to pursuing their core mission of achieving performance outcomes, adapt to drug testing, be more inclusive of athletes with diverse identities, concussion prevention and intervention, and, now, maltreatment. Supporting sport leaders through these adaptations will be necessary to achieve progress in advancing Safe Sport. However, we are confident that these concerns can be fully addressed.

To date, the efforts to advance child protection in sport have been devoted to articulating egregious behaviours and identifying complaint mechanisms to address these behaviours when they occur. The current landscape of Safe Sport in Canada may be best characterized at this time as being reactive—addressing maltreatment once it occurs but remaining relatively silent on prevention and the underlying influences that encourage or enable maltreatment in sport. Specifically, the efforts to-date have failed to address the culture of sport as it relates to healthy child development, including the development of athletic talent in young people. Nor have the funding structures that encourage performance success over all else been addressed in any substantial manner. Important opportunities to realize the potential and promise of sport will be lost without attention to these underlying cultures and structures. Researchers have problematized the autonomy of sport, funding models connected to performance success, win-at-all costs attitudes, and authoritarian coaching and leadership; however, their critiques have not altered the culture of sport in significant ways.

To advance child protection in sport, we need to challenge the prevailing culture of control that perpetuates the autonomous nature of sport, as well as associated assumptions that the sport context is somehow different from other domains in which young people reside. In fact, sport is the only child-populated domain in Canadian society that is completely autonomous and self-regulating. Traditionally accepted and prevalent coaching methods, such as the use of punishments, degrading and humiliating comments, and environments characterized by one-on-one interactions with young people, would not be tolerated in other domains populated by young people, such as educational settings. Normative conduct in sport needs to be aligned with the standards and norms of society at-large, including the adoption of the assumption that optimal performance results from health and well-being, not at the expense of health and well-being. As illustrated in educational settings for youth, traditional authoritarian teaching styles and the use of punitive strategies have been replaced with child-centred approaches, recognizing that when teaching is based on the child's developmental needs and when children feel supported, optimal learning occurs. Youth in sport would benefit from a similar shift in approach. Abandoning traditional approaches to coaching and leadership for approaches that have, at their core, the developmental needs and rights of young people would not only help to prevent experiences of maltreatment but would also facilitate performance.

Ideally, funding structures need to reflect such a focus. Imagine the outcomes for young people if coaches and sport administrators were evaluated on the basis of their athletes' physical and psychological health, as well as athletes' assessments of the quality of their sport experiences, both during and after their athletic careers. With such a funding model, adults in positions of trust for the care of young people would have an extended responsibility to consider the influence of sport experiences on young people long after sport participation has ended. Furthermore, we posit that optimal athletic performances are realized only when athletes are healthy, have a strong sense of self, exert autonomy, and feel well-supported. In conclusion, only with independent oversight and a funding model and educational programmes that prioritize the promotion of athlete development, health, and well-being will we advance Safe Sport and realize the potential and promise of sport.

Author Contributions: Conceptualization: G.K., B.K., and P.D.; historical account: B.K.; writing of original draft preparation: G.K.; writing—review and editing, B.K. and P.D. All authors have read and agreed to the published version of the manuscript.

Funding: This research received no external funding.

Conflicts of Interest: The authors declare no conflict of interest.

References

Alexander, Kate, Anne Stafford, and Ruth Lewis. 2011. *The Experiences of Children Participating in Organized Sport in the UK*. London: NSPCC.

Atkinson, Michael, and Kevin Young. 2008. *Deviance and Social Control in Sport*. Champaign: Human Kinetics.

Axon, Rachel, Nancy Armour, and Tim Evans. 2018. USA Gymnastics Files for Bankruptcy, a Move Related to Larry Nassar's Sexual Abuse Lawsuits. USA Today. Available online: https://www.usatoday.com/story/sports/olympics/2018/12/05/usa-gymnastics-files-bankruptcy-nassar-lawsuits/2218546002/ (accessed on 10 January 2020).

BBC News. 2018. Football sex abuse: Who is Barry Bennell? *BBC News*. February 15. Available online: https://www.bbc.com/news/uk-38104681 (accessed on 15 February 2020).

Bennett, David. 2018. Independent Review of Coaching Culture for Wrestling Canada Lutte. Available online: https://wrestling.ca/wp-content/uploads/2018/12/FINAL-WCL-Report-for-Release-December-2-2018.pdf (accessed on 18 January 2020).

Brackenridge, Celia. 2001. *Spoilsports: Understanding and Preventing Sexual Exploitation in Sport*. New York: Routledge.

Bruyninckx, Hans. 2011. Obsession with rules vs. mistrust in being ruled. Paper presented at Play the Game Conference, Cologne, Germany, October 3–6.

Canadian Association for the Advancement of Women and Sport (CAAWS). 1994. Harassment in Sport: A Guide to Policies, Procedures and Resources. Available online: http://www.caaws.ca/e/archives/article.cfm?id=1289&search=harassment (accessed on 30 January 2012).

Canadian Centre for Child Protection. n.d. Commit to Kids—Keeping Kids Safe in Sport. Available online: https://www.protectchildren.ca/en/programs-and-initiatives/commit-to-kids-children-in-sport/ (accessed on 1 February 2020).

Christie, James. 1997. Amateur sports co-operate to deal with sexual abuse. *Globe and Mail*, January 31, A13, A14.

Coaching Association of Canada. 2019. National Sport Organization Safe Sport Working Group Presents Consensus Statements on Pan-Canadian Safe Sport on the Prevention of Abuse and Harassment. May 10. Available online: https://coach.ca/national-sport-organization-safe-sport-working-group-presents-consensus-statements-pan-canadian-0 (accessed on 17 January 2020).

Coakley, Jay. 2015. Assessing the Sociology of Sport: On Cultural Sensibilities and the Great Sport Myth. *International Review for the Sociology of Sport* 50: 402–6. [CrossRef]

Connor, James. 2009. The athlete as widget: How exploitation explains elite sport. *Sport in Society* 12: 1369–77. [CrossRef]

Coser, Lewis. 1974. *Greedy Institutions: Patterns of Individual Commitment*. New York: Free Press.

Crooks, Claire, and David Wolfe. 2007. Child Abuse and Neglect. In *Assessment of Childhood Disorders*, 4th ed. Edited by Eric Mash and Russell Barkley. New York: Gilford Press, pp. 649–84.

Donnelly, Peter. 1993. Problems associated with youth involvement in high performance sport. In *Intensive Participation in Children's Sports*. Edited by Bernard Cahill and Arthur Pearl. Champaign: Human Kinetics, pp. 95–126.

Donnelly, Peter. 1996. Prolympism: Sport monoculture as crisis and opportunity. *Quest* 48: 25–42. [CrossRef]

Donnelly, Peter, and Leanne Petherick. 2004. Workers' playtime: Child labour at the extremes of the sporting spectrum. *Sport in Society* 7: 301–21. [CrossRef]

Donnelly, Peter, and Kevin Young. 2004. Sport violence and the culture of control. Paper presented at the Olympic Scientific Congress, Thessaloniki, Greece, August 5–10.

Donnelly, Peter, Gretchen Kerr, Amanda Heron, and Danielle DiCarlo. 2016. Protecting Youth in Sport: An Examination of Harassment Policies. *International Journal of Sport Policy and Politics* 8: 33–50. [CrossRef]

Donnelly, Peter, Erin Willson, Paul Melia, Bruce Kidd, and Ashley LaBrie. 2019. The Struggle for Safe Sport in Canada. Paper presented at Play the Game Conference, Colorado Springs, CO, USA, October 13–16.

Elias, Norbert. 2000. *The Civilizing Process. Sociogenetic and Psychogenetic Investigations*, Revised ed. Oxford: Blackwell Press.

Ewing, Lori. 2018. *Canadian Wrestlers Want an Independent Body on Safe Sport Issues*. Toronto: The Canadian Press, Available online: https://www.cbc.ca/sports/olympics/summer/canadian-wrestlerswant-an-independent-body-on-safe-sport-issues-1.4949823 (accessed on 5 January 2020).

Fleury, Theoren, and K. McLellan Day. 2010. *Playing with Fire: The Highest Highs and the Lowest Lows of Theo Fleury*. Toronto: Harper Collins.

Freeh Sporkin and Sullivan. 2012. *Report of the Special Investigative Counsel Regarding the Pennsylvania State University Related to the Child Sexual Abuse Committed by Gerald A. Sandusky*. July 12. Available online: https://media.pennlive.com/midstate_impact/other/REPORT_FINAL_071212.pdf (accessed on 10 January 2020).

Garland, David. 2001. *The Culture of Control: Crime and Social Order in Contemporary Society*. Oxford: Oxford University Press.

Glaser, Danya. 2002. Emotional abuse and neglect (psychological maltreatment): A conceptual framework. *Child Abuse and Neglect* 26: 697–714. [CrossRef]

Goffman, Erving. 1961. *Asylums: Essays on the Social Situation of Mental Patients and Other Inmates*. London: Penguin.

Government of Canada. 2003. Justice Laws website. Physical Activity and Sport Act S.C. 2003, c. 2 Assented to 2003-03-19. Available online: https://laws-lois.justice.gc.ca/eng/acts/p-13.4/index.html (accessed on 5 January 2020).

Government of Canada. n.d. The Role of Sport Canada. Available online: https://www.canada.ca/en/canadian-heritage/services/role-sport-canada.html (accessed on 5 January 2020).

Gruneau, Richard. 2017. *Sport and Modernity*. Cambridge: Polity.

Heroux, Devin. 2019. Canadian Athletes Want the Lip Service around Safe Sport to Stop. Respect Group Inc. Available online: https://www.respectgroupinc.com/2019/05/01/canadian-athletes-want-the-lip-service-around-safe-sport-to-stop/ (accessed on 20 February 2020).

Heroux, Devin, Dave Seglins, and Rachel Houlihan. 2018. Ex-U.S. athlete tells Speed Skating Canada of head coach's alleged sexual relationships with skaters. *CBC News*. Available online: https://www.cbc.ca/news/canada/crowe-speed-skating-1.4495942 (accessed on 12 February 2020).

Horwath, Jan. 2013. *Child Neglect*. New York: Palgrave MacMillan.

Howe, David. 2003. *Sport, Professionalism and Pain: Ethnographies of Injury and Risk*. London: Routledge.

Jacobs, Frank, Froujke Smits, and Annelies Knoppers. 2017. 'You don't realize what you see!': The Institutional Context of Emotional Abuse in Elite Youth Sport. *Sport in Society* 20: 126–43. [CrossRef]

Jesse, David. 2019. Michigan State to Pay Record $4.5 Million Fine in Larry Nassar Sexual Assault Scandal. *USA Today*. September 5. Available online: https://www.usatoday.com/story/sports/2019/09/05/larry-nassar-scandal-michigan-state-pay-record-fine/2221059001/ (accessed on 15 February 2020).

Kennedy, Sheldon, and James Grainger. 2006. *Why I Didn't Say Anything: The Sheldon Kennedy Story*. Toronto: Insomniac Press.

Kerr, Gretchen. 2020. Personal communication with CEO of a National Sport Organization. February 1.

Kerr, Gretchen, Bruce Kidd, and Peter Donnelly. 2020. Advancing Safe Sport in Canada: A Statement on 'Independence.' Centre for Sport Policy Studies. Position Paper. Available online: https://kpe.utoronto.ca/sites/default/files/advancingsafesportincanada.pdf (accessed on 5 January 2020).

Kerr, Gretchen, Erin Willson, and Ashley Stirling. 2019. Prevalence of Maltreatment among Current and Former National Team Members. Available online: https://athletescan.com/sites/default/files/images/prevalence_of_maltreatment_reporteng.pdf (accessed on 15 February 2020).

Levinson, Eric. 2018. Larry Nassar Sentenced to up to 175 Years in Prison for Decades of Sexual Abuse. Available online: www.cnn.com/2018/01/24/us/larry-nassarPsentencing/index.html (accessed on 19 December 2019).

Mangan, James A. 2012. Conformity Confronted and Orthodoxy Outraged: The Loom of Youth – Succès de Scandale? In Search of a Wider Reality. *The International Journal of the History of Sport* 29: 1701–14. [CrossRef]

Matthews, Dawn. 2004. The consequences of child abuse and neglect. In *Child Abuse Sourcebook*. Edited by Dawn Matthews. Detroit: Omnigraphics Inc., pp. 139–51.

McCoy, Monica, and Stefanie Keen. 2014. *Child Abuse and Neglect*, 2nd ed. New York: Psychology Press.

Miller-Perrin, Cindy, and Robin Perrin. 2012. *Child Maltreatment*, 3rd ed. Thousand Oaks: Sage.

Prewitt, Alex. 2019. Breaking the Ice: After Revelations of Abuse by Coaches, Hockey Is Facing a Reckoning. *Sports Illustrated*. December 10. Available online: https://www.si.com/nhl/2019/12/11/hockey-reckoning-coaches-abuse-revelations (accessed on 10 December 2019).

Rabson, Mia. 2018. National Sports Organizations Have to Report Allegations of Abuse Immediately or Lose Federal Funding. *Toronto Star*. June 19. Available online: https://www.thestar.com/sports/2018/06/19/national-sports-organizations-have-to-report-allegations-of-abuse-immediately-or-lose-federal-funding.html (accessed on 17 December 2019).

Raisman, Aly. 2018a. Speech Accepting ESPYS Award on Behalf of Survivors of Sexual Abuse by Larry Nassar. In *'Sister Survivors' Moment of Solidarity Accepting Arthur Ashe Courage Award*. ESPYS 2018. Bristol: ESPN, Available online: https://www.youtube.com/watch?v=W9hu5HLoSzM (accessed on 15 January 2020).

Raisman, Aly. 2018b. Full Text of Aly Raisman Impact Statement. *New York Times*. Available online: https://www.nytimes.com/2018/01/20/sports/full-text-of-aly-raismans-statement.html (accessed on 1 February 2020).

Reid, Scott. 2012. Athletes Who Survived Abuse Join together as Advocates. *Orange County Register*. Available online: https://www.ocregister.com/2012/03/18/athletes-who-survivedabuse-join-together-as-advocates/ (accessed on 10 January 2020).

Robidoux, Michael. 2001. *Men at Play*. A Working Understanding of Professional Hockey. Montréal: McGill-Queen's University Press.

Smith, Ronald. 2016. *Wounded Lions: Joe Paterno, Jerry Sandusky and the Crises in Penn State Athletics*. Urbana: University of Illinois Press.

Sport Information Resource Centre. 2019. Red Deer Declaration for the Prevention of Harassment, Abuse and Discrimination in Sport. Available online: https://scics.ca/en/product-produit/red-deer-declaration-for-the-prevention-of-harassment-abuse-and-discrimination-in-sport/ (accessed on 15 December 2019).

Stafford, Anne, Kate Alexander, and Deborah Fry. 2015. 'There was something that wasn't right because that was the only place I ever got treated like that': Children and young people's experiences of emotional harm in sport. *Childhood* 22: 121–37. [CrossRef]

Stirling, Ashley, and Gretchen Kerr. 2015. In the name of performance: Threats, belittlement, and degradation. In *Health and Elite Sport: Is High Performance Sport a Healthy Pursuit?* Edited by Joe Baker, Parissa Safai and Jessica Fraser-Thomas. London: Routledge, pp. 83–98.

The Canadian Press. 2015. A Timeline of Graham James's Legal History. Available online: https://globalnews.ca/news/2016827/a-timeline-of-graham-jamess-legal-history/ (accessed on 10 February 2020).

The Canadian Press. 2019. Sex Abuser, Ex-Ski Coach Bertrand Charest 'Continues to Trivialize His Conduct'. *Appeal Judges Say.* August 22. Available online: https://www.cbc.ca/news/canada/montreal/appeals-bertrand-charest-1.525641 (accessed on 10 January 2020).

Vertommen, Tine, Nicolette Schipper-van Veldhoven, Kristien Wouters, Jarl K. Kampen, Celia H. Brackenridge, Daniel J. A. Rhind, Karel Neels, and Filip Van Den Eede. 2016. Interpersonal violence against children in sport in the Netherlands and Belgium. *Child Abuse & Neglect* 51: 223–36.

Vine, Cathy, and Paul Challen. 2002. *Gardens of Shame: The Tragedy of Martin Kruze and the Sexual Abuse at Maple Leaf Gardens.* Vancouver: Greystone Books.

Ward, Lori, and Jamie Strashin. 2019. *Sex Offences against Minors: Investigation Reveals More Than 200 Canadian Coaches Convicted in Last 20 years.* Toronto: Canadian Broadcasting Corporation, Available online: https://www.cbc.ca/sports/amateur-sports-coaches-sexual-offences-minors-1.5006609 (accessed on 15 February 2020).

World Health Organization. 2016. Child Maltreatment. Available online: https://www.who.int/news-room/fact-sheets/detail/child-maltreatment (accessed on 15 February 2020).

Young, Kevin. 2012. *Sport, Violence and Society.* New York: Routledge.

social sciences

MDPI

Article

'Warm Eyes', 'Warm Breath', 'Heart Warmth': Using Aroha (Love) and Warmth to Reconceptualise and Work towards *Best Interests* in Child Protection

Susan Young [1,*], **Margaret McKenzie** [2], **Cecilie Omre** [3], **Liv Schjelderup** [3] **and Shayne Walker** [4]

[1] Social Work and Social Policy, The University of Western Australia, Crawley, WA 6009, Australia
[2] College of Community Development and Personal Wellbeing, The Otago Polytechnic, Dunedin 9016, New Zealand; Margaret.McKenzie@op.ac.nz
[3] Faculty of Social Sciences, The University of Stavanger, Faculty of Social Sciences, 4036 Stavanger, Norway; cecilie.omre@uis.no (C.O.); liv.schjelderup@uis.no (L.S.)
[4] Gender Studies and Criminology, The University of Otago, Sociology, Dunedin 9016, New Zealand; shayne.walker@otago.ac.nz
* Correspondence: susan.young@uwa.edu.au

Received: 11 March 2020; Accepted: 13 April 2020; Published: 17 April 2020

Abstract: The attributes 'warm eyes', 'breathe warm air', 'heart warmth' and aroha (love) guide our work in child protection. These quotes are from a young person from the Change Factory 2020, a MFAMILY student in 2020 and Jan Erik Henricksen Key Note at the 4th International Indigenous Voices in Social Work Conference, Alta, Norway 2017 respectively, to describe the way young people and families want workers to be. We reflect on the child rights and family inclusion provisions of the United Nations *Convention on the Rights of the Child (UNCRoC)*, and the Aotearoa New Zealand (ANZ) legislation *Children, Young Persons and their Families Act* (1989), in contributing to the *best interests* of the child. We examine current events in our locations, Aotearoa New Zealand, Norway and Western Australia, as demonstrating that these joint principles are far from universally used in child protection practice. The sole use of Article 3 of the UNCRoC, in particular, often results in excluding families as legitimate stakeholders. In seeking to achieve the *best interests* of the child, we apply a practice framework to example vignettes. Here, we have added micro-practices to address the identified gaps in relationship building, engagement and enabling practices in working towards the practice of *best interests*.

Keywords: child rights; family inclusion; child protection; co-constructing social work; practice frameworks; young people and children

1. Introduction

Our work as social work educators, researchers and practitioners in Aotearoa New Zealand (ANZ), Norway and Western Australia (WA) with child welfare and protection over many years has led us to question how the *best interests* principle has been applied in our countries. A mantra in policy, legislation and practice, this concept has, in many cases, seemingly become a taken-for-granted rationale for removing children from their parents as a first rather than a last step in the aim of protecting children. Over the years, we have argued that the sole reliance on Article 3 of the United Nations *Convention on the Rights of the Child* (UNCRoC) often has the consequence of excluding parents and family/whanau as legitimate stakeholders in their children's lives, and pits professionals against parents, children against parents and risk-focused approaches against family support measures. We have become increasingly interested in the concept of 'love' as an aspect of practice. As educators, we draw on Honneth (1995) conceptualisation of recognition—of which, the three cornerstones are love, rights and solidarity. As practitioners, we have listened in person to young people in Norway as well as through their reports (Neumann 2016; Sanner 2016; Forandringsfabrikken 2017). The Change Factory in Norway is a network of young people who all have experience of child protection through the mental health, justice, education and health systems. As 'pros' (The young people's's name for themselves as professionals in their own lives.), they present talks to other young people, professional workers, educators, policy makers and politicians to encourage systems and practice change. In particular, they want to be shown warmth and love from those who work with them. Alexander, a pro, speaks for many of the pros when he says:

> *"I would like it if more of the people in the system showed some warmth and love when they encounter us. I would like them to show more humility, be more open, instead of using well-rehearsed methods and conversation techniques," says Alexander.* (Kjellander et al. 2016, p. 55)

Here, it is clear that the pros wish for a more reciprocal relationship, recognition that the young people have an equal part to play in their development, and that workers and young people can have a warm working relationship of benefit to them both. Both 'love' and 'warm eyes' is a common theme in their talks; when they say they look for workers who have 'warm eyes,' they know then they can trust the workers to treat them with care. 'Warm breath' is another concept which encompasses a similar expressed need and was spoken by a young Kenyan social worker from her experience with young people in her country. Young people seek to have the space between the worker and young person filled with warm not cold air, reflecting the ability to be approachable and collaborative. Professional objectivity is experienced as coldness. Having 'heart warmth' is an attribute an Indigenous social work colleague has developed over the years of his practice and forms the centrepiece of his practice framework. All these concepts are saying the same thing: young people in the child protection systems want workers who will work with them showing warmth, and, for the young people of the Change Factory, love.

We are mindful that in some of our countries, to openly express or even use the word 'love' brings dangers. We are also mindful that the young people who are part of the child protection world need to have warmth and love shown to them, especially by professionals who carry the authority for what shall happen to these young people in their hands. It is not an insignificant responsibility, and it requires a more nuanced approach to the rights of the child than relying solely on a professional judgement of what constitutes the *best interests* of the child.

However, perhaps rather than defending the use of 'love', we return to the ANZ concept of aroha. The child protection process in Aotearoa New Zealand tikanga (Māori cultural constructs) (Smith 1999) encompasses customs, ethics, values, culture and principles for living daily life (Mead 2003). As a tikanga, aroha has a multi-layered meaning and is not only an expression of love but also the enacting of care, concern, respect and compassion for others (Barlow 1991). When discussing research with Māori, Smith (1999) encourages us to have aroha kit e tangata (a respect for people). The expression of aroha creates an innate positive effect on others that adds to their experience and meaning in everyday life (Barlow 1991). In Aotearoa New Zealand, workers are encouraged to have an integrated approach in their work with Māori families that is tika (correct in our thinking and knowing), pono (having integrity with what we know) and aroha (acting out of love) (Tate 2010). In practice, aroha is more than just knowing a concept or feeling an abstract emotion, aroha has a doing component that is related to the 'ha' (to breathe, to taste) and the 'aro' (to pay attention, take notice). Those we work with in the child protection process recognise the 'aro' when we take notice, but it is the 'ha' that they remember because we breathe life into the context or situation. In contemporary formal and informal greetings, Māori hongi—they gently press noses together (Barlow 1991; Ka'ai 2004) and some, at the same time, touch foreheads. This intermingling and sharing of the 'ha' is more than a metaphor, it is part of the powhiri (formal welcome) ritual and integral essence of the child protection processes with Māori families. Everyone has the opportunity to breathe into the co-construction. Aroha as a takepu (applied principle) (Pohatu 2004) is an intrinsic part of how we 'become the theory,' as it affects the way we behave with children and young people. Aroha is at the heart of co-construction as we take notice of one another, listening, learning and growing. It creates a whakawatea (to clear a pathway or make way) so that we can work together honestly and deeply. We take these 'warmths' and love as guides to practice with the young people and their families in the child protection system.

2. The United Nations *Convention on the Rights of the Child* (1989) and the Aotearoa New Zealand *Children, Young Persons and Their Families Act* (1989)

Two significant milestones occurred in 2019. The United Nations *Convention on the Rights of the Child* (UNCRoC) (1989) and the Aotearoa New Zealand (ANZ) *Children, Young Persons and their Families Act* (1989) both reached thirty years of operation. The ANZ legislation was momentous, as not only did it enshrine Māori practices, it was the first statute in the Western world to actively include families in the decision-making processes when children were considered to be at risk, only two decades after child abuse, then called 'baby-battering', became a policy matter for child welfare authorities. Sourcing inspiration from Indigenous experiences and practices in the troubled world of race relations was an opportunity for hope. However, the journey related to child welfare and child protection since then, while witnessing some achievements in the countries in which we work, ANZ, Norway and Western Australia (WA), hope-filled child protection policy and practice is becoming little more than a chimera. In each of our countries, and indeed in much of the rest of Western child protection, efforts to retain inclusive, participatory, positive partnerships with families are met with challenges and oppositions (Kojan and Lonne 2012; Hyslop and Keddell 2018; Powell et al. 2020). Times have changed, stresses on families have changed and the preparedness of society to sanction any other than parent-blaming responses seems now a figment of a long distance past. Increasing numbers of children, particularly Indigenous children, are coming into the care of the state, and increasingly families are being faced with reduced time to prove their worthiness before their children are legislatively permanently removed from their care (Keddell 2018; Skivenes and Sørsdal 2018; Mackieson et al. 2019). However, far from abandoning hope, we have been witnesses to practices that signal optimism, and these have led us to develop for our own practice and hopefully for others, a way of conceptualising alternate child protection measures in policy and practice. This article uses the two legislative innovations from 1989 to examine the current state of child welfare and child protection in our jurisdictions and articulate ways of responding in this present century to current challenges for child protection practice, with particular reference to how the *best interests* principle may be enacted to truly meet the *best interests* of the child.

2.1. Enacting the Best Interests Principle in Child Protection

'In the *best interests* of the child' has become somewhat of a mantra in child protection settings (Long and Sephton 2011; Eriksen 2018; Salminen 2018; Leloup 2019; Sandberg 2019) but has proven to be problematic in articulation and implementation. The Article in the Convention which introduces the *best interests* principle is Article 3. Some writers have suggested that this Article is one of four 'foundational principles' (George and Awal 2019) along with Articles 2 (protection against discrimination), 6 (right to life) and 12 (the right to be heard). Article 3 has three subsections, but the most commonly cited is that 'in all actions concerning children, whether undertaken by public or private social welfare institutions, courts of law, administrative authorities or legislative bodies, the *best interests* of the child shall be a primary consideration'. There are three main interconnected issues: the original wording with a lack of definition, the interpretation authority, and the use of Article 3 in isolation. The wording of the Article is itself indeterminate, allowing for different interpretations. The use of 'a primary consideration' rather than 'the' primary consideration, suggests other factors may be considered, and the lack of definition of what constitutes *best interests*, linking it in Article 3(2) to well-being and welfare, provide for considerable latitude in understanding and, by extension, decision making by authorities (George and Awal 2019). The second issue is one of authority. Not only are the main stakeholders, the child and the parents, omitted from this Article, there is no indication as to which of the authorities should have the final say in cases where there are disputes, as there usually are.

Finally, the reliance on Article 3 as the main consideration for decision makers contravenes the original intent of the Committee on the Rights of the Child who showed a much more nuanced consideration of what was to be included in the *best interests* principle. The General Comments show that this principle is to be taken together with 'other articles: article 9: separation from parents; article 10: family reunification; article 18: parental responsibilities; article 20: deprivation of family environment and alternative care; article 21: adoption'. The Committee evidently sought to indicate that *best interests* was inclusive of a range of other rights which had to be given due weight. Further, the General Comment states: 'The Committee has already pointed out that "an adult's judgment of a child's best interests cannot override the obligation to respect *all* the child's rights under the Convention."' (CRC 2013, Section 1.A) (Authors' emphasis). While the Committee did not specifically cite Article 12 in this list, which requires that children have a right to participate and to be heard, the idea that adults, and in the main, professional representatives of authorities, unilaterally have the right to determine what is in the best interests of the child was not the original intent. As there is no weighting as to which of the 'State Parties' or other institutions or authorities shall prevail when there is a dispute as to what constitutes the *best interests* of the child, the subjectivity and value-laden nature of the Article lays it open to many different interpretations. There is no absolute arbiter. Hence, when disputes come to courts, whom are the judges to heed?

Such single applications of the *best interests* principle without reference to other, equally important, rights consolidate the prevailing status quo. The binaries in practice of professionals versus parents, children versus parents and risk-orientated practice versus family support remain firmly entrenched.

The UNCRoC is now almost universally ratified by member nations. Some countries, such as Norway, have written child rights principles into their national laws, while others, such as Australia, which belatedly ratified the Convention, leave reflection of the principles as less specific in their legislation. However, all jurisdictions face the challenges of a loosely defined and ultimately differently interpretable consideration of what constitutes *best interests* and what to do in the *best interests* of the child.

2.2. Participation and Decision Making in Child Protection

The ground-breaking legislation, the *Children, Young Persons and their Families Act* (1989), enshrined Māori practices of family decision making in ANZ, leading to the development of the Family Group Conference (FGC) in a move that was intended to strengthen and encourage family participation in providing safety for children. Family and others, not merely parents, were to be included. These stakeholders were, moreover, considered to be competent—perhaps not in all things, but they could contribute to decisions and practice about keeping children safe. Significantly, there was recognition that a group of people, not just the immediate parents, could perhaps achieve protection for the child together rather than separately. Participation, inclusion and joint decision making were embedded in the legislation. FGC has been subject to criticism from both opponents and advocates (Frost et al. 2014; De Jong et al. 2015; Thørnblad et al. 2016; Dijkstra et al. 2018), with some studies suggesting worker attitudes and access to supportive resources for families are vital for success (Williams et al. 2015). This points to the importance of comprehensive support for programmes including ensuring that there are adequate resources available for both staff and families, invoking Articles 18 and 19 of UNCRoC. That ANZ appears to be currently resourcing the FGC process indicates that, despite the continuing underlying neo-liberal policy context (Keddell 2018), family support remains a policy direction. FGC has been adopted in many countries around the world, with Norway being a strong supporter, having adopted it in the late 1990s—further, by 2016, approximately half of all Norwegian municipalities have reported using FGC. Recent amendments to child welfare law in Norway specify that all families coming to the attention of the Child Welfare Services (CWS) should be offered FGC.

3. Child Protection in Aotearoa New Zealand, Norway and Western Australia

The two legislative prescriptions referred to above provide a background to our enquiry as to how to enact a child protection process in our jurisdictions which pays due homage to their intent of participation, inclusion, collaboration and partnership. For, if child rights as envisaged by the UNCRoC and family inclusion as intended by the CYP&F Act are unattainable, what is the future for child protection practice? This article, then, sets the achievements from thirty years ago in relation to child rights and family inclusion in decision making about their future in juxtaposition to the developments in our respective countries and the on-going debates as to just what *child rights* and *family inclusion* mean.

Country Contexts

The differing social policy heritages of our countries notwithstanding all have regulatory and distributive measures in our welfare states to ensure child safety and child well-being. The Social Democratic tradition in Norway means that child welfare is largely considered as being encompassed within the family service approach (Gilbert 2012) and there is an expectation that *child* welfare includes *family* welfare. Australia is characterised as risk oriented (Skivenes and Sørsdal 2018), while ANZ fell somewhere in between in 1989. Contemporary ANZ aligns much more closely to Western Australia, (which although not an autonomous country does constitutionally have jurisdiction over child welfare matters) where the predominant risk management discourses of child protection (Keddell 2014; Hyslop and Keddell 2018) are rapidly being supplemented by the emerging neuroscience discourse (Lowe et al. 2015), thereby solidifying the medical–social model (Parton 1985), with its resultant (and not entirely intended) parent-blaming consequences.

In both Western Australia and ANZ, the management of child protection changes with government change. A recent example in ANZ is the re-focusing (Oranga Tamariki 2019) of its child welfare services to emphasise early intervention in contrast to remedial services. Researchers (Keddell 2018; Atwool 2019) suggest that the reforms have not altered the neo-liberal philosophy underpinning 'vulnerability' and the social investment of the state in 'good' citizens, continuing to highlight individual responsibility and consequent culpability for the frequent failure to meet societal norms. Although ANZ has been labelled as subscribing to a child and family welfare model, rather than a child safety policy position (Gilbert et al. 2009), the neo-liberal agenda of individualisation remains (Hyslop and Keddell 2018) and there are still unacceptably high numbers of children taken into care, a large proportion of whom are Māori and Pasifika. That the neo-liberal agenda is present in ANZ is indicated by what Keddell, Hyslop and others report as its seemingly entrenched patterns of child protection practice (Beddoe and Joy 2017; Hyslop 2017; Ware et al. 2017; Hyslop and Keddell 2018; Keddell 2018, 2019a). A documentary (Summer Newsroom 2019) about an attempted 'uptake', or removal of an infant at birth, went viral in 2019, forming a talking point in many institutions in Australia, and no doubt elsewhere, where social workers expressed surprise that this should occur in ANZ, while also acknowledging its prevalence in Australia.

The recent active reforms, including changing the name of the child welfare department to Oranga Tamariki (OT), and the legislation title to The Oranga Tamariki Act or the Children and Young Persons Act, which notably omits family from the title, purport to promote the centrality of the paramountcy of a child-centred approach. However, commentators (Keddell 2019a) suggest that protection and safety from risk have displaced participation and the use of the family decision-making process of FGC and this is commensurate with the changed focus and renaming of the government department seen in the legislation title. The proposed law name itself was controversial (Becroft 2016), and universally rejected by Māori and Pakeha (European) for its potential for stigmatising and labelling. Hyslop (2017, p. 11) points out that despite the visionary nature of the Act which led to FGC in giving greater authority to families, ever 'since there have been a succession of enquiries, reviews, and reports proposing changes to the statutory child welfare system in New Zealand,' resulting in continued challenges to the ANZ child protection system. Such actions are in danger of ignoring the relational context of children

(Featherstone et al. 2014). In this context, removal is framed as a gain, invoking a 'child-focused practice', where, as the child is the client, parents and whanau can legitimately be excluded.

Australia and ANZ, therefore, are becoming more, rather than less, similar in child welfare practice, which still remains professionally driven. In Australia, the adoption of a national framework for child protection in 2009 (COAG 2009) used a public health model of primary and universal prevention, but practice remains focused on tertiary prevention, or concentrating predominantly on risk. Arguments for taking the primary route to prevention are still being made (Sanders et al. 2018; Lonne et al. 2019), with community or universally available resources or local supports for families among the more urgent needs (Babington 2016). Pockets of family support approaches exist but are mainly performed by the non-government sector. Examples include programmes run by the Family Inclusion Networks (FINs) around Australia using a Family Inclusion Framework of practice (Ross et al. 2017) and family peer support.

Having jurisdictional authority in child protection practice, recent government changes in Western Australia have re-introduced some significant preventive and early intervention strategies for young people and children. Nevertheless, child abuse notifications and substantiations are increasing and, disturbingly, the proportion of Indigenous and Torres Strait Islander children being removed from their families is the highest for many years, at 54% of all out-of-home placements (O'Donnell et al. 2019). The need now is to formulate appropriate responses that will neither continue nor encourage this trend but instead provide the necessary and culturally appropriate supports so that this is reversed. This is the most urgent need in WA, but practice within the state authority system remains firmly reflective of the risk orientation, where its purpose states: ' . . . to protect children and young people from abuse and neglect; to support families and individuals who are at risk or in crisis' (DCPFS 2017, p. 7). The fact that 54% of all home placements are Indigenous and Torres Strait Islander children suggests that authorities consider care in their homes to be of such concern that they have to be removed for their own safety. This alarming proportion of the population showing signs of risk or crisis in itself surely cannot be read to mean that all individual Indigenous and Torres Strait Islander families are so disproportionally failing as to be constantly causing their children to live in risk environments enveloped in crisis.

The situation in Norway is showing signs of risk and crisis, even with its emphasis on family support. A recent assessment of new developments the authors refer to as 'the New Child Protection' (Kojan et al. 2019) suggests that far from providing the support families with multiple challenges need in order to ensure the well-being and safety of their children, these new measures are on the contrary failing parents who are then constructed as failed parents. Despite strong family support provisions, more children are coming to the attention of the authorities, with Norwegian statistics recording 57,000 notifications in 2018 and 15,000 children receiving placement provisions (Statistisk sentralbyrå 2018). As other countries' experiences attest, out-of-home care places children in particularly vulnerable positions, with results from a systematic review of 20 studies indicating poor outcomes over nine measures (Kääriäläa and Hiilamoa 2017). Although some reports suggest that the Norwegian Child Welfare Services, including the specific child welfare agency (CWS), its workers and judges in the courts, enjoy popular support (Juhasz and Skivenes 2017), they also receive considerable criticism. Such criticism relates to opposition of their ability to and practice of removing children from their families, citing injustices and unprofessional conduct (Stang 2018). Even the comparative study, conducted in 2017, which found populations in the Nordic countries generally have greater confidence in the public systems of child welfare than counterparts in the UK and US, still concluded that trust in these systems was 'alarmingly low' (Juhasz and Skivenes 2017). Recent events, such as the well-publicised removal of a 10-year-old child from his mother in Stavanger, Norway, using five cars and seven police (Bjørå 2020), suggest that the management of child protection cases in Norway is indeed in some disarray.

The immediacy of these concerns is shown in some current adjudications by the European Court of Human Rights, which has before it 36 cases from Norway—of which, it has ruled on 6. While two of these have been dismissed, the judgements in relation to the remaining four are damming. The court criticised the Norwegian courts, citing some examples of when the court considered the authorities to be at fault in their actions:

- *'Severing parent-child ties without adequate decision-making process'* (ECHR 2019;)
- *'the potential negative long-term consequences of losing contact with her mother for A and the positive duty to take measures to facilitate family reunification as soon as reasonably feasible were not sufficiently weighed in the balancing exercise'* (ECHR 2018;)
- *'Regime of contact at variance with aim of family reunification. Authorities' failure to consider possibility of family reunification in light of child's best interests'* (ECHR 2019).

Three main issues have been found: inadequate explanation of decisions and the evidence used for the decisions; reliance on out of date information, for example psychologists' reports that were over two years old; and the propensity to ignore the possibility of reunification in the decision-making process. That CWS did not include all relevant Articles in their decisions as expected by the Committee on the Rights of the Child is shown most clearly in the ECHR judgements. These criticisms—indeed, judgements—clearly demonstrate that in the opinion of the Court, CWS workers are removing children from their families without being adequately able to explain why it is in the *best interests* of the children to do so. There may be many reasons for this tendency, perhaps the most compelling, as found in many jurisdictions, is that child protection work has become risk averse (Laird et al. 2018). Seemingly, the Norwegian courts have 'rubber stamped' the professionals' decisions, reinforcing the problematics of Article 3 of identifying the final arbiter. It is hard to escape the paternalism, risk-averse nature of practice, and judgmental attitudes towards 'failed parents' in these practices, which are not unique to Norway, for we also find these in ANZ and Western Australia.

In our work over these three decades, we have met and worked with many young people and children in different contexts. With increasing dismay, we have watched the retreat from the principles of the UNCRoC and the ANZ legislation. Recently, our attention has been drawn to 'love' as a necessary attribute and action in the lives of children and young people, not just from their families and friends, but also from their workers. 'Warm eyes', 'breathe warm air', and 'heart warmth' are expressions spoken by young people, children and workers as describing the way children want workers to be when they are working with them. Warmth of expression, ensuring the setting for the work is one of warmth and that people working with young people are emotionally close are important to these young people—they do not want us to be their friends, but they do want warmth. Not long after the legislative frameworks for inclusion and participation were developed in 1989, Honneth (1995) realised the importance of love as part of a greater social whole. Along with rights and solidarity, love forms the tripartite foundation for social solidarity and thence recognition, a practice that enables growth and development through the sound formation of identity. Young people in the child protection systems are often torn by conflicting identities or forced to withdraw from a given identity through the actions of those who state they are acting in their *best interests*. Young people want to have workers who can help them retain their identities, to grow positive identities that do not force them to negate the connections they had and above all show understanding of this need with warmth (Cossar et al. 2016; Kjellander et al. 2016; Lefevre 2017). While warmth, along with empathy and other characteristics, has been a founding attribute for social work clinical practice for many years (Rogers 1956) and central to the therapeutic relationship, the recent predisposition in child protection has moved away from showing warmth in the ways young people want to be shown.

We next present examples from our countries which we will use to examine possible ways of practicing to avoid or address binary thinking in practice.

4. Three Vignettes

4.1. Norway

Britt (not her real name) is 17 years old and has been participating as a 'pro' with the Change Factory (Forandringsfabrikken in Norwegian) for a year. 'Pro' is the name the young people in the Change Factory call themselves to indicate that the knowledge they have about their lives is at least equal to that of others, particularly adults and other professionals. They provide education about their lived experiences to other young people, professional workers and policy makers, especially politicians. Their aim is to create change in the policy and practice that governs much of the treatment of young people in the education, mental health, children's services and justice systems. The Change Factory has been operating for 15 years and has recently been successful in adding some of their suggestions and wording to the new Norwegian Child Welfare Legislation. It may be that Norwegian law for the protection of children is the first in the world to include provisions about 'love' in the treatment of young people and children—a word that characterises the way the young people of the Change Factory want to be treated (Kjellander et al. 2016). One of the acts of the young people in response to the events mentioned earlier concerning the police handling of a child removal in Stavanger was to write to politicians and the police to strongly request that child rights be included in police policy and manuals (Editor 2020).

Britt told her story. She was a clever and studious child, advancing rapidly at school which she loved. Her parents separated and she had to spend equal time with each parent, but increasingly her time with her father was difficult and abusive. While there was no evident physical or sexual abuse, Britt began to withdraw, begging her mother to let her stay away from her father. Her mother refused, saying it was the law. Britt started staying away from school, her grades dropped dramatically, she began self-harming and eventually there were several attempts at suicide. She was taken into care and, with the greatest of good fortune, a teacher in the special school which she had to attend found something in her to value and praise. Instead of being told she would amount to nothing and it was a waste of time to teach her, which had been the response from teachers in middle school, this teacher formed a supportive encouraging relationship with Britt. It was so successful that Britt was able to catch up the three years she had missed in the first six months at the school and was now back at the level where she should be. One of the staff at the school mentioned the Change Factory and Britt has been a 'pro' now for a year, giving talks to school children, professional workers and politicians. She eventually wants to work with people, to show them that there is hope.

4.2. Western Australia

A sixth-grade (aged 10) Indigenous student was referred to the school social worker by a teacher for behaviour issues. She was inattentive in class and disruptive to other students with what the teacher considered to be attention-seeking behaviour. She did not complete her school work in a timely manner and was operating at a lower level in her grade than her year. The teacher was also concerned that the student would come to school in less than clean clothes and regularly attended the breakfast club, suggesting that she was not fed at home. The teacher had only ever seen the child's carer, who appeared to be an elderly and frail woman, once.

The social worker attended the class and observed that the student did not appear to be overly distracting but did ask questions loudly and did not appear to respond to the teacher's instructions. Overall, the social worker thought the student presented with low confidence and anxiety and appeared uncomfortable to be singled out by the teacher.

The school files had minimal information, recording only that the student had been enrolled by her grandmother at the school in the past month. No other family details were available.

The social worker arranged to speak to the student, who was quiet throughout the meeting, responding only with 'yes' and 'no' answers to questions and sometimes not at all. After several short sessions with the student, the worker understood that the child had difficulty both understanding and hearing him. He also realised that this student had come from the country, which is home to a wide and diverse set of Indigenous groupings. Both of these realisations led him to silently reflect about the child's background (context). While she was light skinned, the worker knew from his previous studies in his social work course that Indigenous people were very varied in skin colour, which itself did not indicate any particular locational or cultural belonging (Fredericks 2013). He also knew that the prevalence of ear conditions for desert Indigenous children was a concern (Burns and Thomson 2013). However, he knew that he needed more information. Gradually, the child responded sufficiently for the worker to ask whether he could visit the home and talk to her grandmother. The student agreed.

When the worker visited the home, he encountered a frail-looking elderly Indigenous woman whose command of English was rudimentary. The house was sparsely furnished and not well kept. The worker wondered about the ability of the grandmother to care for the child, but he witnessed evident warmth and affection between the two. The grandmother was reluctant to talk to him. The worker explained that he was working with her granddaughter at the school because she did not appear to be able to attend well in class and he wondered whether there was some reason for this. He asked whether the granddaughter had had any ear complaints which might affect her hearing. At this, the grandmother responded more readily and asked whether the worker could do something about this.

The worker gradually gained the grandmother's cooperation and pointedly did not comment on or question her about her ability to look after her granddaughter or why she was doing so. Taking the girl to the health clinic and having her hearing issues addressed started the process of the grandmother beginning to trust the worker and, while they were waiting at the health clinic, they were able to talk about where she came from. Over the following weeks of working with this family, the worker was able to assist in several matters—the issue of the child's interactions with the teacher was effectively resolved with medical treatment for the ear complaint. Other issues included the family's relocation from relatives and supports as a consequence of the death of the child's mother and the need to establish local connections and supports. While not from the metropolitan area, this family did indeed have connections locally which were able to be found (Collective Action and Family Capital). These were able to provide support to the grandmother who was also encouraged to seek medical attention. Although she was initially cautious about being involved with a social worker for fear of the possibility of having the child removed, the worker was able to demonstrate that he could be trusted to work alongside her with her wishes and how she foresaw her and the child's future.

4.3. Aotearoa New Zealand

In November 2018, workers from Oranga Tamariki (OT), the ANZ child welfare department, discovered that a 19-year-old mother who had previously had a child removed was expecting again. In February 2019, they logged a report of concern and it was referred for FGC in mid-March. In March and April, meetings were held with the mother and her whanau (family) support which included a number of Māori NGO workers. The mother clearly expressed her determination to keep this baby and discussion was held regarding the mother's progress and strategies in improving her parenting skills. She entered a residential parenting programme on April 1, and the baby was born on May 1 at Hastings Hospital. The very next day, Oranga Tamariki sought and was granted a 'without notice S78 Custody Order'.

Four days later, on May 6, three team members from Oranga Tamariki attempted to remove the baby (male) from the parents at the Hospital. Those in the room, i.e., parents, whanau and midwives reminded the OT staff of the plan which they thought had been agreed. Meanwhile, the media had been alerted and the whole event was being filmed and recorded on phones. OT workers reluctantly agreed that the mother and baby could stay at the hospital until a whanau hui (meeting) could be convened. A strengthened plan was discussed but, on May 7, the OT team decided to proceed to remove the child and a removal was attempted later that evening. The mother and her whanau support (especially the two midwives) bravely resisted several attempts and the OT workers withdrew after midnight on

May 8. A hui was held later that day and it was agreed that the mother and baby would return to the residential parenting programme and this occurred on May 9 (Oranga Tamariki Professional Practice Review Group 2020).

4.4. Summary

These situations provide a backdrop for our desire to have a process we articulated in 2012 (Young et al.) disseminated more widely. In that article, we introduced our conceptualisation of a process for carrying out child protection work in a way that honoured the principles found in social work practice: positive unconditional regard, non-judgement, the dignity and worth of all people, self-determination, person in environment, and the power of social networks, among others. All these attributes have characterised the practice of social work in the West for over a century. They are now being implemented with practices that are older but until now rejected, those of the Indigenous communities who have had systems of care for millennia. Acknowledging these as having equal status and value in social work education and practice is an ongoing process with greater success in some parts of the world than others. However, there is a growing Indigenous body of scholarship and practice models that is adding to the ability of social work as a profession to work more responsively with Indigenous peoples as well as learn from them in applying approaches to protect children (Ryan 2011; Nietz 2017; Blacklock et al. 2018; Gallagher and Louis 2018; Krakouer et al. 2018; Douglas and Saus 2019; Thomspon and Wadley 2019). We have emphasised FGC as an original Indigenous model, as it still incorporates much of what we would hope to have included in child protection practice—the inclusion and participation of, and partnerships with, families; respect for and acceptance of locally grounded knowledge; the willingness to work with different contexts and situations as described and experienced by the people themselves. All these practices and principles reinforce to us that there are different ways of undertaking the business of protecting children, even when, as they often do, they result in children having to be removed from their parents. We hope that in many of these situations, the relational way of working enables positive relationships to be maintained for, and in, the *best interests* of the children.

5. Constructing and Applying a Framework: The Co-Constructing Social Work Framework

In designing a practice framework, we did not set out for it to be definitive or impositional, being very mindful of one of its elements, which is that of context. How could we seek to impose a universal framework at the same time as upholding the value of acknowledging contextual differences and imperatives? A current example of the way frameworks born from one set of circumstances and principles are changed by a universalist approach comes to mind. The Signs of Safety (SoS) (Turnell and Edwards 1999) model is now used in many countries in child protection practice in addition to that location in which it was developed. Born from a grassroots, bottom–up practice drawn from one of the author's extensive experiences working with Indigenous people in WA, it was intended to be contextually driven and responsive to families and their situations. Its subsequent adoption by the state welfare department with the requirement that all staff had to use it in their work with families deprived it of much of the essence which created it. To all intents and purposes, it became a risk assessment tool rather than a mechanism for engaging with families in order to collaboratively assess what needed to be done to keep children safe—a subtle but important distinction. Adopted at the highest level with mandatory training for all workers, there was, nevertheless some resistance from workers who worked directly with remote Indigenous people. In collaboration with local Indigenous families, they found it necessary to translate the practices so that it could be applied in those settings. Local people were suspicious that the process was merely another way of removing their children.

Frameworks such as SoS are often adopted by agencies to meet their desired goals and policies, but they make no allowance for worker judgement or discretion. The practice of the Oranga Tamariki and Norwegian CWS workers was to follow implied or actual agency directives and expectations. Neither of these situations were found to be in the *best interests* of the child. The workers in remote communities directed to use SoS uncritically found it to be both culturally unresponsive as well as potentially damaging to ongoing relationships with the communities.

An alternative approach is to take practice frameworks as incorporating three forms of knowledge to assist workers to use their professional judgements and make choices (Trevithick 2008). Reflecting the theory–practice–theory continuum that is a foundational principle for our work (Young et al. 2014a), or as Lewin states 'there is nothing as practical as a good theory' (Lewin 1945, p. 129), Trevithick (2008) cites Polanyi's theory of knowledge to formulate the intersection between factual knowledge, theoretical knowledge and practice knowledge. Here, practice informs theory and theory informs practice. The theory–practice cycle means that practice is not reducible to a tick-the-box exercise that is uncritically reliant on agency directives. There will be alternatives in explanations (theory) and choices as to what to do (practice). Using a practice framework means practitioners will need to identify their own values and beliefs. Our beliefs and values have been described elsewhere (Young et al. 2014a) but the principles for our practice rely on and are drawn from the principles contained in the UNCRoC and the ANZ legislation which gave rise to FGC.

We repeat the framework for co-constructing social work here (Table 1), to which we have added another column that includes micro-practices as we found these to be missing from our original framework. It is to give words and ideas to how to incorporate into practice the concepts in our title (warm air, warm breath, heart warmth and aroha). In the first two vignettes, we identified worker actions and attitudes which align to warmth and love. In the ANZ vignette, some of the workers also showed warmth and love in supporting the young family. In their desire to uphold what they considered to be protocol in situations where risk had been identified, other workers were not able to show the same warmth and love. Acting in a statutory CP role, which is often by its nature confrontational and complex, bringing great stress, it was clear that that the key concepts of warm breath, heart warmth, and aroha were absent. This family and these workers were in opposite corners. Despite the many instances of mini engagements witnessed in the documentary describing the events, there was no visible foundation of the statutory workers and the family working together in partnership for the *best interests* of the child in this room. On the day, the Māori Oranga Tamariki workers thought that they were operating on the basis of aroha to protect that baby. It was not how it was perceived or experienced by the whanau. They were absolutely heartbroken over what happen.

We do not underestimate the complexity and stress in such situations as these and we acknowledge the commitment and hard work of many Oranga Tamariki staff on a daily basis. We offer our framework, with its additional practice and reflection elements, to assist in the operationalization of a co-constructing social work framework, which incorporates warm eyes, warm breath, heart warmth and aroha for improved relationship making and participation in the *best interests* of the child.

The framework provides sets of reflective questions as well as practical actions, which we hope workers will use for a more nuanced practice, thereby enacting the theory.

The Key Elements for practice include practices which have long histories of use in the past, such as Collective Action (Hudson 1999; Jack 2006), introduce practices which re-frame commonly presented (but differently applied) concepts, such as Child Centred, and articulate concepts which may not be familiar in the child protection environment, such as Family Capital and Reciprocity. Family Capital will be familiar to those practitioners who routinely use a Strengths approach, but possibly Reciprocity with its connection to Recognition perhaps less so. These concepts and their related practices all speak to how we think the *best interests* of the child may be addressed. We have detailed this in relation to some of the salient Articles of the UNCRoC elsewhere (Young et al. 2012, 2014b) to indicate the complex nature of the work and especially when seeking to apply the Articles in relation to the rights of the child. We do not deal with these in depth here, save to note that our position is that, in line with the discussion above, there are many more considerations to be made when working in the *best interests* of the child using the Articles of the UNCRoC. The Articles underpin the Key Elements and we next apply them to the vignettes described above.

Table 1. Key Elements for practice.

Key Elements	Description	Practice Implications	Principles for Micro-Practices: Building Trust, Engaging, Reciprocity, Enabling and Valuing
Child Centred	Seeking, listening to and acting on the child's definition of his/her daily life	Accepting the competence of the child; Working directly with children as agents in their own right; Including children as partners in the work; The importance of intersubjective recognition	*Listen, ask and learn.* *Listen to the child:* invite the child to tell the story s/he wants to tell *Ask:* What is important to you? Who is important to you? *Learn about this child's life:* Find out about interests, experiences, likes, dislikes, who matters, what matters, and who and what the child would like in his/her life Involve the child and others s/he would like to be involved; be family inclusive, not exclusive; learn the practice skills of walking and talking alongside; strengthen, maintain, support existing relationships and networks. Search for kin and their connections, roles and potential
Contextual	Situatedness (time, place, history, culture)	Using local and specific designs generated from the local context rather than programmes designed elsewhere	In *listening, asking and learning* about the child's life, identify what is important about the people and place. *Ask:* How are things done here? What are your kawa (customs, rules)? Who are the people? What do they do? When and how? Be non-intrusive; respect cultural and family values and beliefs; seek clarification and understanding of diversity; examine own privilege and ask: how is it impacting on this piece of work? What is different here?
Collective Action	The whole is more than the sum of the parts; The whole has greater longevity; Distributed leadership	Engaging in equal partnerships; Learning the practice of "together" and "alongside"; Assisting in developing local leadership; Assisting families and children to design their solutions	*Ask:* Who is it important to involve in what should happen? How do we include them? What should we do together? What has been tried in the past? Enable, include, maintain, advocate, facilitate, value; do not judge, critique, risk assess Seek consensus, be collaborative, and cooperate to co-produce possibilities and plans that are attainable, workable and "fit". Believe in possibilities, value difference and diversity
Reciprocity	The family as theorist; Shared responsibility; Trustworthiness; Recognition	Working with diversity; Listening to the experience of the family; Developing equal partnerships	*Ask:* What can I do what would help? This is what I bring, and resource, and do: Have warm eyes, warm breath, heart warmth, open ears, open mindedness Be an Ally
Family Capital	Family knowledge, history, capability, contacts	Considering the potential of third-generation practices to inform the work; Accepting family expertise	*Ask:* Why do you think this is happening? What have you done that worked? How did you do that? Who was involved, can they be here? What would you like to try? What ideas do you have? Who can help? Who do you call on? Value and support, resource autonomy You are the theorist of your life

6. Discussion

The situations in the three vignettes will be largely recognisable to people working in the child protection arena. Perhaps the most surprising is that of the ANZ example, which when it occurred, in Australia at least, was met with cries of 'how could that happen in New Zealand?', closely followed by recognition that it also occurred on a regular basis in Australia. Less surprising is the expectation that removals and out-of-home placements occur in Norway, although the statistics cited earlier indicate a growing trend there too. Nevertheless, in each case, we identify actual and potential responses which may be offered from the co-constructing social work framework. Perhaps as a summary, we can identify positive Child-Centredness as present in the way that one teacher responded to Britt in contrast to the negative Child-Centredness offered by others. More potent was the Reciprocity, particularly using Recognition, evident in the interactions with Britt and her subsequent emergence into a 'pro'. In the WA example, context was everything, along with the potential for Reciprocity. In the ANZ example, Collective Action was paramount, as was Family Capital. We will discuss these in turn.

Some of Britt's early experience showed that she was not listened to or heard, invited to participate or considered to be competent as an agent in her own right. It was only when one teacher responded positively to her that she was able to re-position her destructive trajectory and gain confidence and hope for her future. The teacher evidenced positive instead of negative Child-Centredness and enabled Britt to respond positively through that engagement. Many practitioners in child protection practice claim to use a Child-Centred approach, but all too often it refers to having the child at the centre of the concern, but not necessarily accepting, believing, or working with the child's interpretations of his or her life, much less considering a child to be a competent agent in that life. Even when practitioners seek to engage children in decisions about their lives, how the children experience that is not necessarily what the practitioners believe is the case. Recent research from Denmark (Hestbæk 2018, p. 135) presents this as a paradox, as practitioners report that they have talked with children extensively about the decisions and processes, to which the children agree, but the children do not experience that as participation.

Reciprocity is perhaps the more salient of the Key Elements to describe Britt's situation. Here, it is useful to invoke Honneth's concept of recognition, particularly in relation to what he refers to as an ethical life in which love, rights and solidarity are the cornerstones. More than self-realisation, recognition is an essentially social entity that requires an acceptance and understanding of the complex sociability of the lived experience of young people (Noble 2009). Häkli et al. (2018) formulate a tripartite framework for what they term 'positive recognition,' which involves the practices of 'getting to know (each other)', 'acknowledging (what matters)' and 'providing support (for contextual agency)'. Operationalizing Honneth's philosophy of recognition adds to its potential and we make use of these understandings here, applied to Britt's circumstances. Evidencing 'love', 'rights' and 'solidarity' as invitations to reciprocity, the teacher, who recognised the potential of a self-realising young woman in Britt, was able to acknowledge what mattered to her and helped her to become contextually agentic in the process of getting to know her. Together, they were able to meet their joint goals of agency. It is also not inappropriate to note the presence of 'love' in Honneth's ethical life, and its central position in the work and being of the young people of the Change Factory, which Britt now represents. In telling her story, Britt identified the 'warm eyes' of the teacher as her turning point in her life.

The second of the vignettes presents a common situation in WA where grandparents are carers for their grandchildren, for many different reasons. In this case, not only is a frail and elderly woman caring for a young child, but they are also located a considerable distance away from their country, which is a significant and potentially damaging separation for Aboriginal and Torres Strait Islander people (Zubrick et al. 2010), and their supports. The concerns of the teacher about the child and the potential inability of the grandparent to adequately care for her may be sufficient for some workers to take the child into alternative care. Instead, the worker realised that he needed more information and researched the Context much more thoroughly. He also needed to gain the trust of the grandmother as well as the young girl. He chose a Child-Centred approach in his interactions with the girl and particularly displayed this in forming a trusting relationship with her before also seeking to form a trusting relationship with her grandmother. The process of recognition mentioned above was used effectively here, leading to Reciprocity, in which there was trust and an opportunity for the grandmother to contribute her theory of her and her granddaughter's life. The worker showed himself to be emotionally open, evidencing 'heart warmth' and willing to work with the everyday life of the grandmother. Together, they were able to formulate plans for support which would include Collective Action with other members of the extended family. The child's hearing improved, both she and her grandmother were supported, and their lives could proceed together until it would be time, if they chose, to return to their country.

The ANZ vignette is significant because it was so public. Being broadcast on national TV, it attracted considerable public scrutiny and criticism. Māori marched in the streets with cries of racism. Four reviews and enquiries were called: the Oranga Tamariki Professional Practice Review Group Practice Review into the Hastings Case (2019); Manaakitia A Tātou Tamariki The Children's Commissioner (2020); Pēpi Māori and the care and protection system; and The Whanau Ora Commissioning Agency (2020) Ko Te Wā Whakawhiti: It's Time For Change, A Māori Enquiry into Oranga Tamariki and The Ombudsman. This last has not yet been released. The findings and recommendations of the Oranga Tamariki Professional Practice Review Group were accepted fully. The review found that indeed there were legitimate concerns for the safety of this baby that warranted statutory involvement with the parents and the whanau, but that alternative measures should have been implemented that presented options and recognised Māori values and culture. They also found that communication and engagement with the whanau to form working relationships had not been effective or used, and that the statutory authority delegated to Oranga Tamariki social workers was not consistently well understood or appropriately applied (Oranga Tamariki Professional Practice Review Group 2020, pp. 5–9). All these findings recall those made by the ECHR about Norwegian practice. Recommendations cited that restorative, site-based and procedural changes be made. These specified that as relationships with the family had been damaged, it was imperative that processes to restore these be undertaken. Instituting changes to the organisational culture which permitted these events to occur were deemed necessary, and these included the use of consultations, advisory panels and supervision, and procedural changes to ensure that proper oversight of statutory actions and implementation is established. Worker training and mentoring in appropriate skills and knowledges were also considered to be paramount. Lastly, a coordinated approach should be taken with other relevant agencies, such as health bodies, Police, etc., to ensure consistency across the country.

All the workers in this event were operating with the same intent in mind, to protect the baby. We cite this case not to find fault with Oranga Tamariki staff and their practice but to apply our co-constructing social work framework and learn from this unfortunate case. Closer examination of the review reveals the approach taken was not Child Centred as the state, through its agents, caused stress to the mother, which potentially stressed the baby. Local Māori (whanau and NGO) solutions within the Context were either ignored or misunderstood. There seemed to be very little understanding and partnership behaviour, and there was an effort to exert 'power over' rather than 'power with' this mother and whanau. Collective Action was entirely possible as the whanau collective (including Māori NGOs) were designing and implementing their own solutions back in March 2019. There was no acknowledgement of the Family (whanau) as theorists, as originally Oranga Tamariki paid what eventuated as lip service to their ideas. Recognition of the mother's willingness and ability to achieve the desired standard of care, and of love, rights and solidarity, which are the foundations for productive partnership work, was lacking. Initially, the state could have shared responsibility in a spirit of Reciprocity and trustworthiness. The family (whanau) had brought a huge amount of Capital into this situation—they had proven capability, knowledge and contacts.

An underlying, if insidious, element is to be found here. Keddell (2019b) calls it the 'weaponisation' of trauma, in which the parent's experience of trauma in their own childhoods is used to justify action against them as their circumstances must by definition be risky. Instead of providing support and care and assistance to overcome what might well have been traumatic childhoods for the sake of their children, if not their own, removals are seemingly the only option.

We did not set out to theorise *best interests* but, in examining our contexts and some of the events occurring there and applying our practice framework, we have arrived at a better understanding of what a future of applying *best interests* might include. First and foremost, the notion of the *best interests* of the child is itself somewhat of a misdirection, as it separates the child from others and, predominantly in practice, from parents. In being the main arbiters of what is considered to be in the *best interests* of the child, professionals also distance themselves from parents in their efforts to be child centred. They also predominantly use strategies which solidify the separations through risk-focused instead of family support approaches. Decisions by child protection workers in the *best interests* of the children often remain unexamined or unexplained, as shown in some of the judgments handed down by the ECHR, except that they are claimed as being in the *best interests* of the child. Taking refuge behind a concept as its own justification is inadequate and potentially damaging. A more appropriate approach to *best interests* is to accept that the entity for consideration is family, not parents **or** children. Starting from a family rather than a child position allows for all views and situations to be considered, even when the final decision is for the child to be removed from the parents. Many jurisdictions recognise the importance of family relationships—indeed the comments from the ECHR noted how some of the decisions in Norway contravened its own policy position by not paying enough attention to family relationships. While there is widespread acknowledgement that these relationships can be fraught, may be challenging to maintain and, in some cases, not appropriate or actively damaging, nevertheless, most children themselves seek to have some sort of relationship with their families of origin. The dual separations—of the children from the parents, and the professional workers from the parents—make establishing and maintaining a working relationship which can result in family restoration, or continuation of parent–child relationships, so much more difficult. Trust is now often lacking, active or passive resistance is more likely, and parents are likely to withdraw and cease to engage (Featherstone and Gupta 2018).

Parents, **as** parents, are not recognised in Honneth's terms as having love, solidarity and rights. They are only recognised for what they do not have, that is the ability to **be** parents, however much their children want them to be. Research (Rambøll Management Consulting A/S 2018 from 2018 shows that 90% of children and youth placed in institutions or foster care often or always feel that their parents love them and 73% said that their parents were very important to them. Parents are emotionally important) to their children, even if they do not have sufficient parenting skills. Articles 8, 18 and 19 all make provision for the state to afford support to ensure that children may have relationships with their parents and for parents to be supported by the state to enable them to do so. The need to manage complex social relationships in these situations requires complex solutions. As Hyslop (2017, p. 1802) reminds us, 'Contrary to the view of child protection expounded by politicians and presented in the popular media, child protection social work involves social understandings of social processes: it is a nuanced, uncertain and applied practice'. As such, it needs nuanced approaches.

7. Conclusions

The aim for this article is to propose a way of conceptualising practice for child protection that meets the imperatives of the two legislative milestones which gave rise to thinking about the *best interests* of the child and family inclusion. We have been dissatisfied with how the two informing Acts have been disregarded or selectively used and our framework for our practice seeks to provide a more comprehensive approach to the business of keeping children from harm. In particular, we believe that child protection practice in our jurisdictions, as well as some others, has reached an impasse beset by binary practice. In setting professionals against parents, children against parents and risk-focused practice against family support practice, there seems to be no end to the destructive and largely irreparable relationships between all these stakeholders in which children, because of their lesser power, are most likely to continue to be the losers. We know that children's trajectories after out-of-home care are most likely to lead them to the most negative of social indicators.

We expressed our wish at the beginning of this paper for a child protection practice that contained hope—hope for positive outcomes for children and their families who had come to the attention of child protection authorities. We offered a reconceptualisation of the *best interests* principle, as it seems to us that concept is misused and inadequately applied. The sole reliance on a professional judgement to make decisions for children serves no interests well, let alone the *best interests* of the child. We have adopted the concepts of warmth and love into our practice, while at the same time being mindful of the challenges of doing so in some of our contexts. Honneth (1995) provides us with the theoretical framework and colleagues from ANZ, Norway and Kenya and the young people from the Change Factory contribute the practical framework, for we aspire to be the theory we espouse, having long embraced Lewin (1945) dictum to practice theory and to theorise practice. Many others before us have expressed the desire—indeed, the need—for a more compassionate, responsive, inclusive and participatory practice with families and children who find themselves in the child protection system (for example, Scott 2000; Jack 2004; Lonne et al. 2008; Featherstone et al. 2014). We add our voices to this list with the addition of some practices we and others have found to be useful in forming and maintaining relationships with families. By adding a final column to our model, that of micro-practices in the form of sets of reflective questions for practitioners, we hope to have drawn attention to how to make progress in the implementation of such nuanced practice. The co-constructing social work framework was designed to attend to the nuances and complexities of child protection work. The framework has been informed by young people and children, both directly and through observation of others' work. We are mindful that children and young people have repeatedly stated that they want relationships with their parents, that they want to be part of families, and that they want workers who will help them achieve that. They want workers who have warm eyes, who breathe warm air into their environments, and who have and show heart warmth. They want to be shown love (aroha). We, as workers, owe it to them to listen and work towards achieving these in our interactions with young people. Our goal is to have warm eyes, breathe warm air and have heart warmth in our interactions with children and families which we enact with love.

Author Contributions: S.Y., conceptualisation and writing—original draft preparation; M.M., conceptualisation, resources, and writing—review and editing; C.O., conceptualisation, resources, and writing—review and editing; L.S., conceptualisation, resources, and writing—review and editing; S.W., conceptualisation, resources, and writing—review and editing. All authors have read and agreed to the published version of the manuscript.

Funding: This research received no external funding.

Acknowledgments: To all the practitioners, children, young people and those with whom we have worked and who have provided, by their examples and experiences, the material used for our practice development. Thanks are also expressed to the anonymous reviewers of this paper.

Conflicts of Interest: The authors declare no conflict of interest.

References

Atwool, Nicola. 2019. Child-Centred Practice in a Bi- and Multi-Cultural Context: Challenges and Dilemmas. *Child Care in Practice* 1–18. [CrossRef]

Babington, Brian. 2016. What road ahead? Directions and challenges for the national framework for protecting Australia's children 2009–2020. *Developing Practice: The Child, Youth and Family Work Journal* 44: 4–15.

Barlow, Cleve. 1991. *Tikanga Whakaaro—Key Concepts in Maori Culture*. Victoria: Oxford University Press.

Becroft, Andrew. 2016. Ministry for Vulnerable Children Name 'Stigmatising and Labelling'. Available online: https://www.stuff.co.nz/national/faces-of-innocents/82699004/ministry-for-vulnerable-children-name-stigmatising-and-labelling (accessed on 25 February 2020).

Beddoe, Liz, and Eileen Joy. 2017. Questioning the uncritical acceptance of neuroscience in child and family policy and practice: A review of challenges to the current doxa. *Aotearoa New Zealand Social Work Review* 29: 65–76. [CrossRef]

Bjørå, T. 2020. Barnevernet startet politiaksjon mot 10-åring. In *Stavanger Aftenblad*. Stavanger: Stavanger Aftenblad.

Blacklock, Aunty Sue, J. Meiksans, G. Bonser, P. Hayden, K. Menzies, and F. Arney. 2018. Acceptability of the Winangay Kinship Carer Assessment Tool. *Child Abuse Review* 27: 108–21. [CrossRef]

Burns, J. F., and N. J. Thomson. 2013. *Review of Ear Health and Hearing among Indigenous Australians*. Mt Lawley: Australian Indigenous HealthInfoNet.

COAG. 2009. *Protecting Children Is Everyone's Business: National Framework for Protecting Australia's Children 2009–2020*. Canberra: Commonwealth of Australia Canberra.

Cossar, Jeanette, Marian Brandon, and Peter Jordan. 2016. 'You've got to trust her and she's got to trust you': Children's views on participation in the child protection system. *Child & Family Social Work* 21: 103–12.

CRC. 2013. *General Comment No. 14 on the Right of the Child to Have His or Her Best Interests Taken as a Primary Consideration (art. 3, para. 1)*. New York: United Nations.

DCPFS. 2017. Annual Report. Available online: https://www.dcp.wa.gov.au/Resources/Pages/AnnualReports.aspx (accessed on 26 February 2020).

De Jong, Gideon, G. Schout, J. Pennell, and T. Abma. 2015. Family Group Conferencing in public mental health and social capital theory. *Journal of Social Work* 15: 277–96. [CrossRef]

Dijkstra, Sharon, H. E. Creemers, F. J. A. van Steensel, M. Deković, G. J. J. M. Stams, and J. J. Asscher. 2018. Cost-effectiveness of Family Group Conferencing in child welfare: A controlled study. *BMC Public Health* 18: 848. [CrossRef] [PubMed]

Douglas, Marcela, and Merete Saus. 2019. Invisible Differentness in Sámi Child Protection Services. *Child Care in Practice* 1–15. [CrossRef]

ECHR. 2018. *Case of Jansen v. Norway*. Application no. 2822/16. Strasbourg: E. C. o. H. Rights.

ECHR. 2019. *Case of Abdi Ibrahim v. Norway*. Application no. 15379/16. Strasbourg: E. C. o. H. Rights.

ECHR. 2019. *Case of K.O. and V.M. v. Norway*. Application no. 64808/16. Strasbourg: E. C. o. H. Rights.

Editor. 2020. de-fleste-politifolk-vil-vi-aldri-kjenne-oss-trygge-på. In *Stavanger Aftenblad*. Hjelmeland Kommune: Stavanger Aftenblad.

Eriksen, Evelyn. 2018. Democratic participation in early childhood education and care-serving the best interests of the child. *Tidsskrift for Nordisk barnehageforskning* 17. [CrossRef]

Featherstone, Brid, and Anna Gupta. 2018. *Protecting Children: A Social Model*. Bristol: Policy Press.

Featherstone, Brid, K. Morris, S. White, and S. White. 2014. *Re-Imagining Child Protection: Towards Humane Social Work with Families*. Bristol: Policy Press.

Forandringsfabrikken. 2017. About us (English) Forandringsfabrikken = The Change Factory. Available online: https://www.forandringsfabrikken.no/article/about-us-english (accessed on 10 June 2019).

Fredericks, Bronwyn. 2013. 'We don't leave our identities at the city limits': Aboriginal and Torres Strait Islander people living in urban localities. *Australian Aboriginal Studies* 2013: 4–16.

Frost, Nick, Fiona Abram, and Hannah Burgess. 2014. Family group conferences: context, process and ways forward. *Child & Family Social Work* 19: 480–90.

Gallagher, R., and K. Louis. 2018. Making space: Prioritizing aboriginal practices in aboriginal child protection case conferences. *Advocate (Vancouver Bar Association)* 76: 181–88.

George, M., and N. A. M. Awal. 2019. The best interest principle within Article 3(1) of the United Nations Convention on the Rights of the Child. *International Journal of Business, Economics and Law* 19: 30–36.

Gilbert, N. 2012. A comparative study of child welfare systems: Abstract orientations and concrete results. *Children and Youth Services Review* 34: 532–36. [CrossRef]

Gilbert, Ruth, A. Kemp, J. Thoburn, P. Sidebotham, L. Radford, D. Glaser, and H. L. MacMillan. 2009. Recognising and responding to child maltreatment. *The Lancet* 373: 167–80. [CrossRef]

Häkli, Jouni, Riikka Korkiamäki, and Kirsi Pauliina Kallio. 2018. 'Positive recognition' as a preventive approach in child and youth welfare services. *International Journal of Social Pedagogy* 7: 5. [CrossRef]

Hestbæk, Anne-Dorthe. 2018. The rights of children placed in out-of-home care. In *Human Rights in Child Protection*. Berlin: Springer, pp. 129–46.

Honneth, Axel. 1995. *The Struggle for Recognition*. Cambridge: Polity Press.

Hudson, Pete. 1999. Community development and child protection: a case for integration. *Community Development Journal* 34: 346–55. [CrossRef]

Hyslop, Ian. 2017. Child protection in New Zealand: A history of the future. *British Journal of Social Work* 47: 1800–17. [CrossRef]

Hyslop, Ian, and Emily Keddell. 2018. Outing the elephants: Exploring a new paradigm for child protection social work. *Social Sciences* 7: 105. [CrossRef]

Jack, Gordon. 2004. Child protection at the community level. *Child Abuse Review* 13: 368–83. [CrossRef]

Jack, Gordon. 2006. The area and community components of children's well-being. *Children & Society* 20: 334–47.

Juhasz, Ida, and Marit Skivenes. 2017. The population's confidence in the child protection system—A survey study of England, Finland, Norway and the United States (California). *Social Policy & Administration* 51: 1330–47.

Ka'ai, Tania. 2004. Te mana o te reo me nga tikanga: power and politics of the language. In *Ki Te Whaiao: An Introduction to Maori Culture and Society*. Edited by T. M. Ka'ai, J. C. Moorefield, M. Reilly and S. Mosely. Auckland: Pearson Press, pp. 201–6.

Kääriäläa, Antti, and Heikki Hiilamoa. 2017. Children in out-of-home care as young adults: A systematic review of outcomes in the Nordic countries. *Children and Youth Services Review* 79: 107–14. [CrossRef]

Keddell, Emily. 2014. The ethics of predictive risk modelling in the Aotearoa/New Zealand child welfare context: Child abuse prevention or neo-liberal tool? *Critical Social Policy* 35: 69–88. [CrossRef]

Keddell, Emily. 2018. The vulnerable child in neoliberal contexts: the construction of children in the Aotearoa New Zealand child protection reforms. *Childhood* 25: 93–108. [CrossRef]

Keddell, Emily. 2019a. Harm, care and babies: An inequalities and policy discourse perspective on recent child protection trends in Aotearoa New Zealand. *Aotearoa New Zealand Social Work* 31: 18–34. [CrossRef]

Keddell, Emily. 2019b. Shouting into an echo chamber: confirmation bias and its system conditions in the Hawkes Bay Case review. In *Reimaging Social work in Aotearoa New Zealand*. Available online: http://www.reimaginingsocialwork.nz/author/liz-beddoe/ (accessed on 5 March 2020).

Kjellander, Tove, Nina B. Jørgensen, and Jenny Westrum-Rein. 2016. *Do Rights! Nordic Perspectives on Child and Youth Participation*. Copenhagen: Nordic Council of Ministers.

Kojan, Bente Heggem, and Bob Lonne. 2012. A comparison of systems and outcomes for safeguarding children in Australia and Norway. *Child & Family Social Work* 17: 96–107.

Kojan, Bente Heggem, Edgar Marthinsen, and Graham Clifford. 2019. Combining Public Health Approaches with Increased Focus on Risk and Safety: A Norwegian Experience. In *Re-Visioning Public Health Approaches for Protecting Children*. Berlin: Springer, pp. 455–69.

Krakouer, Jacynta, Sarah Wise, and Marie Connolly. 2018. "We live and breathe through culture": Conceptualising cultural connection for Indigenous Australian children in out-of-home care. *Australian Social Work* 71: 265–76. [CrossRef]

Laird, S. E., K. Morris, P. Archard, and R. Clawson. 2018. Changing practice: The possibilities and limits for reshaping social work practice. *Qualitative Social Work* 17: 577–93. [CrossRef]

Lefevre, Michelle. 2017. Learning and development journeys towards effective communication with children. *Child & Family Social Work* 22: 86–96.

Leloup, Mathieu. 2019. The principle of the best interests of the child in the expulsion case law of the European Court of Human Rights: Procedural rationality as a remedy for inconsistency. *Netherlands Quarterly of Human Rights* 37: 50–68. [CrossRef]

Lewin, Kurt. 1945. The research center for group dynamics at Massachusetts Institute of Technology. *Sociometry* 8: 126–36. [CrossRef]

Long, Maureen, and Rene Sephton. 2011. Rethinking the "Best Interests" of the Child: Voices from Aboriginal Child and Family Welfare Practitioners. *Australian Social Work* 64: 96–112. [CrossRef]

Lonne, Bob, N. Parton, J. Thomson, and M. Harries. 2008. *Reforming Child Protection*. London: Routledge.

Lonne, Bob, D. Scott, D. Higgins, and T. I. Herrenkohl, eds. 2019. *Re-Visioning Public Health Approaches for Protecting Children*. Berlin: Springer.

Lowe, Pam, Ellie Lee, and Jan Macvarish. 2015. Biologising parenting: neuroscience discourse, English social and public health policy and understandings of the child. *Sociology of Health & Illness* 37: 198–211.

Mackieson, Penny, Aron Shlonsky, and Marie Connolly. 2019. Permanent Care Orders in Victoria: A Thematic Analysis of Implementation Issues. *Australian Social Work* 72: 419–33. [CrossRef]

Mead, Hirini Moko. 2003. *Tikanga Maori, living by Maori values*. Wellington: Huia Publications.

Neumann, Cecilie Basberg. 2016. Children's quest for love and professional child protection work: the case of Norway. *International Journal of Social Pedagogy* 5: 104–23. [CrossRef]

Nietz, Heidi. 2017. "Reframing" relation-based practice in the child protection sector in remote Aboriginal communities of Australia. *Journal of Social Work Practice* 32: 251–63. [CrossRef]

Noble, Greg. 2009. 'Countless acts of recognition': young men, ethnicity and the messiness of identities in everyday life. *Social & Cultural Geography* 10: 875–91.

O'Donnell, M., S. Taplin, R. Marriott, F. Lima, and F. J. Stanley. 2019. Infant removals: The need to address the over-representation of Aboriginal infants and community concerns of another 'stolen generation'. *Child Abuse & Neglect* 90: 88–98.

Oranga Tamariki. 2019. *Our Focus*. Auckland: Ministry for Children.

Oranga Tamariki Professional Practice Review Group. 2020. Review, Oranga Tamariki Professional Practice Review Group. Available online: https://orangatamariki.govt.nz/news/hawkes-bay-practice-review/ (accessed on 9 April 2020).

Parton, Nige. 1985. *The Politics of Child Abuse*. Basingstoke: Macmillan.

Pohatu, Taina Whakaatere. 2004. Ata: growing respectful relationships. *He Pukenga Korero* 8: 1–8.

Powell, Mary Ann, A. Graham, A. Canosa, D. Anderson, T. Moore, S. Robinson, N. P. Thomas, and N. Taylor. 2020. Child safety in policy: Who is being kept safe and from what? *Social Policy & Administration*. [CrossRef]

Rambøll Management Consulting A/S. 2018. Angbragte børn og unges trivsel 2018. Available online: https://sim.dk/media/27479/rapport_anbragte_boern_og_unges_trivsel_2018_.pdf (accessed on 25 February 2020).

Rogers, Carl R. 1956. Client-centered therapy: A current view. *Progress in Psychotherapy* 1: 199–209.

Ross, Nicola, J. Cocks, L. Johnston, and L. Stoker. 2017. 'No Voice, No Opinion, Nothing': Parent Experiences when Children Are Removed and Placed in Care. Available online: http://www.lwb.org.au/assets/Parent-perspectives-OOHC-Final-Report-Feb-2017.pdf (accessed on 22 September 2018).

Ryan, Fiona. 2011. Kanyininpa (Holding): A Way of Nurturing Children in Aboriginal Australia. *Australian Social Work* 64: 183–97. [CrossRef]

Salminen, Kirsikka. 2018. Is mediation in the best interests of a child from the child law perspective. In *Nordic Mediation Research*. Cham: Springer, pp. 209–22.

Sandberg, Kirsten. 2019. Best interests of the child in the Norwegian Constitution. In *Children's Constitutional Rights in the Nordic Countries*. Leiden: Brill Nijhoff, pp. 133–58.

Sanders, Matthew, Daryl Higgins, and Ronald Prinz. 2018. A population approach to the prevention of child maltreatment: Rationale and implications for research, policy and practice. *Family Matters* 100: 62–70.

Sanner, M. 2016. About the Change Factory on You Tube. Available online: http://www.forandringsfabrikken.no/article/about-us-english (accessed on 10 June 2019).

Scott, Dorothy. 2000. Embracing what works: building communities that strengthen families. Keynote address at the Family Strengths Conference, University of Newcastle, 23 November 1999. *Children Australia* 25: 4–9. [CrossRef]

Skivenes, Marit, and Line Marie Sørsdal. 2018. The child's best interest principle across child protection jurisdictions. In *Human Rights in Child Protection*. Implications for Professional Practice and Policy. Edited by A. Backe-Hansen and E. Backe-Hansen. London: Palgrave Macmillan, pp. 59–88.

Smith, Linda Tuhiwai. 1999. *Decolonising Methodologies: Research and Indigenous Peoples*. London: Dunedin, Zed Books and University of Otago Press.

Stang, Edda. 2018. Resistance and protest against Norwegian Child Welfare Services on Facebook—Different perceptions of child-centring. *Nordic Social Work Research* 8: 273–86. [CrossRef]

Statistisk sentralbyrå, S. N. 2018. Child Welfare. Available online: https://www.ssb.no/en/barneverng/ (accessed on 25 February 2020).

Summer Newsroom. 2019. NZ's Own 'Taken Generation'. Available online: https://www.newsroom.co.nz/@investigations/2019/06/11/629363/nzs-own-taken-generation (accessed on 25 February 2020).

Tate, H. 2010. Towards some foundations of Maori theology. Ph.D. thesis, Melbourne College of Divinity, Kew Vic, Australia.

Thomspon, Lester J., and David Wadley. 2019. Integrating Indigenous approaches and relationship-based ethics for culturally safe interventions: Child protection in Solomon Islands. *International Social Work* 62: 994–1010. [CrossRef]

Thørnblad, Renee, A. Strandbu, A. Holtan, and T. Jenssen. 2016. Family group conferences: from Maori culture to decision-making model in work with late modern families in Norway. *European Journal of Social Work* 19: 992–1003. [CrossRef]

Trevithick, Pamela. 2008. Revisiting the Knowledge Base of Social Work: A Framework for Practice. *British Journal of Social Work* 38: 1212–37. [CrossRef]

Turnell, Andrew, and Steve Edwards. 1999. *Signs of Safety: A Solution and Safety Oriented Approach to Child Protection Casework*. New York: W. W. Norton & Company.

Ware, Felicity, Mary Breheny, and Margaret Forster. 2017. The politics of government 'support' in Aotearoa/New Zealand: Reinforcing and reproducing the poor citizenship of young Māori parents. *Critical Social Policy* 37: 499–519. [CrossRef]

Williams, J. R., L. Merkel-Holguin, H. Allan, E. J. Maher, J. Fluke, and D. Hollinshead. 2015. Factors associated with staff perceptions of the effectiveness of family group conferences. *Journal of the Society for Social Work and Research* 6: 343–66. [CrossRef]

Young, Susan, M. McKenzie, L. Schjelderup, and C. Omre. 2012. The rights of the child enabling community development to contribute to a valid social work practice with children at risk. *European Journal of Social Work* 15: 169–84. [CrossRef]

Young, Susan, M. McKenzie, C. Omre, L. Schjelderup, and S. Walker. 2014a. Practicing from Theory: Thinking and Knowing to "Do" Child Protection Work. *Social Sciences* 3: 893–915. [CrossRef]

Young, Susan, M. McKenzie, L. Schjelderup, C. Omre, and S. Walker. 2014b. What Can We Do to Bring the Sparkle Back into this Child's Eyes? Child Rights/Community Development Principles: Key Elements for a Strengths-based Child Protection Practice. *Child Care in Practice* 20: 135–52. [CrossRef]

Zubrick, Stephen R., P. Dudgeon, G. Gee, B. Glaskin, K. Kelly, Y. Paradies, C. Scrine, and R. Walker. 2010. Social determinants of Aboriginal and Torres Strait Islander social and emotional wellbeing. In *Working Together: Aboriginal and Torres Strait Islander Mental Health and Wellbeing Principles and Practice*. Canberra: Commonwealth of Australia, pp. 75–90.

social sciences

MDPI

Review

The Potential of Networks for Families in the Child Protection System: A Systematic Review

Sara Pérez-Hernando * and Nuria Fuentes-Peláez

Department of Methods of Research and Diagnosis in Education, Faculty of Education, University of Barcelona, Pg de la Vall d'Hebron, 171, 08035 Barcelona, Spain; nuriafuentes@ub.edu
* Correspondence: sara.perez@ub.edu; Tel.: +34-934035010

Received: 1 March 2020; Accepted: 28 April 2020; Published: 6 May 2020

Abstract: There has recently been increased interest in the potential for formal and informal networks to aid interventions with biologic families in helping them achieve reunification in the context of the child protection system. When group support is provided to families, the creation of a network of social support seems to be a consequence. The article analyzes the conceptualization of social support in order to create social support networks and the benefits on the intervention with families in the framework of the child protection system through a systematic review. From a wide search 4348 documents, finally 14 articles were included in the reviews. Results show that social support is considered a process by which social resources are provided from formal (professional services and programs associated with those services in any off the protection, health of educational systems) and informal (extended family, friends, neighbors and acquaintances) networks, allowing the families to confront daily moments as well as in crisis situations. This social support is related to emotional, psychological, physical, instrumental, material and information support that allow families to face their difficulties. Formal and informal networks of child protection systems contribute to social support, resilience, consolidation of learning and the assistance of families to social intervention programs.

Keywords: family support; child protection; group intervention

---

1. Introduction

Family reunification in child protection systems refers to the experiences a child has when they return to live with their family of origin after a temporary separation as a result of a measure of protection of foster care and/or residential foster care (Balsells et al. 2016a). However, the process is more complex than this definition, since it is important to understand reunification as the set of considerations, strategies and actions necessary to achieve the return of the child to the home and family safely (Nager 2010), which involves resolving conflict situations, maintaining the emotional ties of the children and their parents, improving their parental skills and, especially, ensuring that the family provides a stable, safe and affectionate environment.

To achieve stable family reunification, a series of interventions and resources are launched, such as the provision of economic, social, school, home or even therapeutic support if there is a problem of mental health or substance addiction, in addition to a possible intervention of socio-educational character aimed at improving parental skills (Balsells et al. 2016a). Facilitating birth parents' access to the full continuum of services and integrating them into the overall case plan is crucial to resolving concerns to ensure the child's safety and eventual reunification (Fernandez 2014).

In this way, programs that seek to support the specific parental competencies that families have to develop in a process of reception and reunification represent a necessary strategy for the improvement in the exercise of parenthood (Child Welfare Information Gateway 2011).

The group methodology offers professionals and families a new way of addressing learning situations in a more satisfactory and effective way (Amorós et al. 2009). This intervention format offers important opportunities to help families through the significance of their strengths, to reduce stigma and the sense of social isolation, in addition to increasing the training and social support of families (Balsells et al. 2016a). In the same way, group work allows the creation of support dynamics among group members that help fathers and mothers feel more valued and more comfortable (Balsells 2006).

These support dynamics can involve the creation of a social support network, understood as the process by which social resources are endowed from formal and informal networks in everyday moments, as well as in crisis situations. This social support is related to emotional, psychological, physical, instrumental, material and information support that promote overcoming the difficulties families encounter (Lin and Ensel 1989). The benefits of having or receiving support from various sources are associated with the prevention of relapses, the strengthening of the capacities of the family system and the maintenance and improvement of family functioning (Fuentes-Peláez et al. 2014).

In the welfare system formal networks connect with informal ones to cause effects on those targeted. Agents of the formal network are understood to be those institutions and services in charge of the social and educational intervention with families, as well as those that do paid professional work within those institutions, including everyone from the professionals working directly on the intervention to those working on management of it, offering services of coordination and organization of the service and as supporting agents of the informal network, families, groups, communities or family community or social surroundings of the people receiving the social intervention.

In terms of building resilience, social support enhances well-being and health, as social relationships provide the individual with a set of identities and positive evaluations (Fuentes-Peláez et al. 2014). In this sense, combined social resources, formal and informal support networks, help families to cope from day to day or in crisis situations (Lin and Ensel 1989).

These social support networks, whether formal or informal, represent an important resilience factor for families in situations of social vulnerability (Lietz and Strength 2011), as they help to deal with stressful life situations (Armstrong et al. 2005), improve well-being and health, reduce the rates of depression and emotional distress after traumatic events, while providing a different perspective on the intervention of professionals working in the child protection system (Lietz et al. 2011).

2. Methods

This review aims to know the elements of the group methodology that promote social support in the development of group intervention programs in the protection system and child welfare.

2.1. Search Strategy

In order to respond to this objective, we decided to do a systematic review by searching in different databases. Anglo–Saxon, Hispanic and French databases were selected (PsycINFO, Educational Resource Information Center—ERIC, Web of Science, Scopus, Dialnet and Francis). However, no articles were selected from the Hispanic and French databases. The following keywords were used to perform the search (a) group intervention, (b) social support, (c) social network and family reunification. The Table 1 shows the results of the search. It describes the results by the databases and the keywords used.

Table 1. Results of the search.

	PsycINFO	ERIC	Web of Science	Scopus	
"group intervention" AND "social support"	368	2393	441	498	
"group intervention" AND reunification	6	0	2	1	
"social support" AND reunification	47	11	51	51	
"group intervention" AND protection	73	13	30	247	
"group intervention" AND "social network"	68	9	15	24	
Total	**562**	**2426**	**539**	**821**	**4348**

2.2. Exclusion Criteria

To be included in the review, studies had to be published after the year 2000 in a journal with impact factor. On the main theme, the articles had to refer to group intervention. It was decided to exclude those articles in which the group intervention was therapeutic. It was decided to include only the articles that studied the group intervention with families or children who were in a vulnerable situation or in the child protection system.

Figure 1 reflects the articles selection process. The total search involved reviewing more than four thousand article titles, of which 201 were selected. After reviewing the abstracts, we selected 74 articles to read completely. The final selection is composed of 13 articles. Finally, we decided to include one more article that was suggested by the experts.

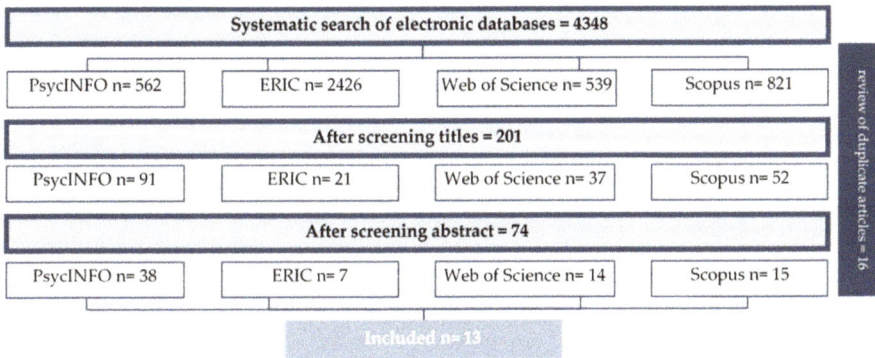

Systematic search of electronic databases = 4348			
PsycINFO n= 562	ERIC n= 2426	Web of Science n= 539	Scopus n= 821
After screening titles = 201			
PsycINFO n= 91	ERIC n= 21	Web of Science n= 37	Scopus n= 52
After screening abstract = 74			
PsycINFO n= 38	ERIC n= 7	Web of Science n= 14	Scopus n= 15
Included n= 13			

review of duplicate articles = 16

Figure 1. Selection process.

3. Results

3.1. Description of the Studies Used in the Review

Table 2 summarizes the principal characteristics and results of the selected studies. Specifically, the country in which the research is carried out, the objective and methodology of the article, the sample and the main results obtained are presented.

Table 2. Characteristics of the studies.

	Reference	Country	Purpose	Method	Respondents	Main Results
1	McDonald et al. (2009)	Canada	Evaluate the program in relation to (1) engaging the teenage mothers into a socially inclusive experience that may challenge the social disapproval they often experience, (2) enhancing the mother–infant bond while increasing her feelings of parental efficacy and (3) reducing stress, social isolation and intergenerational family conflict for the young mothers.	It is a mixed-method approach. Quantitative outcome evaluation used a repeated measure, nonexperimental design with two raters (the teenage mothers and the grandmother) and qualitative data included both written responses to open-ended questions and a service–user panel at the end.	The participants were 17 groups of six people from different areas of Canada.	(1) Stress reduction. There were statistically significant reductions in stress levels of mother and grandmother, social isolation and intergenerational family conflict. (2) Increased support. They also reported significant increase in tangible support, meaning, help from other people to get things done and in total support scores. (3) Protective factors. Multi-family groups provide an opportunity to address the risk factors of relationships with conflict and social isolation, while also building the protective factors of social inclusion and social connection within the family and across families.
2	Berrick et al. (2011)	California (USA)	Understand the mechanisms by which mentors may be effective in promoting positive outcomes for parents who have their children in the child welfare system.	It is a qualitative approach through discussion groups and interviews with those parents who could not attend the group for work.	Seven focus groups were conducted with parents who worked with a peer mentor. In total, 25 parents participated, including 21 women and 4 men.	(1) Value of shared experience. Parents referred to the notion that their peer mentor was capable of helping them because they "had been there" and could fully understand and appreciate the parents' experiences of having their child removed. Three prominent subthemes emerged: encouragement, trust and hope. (2) Communication. Peer mentors' particular style and process was another major theme that repeatedly surfaced during the focus groups. The communication was made easy by its clarity, availability and frequency. (3) Support. Parents suggested that they felt supported by their peer mentor, particularly in times of need. This support included: emotional support, specific support, support in developing self-reliance and support regarding substance abuse.

Table 2. *Cont.*

Reference	Country	Purpose	Method	Respondents	Main Results
6 Jones and Bryant-Waugh (2012)	UK	The aim of piloting the skills and-support group intervention was to test the following hypotheses: mothers of children with FP would have clinically significant levels of anxiety, depression and parenting stress and would show reliable and clinically significant reductions in anxiety, depression and parenting stress following the intervention; mothers would show reductions in parenting concerns and maladaptive behavior related to feeding following the intervention; mothers would find the group supportive, feasible and acceptable.	On the one side, participants were asked to record weekly significant events related to their child, themselves or their family in order to detect significant behaviors or change and track events external to the study which may have an effect. On the other side, there were 4 tools used: - Hospital Anxiety and Depression Scale - Parenting Stress Inventory - Behavioral Pediatrics Feeding Assessment - Parenting Concerns Scale	Of 24 mothers invited to take part in the study, fifteen indicated an interest in taking part, yielding a response rate of 62.5%. Ten mothers met criteria and gave consent.	(1) Emotional relief. Participants valued the opportunity to express difficult emotions and reported a sense of relief at this emotional expression. (2) Emotional support. Participants reported a sense of being supported by one another and of having their feelings validated; this had a positive effect on mood even between sessions. (3) Reduction of guilt and self-blame. Participation appeared to alleviate feelings of guilt in relation to mother–child interactions. (4) Competence and relaxation. Participants reported feeling more relaxed, competent and aware of their own behavior. (5) Shared experience and reduced isolation. Participant's comments suggested that the opportunity to talk with others was more helpful than any specific topic. All participants commented on the powerful effect of realizing that they were not alone in struggling to cope and were not "neurotic" or "mad".

Table 2. *Cont.*

	Reference	Country	Purpose	Method	Respondents	Main Results
7	Fuentes-Peláez et al. (2014)	Spain	The main aim is to know what kind of social support, formal and informal, the kinship foster families had before and after participating in a specific support program called 'Kinship Foster Care Families Training Program'.	The study is based on 147 semi-structured interviews; 85 interviews before the families took part in the LPKFF program and 62 interviews after the same families had participated in the program. In addition, eight focus groups took place 6 months after the families had participated in the LPKFF.	The sample of 62 kinship foster families to participate in the LPKFF was recruited by the child protection social services. The families came from four distinct areas of Spain.	(1) Formal support. The perception of formal support improved considerably after participating in the program. Families taking part in the program have a better understanding of formal support on offer. On completion of the program the families were able to rely on a formal support network and to make regular use of it. They are able to ask for help when they need it and to seek support regularly. (2) Informal support. In comparison with formal support, informal support changed less as a result of the program. There remained a considerable number of families who could still be described as poorly integrated and socially isolated at the end of the program. Results indicated that the LPKFF program increased the levels of informal support from extended family moderately. However, the families valued the LPKFF program as a source of informal support. (3) The families made a link between formal and informal support. They transformed the program into a forum of informal support where they could share experiences with those in a similar situation. The bonding of the families who participated was a key factor of the program, sharing experiences reassured them that they were not alone.
8	Gesell et al. (2016)	California (USA)	This study examined the relationship between social network ties and group cohesion in a group-based intervention to prevent obesity in children.	The data reported are process measures from an ongoing community-based randomized controlled trial. Two measures were collected: a social network survey (people in the group with whom one discusses healthy lifestyles);	305 parents with a child (3–6 years) at risk of developing obesity that were assigned to an intervention that taught parents healthy lifestyles.	(1) Group cohesion. Cohesion increased from 6.51 to 6.71. Network nominations tended to increase over the 3-week period in each network. Number of new network nominations at week 6 was positively related to cohesion. (2) Social network and group cohesion. Being able to name new network contacts was associated with feelings of cohesion. Network changes affect perceived group cohesion within a behavioral intervention. Given that many behavioral interventions occur in group settings, intentionally building new social networks could be promising to augment desired outcomes.

Soc. Sci. **2020**, 9, 70

Table 2. *Cont.*

	Reference	Country	Purpose	Method	Respondents	Main Results
9	Balsells et al. (2015)	Spain	This article presents the results of research with the goal of using the voices of the protagonists to examine the needs of parents who are susceptible to a positive family intervention that contributes to the consolidation of family reunification.	This study is qualitative, with descriptive explanatory goals. It includes an exploratory design using discussion groups and semi structured interviews with multiple informants.	This study drew on a total of 135 participants. Sixty-three were professionals who worked in the children's protection services, 42 were parents either recently reunified or with plans for reunification and 30 were children or adolescents who had passed through a process of either family or residential care.	(1) Emotional management. The results show that although there are feelings of happiness and responsibility, feelings related to insecurity and fear predominate. The family has been separated for a period and the parents feel insecure because they see their children as strangers with whom they will have to learn to live. (2) Helping other families. Most of those interviewed comment that they would like to participate in group activities that would allow them to spend time with other families. Professionals agree, noting the need for space in common with other people, preferably people who have experienced the same situation, who can give advice and explain what to expect. Furthermore, professionals believe that such a space would be interesting not only during reunification but also during the entire process. (3) Social support after returning home. Once a family has been reunified, continuity of assistance requires parents and children to continue thinking of professionals as a source of support. However, Spain's child-protection system does not stipulate either a tracking time or supervision after returning home. According to professionals, the tendency is to see reunification as an end, as a closure.
10	Aschbrenner et al. (2016)	New Hampshire (USA)	The purpose of this study was to explore peer-to-peer support among individuals participating in a group lifestyle intervention that included social media to enhance in-person weight management sessions.	A mixed method study design was used to explore participants' perceptions and experiences of support from other group members during a 6-month group lifestyle intervention.	Twenty-five individuals with serious mental illness reported their perceptions of the peer group environment and social support during the intervention. Seventeen of these individuals also participated in focus group interviews further exploring their experiences with group members.	(1) Group participation. More than 80% of participants agreed that other group members were trustworthy and dependable and 92% reported a high level of shared purpose and active participation in the group. (2) Group support. Participants described how shared learning and group problem-solving activities fostered friendships and provided essential support for health behavior change. (3) Different kinds of support. Sharing information, personal successes and challenges and "being in the same boat" as other group members were key features of peer-to-peer support. (4) Collaborative learning. Findings from this exploratory study suggest that participants enrolled in a group-based lifestyle intervention for people with serious mental illness experience peer-to-peer support in various ways that promote health behavior change. These findings highlight opportunities to enhance future lifestyle interventions with collaborative learning and social network technologies that foster peer support among participants.

Table 2. *Cont.*

	Reference	Country	Purpose	Method	Respondents	Main Results
11	Balsells et al. (2016b)	Spain	The aims of this study were (1) To evaluate the skill development of the professionals involved regarding establishing a supportive relationship with the families, management skills and group dynamics and knowledge and personal social skills to work in kinship fostering. (2) To observe the changes in the practice of professionals who have been leaders in support groups for kinship foster families and have taken part in the process of cooperative action-research.	The study adopted a complementary methodology. Quantitative data were collected by means of a questionnaire about professional skills and qualitative data were collected from the discussion groups.	39 professionals from the Child Protection System from different regions of Spain participated in the study. Of the professionals involved, 83.8% were women and 16.2% were men. The professionals who applied PFAFE were mostly psychologists and social workers, while a smaller number were social educators and educators.	(1) Competences. Data show an improvement in the development of the competences necessary to establish a supportive relationship with families, management and group dynamics. (2) Crystallization. These findings highlight the crystallization of attitudinal changes in professional practices.
12	Karjalainena et al. (2019)	Finland	The purpose of this study was to research the effectiveness of the structured, group-based parenting program on children's behavioral problems and parenting practices in families involved with child protection and other family support services.	Randomized controlled trial was conducted in seven municipalities across Finland, representatives of which were invited to participate due to their experience and knowledge of the IY parenttraining intervention.	The participants were 102 children with behavioral problems and their parents, from seven municipalities in Finland. Families were currently clients of child protection services or clients of social services indicated to need support in parenting.	(1) Positive parenting. The results suggest that the parent training intervention increased positive parenting and reduced child behavioral problems in these families with special needs. (2) Reduction in children's externalizing behavior. The results regarding the effects on child externalizing behavioral problems are in line with the theorical approach. IY intervention studies conducted in child welfare services, social services, families reporting a history of child maltreatment and families in child welfare services receiving Triple-P intervention have also all shown a reduction in children's externalizing behavior.

Table 2. *Cont.*

	Reference	Country	Purpose	Method	Respondents	Main Results
13	Balsells et al. (2018)	Spain	This article presents the results of a qualitative study that explores parenting skills when a child returns home after a period of foster care in the child protection system.	The design of the research is qualitative with descriptive and explanatory purposes. The perspective focused on parents, children and professionals as experts in the reunification process and essential to its improvement. The design is based on conducting focus groups and semi-structured interviews to multi-informants: professionals, parents and children.	The total sample included 135 people and comprised 42 parents on child welfare plans or recently reunited (for less than one year), 63 childcare professionals and 30 children and adolescents who had undergone a foster process, whether kinship or residential.	(1) The results of the research highlight five dimensions that favor the process of family reunification: adjustment of parenting skills, adapting to the child's needs, social support, accurate perception of the parental role and parental self-efficacy. (2) The study shows that there is a relationship between the specific dimensions of parental skills (adjustment of parenting skills, ability to adapt to the child's needs and social support) and transversal skills (accurate perception on the parental role and parental self-efficacy).
14	Chambers et al. (2018)	California (USA)	This research study explored a program that included three core components: Family to Family program model, reduced worker caseloads and caseworker continuity. The study aimed to answer three research questions: how the program was envisioned, the program and what were created and implemented, what were staff members' experiences implementing the program and what were parents' experiences receiving services from this program.	A mixed method study design was used. Interviews were conducted with staff members and surveys were distributed to parents who had previously or were currently participating at the time of the survey. In addition, written documentation, such as policies, procedures, manuals and job descriptions for staff were collected and analyzed.	Thirteen members of staff participated in semi-structured interviews that were conducted individually and face-to-face at an agency office. On the other hand, a standardized family satisfaction scale was used to collect data from seventeen parent participants.	(1) Perceived effectiveness. Findings indicated that the implementation of the pilot program was consistent with the original program design. Both staff and parents perceived the program to be valuable and effective. (2) Perception of formal support. Participants highlighted how the program's unique structure helped families reunify, especially by fostering trusting relationships between caseworkers and parents and close collaboration between the child welfare agency and the local community. (3) Recommendations. Results from the study offer recommendations regarding alternative approaches to achieving family reunification or permanency for children. Implications for child welfare practice, policy and research are provided.

3.2. Data from Studies Selected for Systematic Review

The authors identify different elements of group intervention that favor the possible creation of an informal support network. It was decided to divide these elements into five large groups: (1) Changes in participants, (2) Changes in the development and results of the program, (3) Changes in the perception of formal and informal support, (4) Desire to offer support to other families in the same situation and (5) Evaluation. Table 3 summarizes the elements identified according to the emerging categories mentioned.

Table 3. Elements identified in the selected articles.

Emergent Categories	Elements of Group Intervention That Favor the Possible Creation of an Informal Support Network	Articles
Changes in participants	Reduction of stress and social isolation	McDonald et al. (2009) Berrick et al. (2011) Jones and Bryant-Waugh (2012)
	Reduction of feelings of guilt and shame and improvement of self-esteem	
	Improvements in the sense of social inclusion	
Changes in the development and results of the program	Communication improvements	Berrick et al. (2011) Wei et al. (2012) Jones and Bryant-Waugh (2012) Fuentes-Peláez et al. (2014) Aschbrenner et al. (2016) Karjalainena et al. (2019)
	Positive assessment of "shared experiences" (they do not feel judged, they feel understood)	
	Collaborative learning among group members improves the effectiveness of the socio-educational intervention program.	
Changes in the perception of formal and informal support	Perception of support, especially emotional and instrumental, particularly in times of crisis or need	McDonald et al. (2009) Berrick et al. (2011) Lietz et al. (2011) Byrne et al. (2012) Jones and Bryant-Waugh (2012) Fuentes-Peláez et al. (2014) Chambers et al. (2018)
	References to intrafamily support (from the nucleus or family unit) and external (from the extended family, neighbors, support group, aid associations, etc.)	
	Change of view of formal support	
Desire to offer support to other families in the same situation	Importance of not only receiving but also being sources of support for other families, which in turn promoted family resilience	Lietz et al. (2011) Balsells et al. (2015)
Evaluation	Most studies use traditional techniques such as questionnaires, interviews and discussion groups. That is, quantitative and qualitative methodologies. Often combining both methodologies	Gesell et al. (2016)
	Gesell et al. (2016) introduce Social Network Analysis as a method for the evaluation of the group intervention program with families	Gesell et al. (2016)

4. Discussion

In the cases where support networks have been built, research shows that the families expressed significant reductions in stress levels and social isolation (McDonald et al. 2009). Participation in group intervention programs also appeared to alleviate feelings of guilt and self-blame associate to the situation of neglect or abuse that originates the enter in the child protection system. The support group provided a sense of having something in common with others (Berrick et al. 2011; Jones and Bryant-Waugh 2012).

In reference to changes in the development and results of the program, Karjalainena et al. (2019) alluded to the effectiveness of the intervention being likely to be associated with the context of the group intervention.

Parents stated that the other families were capable of helping them because they "had been there" and could fully understand and appreciate the parents' experiences of having their child removed (Jones and Bryant-Waugh 2012). They also stated that communication was made easy by its clarity, availability and frequency. In this sense, families suggested that the opportunity to talk with others was more helpful than any specific topic (Berrick et al. 2011). In some cases, parents transformed the program into a forum of informal support where they could share experiences with those in a similar situation. The bonding of the families who participated was a key factor of the program (Fuentes-Peláez et al. 2014). Finally, studies show that collaborative learning among group members seems to have improved the effectiveness of socio-educational intervention programs (Wei et al. 2012; Aschbrenner et al. 2016).

One of the results is that the families change their perception of formal and informal support after having participated in the group intervention programs. The families are able to identify instrumental and emotional support provided by other families (Berrick et al. 2011). On the other hand, families refer to the informal external support they receive as extended family, friends and neighbors, etc. Families also highlighted the importance of intrafamilial social support, referring to the encouragement and practical help that comes from the family unit (McDonald et al. 2009). Families taking part in group programs had a better understanding of formal support (Fuentes-Peláez et al. 2014). They were able to ask for help when they need it and to seek support regularly. They also increased the use of those resources of support that were rarely used at the beginning of the program: such as police, neighborhood associations, child protection services and other institutions (Lietz et al. 2011; Byrne et al. 2012).

The studies emphasize, not only the support that families receive, but the support they can offer. These narratives included the role that giving social support or helping others played in maintaining healthy functioning post-reunification. As families moved past the crisis, many discussed their desire to give back or contribute in some way to helping others (Lietz et al. 2011; Balsells et al. 2015).

The study of support networks was mainly carried out with traditional techniques such as questionnaires, interviews and focus groups. That is, quantitative and qualitative methodologies. Often combining both methodologies. However, Gesell et al. (2016) introduce Social Network Analysis as a method for evaluating the group intervention program with families.

The Social Network Analysis is a tool to measure and analyze the social structures that arise from the relationships between different social actors. In this sense, network analysis pays special attention to the study of social structures, paying more attention to the understanding of interactions between individuals than to what individuals can or cannot do.

As a summary, the provision of support to biologic parents is viewed as a legally mandated responsibility of Child welfare agencies as these services are aimed at the preservation of families or to work towards reunification (Barth et al. 2005). Lack of support from extended family or neighbors is associated with higher risk of return failure (Thoburn 2009). For this reason, support during the initial months of reunification is important for the stability of the reunification. In this sense, support groups reduce the isolation of caregivers and allow newer parents to seek practical advice from more seasoned parents (Sauls and Faheemah 2015). These support systems provide parents with emotional, material and financial support, helping them to create stability, which is important for family reunification (Potgieter and Hoosain 2018).

5. Conclusions

Studies of family resilience discover that families are capable of generating positive relationships, which help to optimize their possibilities and resources (Walsh 2002). Social support is considered a protective factor for families in a social risk situation (Balsells et al. 2016b).

Regarding informal support, although such support is considered to be indispensable to the reunification process, various studies have found that families at risk (Rodrigo et al. 2007; Fuentes-Peláez et al. 2014) and families under the care of the protection system typically have a poor, insufficient network of informal support to call on when addressing the difficult circumstances and changes to which they must respond.

After participation in the group intervention programs, the studies show that the support received from the new informal support networks is mainly instrumental (like accompanying other members of the group with transport difficulties) or emotional (making them feel understood and not judged) (Berrick et al. 2011).

Furthermore, we can see that there is a change in the way the families view the support offered by the formal network services. Although the studies do not show differences between the support received at the beginning and the end of the group intervention programs, the families have a much more positive view of the help that these services can offer them. In some cases, the families started the programs facing the formal networks due to measures that these services have taken (for example the removal of their children) (Lietz et al. 2011), and by the end of their participation in social intervention programs, they are able to understand the circumstances that lead the professionals to separate the family. In other cases, the families increased the use of the services of the formal network that they did not intend to use at the beginning of the intervention program, such as police, neighborhood associations, child protection services and other institutions (e.g., mental health services, Red Cross) (Byrne et al. 2012).

These changes can also be seen in the effectiveness and the results of the group intervention programs with the families. The families feel listened to and not judged which makes them more open to talking about their stories and working on them (Berrick et al. 2011; Balsells et al. 2016b). Moreover, collaborative earning among group members improves the effectiveness of the socio-educational intervention program (Aschbrenner et al. 2016; Karjalainena et al. 2019).

The authors not only emphasize the importance of families receiving the formal and informal support offered to them, they also come to be seen as sources of informal support in themselves for the rest of the group (Balsells et al. 2015). This change of perspective may be a factor of family resilience.

Scientific evidence demonstrates that group methodology favors this type of support, promoting the development of support networks and mutual help. In this sense, it seems necessary to continue studying the methodologies that favor these networks. This review also shows that these networks can be studied, not only with traditional methodologies, but also with other methodologies such as social network analysis.

6. Limitations

One of the key limitations of the revision was finding research that refers directly to group intervention for family reunification. Furthermore, not all of the articles present the same information, which has made it difficult to compare the studies. Another limitation was not being able to search French and German databases. Finally, it is possible that other sources of social support exist and that have not been considered, for example support via technological tools.

Author Contributions: All authors have contributed equally to the study. All authors have read and agreed to the published version of the manuscript.

Funding: This research received external funding. Funding Reference RTI2018-099305-B-C22 (Ministerio de Ciencia, Innovación y Universidades, Spanish Government).

Conflicts of Interest: The authors declare no conflict of interest.

References

Amorós, Pere, Maria Àngels Balsells, Nuria Fuentes-Peláez, Crescencia Pastor, Maria Cruz Molina, and Maria Isabel Mateos. 2009. Programme de formation pour familles d'accueil. Impact sur la qualité des enfants et la résilience familiale. In *Resilience, Regulation and Quality of Life*. Edited by Nader-Grosbois. Louvain: UCL Presses Universitaires de Louvain, pp. 187–93.

Armstrong, Mary I., Shelly Birnie-Lefcovitch, and Michael T. Ungar. 2005. Pathways Between Social Support, Family Well Being, Quality of Parenting, and Child Resilience: What We Know. *Journal of Child and Family Studies* 14: 269–81. [CrossRef]

Aschbrenner, Kelly A., John A. Naslund, and Stephen J. Bartels. 2016. A Mixed methods study of peer-to-peer support in a group-based lifestyle intervention for adults with serious mental illness. *Psychiatric Rehabilitation Journal* 39: 328–34. [CrossRef]

Balsells, Maria Àngels. 2006. Québec y Cataluña: Redes y profesionales para la acción socioeducativa con familias, infancia y adolescencia en situación de riesgo social. *Revista Española de Educación Comparada* 12: 365–87.

Balsells, Maria Àngels, Crescencia Pastor, Ainoa Mateos, Eduard Vaquero, and Aida Urrea. 2015. Exploring the needs of parents for achieving reunification: The views of foster children, birth family and social workers in Spain. *Children and Youth Services Review* 48: 159–66. [CrossRef]

Balsells, Maria Àngels, Crescencia Pastor, Maria Cruz Molina, Nuria Fuentes-Peláez, and Noelia Vázquez. 2016a. Understanding Social Support in Reunification: The Views of Foster Children, Birth Families and Social Workers. *British Journal of Social Work* 47: 812–27. [CrossRef]

Balsells, Maria Àngels, Nuria Fuentes-Peláez, Maria Isabel Mateo, Joseo Maria Torralba, and Violeta Violant. 2016b. Skills and professional practices for the consolidation of the support group model to foster families. *European Journal of Social Work* 20: 253–64. [CrossRef]

Balsells, Maria Àngels, Ainoa Mateos Inchaurrondo, Aida Urrea Monclús, and Eduard Vaquero Tió. 2018. Positive parenting support during family reunification. *Early Child Development and Care* 188: 1567–79. [CrossRef]

Barth, Richard P., John Landsverk, Patricia Chamberlain, John B. Reid, Jennifer A. Rolls, Michael S. Hurlburt, Elizabeth M. Z. Farmer, Sigrid James, Kristin M. McCabe, and Patricia L. Kohl. 2005. Parent-Training Programs in Child Welfare services: Planning for a More Evidenced-Based Approach to serving Biological Parents. *Research on social Work Practice* 15: 353–71. [CrossRef]

Berrick, Jill D., Elizabeth W. Young, Ed Cohen, and Elizabeth Anthony. 2011. "I am the face of success": *Peer* mentors in child welfare. *Child and Family Social Work* 16: 179–91. [CrossRef]

Byrne, Sonia, María José Rodrigo, and Juan Carlos Martín. 2012. Influence of form and timing of social support on parental outcomes of a child-maltreatment prevention program. *Children and Youth Services* 34: 2495–503. [CrossRef]

Chambers, Ruth M., Rashida M. Crutchfield, Stephanie G. Goddu Harper, Maryam Fatemi, and Angel Y. Rodriguez. 2018. Family reunification in child welfare practice: A pilot study of parent and staff experiences. *Children and Youth Services Review* 91: 221–31. [CrossRef]

Child Welfare Information Gateway. 2011. *Family Reunification: What the Evidence Shows (June)*. Washington, DC: Child Welfare Information Gateway.

Fernandez, Elizabeth. 2014. Child Protection and Vulnerable Families: Trends and Issues in the Australian Context. *Social Sciences* 3: 785–808. [CrossRef]

Fuentes-Peláez, Nuria, Maria Àngels Balsells, Josefina Fernández, Eduard Vaquero, and Pere Amorós. 2014. The social support in kinship foster care: A way to enhance resilience. *Child and Family Social Work* 21: 1–10. [CrossRef]

Gesell, Sabina B., Shari L. Barkin, Evan C. Sommer, and Jessica R. Thompson. 2016. Increases in New Social Network Ties are Associated with Increased Cohesion among Intervention Participants. *Health Education Behaviour* 43: 208–16. [CrossRef]

Jones, Ceri J., and Rachel Bryant-Waugh. 2012. Development and pilot of a group skills-and-support intervention for mothers of children with feeding problems. *Appetite* 58: 450–56. [CrossRef]

Karjalainena, Piia, Olli Kiviruusu, Eeva T. Aronen, and Päivi Santalahti. 2019. Group-based parenting program to improve parenting and children's behavioral problems in families using special services: A randomized controlled trial in a real-life setting. *Children and Youth Services Review* 96: 420–29. [CrossRef]

Lietz, Cynthia A., and Margaret Strength. 2011. Stories of Successful Reunification: A Narrative Study of Family Resilience in Child Welfare. *Families in Society* 92: 203–10. [CrossRef]

Lietz, Cynthia A., Jeffrey R. Lacasse, and Joanne Cacciatore. 2011. Social Support in Family Reunification: A Qualitive Study. *Journal of Social Work* 14: 13–20. [CrossRef]

Lin, Nan, and Walter M. Ensel. 1989. Life stress and health: Stressors and resources. *American Sociological Review* 54: 382–99. [CrossRef]

McDonald, Lynn, Tammy Conrad, Anna Fairtlough, Joan Fletcher, Liz Green, Liz Moore, and Betty Lepps. 2009. An evaluation of a groupwork intervention for teenage mothers and their families. *Child and Family Social Work* 14: 45–57. [CrossRef]

Nager, Alan L. 2010. Family Reunification. Concepts and Challenges. *Clinical Pediatric Emergency Medicine* 3: 195–207. [CrossRef]

Potgieter, Anesta, and Shanaaz Hoosain. 2018. Parents' experiences of family reunification services. *Social Work* 54: 438–51. [CrossRef]

Rodrigo, María José, Juan Carlos Martín, María Luisa Máiquez, and Guacimara Rodríguez. 2007. Informal and formal supports and maternal child-rearing practices in at-risk and non at risk psychosocial contexts. *Children and Youth Service Review* 29: 329–47. [CrossRef]

Sauls, Heidi, and Esau Faheemah. 2015. *An Evaluation of Family Reunification Services in the Western Cape: Exploring Children, Families and Social Workers' Experiences of Family Reunification Services within the First Twelve Months of Being Reunified*; Cape Town: Directorate Research, Population and Knowledge Management, Western Cape Government.

Thoburn, June. 2009. *Reunification of Children in Out-Of-Home Care to Birth Parents or Relatives: A Synthesis of the Evidence on Processes, Practice and Outcomes*. Norwich: University of East Anglia.

Walsh, Froma. 2002. A family resilience framework: Innovative practice applications. *Family Relations* 51: 130–37. [CrossRef]

Wei, Ying-Shun, Hsin Chu, Chiung-Hua Chen, Yu-Jung Hsueh, Yu-Shiun Chang, Lu-I. Chang, and Kuei-Ru Chou. 2012. Support groups for caregivers of intellectually disabled family members: Effects on physical–psychological health and social support. *Journal of Clinical Nursing* 21: 1666–77. [CrossRef] [PubMed]

social sciences

MDPI

Article

"If I'm Here, It's Because I Do Not Have Anyone": Social Support for the Biological Family during the Foster Care Process

Eduard Vaquero [1,*], M. Àngels Balsells [1], Carmen Ponce [2], Aida Urrea [3] and Alicia Navajas [1]

[1] Department of Pedagogy, Faculty of Education, Psychology and Social Work, University of Lleida, Av. Estudi General 4, 25001 Lleida, Spain; mangels.balsells@udl.cat (M.À.B.); alicianavahurta@gmail.com (A.N.)
[2] Department of Pedagogy, Faculty of Education Sciences and Psychology, University Rovira i Virgili, Carretera de Valls, s/n Campus Sescelades, 43007 Tarragona, Spain; carmen.ponce@urv.cat
[3] Department of Educational Theory and Social Pedagogy, Faculty of Education Sciences, Autonomous University of Barcelona, Campus de la UAB, 08193 Bellaterra, Spain; aida.urrea@uab.cat
*   Correspondence: eduard.vaquero@udl.cat

Received: 19 February 2020; Accepted: 19 March 2020; Published: 20 March 2020

Abstract: Social support is a crucial element for families in vulnerable situations, especially for those with children in foster care processes. This support is key to the acceptance of the protection measure in the initial moments and to laying the foundations for collaboration towards reunification. However, the social support of these families is limited, and families' use of support elements is strongly related to their attitude towards them. The aims of this article were to identify the types and characteristics of social support and to analyze what elements influence families' attitudes towards these supports. The qualitative study research was carried out in Spain through focus groups and interviews with 135 participants: 63 professionals from child protection services, 42 parents, and 30 children and adolescents who had been in foster care measures. Results show the diversity of social support resources available to families and demonstrate that families make unequal use of such resources depending on factors such as their experiences in the process of formalization and communication of the protection measure or their predisposition to receive support, among others. The important role played by social support resources in the promotion of factors that allow for successful reception and reunification is highlighted.

Keywords: social support; foster care; child welfare; family needs; content analysis

---

1. Introduction

The Spanish Child Protection System understands its actions as being a consequence of a situation of helplessness that endangers the psychological, emotional, and/or physical well-being of children. The Organic Law for the Legal Protection of Minors (Ley Orgánica de Protección Jurídica del Menor) (Law 26/2015) includes various provisional separation measures, during which the child lives in foster care with extended family, foster care, or residential foster care, while his/her family is involved in a plan of a case that may allow family reunification and the child's return home. The decision that involves the separation of a family is of special relevance in the lives of children given the short and long-term effects it has on their lives (Farmer 2014). The initial moments in which the decision is made to apply a protection measure deserve detailed attention. In this situation, social support is a key element for families to promote their acceptance of the established measure and demonstrate a collaborative attitude.

Social support is defined as the process by which the social resources provided by informal and formal networks allow for personal and family instrumental and expressive needs to be satisfied, both in everyday situations and in crisis situations. (Lin and Ensel 1989). Such support is related to emotional, psychological, physical, informative, instrumental, and material support provided by others to maintain well-being or promote adaptations to difficult life events (Dunst et al. 1988). Moreover, social support comprises the networks of formal and informal support of social resources that help families cope with day-to-day life or in crisis situations (Lin and Ensel 1989).

In the case of families in the Child Protection System, research has indicated how the social support available to families to positively address the processes of foster care and reunification has been associated with a lower rate of return to the Protection System (Farmer and Wijedasa 2013). The family resilience model in cases of family reunification, developed by Lietz and Strength (2011), identifies social support as one of the strengths that helps in overcoming this initial moment of separation of children from their biological family. Additionally, Walsh (2002) notes the ability of families to generate positive relationships that help optimize their possibilities and resources as a mechanism of family resilience. In contrast, Kimberlin et al. (2009) show that the lack of social support could be considered as a risk factor for successful reunification. Other authors suggest that having or receiving this social support entails benefits that are associated with relapse prevention and strengthening the capabilities of the family system (Lee et al. 2010) and with maintaining and improving family functioning (Lietz et al. 2011; Ordoñez 2009).

Social support comprises formal and informal support. Informal support comes from those nonprofessional relationships established with family, friends, neighbors, etc. (Spilsbury and Korbin 2013). Various studies (Lietz and Strength 2011; Maluccio and Ainsworth 2003; Terling 1999; Maluccio et al. 2000; Lee et al. 2010) have indicated that this type of support plays a preeminent role in foster care and family reunification. According to Simard (2008), it is important to consolidate children's family networks when enacting protective measures to obtain positive results in reunification. However, despite the benefits of this type of support, the findings of different studies suggest that families at risk (Rodrigo et al. 2007) and those receiving attention from the Protection System (Fuentes-Peláez et al. 2016) often have an informal and poor support network to address their difficult situations and the changes to which they must respond.

Formal support comes from professionals, services, agencies, or institutions (Spilsbury and Korbin 2013). Among the studies on this type of support, one by Balsells et al. (2013) found that the families involved in the Protection System considered it essential to receive formal support from the institutions. More specifically, parents used support with various objectives, such as knowing what changes they had to make and in what way, expressing their emotions and feeling accompanied. In addition, Fuller et al. (2014) found that what helped most parents was the emotional support provided by professionals in child protection services. Such support was useful to normalize their feelings and their situation and to help them feel more secure in having someone to facilitate certain arrangements. Moreover, Barth et al. (2008) noted that some of the most successful formal support strategies in foster care and reunification are mentoring or socioeducational programs for parents.

Both formal and informal support are useful to address the acceptance of the protective measures in the initial phase of separation and foster care. Properly handling this phase is one of the most relevant issues to ensure that the family understands the situation and acquires a greater degree of awareness of the problem and commitment to change. Authors such as Amorós et al. (2003), Schofield et al. (2011) and Ellingsen et al. (2011) emphasize the role of an adequate understanding of family difficulties; i.e., the importance of parents being aware of the situation and understanding the reasons for the separation. Balsells et al. (2014) found that the acquisition of this ability originates progressively and at different moments of the process of foster care and family reunification. They agree with the previous authors in mentioning that, at first, it is important to work on the understanding of the reason for the separation and the assimilation of that reason with the case plan. It is important that parents understand how to adapt, are open to change and remain flexible in the face of this situation. It is also crucial that they consider the measure of protection as positive and providing a personal gain for them and for their children, and at the same time, they must acquire confidence, security, and autonomy in themselves to overcome the situation (Schofield et al. 2011; Thomas and Reifel 2005). Balsells et al. (2011) also found that families placed great importance on their commitment and willingness to accept and carry out the necessary changes to regain the guardianship of their children, demonstrating a commitment and an unquestionable desire of the family to be reunited (Lietz and Strength 2011; Ordoñez 2009; Farmer 1996).

However, families' use of a support is strongly related to their attitude towards this support. It is known that, in this first phase, parents can demonstrate hostility towards the protection measure, towards the professionals who have made the decision to enact such measures, and, ultimately, towards all the formal support resources that have been involved in the separation. (Forrester et al. 2012) indicate five reasons why parents tend to show resistance and little collaboration in these circumstances: (1) the parents' social disadvantage, (2) the working context of the Protection System, (3) the resistance to change, (4) the denial or minimization of abuse, and (5) the behavior of the professionals themselves. Studies (Smithson and Gibson 2016) have also collected the voices of parents, indicating how they feel judged, self-conscious, not considered in decision-making, frustrated by waiting periods and changes in requirements for reunification, emotionally poorly understood, and stressed. Such studies call for more support from professionals and offer examples of good practices, such as comprehensive attention to families' problems, viewing the family as a family and not merely a case, and ensuring that parents are heard and informed in a timely manner, among other issues (Smithson and Gibson 2016). Parents tend to demonstrate less reluctance towards informal support because, for example, relationships with other families in the same situation or who have undergone a process similar to their own reduce the feelings of isolation and solitary experience that these families often suffer when separated from their children (Serbati and Milani 2012; Balsells et al. 2015).

In summary, social support is a fundamental element for the development of families who are in foster care processes, especially in the initial moments when the communication of the measure occurs. In this phase, families need more intense and specific support to lay the foundations for good collaboration, involvement, and participation throughout the process (Fernández-Simo and Cid-Fernandez 2018), which will mark the success of the possible reunification. However, these needs raise questions such as the following: What types of support are more relevant? What characteristics do these supports have? What attitudes do families have regarding social support?

To answer these questions, the present article aims to (a) identify social support and its characteristics in the initial stages of a foster care process and (b) analyze the elements that influence birth families' attitudes towards social support.

2. Methods

The present research is qualitative in nature, with a descriptive–explanatory purpose. The study included an exploratory design using discussion groups and semistructured interviews with multiple informants: professionals from the Child Protection Service, parents with children in protective measures, and children and adolescents involved in foster care processes. The perspective focused on these participants as experts in the reunification process (Stolz et al. 2013) and who are essential to its improvement. This methodological design was deemed necessary to deepen and better understand the role of social support in the processes experienced by families in the child protection system (Lin 2014). This multi-informant nature made it possible to find relevant aspects from different perspectives.

2.1. Participants

The research was conducted with a total of 135 participants from four different regions of Spain: Catalonia, Balearic Islands, Cantabria and Galicia. In total, 63 of them were professionals who worked in public agencies of the Child Protection Service, 42 were parents with reunification plans or had been recently reunified, and 30 were children and adolescents who had gone through a family or residential foster care process. The participants were families who went through the whole process in order to identify the protective factors that had an impact over time and which the families themselves valued as important strengths linked to social support and family resilience in the early stages of the process: foster care and reunification. Participants were selected according to different criteria. The selection criteria for professionals were the following: participants (1) worked in the Child Protection System; (2) had a minimum of two years of experience in residential or family foster care; and (3) represented the multidisciplinary nature of the professionals—that is, they had different roles, such as being social educators, pedagogues, psychologists, social workers, etc. Table 1 shows the characteristics of the participating professionals.

Table 1. Characteristics of the participating professionals.

Characteristics	Professionals (N = 63)
Gender	
Women	47 (74.60%)
Men	16 (25.40%)
Age	
Between 25 and 35 years	16 (25.80%)
Between 36 and 45 years	29 (45.16%)
More than 46 years	18 (29.04%)
Title	
Social educators	20 (31.75%)
Pedagogues	10 (15.87%)
Psychologists	20 (31.75%)
Social workers	13 (20.63%)
Intervention with	
Biological family	37 (58.73%)
Residential foster care	16 (25.40%)
Family foster care	10 (15.87%)

Source: Prepared by the authors.

The selection criteria for parents were as follows: (1) families that were already reunified or waiting to be reunited in one or two months; (2) families who had created or were carrying out a reunification plan; (3) families with a predisposition to and attitude of collaboration with professionals at the time of data collection; (4) families with different characteristics of age, family structure, etc.; and (5) families that did not have any physical, mental, or sensory disabilities. Table 2 shows the characteristics of the participating parents.

Table 2. Characteristics of participating parents.

Characteristics	Parents (N = 42)
Gender	
Women	32 (76.19%)
Men	10 (23.81%)
Family situation	
Reunified	37 (88.09%)
In the process of reunification	05 (11.91%)

Source: Prepared by the authors.

The selection criteria for children or adolescents were the following: (1) over six years old, (2) already reunified or waiting to be reunited in one or two months; (3) different characteristics of age, family structure, etc.; and (4) no physical, mental, or sensory disabilities. Table 3 shows the characteristics of the participating parents.

Table 3. Characteristics of participating children and adolescents.

Characteristics	Children and Adolescents (N = 30)
Gender	
Girls	16 (53.33%)
Boys	14 (46.67%)
Age	
Between 6 and 11 years	05 (16.66%)
Between 12 and 17 years	17 (56.67%)
More than 18 years	08 (26.67%)
Family situation	
Reunified	21 (70.00%)
In the process of reunification	09 (30.00%)

Source: Prepared by the authors.

The recruitment of parents and children, as a participant in the study, was proposed by the reference professional of each family of the child protection agency, according to the cited criteria.

2.2. Instruments

Discussion groups and semistructured interviews were used to collect data. This technique has been considered appropriate for use with vulnerable population groups (Ayón and Villa 2013), particularly families in the child protection system (Balsells et al. 2011) as well as with professionals who work with families (Stolz et al. 2013). A guide was prepared that included several instruments: (1) an identification card to collect participants' basic data; (2) a script of questions for the development of discussion groups and semistructured interviews; and (3) a summary record, in which the researchers gathered aspects related to the development of the group, such as the date, duration and place of performance, participants' motivation, group cohesion, and dynamics.

The scripts were developed as a result of a review of the scientific literature on the subject, which revealed key elements to be investigated. The focus of the questions was intended to prompt participants to share their experiences about the process of foster care and reunification, including the initial stages of the protection measure: how it was produced, what feelings surfaced, what help was given, etc. The questions were formulated from the perspective of the different participants involved: parents, children, and professionals. Thus, different questions about formal and informal support were asked of each participant, adjusting aspects such as the technical vocabulary or type of information that professionals, parents or children could provide in each case.

2.3. Procedure and Data Analysis

A total of 22 discussion groups were conducted: nine with professionals (average of seven professionals per group), eight with parents (average of five parents per group) and five with children and adolescents (average of three children per group). Moreover, a total of 18 semi-structured interviews with children and adolescents were carried out. All of them were audio-recorded and subsequently transcribed. Two researchers from the research team went to each Child Protection Service that collaborated in the project. One investigator was in charge of the group dynamics, while the other was in charge of recording and verifying that the criteria established in the instructions were followed.

The content analysis was performed following the bottom-up system and focused on two dimensions: (a) social support and its characteristics in the initial stages of a foster care process, and (b) elements that influence birth families' attitudes towards social support. Content analysis was used to analyze the information by the preparation of codes to be evaluated by seven judges. The first stage of analysis was textual, selecting paragraphs, fragments, and important quotes from the transcripts of the interviews and focus groups. The second stage was conceptual and identified the categories and subcategories that were potentially interrelated. Both stages were subjected to review by judges. The process of extracting codes and categories was evaluated through a validation process. The content analysis was reviewed to seek consensus and achieve maximum reliability of the extracted data. Categories and subcategories were defined when the data reached saturation. The categories were considered saturated when (1) no new data emerged in a category, (2) the category was well developed and showed variation and (3) the relationships between the categories were established and validated.

The software Atlas.ti 6.2 was used to process qualitative data. A Hermeneutic Unit Editor was created in which the literal transcriptions of the focus group and interviews (primary documents) were included. Each category was assigned a code (code), and textual notes were included (memos). A conceptual network (network) was created to analyze the data as a basis for the connections established between the codes of the hermeneutic unit.

2.4. Ethical Considerations

Numerous ethical considerations were involved in the development of the research. An informed consent document was developed for professionals and parents to ensure that they knew what they were involved in and could offer their consent. This document clearly explained the scientific purpose of the research, their rights as participants, and the confidential treatment of the data collected. Before interviews were conducted, participants were encouraged to ask any questions or request clarifications to support their understanding and willingness to participate. Similarly, the fact that participants had the right not to answer any question they did not wish to was emphasized. In the case of children, authorization and consent were requested from parents or from the Public Administration that had legal guardianship at that time. Before starting data collection, children were informed in detail about the purpose of the study, adjusting the vocabulary and language, and were also encouraged to state any doubts they had; furthermore, explicit assent was requested before beginning the data collection.

3. Results

The content analysis of the voices of the parents, children, and professionals made it possible to identify and answer two key questions related to formal and informal support: (a) What types of support are more relevant, and what are their characteristics? and (b) What are families' attitudes regarding social support?

3.1. What Types of Support Are More Relevant, and What Are Their Characteristics?

The results show a diverse range of formal support resources that families use when a separation and fostering measure is initiated: (a) the formal supports provided by the Protection System (the interdisciplinary team that runs the case plan, the reception center, or the service for foster families, among others) and other formal supports (doctors, teachers, etc.) or specialized support (psychologists, psychiatrists, specialists or therapists, etc.); and (b) the informal supports provided by community social services, extended family, friends, etc..

Regarding formal support, the results suggest that this type of resource is not always used to equal extents or in the same way by families. In this phase of foster care, there are families that make little use of the support provided by the Protection System and even reject it. Other families, in contrast, use these supports positively from the beginning, especially those who go to social services to voluntarily apply for the administrative guardianship of their children.

> "At the beginning, I rejected it, I was blocked, I only received help from the director of the center where I was rehabilitating, but then, when I left, it is true that I was with some psychologists and educators who helped me, but maybe it was because by then, I listened to them more." (quote from a mother)

Standardized or specialized formal supports are used selectively by families according to their needs; notably, their use might also be influenced by the type of relationship established between the family and professionals. In this sense, trust, mutual knowledge, and bonding are crucial aspects associated with this relationship.

> "I arrived mid-year, the teacher took care of me very well, they gave me affection, they were very attentive to me, they treated me very well." (quote from an adolescent)

The results indicate the formal supports that are most requested by parents are economic and psychological support. In the case of economic support, families, children, and interviewed professionals emphasized the need to increase this type of aid. In the case of psychological support, the results indicate that this is recognized as one of the most notable sources of formal support in this phase of foster care.

> "You cannot tell a family with €400 to take good care of three children and that is it, because it is impossible...because sometimes things are sustained by something material." (quote from an adolescent)

> "Social workers bet a lot on me. In addition, then, the psychologists made me see the reason why they had taken the children away from me." (quote from a father)

With regard to informal support, the results demonstrate that it has a low presence in the initial moments of the foster care process. Support from family, friends, or neighbors is often considered insufficient. Particularly in the case of the extended family, absence usually corresponds to deteriorating family relationships or distance from relatives. In spite of everything, some participants recognized that informal support is a fundamental element in the well-being of their children and for the stability of the family. In this sense, they stated that if they had had this type of support in the past, perhaps the situation of separation from their children could have been avoided.

> "At first, I had my whole family against me, and it was very hard; I was alone and they had taken my daughter away from me. Then, I called social services to get my family together, we sat down, we talked, and from then on the thing began to be solved...now I think that if I had had the relationship I have now with my family, perhaps none of this would have happened to us." (quote from a mother)

> "When you ask some families – Do you have someone who...? The majority tell you – if I'm here, it's because I do not have anyone." (quote from a professional)

3.2. What Are Families' Attitudes Regarding Social Support?

The results show that the attitude of families towards support depends on how the protection measure is formalized and how it is communicated to families. As this separation process takes place, a set of feelings are generated among the family members that determines their attitude towards support.

With regard to the attitude of families regarding formal support, families tend to be more collaborative and receptive towards formal support when they voluntarily request that the guardianship and custody of their children be exercised by the Administration. In contrast, when the decision is not made by families, and they do not accept the protection measures, two types of attitudes that lead to less collaboration are usually observed: anger and aggressiveness or passivity and indifference.

Although the results indicate that families who are angry and agitated at the beginning are most reluctant to collaborate in the early stages, they do suggest that this may be a reaction to regaining guardianship for children, which can lead to reunification, as it may indicate—in terms of involvement and participation—that there is genuine interest in the future of the children and the re-establishment of family and contextual conditions for optimal parenting. In contrast, those who accept separation and who do not show interest in understanding the elements that led to the separation may have lower expectations of reunification. However, the latter make up a minority of the families in foster care.

"I have met very few families who are 'abandoning'; if I think of the twenty years that I have been working on the team, I might have known one or two." (quote from a professional)

The results also indicate that the acceptance of these formal supports is related to three elements: the acceptance of the foster care measure, the family's perception of professionals as a help resource, and the predisposition to receive support.

To promote acceptance of the measure, both an awareness of the problem that caused the separation and feeling responsible for the situation are considered key. In this sense, results suggest that awareness of the reasons for separation is acquired through a gradual process of understanding that is linked to the motivation for change. When parents understand the reasons for the separation, they begin to be motivated to make the necessary changes.

"I began to see them as useful after eight months or so, not before, because I saw that they wanted to help me get my children back and be well." (quote from a mother)

For parents to accept formal support, it is necessary for them to consider professionals as an element of help and not as a controlling element. For this change in perspective and attitude to occur, a crucial aspect is trust, which is also acquired through a gradual and temporal process.

"First it sounds strange, then you start to listen. It is like a process, right? And then the time comes because they talk to you, and you start accepting a little bit, then you get used to it slightly more, until there comes a time when you get to trust them." (quote from a father)

Another essential element associated with accepting support consists of the predisposition and openness of parents to receive help. In this regard, all participants believed that collaboration begins when parents are aware that the first step towards progress lies in a receptive attitude to be helped:

"I personally was very negative about listening to anyone, I did not want anyone to help me, but when I realized everything I had lived, I understood, I opened my heart so that the teacher I had could help me. Then, I was open to all the corrections, to everything that was said to me." (quote from a mother)

"You have a great team around, a great team that supports you, that guides you...but it is you who have to accept it and swallow your pride." (quote from a father)

In addition to these elements, the results indicate that families' attitudes are also influenced by the feelings that are generated in the initial moments of the foster care experience. In general, families harbor intense, ambivalent, and even negative feelings due to the separation from their children. The results show that the most frequent feelings might be anxiety, loneliness, disorientation, shock, emotional blockage, pain, suffering, anger, helplessness, fear, tension, and depression. Some of these feelings seem to be generators or propellers of intentions for change in families.

"Families tend to be reactive, but behind this reaction, there are feelings of fear and helplessness, of anger...and these are the ones that end up 'clicking' before." (quote from a professional)

"I felt I was a bad father, and since I felt a bad father because no one told me anything, well, I would leave the girl...So, when they took my daughter away, the world sank. I fell into a dark pit." (quote from a father)

With regard to the attitude of families regarding informal support, the parents and professionals interviewed affirm that if foster care occurs in extended families, the situation is usually experienced in a less traumatic way, which might imply that the family's attitude towards informal support is also more positive.

"If it is in the family environment because it stays in the extended family, it is not so traumatic; it is within its scope." (quote from a professional)

Finally, the results indicate that families' most frequent feelings towards informal support are shame, fear, and distrust, which makes them reject this type of support due to the fear of "what they will say" and the perception that asking for help is a symptom of weakness.

"When they return home, there are those who do not ask for help because they fear that they will take their children away from them again." (quote from a professional)

"If they had been there, it would have been very different; a single person [family] is not capable without help from someone they trust." (quote from a mother)

4. Discussion and Implications for Practice

This study has analyzed two of the key elements linked to the social support of families in foster care processes: the type and characteristics of support and families' attitudes towards them. As has been observed in this study and those of different authors (Rodrigo et al. 2007; Lietz et al. 2011), social support is a key factor before (to prevent separation), during (to promote change during foster care) and after (to promote and strengthen family reunification and the children's return home) the process. These aspects are associated with the strengths of the stages of the process of family resilience (Lietz 2006; 2009; Lietz and Strength 2011). Social support is a relevant key factor for family resilience during all of the foster and reunification process but is particularly important in the early days following placement where not only do families need to receive confident and trusted formal support, but they have to face different challenges to build an informal network progressively that will help them to succeed in fostering and reunification.

The research shows that formal support is especially important at the beginning of a protection measure. This type of support is demanded by some families but also rejected by others, who may initially harbor intense feelings and ambivalence, or even reject some support. This finding supports and extends the results of other studies that point to the relationship between professionals and the family as an element that favors the commitment of the family to reunification (Child Welfare Information Gateway 2011). When parents consider professionals to be help elements, the process of fostering and returning their children to their homes is favored (Bravo and Del Valle 2009). This view of the professional as a reference for help is obtained through a gradual process in which the acceptance of the foster care measure and the establishment of a relationship of trust and communication are crucial factors (Balsells et al. 2014).

Regarding informal support, the results underscore the important role played by family members, neighbors, or friends. According to Spilsbury and Korbin (2013), this type of support can help reduce and mitigate the impact of certain vulnerability factors by providing emotional resources, protecting families from the stresses of daily life, and helping them cope with crisis situations. However, the results confirm the weak informal support network of these families, especially regarding the support received from the extended family, despite its importance as reflected in other studies (Lietz et al. 2011).

In addition, the voices of the participants confirm that the family's attitude towards support is linked to the family's other feelings, especially the reticence and fears that parents and their children may have regarding asking for help. In other studies, parents do not want to be vulnerable because "they might feel guilt, shame or anger" (Bravo and Del Valle 2009, p. 130), which makes it difficult for them to apply for and receive help.

The relevance of formal support to help families successfully face foster care and reunification leads professionals to adopt new forms of relationships and communication. Our results align with those indicated by the Child Welfare Information Gateway (2011) and Ward et al. (2012) in terms of the challenges that arise: working collaboratively with parents, helping them understand the changes they need to face, building on their strengths, showing sensitivity, explaining the consequences of breaking agreements, and explaining "bad news" where necessary. Similarly, the results confirm how certain skills and attitudes displayed by the professional help mitigate families' fears and build the necessary relationship for a quality placement, such as open and honest communication with parents (Yatchmenoff 2005) or a real commitment to the case (Cheng 2010).

Therefore, some orientations and implications for practice linked to social support in foster care processes emerge:

a. Offer greater formal support based on understanding and emotional support, treating families with empathy and showing open, sincere, and constant communication to foster trust with professionals.

b. Promote the informal network of friends, family, and groups of families who have been through the same situation such us family group conference as a strategy to begin to foster greater informal support during the early days following placement.

c. Encourage the professionals of the Child Protection System to be a reference figure in whom families find a person who can provide them with support.

d. Work with the whole family, including the extended family as much as possible; i.e., conduct comprehensive work with the family with the possible inclusion of informal support.

Author Contributions: Conceptualization, M.À.B.; methodology, E.V. and M.À.B.; formal analysis, E.V.; C.P.; A.U. and A.N.; investigation, M.À.B.; data curation, E.V.; A.U.; C.P. and A.N.; writing—original draft preparation, E.V.; M.À.B.; C.P.; A.U. and A.N.; writing—review and editing, E.V. All authors have read and agreed to the published version of the manuscript.

Funding: This research was funded by the Ministry of Science, Innovation and Universities, grant number RTI2018-099305-B-C21 and the Ministry of Economy and Competitiveness, grant number EDU2014-52921-C2-1-R of the Government of Spain, and the Agency for Management of University and Research Grants of the Generalitat of Catalonia, grant number 2017SGR905.

Acknowledgments: The researchers are grateful for the participation of the children, parents and professionals in the study.

Conflicts of Interest: The authors declare no conflict of interest. The funders had no role in the design of the study; in the collection, analyses, or interpretation of data; in the writing of the manuscript, or in the decision to publish the results.

References

Amorós, Pere, Jesús Palaciós, Nuria Fuentes-Peláez, Esperanza León, and Alicia Mesas. 2003. *Famílies Cangur. Una Experiència de Protecció a La Infància*. Col·lecció Estudis Socials. Barcelona: Fundació 'la Caixa', Available online: https://obrasociallacaixa.org/documents/10280/240906/vol13_ca.pdf/3307dbe2-dc75-4dfe-b622-8bd84104115f (accessed on 20 March 2020).

Ayón, Cecilia, and Annia Quiroz Villa. 2013. 'Promoting Mexican Immigrant Families' Well-Being: Learning From Parents What Is Needed to Have a Strong Family'. *Families in Society: The Journal of Contemporary Social Services* 94: 194–202. [CrossRef]

Balsells, M. Àngels, Pere Amorós, Nuria Fuentes-Peláez, and Ainoa Mateos. 2011. 'Needs Analysis for a Parental Guidance Program for Biological Family: Spain's Current Situation'. *Revista de Cercetare Si Interventie Sociala* 34: 21–37. Available online: http://repositori.udl.cat/bitstream/handle/10459.1/48290/016882.pdf?sequence=1&isAllowed=y (accessed on 20 March 2020).

Balsells, M. Àngels, Crescencia Pastor, María Cruz Molina, Nuria Fuentes-Peláez, Eduard Vaquero, and Anna Mundet. 2013. 'Child Welfare and Successful Reunification: Understanding of the Family Difficulties during the Socio-Educative Process'. *Revista de Cercetare Si Interventie Sociala* 42: 809–26. Available online: https://repositori.udl.cat/bitstream/handle/10459.1/48294/020021.pdf?sequence=1&isAllowed=y (accessed on 20 March 2020).

Balsells, M. Àngels, Crescencia Pastor, Pere Amorós, Ainoa Mateos, Carmen Ponce, and Alicia Navajas. 2014. 'Child Welfare and Successful Reunification through the Socio-Educative Process: Training Needs among Biological Families in Spain'. *Social Sciences* 3: 809–26. [CrossRef]

Balsells, M. Àngels, Crescencia Pastor, Pere Amorós, Nuria Fuentes-Peláez, María Cruz Molina, Ainoa Mateos, and Eduard Vaquero. 2015. *Caminar En Familia: Programa de Competencias Parentales Durante El Acogimiento y La Reunificación Familiar*. Madrid: Ministerio de Sanidad, Servicios Sociales e Igualdad. Centro de Publicaciones, Available online: https://www.mscbs.gob.es/ssi/familiasInfancia/ayudas/docs2013-14/docs2016/CaminarenFamilia.pdf (accessed on 20 March 2020).

Barth, Richard, Elizabeth Weigensberg, Philip Fisher, Becky Fetrow, and Rebecca Green. 2008. 'Reentry of Elementary Aged Children Following Reunification from Foster Care'. *Children and Youth Services Review* 30: 353–64. [CrossRef] [PubMed]

Bravo, Amaia, and Jorge Fernández Del Valle. 2009. *Intervención Socioeducativa En Acogimiento Residencial*; Santander: Gobierno de Cantabria. Consejería de empleo y bienestar social. Dirección General de Políticas Sociales.

Cheng, Tyrone Chiwai. 2010. 'Factors Associated with Reunification: A Longitudinal Analysis of Long-Term Foster Care'. *Children and Youth Services Review* 32: 1311–16. [CrossRef]

Child Welfare Information Gateway. 2011. 'Family Reunification: What the Evidence Shows'. Washington, DC, June. Available online: https://secure.ce-credit.com/articles/101406/family_reunification.pdf (accessed on 20 March 2020).

Dunst, Carl, Carol Trivette, and Angela Deal. 1988. *Enabling and Empowering Families*. Cambridge: Brookline Books.

Ellingsen, Ingunn Tollisen, David Shemmings, Ingunn Størksen, and Ingunn Storksen. 2011. 'The Concept of "Family" Among Norwegian Adolescents in Long-Term Foster Care'. *Child and Adolescent Social Work Journal* 28: 301–18. [CrossRef]

Farmer, Elaine. 1996. 'Family Reunification with High Risk Children: Lessons from Research'. *Children and Youth Services Review* 18: 403–24. [CrossRef]

Farmer, Elaine. 2014. 'Improving Reunification Practice: Pathways Home, Progress and Outcomes for Children Returning from Care to Their Parents'. *British Journal of Social Work* 44: 348–66. [CrossRef]

Farmer, Elaine, and Dinithi Wijedasa. 2013. 'The Reunification of Looked After Children with Their Parents: What Contributes to Return Stability? ' *British Journal of Social Work* 43: 1611–29. [CrossRef]

Fernández-Simo, Deibe, and Xose Manuel Cid-Fernandez. 2018. 'Longitudinal Analysis of the Transition to Adulthood of People Separated from the Child and Adolescent Welfare System'. *Bordón. Journal of Education* 70: 25–38. [CrossRef]

Forrester, Donald, David Westlake, and Georgia Glynn. 2012. 'Parental Resistance and Social Worker Skills: Towards a Theory of Motivational Social Work'. *Child & Family Social Work* 17: 118–29. [CrossRef]

Fuentes-Peláez, Nuria, Maria Àngels Balsells, Josefina Fernández, Eduard Vaquero, and Pere Amorós. 2016. 'The Social Support in Kinship Foster Care: A Way to Enhance Resilience'. *Child & Family Social Work* 21: 581–90. [CrossRef]

Fuller, Tamara, Megan Paceley, and Jill Schreiber. 2014. 'Differential Response Family Assessments: Listening to What Parents Say about Service Helpfulness'. *Child Abuse & Neglect*. [CrossRef]

Kimberlin, Sara, Elizabeth Anthony, and Michael Austin. 2009. 'Re-Entering Foster Care: Trends, Evidence, and Implications'. *Children and Youth Services Review* 31: 471–81. [CrossRef]

Lee, Bethany, Charlotte Lyn Bright, Deborah Svoboda, Sunday Bolanle Fakunmoju, and Richard Barth. 2010. 'Outcomes of Group Care for Youth: A Review of Comparative Studies'. *Research on Social Work Practice* 21: 177–89. [CrossRef]

Lietz, Cynthia. 2006. 'Uncovering Stories of Family Resilience: A Mixed Methods Study of Resilient Families, Part 1'. *Families in Society* 88: 147–55. [CrossRef]

Lietz, Cynthia. 2009. 'Examining Families' Perceptions of Intensive in-Home Services: A Mixed Methods Study'. *Children and Youth Services Review* 31: 1337–45. [CrossRef]

Lietz, Cynthia, and Margaret Strength. 2011. 'Stories of Successful Reunification: A Narrative Study of Family Resilience in Child Welfare'. *Families in Society* 92: 203–10. [CrossRef]

Lietz, Cynthia, Jeffrey Lacasse, and Joanne Cacciatore. 2011. 'Social Support in Family Reunification: A Qualitative Study'. *Journal of Social Work* 14: 13–20. [CrossRef]

Lin, Ching Hsuan. 2014. 'Evaluating Services for Kinship Care Families: A Systematic Review'. *Children and Youth Services Review* 36: 32–41. [CrossRef]

Lin, Nan, and Walter Ensel. 1989. 'Life Stress and Health: Stressors and Resources'. *American Sociological Review* 54: 382–399. [CrossRef]

Maluccio, Anthony, and Frank Ainsworth. 2003. 'Drug Use by Parents: A Challenge for Family Reunification Practice'. *Children and Youth Services Review* 25: 511–33. [CrossRef]

Maluccio, Anthony, Frank Ainsworth, and June Thoburn. 2000. *Child Welfare Outcome Research in the United States, the United Kingdom, and Australia*. Washington, DC: Child Welfare League of America.

Ordoñez, María Dolores. 2009. 'Factores Que Influyen En El Éxito de La Reunificación Familiar'. *Revista Internacional de Ciencias Sociales y Humanidades SOCIOTAM* XIX: 139–61.

Rodrigo, María José, Juan Carlos Martín-Quintana, María Luisa Máiquez, and Guacimara Rodríguez-Suárez. 2007. 'Informal and Formal Supports and Maternal Child-Rearing Practices in at-Risk and Non at-Risk Psychosocial Contexts'. *Children and Youth Services Review* 29: 329–47. [CrossRef]

Schofield, Gilian, Bente Moldestad, Ingrid Höjer, Emma Ward, Dag Skilbred, Julie Young, and Toril Havik. 2011. 'Managing Loss and a Threatened Identity: Experiences of Parents of Children Growing Up in Foster Care, the Perspectives of Their Social Workers and Implications for Practice'. *British Journal of Social Work* 41: 74–92. [CrossRef]

Serbati, Sara, and Paola Milani. 2012. 'La Genitorialità Vulnerabile e La Recuperabilità Dei Genitori'. *Minorigiustizia* 3: 111–19. [CrossRef]

Simard, Marie-Claude. 2008. 'La Reunificazione Familiare Di Adolescenti in Affidamento. Prospettive per i Servizi per La Ricerca'. In *Conoscere i Bisogni e Valutare l'efficacia Degli Interventi Bambini e Famiglie*. Edited by Cinzia Canali, T. Vecchiato and J. K. Wittaker. Padova: Fondazione 'Emanuela Zancan', pp. 74–76.

Smithson, Rosie, and Matthew Gibson. 2016. 'Less than Human: A Qualitative Study into the Experience of Parents Involved in the Child Protection System'. *Child & Family Social Work*. [CrossRef]

Spilsbury, James, and Jill Korbin. 2013. 'Social Networks and Informal Social Support in Protecting Children from Abuse and Neglect: Community Ties and Supports Promote Children's Safety'. *Child Abuse & Neglect* 37: 8–16. [CrossRef]

Stolz, Heidi, Mary Denise Brandon, Heather Wallace, and Patricia Roberson. 2013. 'Understanding and Addressing the Needs of Parenting Educators: A Focus Group Analysis'. *Families in Society: The Journal of Contemporary Social Services* 94: 203–10. [CrossRef]

Terling, Toni. 1999. 'The Efficacy of Family Reunification Practices: Reentry Rates and Correlates of Reentry for Abused and Neglected Children Reunited with Their Families'. *Child Abuse & Neglect* 23: 1359–70. [CrossRef]

Thomas, David Chenot, and Barbara Reifel. 2005. 'A Resilience-Based Model of Reunification and Reentry: Implications for out-of-Home Care Services'. *Families in Society* 86: 235–43. [CrossRef]

Walsh, Froma. 2002. 'A Family Resilience Framework: Innovative Practice Applications'. *Family Relations* 51: 130–37. [CrossRef]

Ward, Harriet, Rebeca Brown, and David Westlake. 2012. *Safeguarding Babies and Very Young Children from Abuse and Neglect*. London: Jessica Kingsley.

Yatchmenoff, Diane. 2005. 'Measuring Client Engagement From the Client's Perspective in Nonvoluntary Child Protective Services'. *Research on Social Work Practice* 15: 84–96. [CrossRef]

![social sciences logo] *social sciences*

MDPI

Article

A Framework to Inform Protective Support and Supportive Protection in Child Protection and Welfare Practice and Supervision

Caroline McGregor [1,*] and Carmel Devaney [1,2]

[1] UNESCO Child and Family Research Center, The National University of Ireland, H91 C7DK Galway, Ireland; carmel.devaney@nuigalway.ie

[2] School of Political Science and Sociology, The National University of Ireland, H91 C7DK Galway, Ireland

* Correspondence: caroline.mcgregor@nuigalway.ie

Received: 1 March 2020; Accepted: 29 March 2020; Published: 7 April 2020

Abstract: In this article, our intention is to provide an in-depth framework to inform the management of the inevitable complexity of day-to-day practice and supervision in child protection and welfare. It is based on what is now well evidenced about child protection and welfare literature in relation to risk, relationships, family support, supervision, and professional development. Using Ireland as a case example for illustration and application, we introduce an emerging framework based on a dualism of 'protective support and supportive protection' developed in previous work. We avail of Bronfenbrenner's bio-ecological framework and network theories to progress this ongoing 'work in progress' to inform social work and social care practice and supervision in a global context as and where appropriate. We emphasize the importance of context specific approaches, the relevance of range of actors, practitioner and supervisor expertise through experience, and proactive partnership based engagement with children, families, and relevant communities in all aspects of service delivery, including evaluation. We reflect on the challenges and possible obstacles to how such a framework can inform practice and supervision. We argue that practitioners can best activate and apply the framework using a practice research approach.

Keywords: child abuse; child protection and welfare; public protection; family support; bio-ecological; networks and networking

---

1. Introduction

1.1. Setting the Scene

"The closer we can get to ensuring that children and families, no matter what point they come into contact with 'the system' or 'the state,' are responded to in a manner that promotes strengths, offers partnership working, supports while it asserts and prosecutes as needed to protect, the more likely we are to achieve the goal of reducing abuse and neglect and enhancing family well-being" (McGregor and Devaney 2020, p. 284).

In this article, using Ireland as a case example, we propose a framework of protective support and supportive protection that can be used to inform practice and supervision in different global contexts to complement existing approaches. We present this as a conceptual paper to inform supervision and practice development. We propose that a practice research approach can advance the proposed framework further.

This first section provides a commentary on the current literature relating to the relationship between child protection and family support showing a complex range of considerations for practitioners to be aware of. We then consider the Irish context as a specific illustration of child welfare and protection practice. In the results section, we set out our framework for protective support and supportive protection as a way to manage the complex demands of supporting and protecting children, young people, and families. To advance this, we consider the relationship between family support and child protection within the context of Bronfenbrenner and Morris (2006) bio-ecological approach. In particular, we avail of their use of PPCT (person, process, context, and time) to articulate strengths and challenges in supporting and protecting families within the Irish system. We combine this with relevant network theories to inform practice. To assist in the application to practice, we have developed tools to illustrate how this can be used to inform practice development and supervision conversations (see Appendices A–C). We propose that the next step is to implement this framework using a practice research approach (Appendix D) that enables the use of the framework to influence and be influenced by day-to-day practice.

There are multiple stories to tell about child protection and family support with numerous publications that inform how the current challenges in child protection can be addressed (e.g., Parton 2015a, 2015b, 2015c). This includes the importance of relational social work and growing evidence of a link between the strength of partnership/collaboration with parents and better outcomes/reductions in child maltreatment. There is concrete evidence of the dominance of social factors of inequality, poverty, and disadvantage as contributing factors to child neglect and child welfare concerns (Bywaters et al. 2018; Morris et al. 2018). The impact of adverse childhood experiences (ACES's) (Spratt et al. 2019; Joy and Beddoe 2019), trauma (Lotty et al. 2020), difficulties with disorganized attachment (Shemmings and Shemmings 2011), and working with parents with severe and enduring mental illness (Killion 2020) are significant contemporary concerns. We have advanced knowledge, research, and practice guidance relating to assessment, risk, and decision making (McCafferty and Taylor 2020). A welcomed emphasis on the wider social conditions of child welfare in research (Parton 2014; Featherstone et al. 2018), public health approaches to child protection (Lonne et al. 2019; Canavan et al. 2019), and community development approaches (Liebenberg and Hutt-Macleod 2017) is evident. Sophisticated differential analysis of different aspects of child abuse and neglect are widely available such as child sexual exploitation (Pearce 2019), child to parent violence (Coogan 2017), child protection and domestic violence (Overlien and Holt 2019; Holt et al. 2018; Buckley 2018), and digital and on-line abuse (McAlinden 2012). A long-standing concern about how to intervene sensitively with different cultures and differences within cultures continues (e.g., Bartley and Beddoe 2018; Ferguson et al. 2018; Munford and O'Donoghue 2019) which has helped to orient global practice towards greater awareness of cultural humility (Mafile'o 2019), alongside other related concepts of cultural competence, awareness, and sensitivity. This adheres well with principles of partnership and participation now embedded in child protection practices (Bell 1999; Slettebø 2013). The need for strategic leadership that takes account of the complexity of child protection practice (e.g., Morrison 2010) and the possibility of child protection social work transforming from a siloed to a networked profession (Frost 2017) are important further considerations. Gradually, the voice of service users and those who have experienced services is gaining more ground in literature relating to practice (e.g., Buckley et al. 2011; Brown 2019) and education (Tanner et al. 2017; Sapouna 2020). Further co-construction of theory and practice to combine intellectual and theoretical constructs with evidence, data, and practice wisdom is clearly required. So too is a critical appraisal of an overly technical application of practice models and a recognition of the complexity and systemic nature of child welfare concerns and necessary interventions.

While we have a strong body of global evidence, the challenge of responding to the complex field of child welfare and protection remains ongoing. Despite many publications and approaches on child protection internationally, it is clear that child abuse and neglect—or child maltreatment—is still a major social problem that authors such as Parton discussed in work focused on child protection social work and social systems (e.g., Parton 1991, 2014). Ongoing critiques of practice, especially within the legal domain and in high profile tragedies, diminishes public and media confidence in the capacity of systems and professionals working within them to respond appropriately, neither over-interfering with family life nor being so laissez-faire that children are left in harmful and dangerous living conditions (Gibbons 2010). And, particularly relevant for this paper, the relationship between family support and child protection remains a complex and evolving one across many jurisdictions (see, Gilbert et al. 2011; Merkel-Holguin et al. 2019; Connolly and Katz 2019).

It can be difficult to avoid a pessimistic perspective that implies the problem of child abuse and neglect, and responses to it, are not only "wicked" (Devaney and Spratt 2009) but also intractable and un-addressable and/or toxic (Wilkins 2012). There is concern in some jurisdictions that child protection is becoming too narrowly focused and separated from wider discourses of social work (Higgins 2017). However, there is much evidence in literature also to show that optimism can be found in the increased visibility of practice-led research (Satka 2020) and more diverse indigenous perspectives which are potentially transformative (Libesman 2004; Bartley and Beddoe 2018). Increasingly perspectives from young people and families give clear and achievable guidance on what we need to do differently (e.g., Tierney et al. 2018). Even if not practiced as such, there is an overall conceptual shift towards recognizing that good child protection happens in the context of excellent prevention and family support (see Daro 2016, 2019; Devaney 2017) and that we need a stronger recognition of the need to address structural inequality and the problems that parents face (addiction, alcohol abuse, disability, etc.) (see, for example, Dolan and Nick 2017).

One important mechanism to maximize the potential for transformative practice is practice development and supervision (O'Donoghue 2019; McGregor 2016). Supervision and support with professional development is essential to support child protection and child welfare practice. Morrison's four stage model of supervision is commonly used which involves management, development, support, and mediation. McPherson's in-depth study in the Australian context shows that, in addition to Morrison's four functions, a fifth requirement was to provide safety for the workers (McPherson and MacNamara 2017). In recent years in Ireland, supervision has become more systematic and integrated into agency policy. Linked to supervision, registration requirements for social workers in place since 2012 in Ireland put greater emphasis on continuing professional development (CPD) (www.coru.ie). Workers are expected to develop their own individual learning plan that compliments a wider team and agency training and support program and access to evidence based program support (e.g., https://www.effectiveservices.org/work/tusla-empowering-practitioners-and-practice-initiative). We argue that the framework presented here can best be developed and applied through being used as a tool for supervision and continuing professional practice development.

1.2. Introduction to Irish Child Protection and Welfare System

Ireland has had a national child protection system since the Health Act 1970. Prior to that, it held statutory responsibility for some children in care (e.g., workhouses, county homes, and some children in industrial schools) and some children who were adopted. From 1970 to 2014, child protection and welfare services were part of a wider health and social services structure (see Burns and Caroline 2019). Ireland has always relied heavily on voluntary services to deliver core features of the system and child welfare, protection, and family support is made up of a network of statutory and voluntary/third sector and more recently private care organizations. In 2014, the Child and Family Agency (Tusla) was established as an independent statutory authority. In Q3 of 2019, the most recently reported data, there were 15,401 referrals for child protection and welfare to Tusla (from a child population of 1,251,796 as of Census 2016). Referrals are categorized as 'abuse and neglect' (emotional, physical, sexual, neglect) or 'welfare' (children and families in need). Overall, there is a 44%–56% split between referrals for 'abuse and neglect' and those categorized as 'welfare.' In addition to addressing 'welfare' (high need) through the child protection process, the system also provides a family support response focused on early intervention and prevention. In Q2 2019, 17,879 children were in receipt of family support services (Tusla Q3 report 2019). Tusla also provides alternative care to 5983 children (Tusla 2019). Care in Ireland is made up mostly of foster care - general and relative - accounting for 91% of all children. Tusla organizes its service on a continuum of help-support covering universal family support services to child protection interventions across four levels. A more integrated approach to support and protection is reflected especially with the mainstreaming of a program of prevention, partnership, and family support (PPFS) (see Malone and Canavan 2018). This article continues the themes developed to inform the Irish system which has resonance for child protection and welfare practice more widely.

2. Results

2.1. Introduction

In McGregor and Devaney (2020) we argued that for front line practice it is essential that those who have a responsibility to deliver support and protection to children and families "have the capacity to work in a manner that puts the child at the center and the skills and values to engage effectively in protective support work and supportive child protection" (p. 8). We argued that while family support and child protection are often treated separately, they have a shared history and a complimentary and reflexive relationship. We have further argued that the notion of 'protective support and supportive protection' can be used as an overarching conceptual framework for practice. This framework can inform the implementation of a range of support and protection practice models like, in Ireland, Meitheal and Signs of Safety. Our aim in this paper is to advance further this framework focused on the dualism of 'protective support and supportive protection' (McGregor and Devaney 2020) by setting it within a bio-ecological frame and emphasizing the importance of networking skills in this context. We are interested in how this work can inform practice development and supervision with child protection and welfare practitioners and we provide some tools for practitioners to use to apply and then test and critique the conceptual framework to practice (Appendices A–D)

We have four main sections to the framework as follows. In Section 2.2, we set out our main argument that a 'protective-support and supportive-protection' conceptual framework offers a broad overarching approach to inform child welfare practice. We then summarise the knowledge base underpinning this in Section 2.3. In Section 2.4, we argue that consideration of this as a process within the bio-ecological context helps to capture the multi-faceted nature of practice especially allowing for more focus on extrinsic factors that impact on the causes and responses to child protection concerns. In Section 2.5, we propose that to activate our framework further, an emphasis on the skills of networking and the use of informal and formal networks to enable specific and focused interaction between micro-meso and exo-macro systems is necessary. Throughout, we offer some suggestions for how this can be used in supervision and practice development (Appendices A–C). In the discussion and conclusion, we argue that the conceptual framework, while beneficial to guide discussions and case planning, remains limited because it resides mostly in the academic domain. To test and develop the framework, we argue that a practice research approach (Marthinsen and Julkunen 2012) is essential so that practitioners can consider the knowledge emerging from the conceptual work, apply and critique it in collaboration with each other and with service users. Appendix D offers guidance to inform this development. We argue that the unique contribution we make is to provide an applicable framework capable of dealing with the complex layers of child protection and welfare practice that can be used irrespective of specific models and methods of practice.

2.2. Summary of 'Protective Support-Supportive Protection' Framework

In McGregor and Devaney (2020), we adapted Hardiker et al.'s (1991) model of preventative practice. We used our discussion in relation to child protection and welfare in Ireland to challenge the notion of 'interface' when we refer to support and protection and suggest instead that they are complementary practices that most often go hand in hand (see also Devaney and McGregor 2017). We identified the problem that relationships between support and protection are often not integrated or, when they are, are done so in a linear way, and we wanted to offer an alternative framework that better reflects the nature of practice. We argued that while Levels 2 to 4 in Hardiker et al. denote different thresholds of need and risk, most families are 'in the middle' with a level of need between support and protection.

We made the case for developing Hardiker et al. (1991) to take more account of three core aspects of practice by breaking down Levels 4 and 1 and integrating Levels 2–4a. Specifically we suggested that the following levels reflect current practice:

- Levels 2–4a: These levels relate to what we referred to as 'families in the middle' who make up the majority of users of child welfare services needing support and/or protection at a point in time or over a life-time. These are families with high levels of need and/or risk concerns.
- Level 4b: Families who need more formal civic and criminal legal intervention that requires an explicit socio-legal intervention in partnership with courts and police services. While the commitment to protective support and supportive protection is still present, it is overlaid with explicitly socio-legally mandated work. This includes working in contexts where the 'potential subjectivity' (See Philp 1979; Skehill 2004; Hyslop 2018) or possibility of change in the interests of the child is outweighed by objective harmful and/or illegal behavior that requires civil and criminal legal interventions.
- Levels 1a and 1b: These relate to universal services and the public, which are differentiated between formal universal services and informal natural networks and supports. We argued that more emphasis should be placed on strengthening both formal and informal aspects of these levels.

There are other threshold models that can be applied (see Connolly and Katz 2019). There are also critical warnings about the limits of a thresholds approach (Devaney 2018) and models specifically developed within family support (Dolan et al. 2006) and framed differently in other jurisdictions (see Dunst et al. 2002). In line with the United Nations Convention on the Rights of the Child, in many jurisdictions, family support and child protection are triangulated with children's rights (Gilbert et al. 2011; Merkel-Holguin et al. 2019; Connolly and Katz 2019). With reference to Daly et al. (2015), the authors acknowledge the complex differences between child welfare systems internationally but contend that one common feature throughout is evidence of 'orientation' or 'balance' between supporting children, youth, and families, and child protection. Our argument is that a commitment to a process that prioritizes doing protective work supportively and doing supportive work protectively helps to bring together distinct practices between 'support' workers and 'protection' workers across all threshold levels. The majority of intervention involves explicit support and protection practice vacillating often between high levels of need and harm (Levels 2 to 4a). This interconnects with the more legal and criminal context of the child that we called 4b, and with the wider public and universal services outside of the specific child and family agency (formal and informal at Levels 1a and 1b). The child protection worker has to have the skills, knowledge, and values to span this full scale of support and practice, within a socio-legal context. We propose that this framework, as developed here using ecological and network theories, can provide greater scope than heretofore available, to inform supervision discussions about child protection practice and skills development.

2.3. Knowledge Base Informing the Framework

We come from the position that child protection practice is essentially a practice of mediation in the social. As Parton has charted, child protection has evolved over time being influenced in the mid-20th century by a focus on medico-social discourse (e.g., the battered baby syndrome) to socio-legal discourses in the advancement and development of child care legislation (Parton 1991). In the past 50 years, at a varying pace in different contexts, a welcome legal emphasis in child protection has been the shift from intervention where there is evidence of harm to intervening when there is evidence of likelihood or risk of harm. This focus on risk is reflective of wider societal developments (see Beck 1992). One example in Ireland relates to the introduction of legislation to intervene on the basis of risk of significant harm under the Child Care Act 1991 which reformed the Children Act 1908 which only allowed for intervention where evidence of harm existed. This legal limit, linked with the family-centric (if married) constitution, was directly seen to have affected failure to intervene in one of the first child abuse inquiries in Ireland, the Kilkenny Incest Investigation (Mc Guinness 1993). However, while we should welcome this greater scope of intervention for protecting children at risk—in the sense that it gives more scope to protect a child from harm—it also brings with it increased anxiety and pressure as it links with theories of chance and probability which by nature, do not have certainty. A focus on risk brings with it the need for advanced skills, knowledge, and values for child protection workers to be able to predict the future and make judgments not only on what has happened but what is likely to happen (Wilkins and Forrester 2020). Assessing, managing, and balancing risk are key influential factors in decision-making in child protection (McCafferty and Taylor 2020), and living with uncertainty is easier to say than do when one is engaged professionally and empathically with children, young people, and families on a one-to-one basis. Rather than becoming more comfortable with living with a risk environment, there is evidence in Ireland of increasingly risk averse policy making in the areas, for example, of retrospective disclosure of child abuse (Mooney 2018) and responding to past practices in institutions such as mother and baby homes (Buckley and McGregor 2019).

It was indeed the over-emphasis on risk also seen in England that led to the review of child protection triggered by the Baby P case (Munro 2011). This created a re-emphasis on relationships in child protection practice as a means of ensuring that where there is the need for regulation and risk management this is done in a way that emphasizes the importance and centrality of doing so through relationships (Ruch et al. 2017; Ferguson et al. 2020). A stronger emphasis on relationships, and attachment in particular, emerged also in Ireland after the Roscommon Child Abuse Inquiry (Gibbons 2010) which found that observations of disorganized attachment were mistaken as strong attachment. This strongly influenced decision making about the continuum of good-enough conditions at home versus removal of children into a care setting. In some other jurisdictions, the emphasis on risk has emerged through changing social conditions (e.g., Harrikari and Rauhala 2019), while in others—for example, the Pacific regions—other core principles like relationships, love, and humility (Mafile'o 2019) are the leading discourses of practice.

One of the means towards improving relational practices is to focus on the use of family support principles, practices, and values in child protection. It is interesting to note that while we have some good examples of publishing relating to child protection and family support (e.g., Parton 1997; Corby 1998; Fargion 2014; Devaney 2011; Devaney 2017; Devaney and McGregor 2017; Pinkerton et al. 2019), this area is surprisingly under-developed given the duality of support and protection inherent in child welfare practice. Inexplicably, parenting support is also often seen as separate policy and practice orientation (Connolly and Devaney 2018). As mentioned earlier, services in Ireland are organized and divided between child protection (intake, assessment and intervention, children in care, fostering) and family support services although there has been greater integration in recent years. Family support practitioners may include professional social workers but are more likely to be social care trained (Devaney and McGregor 2017). A Master's degree in family support studies exists at the National University of Ireland, Galway (Devaney 2015) and otherwise, child protection resides primarily in social work Degree and Master programs. Youth and Community Work are separated as distinct qualifications and activities and graduates tend to be employed more within the voluntary and third sector.

Based on this knowledge base, we argue that greater integration of family support and child protection conceptually and practically is essential in child protection practice. It seems to align with a constant in child protection practice of mediating in the social (Parton 1991; Philp 1979; Skehill 2004; Hyslop 2018). We favor the model as it shows capability of application to a wider range of contexts which will have different orientations and approaches to balancing between support and protection. However, without a further device to critically analyze how support is perceived and how protection is legislated for, it may prove difficult to apply as an additional framework to existing practice models. The diversity of context for Ireland alone requires this nuanced approach. In order to provide a framework to capture and develop this complexity, we think that the bio-ecological model offers an appropriate next step as discussed below.

2.4. Using Bio-Ecological Model to Develop Further a Practice and Supervision Framework

2.4.1. Brief Overview

Bronfenbrenner (1979) introduced an ecological model for understanding human development that has gained wide appeal in many fields, including social work and social care. Over time, Bronfenbrenner focused more on the bio-ecological (Bronfenbrenner and Ceci 1994; Bronfenbrenner and Morris 1998, 2006) and this is the specific framework we have chosen to apply here. While application of the ecological model is not without its critics (see Tudge et al. 2009), it does offer a way to deepen the 'person-in-environment' relationship and serves as an excellent tool for mapping influences and planning interventions. The ecological model has been influential in informing child protection and welfare assessment frameworks and family support models of practice for decades (e.g., Jack 2000). In Ireland, recent adaptations of the ecological model include a study on child protection decision making (McCormack et al. 2020) and outcomes for permanence and stability for children in care (Devaney et al. 2018).

The model is based on PPCT—person, process, context (micro, meso, exo, and macro), and time (chrono and moments). The focus is on interactions and 'proximal processes.' It is this interactive component that we find most useful as a guide for practice development and supervision. It starts with person, then process; in this instance, this is mediating protective support and supportive protection. This is followed by context which relates to the levels of micro, meso, exo, and macro. We talk about time which adds the chrono level—trends in time, for example—and some discussion on time itself. Appendix A provides a sample table that practitioner and/or supervisor can use to frame critical discussion on themes pertinent under each of the headings briefly discussed below.

2.4.2. Person(s)

One of the major contributions from Ireland to child and family practice has been the introduction of the Meitheal practice model (Rodriguez et al. 2018). This placed the child at the center of the process and requires that all planning and decision making is influenced by this positioning. Current work relating to the day-to-day experiences of social work such as Winter and Cree (2016) and Ferguson et al. (2020) shows the intensity of interactions at a person-to-person level for worker and service users. By applying the P to the PPCT in the protection-support framework, we emphasize the distinctiveness of practice starting at the micro with the person and practitioner's own personhood and self-awareness in this process. This argument is further developed below in the discussion on the micro level

Thinking about the person should also be applied to the worker. It is now well-established that child protection and welfare work, by its nature and intensity, can lead to burnout and vicarious trauma for the practitioner involved. In Ireland, Burns (2011) has highlighted the factors that impact on staff retention in child protection and how they might be addressed. A balance in supervision and support between building resilience and strength to withstand the challenges of the work is required, while also recognizing the need to address the wider impact on persons in their work environment such as lack of resources, an over-focus on business processes, a lack of awareness of impact of dealing with traumatic issues, and denial of organizational factors thus leading to a blame culture on a worker deemed not to be 'coping.' Emotional intelligence needs to be balanced with emotional support similar to the arguments made in Australia regarding the role of supervision in creating safe space for practitioners (McPherson and MacNamara 2017).

2.4.3. Process

The importance of process, relationships, risk management, and mediation in the social have already been discussed. In this case, the process is engaging through a protective support and supportive protection framework. The specific country, agency context, and existing practice models must determine the scope of intervention. For example, Signs of Safety, developed in Australia (Turnell and Murphy 2017) has come to influence many jurisdictions including Ireland and it is now the favored child protection practice model in which many relevant practitioners are trained. Signs of Safety focuses on strengths and safety planning and shares principles with support and prevention models such as Meitheal in Ireland (Malone et al. 2018). We argue that whatever the specific model being used, a continuity framing practice as protective support and supportive protection offers a way to combine important practices of family support and socio-legal interventions that works with the majority of service users. Activating this complex process is aided, we suggest, by considering the different levels of context as outlined below.

2.4.4. Context

In this framework, context can be used to differentiate cause and focus of a presenting child welfare concern from micro through to the macro level (see Bywaters et al. 2018). Context can also be used to decide on levels of intervention from focused individual and direct work with children, youth, parents, and families, to wider policy and political engagement (Marston and McDonald 2012). Appendix A maps how this can be used in supervision and practice skills development. For example, at the micro level, this overlaps with reference to person above and encourages a focus in the interactions from the micro system into the wider meso/exo and macro level. Micro interactions encompass a range of intrinsic (e.g., mental health and wellbeing, personality, attachment, trauma) and extrinsic (personality, relationships, home, siblings) dimensions connecting strongly with the surrounding meso level—the inner circle of micro relations. Awareness of the nature of family relations within and between individuals and cultures is crucial here to maximize the potential for close partnership working with families appropriate to the specific cultural contexts of engagement (Ruch et al. 2017). Meso interactions can include both informal/natural relations (within family, friends, extended family, local community worker) and formal individual relations (e.g., with school teacher, resource worker, individual social worker(s), police, solicitors). The connection between micro to meso goes outwards also to exo, towards the formal structures from which many of the formal relations come from (e.g., the social work agency, child welfare office, school, solicitors office, legal aid services, police service) as well as the wider community and extended family environment (welfare office, community group, family resource centre, early years provider). It is often at this level of interaction that detailed actions relating to individual cases can be difficult to break down. Appendix A should be especially useful for developing interactions with the wider exo and macro level.

For example, increasingly in Ireland, better structures exist to engage at the exo level of practice, such as local child and family support networks and children's services committees that bring together relevant personnel from statutory, voluntary, and third sector domains to work together (see Rodriguez et al. 2018). The child welfare organization itself has expanded its teams and structures as well as related training and policy development (Tusla 2020). The macro level then denotes the wider policy and legal contexts that shape people's interactions with the system and with wider society.

Another major challenge presently in the wider context of the Irish system is how to connect government department of Department of Children and Youth Affairs with related departments of welfare, housing and the environment, justice, and health to address wider social issues affecting individual service users (McGregor and Gabhainn 2018). In Ireland, these presently include increases in child poverty, family homelessness, inadequate child and youth mental health services, and inadequate services for families seeking asylum. There is also a disconnect between disability and child protection services and evidence of discrimination and inequity experienced by many individuals and groups in Ireland including Travellers, (European Commission Against Racism and Intolerance (ECRI) 2019), persons with disability (Flynn 2020), asylum seekers, and unaccompanied minors (Ní Raghallaigh 2018). Another major macro and exo level challenge relates to the Irish legal system. As evidenced in the work of Coulter (2015, 2018) and Halton et al. (2018), there are significant issues arising with regard to knowledge and understanding of child welfare and family relations within the legal system.

The key to using the bio-ecological model effectively in this context is to use it as a visual and adaptable mapping tool with children, youth, and families to pinpoint both causes of concern and focus for intervention. This can also be used in supervision to inform case review and planning. Strengths, risk factors, and plans for intervention denoted in approaches like Signs of Safety, mostly focused on the micro-meso level (see Keddell 2014), can be further strengthened with explicit and sophisticated use of the ecological or similar system level models by strategic and collaborative usage to ensure the target of concern is more carefully considered. The scope to identify concrete actions at exo and macro level is especially important here.

2.4.5. Time-Chrono

The chrono level is usually denoted as a fifth concentric 'circle' in the ecological model. This refers to trends and changes in society. For example, the influence of digital and online platforms is changing the nature of risk for children and potential ways to address. Other important chrono factors in Ireland include the introduction of stronger children's rights into a traditional Parsonian and Catholic family-favoring constitution and the recent passing of a marriage referendum to allow same-sex couple marriages. Travellers in Ireland, our indigenous ethnic minority, who continue to experience over-representation in child protection and care statistics and experience ongoing racism and discrimination have recently (and finally) received recognition as a distinct ethnicity, thus allowing more scope to use rights and legal based approaches to address the ongoing discrimination in this area. As well as trends, time is also about moments and connects, in our view, to processes and relationships. Ample evidence abounds that tells us that people's direct experience of worker interventions strongly influences their positive or negative perceptions of the child welfare and protection system (see, for example, Buckley et al. 2011).

2.4.6. Reflections on the Bio-Ecological Framework

Recent developments in Ireland offer a welcome opportunity for greater collaboration across different practices, disciplines, and professions from micro to macro levels. But there are notable challenges to implementing a framework of protective support and supportive protection that we have advocated for here. These relate especially to the context level from micro to macro. Here the key challenge is to intervene at the right point (threshold) from the viewpoint of child, youth, and family. We have argued that most child protection and family support happens with 'families in the middle.' Child protection and welfare workers are also often in the middle—supporting and protecting—while interacting with the wider context at Levels 1a and 1b and Level 4b. While the ecological model is well developed as an assessment and mapping tool, we have argued here for the need for a more dynamic engagement with the PPCT model (Bronfenbrenner and Morris 1998, 2006; Bronfenbrenner and Ceci 1994) and its use as a supervision and practice development tool. Taking into account this framework, practitioners need a wide range of skills to identify and protect and support directly through therapeutic or socio-legal work as well as indirectly through agency and organizational structures and related organizations. Excellent ability to work collaboratively with the public and universal services, to mediate support and protection with families who come into the system, and to confidently and assertively engage more explicitly within the socio-legal domain and work with police and courts to address the injustice of child abuse and neglect are required. Additionally, more explicit attention to factors at exo and macro level issues are urgently needed.

While the bio-ecological model is very useful to map and plan assessment, interventions, and evaluations at the different levels through supervision, alone, we think it is still too broad and general to help focus individual practices sufficiently. In particular, it does not address the question of how workers can influence socio-structural exo and macro factors while also maintaining their micro-meso focus on the child at the center. One way forward, we suggest, is to apply more reflection on network theory and practices of networking in supervision and practice development to activate the framework further.

2.5. Networks and Networking in Child Protection

Social network theory has been applied across many disciplines including management and psychology (see, for example, Kadushin 2012). Social network theory has also been a familiar feature of social work and social care for many decades (see, for example, Sharkey 1989; Timms 1990) and has been influential in many fields of practice, including disability and working with older people. It is important to distinguish between networks as formal and informally occurring structures and networking as a skill and a practice. Social network theory has wider applicability links to theories relating to social capital as described by Bourdieu (see Houston 2019) and social support theory (Devaney and Dolan 2017).

Here, we embrace the recommendations of Frost (2017) who argues that social work generally needs to move from being a siloed profession and towards a more networked approach to practice as a core feature of practice, and we support this general assertion. We argue that this networked approach will enable practitioners working to protect and support children, young people, and families to more strategically target and address extrinsic factors in particular that impact on children's safety and wellbeing. Frost focused on the practices of co-location and inter-disciplinary work using the area of CSE (child sexual exploitation) which relates to one dimension of networking. This type of networking is crucial but we also argue that, in child protection practice, the scope can be wider with regard to use of network theory, structured networks, and ideas about networking (see, for example, Kadushin 2012), alongside social network interventions with children, young people, and families. We suggest that this emphasis on networks enables the location of specific network activity between workers and service users (micro-meso) and exo and macro 'nodes' to address some of the extrinsic factors that have such a great impact on child protection and welfare practices (see Appendix B). We suggest that there needs to be a range of approaches taken. For example, the newly introduced version of Barnuhus model for child sexual exploitation in Ireland, the One House project, provides a similar opportunity to multi-disciplinary working as Frost (2017) explored in his research. There is strong evidence to support the situation of all professionals involved in Child Sexual Abuse (CSA) including medical, legal, forensic, psychological, police, and social work services (see Dolan and Caroline 2020). In relation to Tusla, child protection and welfare intake services (for example inter-disciplinary and inter-agency relations) developed through networking are also essential given that the child and family agency relies heavily on voluntary services commissioned to deliver key early intervention and prevention programs. Using Appendix B, a network plan can be used to target the relevant organization, formal network, campaign group, service user group, and so on to engage with. Appendix C provides an illustrative list of options to be considered in an Irish context.

An under-utilized network action is the collation of data from casework individually and collectively to influence interactions. Practitioners in child protection can get even closer than ethnography studies to be able to identify and communicate with confidence the nature and appropriate responses needed in individual micro-meso contexts. The expanding range of opportunities for Irish child protection workers to gain support in relation to evidence-based practice, pursue doctoral research in practice, write research, and engage in practitioner research partnerships is crucial. Such practice research activities need to continue to be supported by the organization and the local academic universities and colleges that can support the creation of greater visibility of child protection practitioner expertise and the use of this to continue to deepen and build our network of knowledge to inform future theory, practice, and policy developments (see McGregor 2019, Appendix D).

Networking provides a tool to address both micro-meso and exo-macro level concerns in a systemic way. This begins with practitioners with roles in family support and child protection working together to achieve better outcomes for children and families (see, for example, Devaney and Dolan 2017; Ferguson et al. 2020). By practitioners involved in family support being highly skilled in child protection matters, there is a great opportunity for earlier intervention and prevention. Greater ability to 'hold' and 'manage' risk within a supportive context - with support as needed from child protection colleagues—should prevent some families meeting a threshold for referral into the child protection and welfare aspect of the services under the Irish guidance, Children First 2017, for reporting and address concerns about child abuse and neglect. Generally, as we argued in Devaney and McGregor (2017), practitioners involved in child protection and family support can engage collaboratively and create effective networks and relationships together in training, practice, and supervision processes. We also suggest that networking is best achieved from the micro-meso level outwards and suggest a revised visualization of this relationship in Appendix B. As shown in Appendix C, a number of potential network nodes can be targeted for action through supervision and practice development.

To enable further reach towards engagement at Levels 1a and 1b, broadening of networks with those working more closely with the public in communities, localities, and early intervention and prevention services will enhance their ability to support those who become involved with child protection to engage. Also, the better the network between the early intervention and prevention services, universal services, and child protection, the more likely we are to prevent referrals in the first place, build trust in the system, and enable people to be more confident and less afraid of seeking statutory help with parenting and family support (see Daro 2016, 2019). Use of opportunities such as public awareness activities to run joint events can enhance networking potential and delivery of common messages to the public about family support and child protection. We know from current research (McGregor et al. 2018) that the public still views the statutory child and family agency as mostly about child protection and children in care, but this is beginning to change (McGregor and Gabhainn 2018). Effective networking and support between child protection workers and their wider statutory, voluntary, formal, and informal networks workers has huge further potential (as it is happening) to address public and media misperceptions about the primary function of the system to intervene against parents' wishes or in an overly anti-family way (O'Connor et al. 2018). This perception links best with what we have called the Level 4b aspect of practice. While this represents a minority of cases—most families are between levels 2–4a—it is important to encourage greater awareness for those working outside of child protection of the impact on persons working with some severe and shocking cases of abuse and the need for a robust child and youth centered justice approach to address this.

A particular emphasis needs to be placed on how to use networks and engage at the exo and macro level. While wider engagement with exo and macro factors will not address the range of child abuse and neglect issue that are contained within micro-meso level interactions, it will address significant portions of neglect, child welfare, and related child protection concerns (Bywaters et al. 2018; Morris et al. 2018). Greater partnership work with families to strengthen their own social network, avail of potential social capital in their community (e.g., local advocacy group, local politician) can enhance and add to partnership and collaborative working (Rodriguez et al. 2018; Brady et al. 2020). Social network practice is core to traditional social work and social care and can be drawn on more explicitly to guide child protection and support practices. It can also include engagement through formal structures for childcare networks to reach politicians and policy makers.

Reflecting back to the broad protective support and supportive protection framework, in all of this work, the scope of child protection practice from informal family self-governance through universal and targeted services, needs to be borne in mind. Through taking a networked professional approach, we have greater capacity to differentiate the wider social issues that are contributing to, if not creating, many child welfare referrals. This then leads to greater scope to intervene intensely, through protective support and supportive protection at the micro and meso level on the individual issues that lead to child protection and welfare concerns. Developing a stronger focus on networks and networking in social work will not eradicate child protection concerns but it should reduce those referred and lead to greater prevention and early intervention. This will not replace 'high level' 4b concerns but it could help to re-orientate and reduce harm through better support and respect to the dignity of parents, youth, children, and communities. Differentiated responses require differentiated networking. For Irish child protection and welfare workers, this means building networks with universal and community services where appropriate (e.g., connecting with local schools and building relations with teachers, knowing the GP service of the area), strengthening networks of support and protection that are engaged with most families 'in the middle,' and engaging in more targeted socio-legal networking through collaboration and joint training with those involved in the legal system (e.g., police, solicitors, guardian ad litmus).

Not all workers can or should attempt to extend their networks across all domains. Supervision and practice development can be used to target nature and level of interventions at individual, team, and organizational levels using Appendices B and C for example. Of course, such a networking approach is not a panacea. Turba et al. (2019) for example, based on a study of professional and organizational networks in child protection in Norway, discuss the barriers to professional networks. They argue that the professional and bureaucratic authority of child protection workers and managers, operating within a highly structured context, may make it difficult as this can cause "irritation and anxiety among their co-actors, resulting in the perception of poor collaboration" (p. 1; see also Herrera-Pastor et al. 2019).

If everyone perceived networking (informally and through formal structures) as core to business, then by diffusion, as Kadushin (2012) explains, it is possible to foresee a culture change towards child protection becoming a more networked activity. We argue that an integrated rather than an interfacing conceptualization of family support and child protection that can map interactions at different levels is essential to enable such a development. Diffusion implies that no one person has all of the answers; no one can do it all but we can all do something. There is capacity to gain belief and confidence in addressing what seem like wicked, un-addressable, or toxic issues not as one whole issue but through a multitude of individual networked practices targeting different levels depending on the nature, cause, and response to child protection concerns. In doing this, the focus has to stay on the personhood of the child/young person at the center of concern and the relational aspects of practice. Child protection workers alone cannot, in addition to this, take on the enormous 'big picture' of the exo and macro factors too. As much as child protection workers need to extend their networking skills to interact more with the exo and macro level as core to their work, so too do colleagues and individuals working in community, universal, and early intervention, and family support services need to network into child protection to support and sustain the work.

3. Discussion and Conclusion

In this paper, we have argued that the process and practice of protective support and supportive protection can be framed within a broader bio-ecological framework. To activate and specify interactions, we propose a networking approach. We suggest that in addition to the core practices of sharing information, collaboration, consultation, and full participation (Bell 1999) we can add facilitation of networking with formal and informal systems as another important participatory practice. We have argued that key to operating within a wider ecological framework, with an emphasis on networking for the reasons discussed above, a shift in thinking about the relationship between support and protection as 'interfacing' towards seeing them as 'integrative' is essential. We have sought to offer a way to do this by proposing and developing our 'protective support and supportive protection' model.

Our commentary implies a high level of expectation from child protection workers' skills. This includes ability to directly intervene therapeutically and supportively, to network, to advocate, to challenge, to confidently engage with the courts and police, and to contribute to public understandings of child protection. As a mainly conceptual paper, the next step for this framework is to ask practitioners to progress it further. In using it as a supervision and practice development tool, data and observations could be collated through embedded practice research. The framework so far can be described as 'Mode 1' knowledge production (Rasmussen 2012) derived from traditional scientific hierarchies of knowledge produced through universities and peer review (see also, McGregor 2019). There is now a need to advance the work within a 'Mode 2' framework which refers to an approach where knowledge production is broadened into the field and led by practitioners and service users who apply and experience the knowledge application in practice (Rasmussen 2012; Uggerhoj 2012; Satka 2020). As Marthinsen (2012) argues, this does not mean a rejection of more traditional conceptual approaches like we have used here. Rather it is about developing a relationship with theory to practice whereby practitioners can respond to and speak back to frameworks through incorporating practice research into supervision and practice development (see for example Appendix D). As Rasmussen (2012) argues, practice research can be characterized as a type of knowledge production, referred to as Mode 2, which sits alongside and compliments, rather than displacing Mode 1. At the same time, Mode 2 brings an essential value unattainable through Mode 1 theorization alone as detailed ore in Appendix D. It is also an approach that supports a networked approach:

"When practitioners form networks, they can develop the perspectives, concepts and categories that are relevant to their needs . . . . By generating knowledge gained from different perspectives, such research would be reflexive and well-grounded in specific practices rather than presuming to produce the one right answer to address one pre-described category of problems or methods" (Rasmussen 2012, p. 47).

Thus, we conclude with a humble recognition that our contribution is limited without an essential next step of practitioners and those they work with critically engaging in dialogue, testing, application, critiquing, and recreation of the framework. With this addition, the framework has potential to be transformative in an overarching way to make sense of the complex relationship between child protection and family support informing micro to macro level practice and policy developments.

Author Contributions: All authors contributed equally to this paper. All authors have read and agreed to the published version of the manuscript.

Funding: This research received no external funding.

Conflicts of Interest: The authors declare no conflict of interest.

Appendix A. Sample Discussion Tool for Practice Development and Supervision 1: Mapping Practice with the Bio-Ecological Framework

Note: In the diagram below, these levels are all inter-acting and inter-dependent as reflected in the circular concentric presentation. We provide an adapted version of the ecological model we used for children in care as an example (Devaney et al. 2018). Practitioners should draw their own models that reflect the nature and dynamics of interventions best.

Bio-eco Level		Issues for Specific Practice, e.g.	Issues for Own Professional Development	Skills/Values Comment
Person		E.g., impact of abuse	E.g., empathy impact on self - self-care	Balancing therapeutic and socio-legal skills
Process		What level of support and protection needed	Map own approach to protective support and supportive protection	Balancing assertiveness and supportive skills
Context	Micro	Quality of own network	Mapping individual context with child/young person or parent	Empathy, observation, confidence to draw and use maps
	Meso	Relationship with social worker	Awareness of power of interactions between meso-micro	Mediation skills
	Exo	Impact of lack of community place	What network node can you use, e.g., local Child and Family Support Networks (CFSN)	Confidence, knowledge, relationships
	Macro	Experience of inadequate housing	What resources has individual got, e.g., local politician. What network node, e.g., ask manager to engage with Children and Young People's Services Committees (CYPSC)/local housing department	Critical awareness of issues of housing and link to welfare needs
Time	Chrono	Impact of online bullying	Staff shortages and limited time	Ability to upskill to be aware of new trends and challenges
	Moments	How does person experience your intervention at this moment?	Awareness that your moments of interaction can have great power	Ability to see and analyze power relations

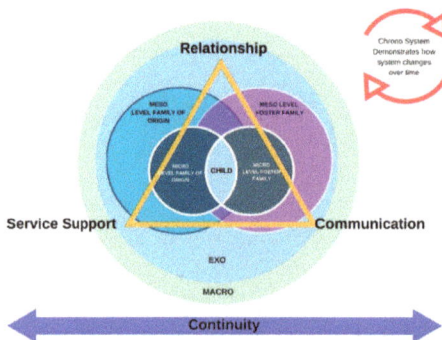

Knowledge Sources: Notes

Research Practice Evaluation: Notes

Appendix B. Sample Discussion Tool for Practice Development and Supervision 2: Networking

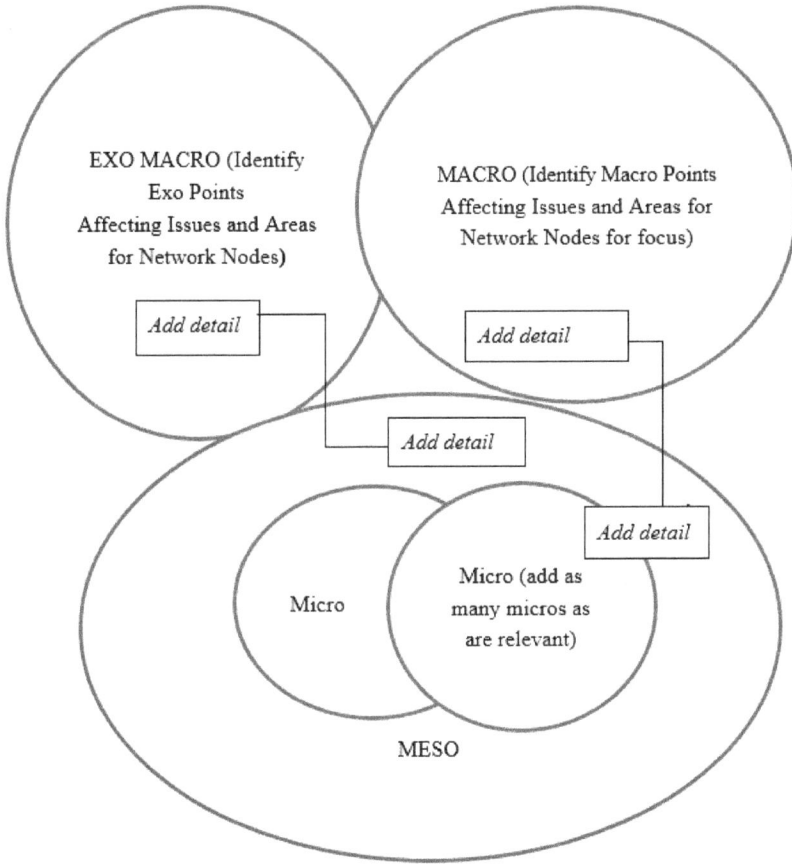

EXO MACRO (Identify Exo Points Affecting Issues and Areas for Network Nodes)

MACRO (Identify Macro Points Affecting Issues and Areas for Network Nodes for focus)

Add detail

Add detail

Add detail

Add detail

Micro

Micro (add as many micros as are relevant)

MESO

Appendix C. Sample Networking Nodes to Target Networking Interactions

Node	
Formal Structures for Networking	In Ireland, two types of network operate in relation to child and family services: Child and family support networks (CFSNs) support the provision of accessible and integrated supports for families by taking a localized, area based approach to coordinating services. A number of CFSNs can operate in any given geographical area depending on population density, levels of need, and service provision (exo level). Children and young people's services committees (CYPSC's) are responsible for securing better outcomes for children and young people in their area through more effective integration of existing services and interventions. Their age remit spans all children and young people aged from 0 to 24 years and there is one in every county in Ireland (exo level).
Children's Participation Strategy	In line with the children's participation strategy and training available relating to this, look for examples of where children and young people can work with individuals and teams to advocate and influence.
Organizational Data Sources	Tusla reports quarterly regional and national performance data. Keep up to date with trends in your region and use the data to support your networking practices.
Campaign Groups	Link in with relevant campaign groups to ask for assistance in raising issues like your observed impact of homelessness on families you work with, your evidence from practice regarding impact of poverty on school attendance; e.g. Children's Rights Alliance, Barnardos, Irish Society for for the Prevention of Cruelty to Children (ISPCC).
Targeted Services	Find the most relevant organization that addresses the issues arising in your practice, such as local and national Traveller movements, Empowering People in Care (EPIC) relating to children in care and leaving care, Support groups in relation to asylum seekers and refugees
Interagency/multi-disciplinary training/learning opportunities.	Engage in any available opportunities to attend cross agency/multi-disciplinary learning or training events in your area. These can be face-to-face/online. Local third level institutions may provide open access seminars, conferences, and training events, and many national organizations (e.g. Barnardos) provide on-line training events.

Appendix D. Guide for Practice Researchers Testing the Application of the Framework for Supervision and Practice Development (*Adapted from Marthinsen E. and Julkunen, I, 2012 Practice Research in Nordic Social Work: Knowledge Production in Transition*)

- "Practice research involves curiosity about practice" (Salisbury statement on practice research in Marthinsen and Julkunen (2012, p. 194)).
- Practice research is not a method in itself, it is an approach to research led by practitioners. It can involve a range of methods depending on the objective and planned outcome of the research.
- While a range of different methods of evaluation can be used, practice research tends to orient towards multi-methods, single case studies, analysis involving reflective and narrative interpretations, and ethnographies (see Julkunen 2012).
- Practice research can be through partnerships between universities and agencies; practitioner led research, and/or practitioner and service user partnership research.
- Practice research requires the same rigor as other forms of research but tends towards a more interactive and collaborative rather than a hierarchical model (see Julkunen 2012).
- The role of the researcher in practice research is similar to that of an academic researcher: As a change agent. The practice researcher tends towards reflections through evaluation and internal validation often involving peer learning and evaluation (see Julkunen 2012).
- Practice research lends itself well to service user involvement in the evaluation and testing of different approaches to practice.
- Practice research, according to Julkunen, 2012, brings forth a new conceptualization of evaluation which is interested in "recovering a sense of making and participating rather than just seeing and finding" (p. 112).
- A practice research approach can be built into supervision and practice development through agreeing a method of recording how the supervision tools are used (e.g., using a narrative method) and committing to evaluating the framework with regard to its applicability to practice skills development.

References

Bartley, Allen, and Liz Beddoe. 2018. *Transnational Social Work: Opportunities and Challenges of a Global Profession.* Chicago: Chicago University Press.

Beck, Uri. 1992. *Risk Society: Towards and New Modernity.* London: Sage.

Bell, Margaret. 1999. Working in Partnership in Child Protection: The Conflicts. *The British Journal of Social Work* 29: 437–55. [CrossRef]

Brady, Bernadine, Carmel Devaney, Rosemary Crosse, Leonor Rodriguez, and Charlotte Silke. 2020. *The Strengths and Challenges of the YAP Community Based Advocate Model.* Galway: UNESCO Child and Family Research Centre.

Bronfenbrenner, Uri. 1979. *The Ecology of Human Development: Experiments by Nature and Design.* Cambridge: Harvard University Press.

Bronfenbrenner, Uri, and Stephen J. Ceci. 1994. Nature-Nuture Reconceptualized in Developmental Perspective: A Bioecological Model. *Psychological Review* 101: 568. [CrossRef]

Bronfenbrenner, Uri, and Pamela A. Morris. 1998. The Ecology of Developmental Processes. In *Handbook of Child Psychology, Vol. 1: Theoretical Models of Human Development*, 5th ed. Edited by William Damon and Richard M. Lerner. New York: Wiley, pp. 993–1023.

Bronfenbrenner, Uri, and Pamela A. Morris. 2006. The Bioecological Model of Human Development. In *Handbook of Child Psychology, Vol. 1: Theoretical Models of Human Development*, 6th ed. Edited by William Damon and Richard M. Lerner. New York: Wiley, pp. 793–828.

Brown, Kate. 2019. Vulnerability and Child Sexual Exploitation: Towards an Approach Grounded In Life Experiences. *Critical Social Policy* 39: 622–42. [CrossRef]

Buckley, Helen. 2018. Editorial: Special Issue on Child Protection and Domestic Violence. *Australian Social Work* 71: 131–34. [CrossRef]

Buckley, Helen, Nicola Carr, and Sadhbh Whelan. 2011. 'Like walking on eggshells': Service user views and expectations of the child protection system. *Child and Family Social Work* 16: 101–10. [CrossRef]

Buckley, Sarah-Anne, and Caroline McGregor. 2019. Interrogating institutionalisation and child welfare: The Irish case, 1939–1991. *European Journal of Social Work* 22: 1062–72. [CrossRef]

Burns, Kenneth. 2011. 'Career preference', 'transients' and 'converts': A study of social workers' retention in child protection and welfare'. *British Journal of Social Work* 41: 520–38. [CrossRef]

Burns, Kenneth, and McGregor Caroline. 2019. Child protection and welfare systems in Ireland: Continuities and discontinuities of the present. In *National Systems of Child Protection: Understanding the International Variability and Context for Developing Policy and Practice.* Edited by Lisa Merkel-Holguin, John D. Fluke and Richard Krugman. Dordrecht: Springer.

Bywaters, Paul, Geraldine Brady, Lisa Bunting, Brigid Daniel, Brid Featherstone, Chantel Jones, Kate Morris, John Scourfield, Tim Sparks, and Calum Webb. 2018. Inequalities in English child protection practice under austerity: A universal challenge? *Child & Family Social Work* 23: 53–61. [CrossRef]

Canavan, John, Carmel Devane, Caroline Mc Gregor, and Aileen Shaw. 2019. A Good Fit? Ireland's Programme for Prevention, Partnership and Family Support as a Public Health Approach to Children Protection. In *Re-Visioning Public Health Approaches for Protecting Children.* Edited by Bob Lonne, Deb Scott, Daryl Higgins and Todd I. Herrenkohl. New York: Springer Publishers.

Connolly, Maria, and Ilan Katz. 2019. Typologies of Child Protection Systems: An International Approach. *Child Abuse Review* 28: 381–94. [CrossRef]

Connolly, Nuala, and Carmel Devaney. 2018. Parenting Support: Policy and Practice in the Irish Context. *Child Care in Practice* 24: 15–28. [CrossRef]

Coogan, Declan. 2017. *Child to Parent Violence and Abuse: Family Interventions with Non-Violent Resistance.* London: Jessica Kingsley.

Corby, Brian. 1998. Child Protection and Family Support. Tensions, Contradictions and Possibilities. *Child and Family Social Work* 3: 215–16. [CrossRef]

Coulter, Carol. 2015. *Final Report of the Child Care Law Reporting Project.* Dublin: Child Care Law Reporting Project.

Coulter, Carol. 2018. *An Examination of Lengthy, Contested and Complex Child Protection Cases in the District Court.* Dublin: Child Care Law Reporting Project.

Daly, Mary, Rachel Bray, Zlata Bruckauf, Jasmina Byrne, Alice Margaria, Ninoslava Pećnik, and Maureen Samms-Vaughan. 2015. *Family and Parenting Support: Policy and Provision in a Global Context.* Florence: UNICEF Office of Research, Innocenti Insight.

Daro, Deborah. 2016. Early Family Support Interventions: Creating Context for Success. *Global Social Welfare* 3: 91–96. [CrossRef]

Daro, Deborah. 2019. A Shift in Perspective: A Universal Approach to Child Protection. *The Future of Children* 29: 17–40. [CrossRef]

Devaney, Carmel. 2011. *Family Support as an Approach to Working with Children and Families in Ireland.* Germany: Lap Lambert Publishing.

Devaney, Carmel, and Pat Dolan. 2017. Voice and Meaning: The Wisdom of Family Support Veterans. *Child & Family Social Work* 22: 10–20. [CrossRef]

Devaney, Carmel. 2015. Enhancing Family Support in Practice through Postgraduate Education. *Social Work Education* 34: 213–228. [CrossRef]

Devaney, Carmel, and Caroline McGregor. 2017. Child protection and Family Support practice in Ireland: A contribution to present debates from a historical perspective. *Child and Family Social Work* 22: 1–9. [CrossRef]

Devaney, Carmel. 2017. Promoting children's welfare through Family Support. In *The Routledge Handbook of Global Child Welfare.* Edited by Pat Dolan and Frost Nick. London: Routledge, pp. 99–109.

Devaney, Carmel, Caroline McGregor, and Lisa Moran. 2018. Outcomes for Permanence and Stability for Children in Care in Ireland: Implications for Practice. *The British Journal of Social Work.* [CrossRef]

Devaney, John. 2018. The Trouble with Thresholds: Rationing as A Rational Choice In Child And Family Social Work. *Child and Family Social Work.* [CrossRef]

Devaney, John, and Trevor Spratt. 2009. Child Abuse as a Complex and Wicked Problem: Reflecting on Policy Developments in the United Kingdom in Working with Children and Families with Multiple Problems. *Children and Youth Services Review* 31: 635–41. [CrossRef]

Dolan, Pat, and Frost Nick, eds. 2017. *The Routledge Handbook of Global Child Welfare.* London: Routledge.

Dolan, Pat, John Canavan, and John Pinkerton, eds. 2006. *Family Support as Reflective Practice.* London: Jessica Kingsley.

Dolan, Pat, and McGregor Caroline. 2020. *Social Support Empathy and Ecology: In J. Pearce Ed Child Sexual Exploitation Why Theory Matters.* Bristol: Policy Press.

Dunst, Carl J., Kimberly Boyd, Carol M. Trivette, and Deborah W. Hamby. 2002. Family-oriented program models and professional helpgiving practices. *Family Relations* 51: 221–29. [CrossRef]

European Commission Against Racism and Intolerance (ECRI). 2019. *ECRI Report on Ireland: Fifth Monitoring Report.* Strasbourg: Council of Europe.

Fargion, Silvia. 2014. Synergies and Tensions in Child Protection and Parent Support: Policy lines and Practitioners Cultures. *Child and Family Social Work* 19: 24–33. [CrossRef]

Featherstone, Brid, Anna Gupta, Kate Morris, and Sue White. 2018. *Protecting Children: A Social Model.* Bristol: Policy Press.

Ferguson, Ian, Vasilios Ioakimidis, and Michael Lavlette. 2018. *Global Social Work in a Political Context: Radical Perspectives.* Bristol: Policy Press.

Ferguson, Harry, Lisa Warwick, Tarsem Singh Cooner, Leigh Jadwiga, Liz Beddoe, Tom Disney, and Gillian Plumridge. 2020. The nature and culture of social work with children and families in long-term casework: Findings from a qualitative longitudinal study. *Child and Family Social Work.* [CrossRef]

Flynn, Susan. 2020. Towards Parity in Protection: Barriers to Effective Child Protection and Welfare Assessment with Disabled Children in the Republic of Ireland. *Child Care in Practice.* [CrossRef]

Frost, Nick. 2017. "From "silo" to "network" profession—A multi-professional future for social work. *Journal of Children's Services* 12: 174–83. [CrossRef]

Gibbons, Norah. 2010. *Roscommon Child Care Case.* Dublin: HSE.

Gilbert, Neil, Nigel Parton, and Marit Skivenes. 2011. *Child Protection Systems: International Trends and Orientations.* New York: Oxford University Press. [CrossRef]

Halton, Carmel, Gill Harold, Aileen Murphy, and Edel Walsh. 2018. *A Social and Economic Analysis of the Use of Legal Services (SEALS) In the Child and Family Agency (Tusla).* Cork: University College Cork.

Hardiker, Pauline, Kenneth Exton, and Mary Barker. 1991. *Policies and Practices in Preventive Child Care*. Aldershot: Avebury.

Harrikari, Timo, and Pirkko-Liisa Rauhala. 2019. *Towards Glocal Social Work in the Era of Compressed Modernity*. London & New York: Routledge.

Herrera-Pastor, David, Juárez Jesús, and Cristóbal Ruiz-Román. 2019. Collaborative leadership to subvert marginalisation: The workings of a socio-educational network in *Los Asperones*, Spain. *School Leadership & Management*. [CrossRef]

Higgins, Martyn. 2017. Child Protection Social Work in England: How Can It Be Reformed? *The British Journal of Social Work* 47: 293–307. [CrossRef]

Holt, Stephanie, Carolina Overlien, and John Devaney, eds. 2018. *Responding to Domestic Violence Emerging Challenges for Policy, Practice and Research in Europe*. London: Jessica Kingsley Publishers.

Houston, Stanley. 2019. Extending Bourdieu for Critical Social Work. In *Routledge Handbook of Critical Social Work*. Edited by Stephen Webb. London: Routledge.

Hyslop, Ian. 2018. Neoliberalism and social work identity. *European Journal of Social Work* 21: 20–31. [CrossRef]

Jack, Gordon. 2000. Ecological Influences of Parenting and Child Development. *British Journal of Social Work* 30: 703–20. [CrossRef]

Joy, Eileen, and Liz Beddoe. 2019. Aces, Cultural Considerations and 'Common Sense' In Aotearoa New Zealand. *Social Policy and Society* 18: 491–97. [CrossRef]

Julkunen, Ilse. 2012. Critical Elements in evaluating and developing practice in social work: An exploratory overview. In *Practice Research in Nordic Social Work: Knowledge Production in Transition*. Edited by Edgar Marthinsen and Isle Julkunen. London: Whiting and Birch, pp. 95–116.

Kadushin, Charles. 2012. *Understanding Social Networks: Theories, Concepts, and Findings*. Oxford: Oxford University Press.

Keddell, Emily. 2014. Theorising the signs of safety approach to child protection social work: Positioning, codes and power. *Children and Youth Services Review* 47: 70–77. [CrossRef]

Killion, Mary G. 2020. Family Focused Practices in Irish Mental Health. In *Irish Social Worker*. Dublin: Irish Association of Social Workers.

Libesman, Terri. 2004. Child welfare approaches for Indigenous communities: International perspectives. Child Abuse Prevention Issues. *Australian Institute of Family Studies* 20: 1–39.

Liebenberg, Linda, and Daphne Hutt-Macleod. 2017. Community Development Programmes in Response to Neo-liberalism. In *The Routledge Handbook of Global Child Welfare*. Edited by Pat Dolan and Nick Frost. London: Routledge.

Lonne, Bob, Deb Scott, Daryl Higgins, and Todd Herrenkoh, eds. 2019. *Re-Visioning Public Health Approaches for Protecting Children*. Cham: Springer International Publishing, Volume 9, ISBN 978-3-030-05857-9.

Lotty, Maria, Audrey Dunn Galvin, and Eleanor Bantry White. 2020. Effectiveness of a trauma-informed care psychoeducational program for foster carers—Evaluation of the Fostering Connections Program. *Child Abuse and Neglect*. [CrossRef]

Mafile'o, Tracie. 2019. Social Work with Pacific Communities. In *New Theories for Social Work Practice: Ethical Practices for Working with Individuals, Families and Communities*. Edited by Robyn Munford and Kieran O'Donoghue. London: Jessica Kingsley Publishers, pp. 212–30.

Malone, Patrick, and John Canavan. 2018. *Systems Change: Final Evaluation Report on Tusla's Prevention, Partnership and Family Support Programme*. Galway: UNESCO Child and Family Research Centre, National University of Ireland Galway.

Malone, P., J. Canavan, C. Devaney, and C. Mc Gregor. 2018. *Comparing areas of commonality and distinction between the national practice models of Meitheal and Signs of Safety*. Galway: UNESCO Child and Family Research Centre.

Marston, Greg, and Catherine McDonald. 2012. Getting Beyond 'Heroic Agency' in Conceptualising Social Workers as Policy Actors in the Twenty-First Century. *The British Journal of Social Work* 42: 1022–38. [CrossRef]

Marthinsen, Edgar. 2012. Social Work Practice and Social Science History. In *Practice Research in Nordic Social Work: Knowledge Production in Transition*. Edited by Edgar Marthinsen and Isle Julkunen. London: Whiting and Birch, pp. 1–26.

Marthinsen, Edgar, and Isle Julkunen, eds. 2012. *Practice Research in Nordic Social Work: Knowledge Production in Transition*. London: Whiting and Birch.

McCormack, Cheryl, Marie Gibbons, and McGregor Caroline. 2020. An Ecological Framework for Understanding and Improving Decision Making in Child Protection and Welfare Intake (Duty) Practices in the Republic of Ireland. *Child Care in Practice.* 26: 146–62. [CrossRef]

McGregor, Caroline. 2019. Paradigm Framework for social work in the 21st century. *The British Journal of Social Work* 49: 2112–29. [CrossRef]

McGregor, Caroline. 2016. Balancing Regulation and Support in Child Protection: Using Theories of Power to Develop Reflective Tools for Practice. In *Irish Social Worker*. Dublin: Irish Association of Social Workers, pp. 11–16.

McGregor, Caroline, and Carmel Devaney. 2020. Protective support and supportive protection for families "in the middle": Learning from the Irish context. *Child & Family Social Work* 25: 277–85.

McGregor, Caroline, and Saoirse Nic Gabhainn. 2018. *Public Awareness*. Galway: UNESCO Child and Family Research Centre, National University of Ireland Galway.

McGregor, Caroline, John Canavan, and Patricia O'Connor. 2018. *Public Awareness Work Package Final Report: Tusla's Programme for Prevention, Partnership and Family Support*. Galway: UNESCO Child and Family Research Centre, National University of Ireland Galway.

Mc Guinness, Catherine. 1993. *Report of the Kilkenny Incest Investigation*; Dublin: Government Publications Stationery Office.

McAlinden, Anne-Marie. 2012. *'Grooming' and the Sexual Abuse of Children: Institutional, Internet, and Familial Dimensions*. Oxford: Oxford University Press.

McCafferty, Paul, and Brian Taylor. 2020. Risk, Decision-making and Assessment in Child Welfare. *Child Care in Practice* 26: 107–10. [CrossRef]

McPherson, Lynn, and Noel MacNamara. 2017. *Supervising Child Protection Practice: What Works?* Cham: Springer International Publishing.

Merkel-Holguin, Lisa, John. D. Fluke, and Richard. D. Krugman, eds. 2019. *National Systems of Child Protection: Understanding the International Variability and Context for Developing Policy and Practice*. New York: Springer.

Mooney, Joe. 2018. Adult Disclosures of Childhood Sexual Abuse and Section 3 of the Child Care Act 1991: Past Offences, Current Risk. *Child Care in Practice* 24: 245–57. [CrossRef]

Morris, Kate, Will Mason, Paul Bywaters, Brid Featherstone, Brigit Daniel, Geraldine Brady, and Calum Webb. 2018. Social Work, Poverty, and Child Welfare Interventions. *Child & Family Social Work* 23: 364–72.

Morrison, Tony. 2010. The Strategic Leadership of Complex Practice: Opportunities and Challenges. *Child Abuse Review* 19: 312–29. [CrossRef]

Munford, Robyn, and Kieran O'Donoghue. 2019. *New Theories for Social Work Practice: Ethical Practices for Working with Individuals, Families and Communities*. London: Jessica Kingsley Publishers, pp. 212–30.

Munro, Eileen. 2011. *The Munro Review of Child Protection: Final Report. A Child-Centred System*. London: Department of Education.

Ní Raghallaigh, Muireann. 2018. The integration of asylum seeking and refugee children: Resilience in the face of adversity. In *Research Handbook on Child Migration*. Edited by Jacqueline Bhabha, Jyothi Kanics and Daniel Senovilla Hernández. Elgar: Cheltenham, pp. 351–87.

O'Connor, Patricia, Caroline McGregor, and Carmel Devaney. 2018. *Newspaper Content Analysis: Print Media Coverage of Ireland's Child and Family Agency (Tusla) 2014–2017*. Galway: The UNESCO Child and Family Research Centre, National University of Ireland Galway.

O'Donoghue, Kirean. 2019. Supervision and Evidence Informed Practice. In *New Theories for Social Work Practice: Ethical Practices for Working with Individuals, Families and Communities*. Edited by Robyn Munford and K. O'Donoghue. London: Jessica Kingsley Publishers, pp. 271–88.

Overlien, Carolina, and Stephanie Holt. 2019. Editorial: European Research on Children, Adolescents and Domestic Violence: Impact, Interventions and Innovations. *Journal of Family Violence* 34: 365–69. [CrossRef]

Parton, Nigel. 1991. *Governing the Family*. London: MacMillan.

Parton, Nigel. 1997. Child protection and family support: Current debates and future prospects. In *Child Protection and Family Support: Tensions, Contradictions and Possibilities*. Edited by Nigel Parton. London: Routledge.

Parton, Nigel. 2014. Social Work, Child Protection and Politics: Some Critical and Constructive Reflections. *British Journal of Social Work* 44: 2042–56. [CrossRef]

Parton, Nigel, ed. 2015a. *Contemporary Developments in Child Protection. Vol 1 Policy Changes and Challenges*. Basel: MDPI.

Parton, Nigel, ed. 2015b. *Contemporary Developments in Child Protection. Vol 2 Issues in Child Welfare*. Basel: MDPI.

Parton, Nigel, ed. 2015c. *Contemporary Developments in Child Protection. Vol 3 Broadening Challenges in Child Protection*. Basel: MDPI.

Pearce, Jenny. 2019. *Child Sexual Exploitation: Why Theory Matters*. Bristol: Policy Press.

Pinkerton, John, Canavan John, and P. Dolan. 2019. Family Support and Social Work Practice. In *New Theories for Social Work Practice: Ethical Practice for Working with Individuals, Families and Communities*. Edited by R. Munford and K. O'Donoghue. London: Jessica Kingsley Publishing, pp. 44–62.

Philp, Mark. 1979. Notes on the Forms of Knowledge in Social Work. *Sociological Review* 27: 83–111. [CrossRef]

Rasmussen, Tove. 2012. Knowledge production and social work: Forming knowledge production. In *Practice Research in Nordic Social Work: Knowledge Production in Transition*. Edited by Edgar Marthinsen and Isle Julkunen. London: Whiting and Birch, pp. 43–66.

Rodriguez, L., A. Cassidy, and C. Devaney. 2018. *Meitheal Process and Outcomes Study*. Galway: UNESCO Child and Family Research Centre, National University of Ireland Galway.

Ruch, Gillian, Karen Winter, Viv Cree, Sophie Hallet, Fiona Morrisson, and Mark Hadfield. 2017. Making meaningful connections: Using insights from social pedagogy in statutory child and family social work practice. *Child and Family Social Work* 22: 1015–23. [CrossRef]

Sapouna, Lydia. 2020. Service-user narratives in social work education; Co-production or co-option? *Social Work Education*. [CrossRef]

Satka, Mirja. 2020. Pragmatist knowledge production in practice research. In *The Routledge Handbook of Social Work Practice Research*. Edited by Lynette Joubert and Martin Webber. London: Routledge.

Sharkey, Peter. 1989. Social Networks and Social Service Workers. *The British Journal of Social Work* 19: 387–405. [CrossRef]

Shemmings, David, and Yvonne Shemmings. 2011. *Understanding Disorganized Attachment: Theory and Practice for Working with Children and Adults*. London: Jessica Kingsley Publishers.

Slettebø, Tor. 2013. Partnership with Parents of Children in Care: A Study of Collective User Participation in Child Protection Services. *The British Journal of Social Work* 43: 579–95. [CrossRef]

Skehill, Caroline. 2004. *History of the Present of Child Protection and Welfare Social Work in Ireland*. Lapmeter: Edwin Mellen.

Spratt, Trevor, John Devaney, and John Frederick. 2019. Adverse Childhood Experiences: Beyond Signs of Safety; Reimagining the Organisation and Practice of Social Work with Children and Families. *British Journal of Social Work* 49: 2042–58. [CrossRef]

Tanner, Denise, Rosemary Littlechild, Joe Duffy, and David Hayes. 2017. 'Making It Real': Evaluating the Impact of Service User and Carer Involvement in Social Work Education. *British Journal of Social Work* 47: 467–68. [CrossRef]

Tierney, Edel, Danielle Kennan, Cormac Forkan, Bernadine Brady, and Rebecca Jackson. 2018. *Children's Participation Work Package Final Report: Tusla's Programme for Prevention, Partnership and Family Support*. Galway: UNESCO Child and Family Research Centre, National University of Ireland Galway.

Timms, Elizabeth. 1990. Social Networks and Social Service Workers: A Comment on Sharkey. *The British Journal of Social Work* 20: 627–31. [CrossRef]

Tudge, Johnathan, Irina Mokrova, Bridget E. Hatfield, and Rachana B. Karnik. 2009. Uses and Misuses of Bronfenbrenner's Bioecological Theory of Human Development. *Journal of Family Theory & Review* 1: 198–210.

Turba, Hannu, Janne Paulsen Breimo, and Christian Lo. 2019. Professional and Organizational Power Intwined: Barriers to Networking? *Children and Youth Services Review*. [CrossRef]

Turnell, Andrew, and Terry Murphy. 2017. *Signs of Safety Comprehensive Briefing Paper*, 4th ed. Perth: Resolutions Consultancy Pty Ltd.

Tusla. 2019. *Third Quarterly Performance Data Report*. Dublin: Tusla.

Tusla. 2020. Available online: www.tusla.ie (accessed on 30 March 2020).

Uggerhoj, Lars. 2012. Theorising practice research in social work. In *Practice Research in Nordic Social Work: Knowledge Production in Transition*. Edited by Edgar Marthinsen and Isle Julkunen. London: Whiting and Birch, pp. 67–94.

Wilkins, David. 2012. Disorganised attachment indicates child maltreatment: How is this link useful for child protection social workers? *Journal of Social Work Practice* 26: 15–30. [CrossRef]

Wilkins, David, and Donald Forrester. 2020. Predicting the Future in Child and Family Social Work: Theoretical, Ethical and Methodological Issues for a Proposed Research Programme. *Child Care in Practice* 26: 196–209. [CrossRef]

Winter, Karen, and Viviene E. Cree. 2016. Social Work Home Visits to Children and Families in the UK: A Foucaldian Perspective. *British Journal of Social Work* 46: 1175–90. [CrossRef]

social sciences

MDPI

Article

Safeguarding Children in the Developing World—Beyond Intra-Organisational Policy and Self-Regulation

Afrooz Kaviani Johnson [1,*] **and Julia Sloth-Nielsen** [2,*]

1   Department of Child Law, University of Leiden, 2311 Leiden, The Netherlands
2   Department of Public Law and Jurisprudence, University of the Western Cape, Bellville,
    Western Cape 7535, South Africa
*   Correspondence: a.kaviani.johnson@law.leidenuniv.nl (A.K.J.); jsloth-nielsen@uwc.ac.za (J.S.-N.)

Received: 29 April 2020; Accepted: 29 May 2020; Published: 8 June 2020

Abstract: Safeguarding in the context of development and humanitarian assistance has received heightened international attention since 2018. Emerging literature has not yet investigated the extent to which responses are evolving in the best interests of the child, in line with the treaty-based rights of children. This article makes a unique contribution to scholarship by applying a child rights lens to safeguarding efforts in the aid sector with a focus on the least developed countries in Africa. The article first reviews the safeguarding landscape—providing a snapshot of self-regulatory and standard setting initiatives by non-government organisations (NGOs) and bilateral government donors. Next, the article examines the relevant standards in the Convention on the Rights of the Child and the African Charter on the Rights and Welfare of the Child and respective Committee observations to enrich the safeguarding discussion. Finally, the article discusses key dilemmas and remaining challenges for safeguarding children in the developing world. The article suggests that a rights-based approach provides for a more nuanced and contextualised response, avoiding the temptation of 'tick-box' exercises driven by reputational management and 'programming siloes' imposed by humanitarian and development actors. To support sustained and consistent progress, efforts should go beyond intra-organisational policy and sectoral self-regulation. Child rights law monitoring mechanisms can be leveraged to encourage effective government oversight of NGOs in contact with children, as part of national frameworks for child protection. Donor governments should also consider and increase investment in national and local child protection systems to address risk factors to child abuse and ensure appropriate responses for any child that experiences harm.

Keywords: safeguarding; child protection; child abuse; risk to children; sustainable development goals; convention on the rights of the child; African charter on the rights and welfare of the child; non-government organisations

1. Introduction

The global community has less than a decade to achieve the Agenda for Sustainable Development and Sustainable Development Goals (SDGs). Agenda 2030 envisages a "world which invests in its children and in which every child grows up free from violence and exploitation" (United Nations General Assembly 2015, para. 8) and expressly includes several targets to end all forms of violence against children.[1] Unlike the preceding Millennium Development Goals, Agenda 2030 is grounded in

---

1   Including to eliminate all forms of violence against all women and girls (target 5.2), to take immediate and effective measures
    to secure the prohibition and elimination of the worst forms of child labour, including recruitment and use of child soldiers,

human rights standards and requires that the goals "be implemented in a manner that is consistent with the rights and obligations of States under international law" (United Nations General Assembly 2015, para. 18).

Those obligations relating to children's right to be protected from violence are articulated under several international instruments—most notably the Convention on the Rights of the Child and the Optional Protocol to the Convention on the Rights of the Child on the sale of children, child prostitution and child pornography. The Convention has near universal ratification, except for the United States of America (US). Most African countries have ratified the Optional Protocol (United Nations Human Rights Office of the High Commissioner 2020). In the regional context, the African Charter on the Rights and Welfare of the Child has comparative articles expounding children's right to be protected from violence. Regional policy frameworks include the African Union Agenda 2063 and Africa's Agenda for Children 2040 (African Committee of Experts on the Rights and Welfare of the Child 2018).

Despite the global and regional aspirations, high rates of violence against children persist. There is insufficient investment in tackling root causes and drivers of violence, as well as in those specialised services to support children and families affected by violence. In much of Africa, social welfare and child protection services are largely delivered by non-State actors including non-government organisations (NGOs), faith-based organisations, and community actors. Formal legal systems do not function optimally. In many cases, this enables a culture of impunity for perpetrators (Csáky 2008, p. 20). Not surprisingly, in the least developed countries, cases of child abuse and exploitation perpetrated by those meant to 'help' communities are met with heightened public outrage. This outrage ripples across the Global North in cases which implicate 'Western' offenders, international NGOs and Official Development Assistance.

In early 2018, allegations of the sexual exploitation of women and girls by a senior Oxfam staff member following the 2010 earthquake in Haiti made global headlines (BBC 2018). The revelations triggered critical introspection within the humanitarian and development sector and a flurry of consequent activity. Like the reactions following the 2002 West African 'sex-for-food' scandal (United Nations High Commissioner for Refugees & Save the Children UK 2002), several significant policy commitments on 'safeguarding' emerged, largely from the components of the 'aid chain' headquartered in the Global North. Scholarly engagement with the concept of safeguarding is just emerging (Sandvik 2019, p. 2), and literature has not yet explored the extent to which responses are evolving in the best interests of the child, in line with the treaty-based rights of children. Although the Oxfam investigations were reportedly unable to substantiate the allegations concerning girls (Charity Commission for England and Wales 2019), the risks to children arising from development and humanitarian activity are well known to child protection practitioners and documented by Csáky (2008), amongst others.

This article makes a unique contribution by applying a child rights lens to safeguarding efforts in the aid sector, with a focus on the least developed countries in Africa, from a view in the developing world. The article examines child safeguarding within the public international law framework, taking a child rights, legal theory-based approach, and drawing on international human rights standards and norms set out in the Convention on the Rights of the Child and other relevant instruments. The article also draws on the observations of the Committee on the Rights of the Child and the African Committee of Experts on the Rights and Welfare of the Child and existing legal academic scholarship relating to children's rights. The methodology necessarily employed both legal and interdisciplinary research. The sources reviewed and analysed were identified through comprehensive desk research via databases, journal tracking and review of grey literature, including research reports, conference proceedings, and government documents on thematic areas of child abuse and exploitation, child safeguarding, safeguarding, institutional child abuse, child protection and abuse of power in development and

---

and, by 2025, end child labour in all its forms (target 8.7) and to end abuse, exploitation, trafficking and all forms of violence against and torture of children (target 16.2).

humanitarian contexts, with a focus on Africa. The article is also informed by the authors' professional experience in child rights and protection in Africa and internationally. The article first reviews the safeguarding landscape—providing a snapshot of self-regulatory and standard setting initiatives by the sector over the last three decades. Next, the article examines the relevant standards in the Convention on the Rights of the Child and the African Charter on the Rights and Welfare of the Child and respective Committee observations to enrich the safeguarding discussion. Finally, the article discusses key dilemmas and remaining challenges for safeguarding children in the developing world.

The article suggests that a rights-based approach provides for a more nuanced and contextualised response, avoiding the temptation of 'tick-box' exercises driven by reputational management and 'programming siloes' imposed by humanitarian and development actors. To support sustained and consistent progress, efforts should go beyond intra-organisational policy and sectoral self-regulation. Child rights law monitoring mechanisms can be leveraged to encourage effective government oversight of NGOs in contact with children, as part of national frameworks for child protection. While safeguarding discourse in certain policy arenas has focused on sexual exploitation and abuse, an especially egregious violation of children's rights, a rights-based approach should consider the various intersections between humanitarian and development activity and children's treaty-based rights. This should encompass all risks and harms including those arising in the digital era. Intra-organisational efforts are interlinked and dependent on local and national systems. As such, donor governments should consider and increase investment in child protection systems to address risk factors to child abuse and ensure appropriate responses for any child that experiences harm. At the time of writing, countries in Africa are beginning to deal with secondary impacts of the COVID-19 pandemic and, more than ever, robust social services are required to protect the most vulnerable children.

2. The Safeguarding Landscape—Evolving Self-Regulation and Standard Setting

Safeguarding means different things to different people (Sandvik 2019, p. 4). Until relatively recently, the term was almost exclusively used in the United Kingdom (UK) as a legal definition applied to vulnerable adults and children (HM Government 2018; UK Department for International Development 2019, p. 23). In the context of aid, the term has evolved to focus on the organisational 'duty of care' and responsibility to 'do no harm'. The term remains poorly understood in the Global South (Walker-Simpson 2017, p. 254). While different organisations use different terminologies (Sandvik 2019, p. 2), the broader issue of NGO accountability to the people they serve can be positioned within a context of at least three decades of evolving NGO self-regulation and standard setting. This section provides a snapshot of these efforts.

2.1. Self-Regulatory and Standard Setting Initiatives and the West Africa 'Sex-for-Food' Scandal

The demand for humanitarian relief following the end of the Cold War saw a proliferation of new organisations that were often "inexperienced and unprofessional" (Zarnegar Deloffre 2016, p. 729). Attention was drawn to NGO accountability and the lack of professional standards following a series of "problematic" emergency relief operations, particularly in Ethiopia, Somalia, and Rwanda (Zarnegar Deloffre 2016, p. 729). Industry-wide standards emerged for NGOs to distinguish themselves from "low-quality" organisations (Zarnegar Deloffre 2016, p. 729). These standards included the Sphere Humanitarian Charter and Minimum Standards, People in Aid Code of Conduct, and the Code of Conduct for International Red Cross and Red Crescent Movement (Sandvik 2019, p. 2). The Humanitarian Accountability Project was established in 2000, with the aim of piloting an international aid ombudsman (Hilhorst et al. 2018, p. 15).

The issue of child exploitation perpetrated by humanitarian workers first came to global attention in 2002, with the West African 'sex-for-food' scandal. A United Nations High Commissioner for Refugees (UNHCR) and Save the Children report implicated 67 personnel from 42 agencies in Liberia, Sierra Leone and Guinea in the sexual exploitation of refugee children (United Nations High Commissioner for Refugees & Save the Children UK 2002). The revelations precipitated the development of several policies, codes and procedures by the UN and civil society. While not the focus of this article, those key UN developments deserve mention as they have also guided the policies and standards of NGOs. These include the establishment of the Inter-Agency Standing Committee on sexual exploitation and abuse and subsequent guidance for protection from and response to sexual exploitation and abuse (Inter-Agency Standing Committee n.d.), the UN General Assembly resolution on the investigation into sexual exploitation of refugees by aid workers in West Africa (United Nations General Assembly 2003), and the issuance of a global policy in the form of the Secretary-General's Bulletin, Special measures for protection from sexual exploitation and sexual abuse (United Nations Secretariat 2003). Importantly the Bulletin provides that sexual activity with children (persons under the age of 18) is prohibited regardless of the age of majority or age of consent locally, and that mistaken belief in the age of a child is not a defence. The safeguarding policies of many NGOs and bilateral donors mirror these standards.

Around the same time, a coalition of humanitarian and development NGOs in the UK came together to establish the Keeping Children Safe coalition. The first version of the Child Safeguarding Standards was launched in 2002. The standards call for organisations to: (i) develop a policy describing commitment to prevent and respond appropriately to harm to children; (ii) place clear responsibilities and expectations on staff and associates and support them to understand and act in line with these; (iii) create a child-safe environment through implementing child safeguarding procedures across the organisation; and (iv) monitor and review safeguarding measures (Keeping Children Safe 2014, p. 10). Keeping Children Safe has evolved into an independent NGO, which also provides consultancy services to organisations to improve child safeguarding internationally (Keeping Children Safe n.d.).

The protection of beneficiaries (adults and children) from sexual exploitation and abuse was also integrated into the work of the Humanitarian Accountability Project (HAP) and its successor Core Humanitarian Standards Alliance.[2] The Core Humanitarian Standard on Quality and Accountability sets out nine commitments that organisations and individuals involved in humanitarian response can use to improve the quality and effectiveness of the assistance they provide. The Core Humanitarian Guidance Note draws attention to the issue in five of the nine commitments. Commitment 1 (to ensure assistance appropriate to needs) calls for consideration of protection concerns, such as preventing sexual exploitation and violence. Commitment 3 (to ensure no negative impacts) recognises the "high value of aid resources and the powerful position of aid workers" and requires identification and timely action upon unintended negative effects including sexual exploitation and abuse by staff. Commitment 4 (to provide access to information and participation) explains that people may be vulnerable to exploitation and abuse (including sexual abuse) if they do not know their entitlements, the standards of behavior for humanitarian workers, and how to make a complaint. A child safeguarding policy is expressly recommended under Commitment 5 (complaints mechanisms). As part of guidance to monitor organisational responsibilities, Commitment 8 (well-managed staff and volunteers) includes a question on whether all staff and contractors are required to sign a code of conduct that covers the prevention of sexual exploitation and abuse (Core Humanitarian Standard (CHS)).

On a national level in the Global North, NGO umbrella bodies (such as the Australian Council for International Development in Australia, Bond in the UK, and InterAction in the US) championed codes of conduct, and accreditation, risk management and contracting arrangements of some governments were utilised to enforce standards (Humanitarian Advisory Group 2018). The Australian Government was the first bilateral donor to implement child protection standards for staff and funded partners under its Child Protection Policy, introduced in 2008 (AusAID 2013). The mandatory child protection standards follow five key principles: zero tolerance of child exploitation and abuse; recognition of the best interests of the child; sharing responsibility for child protection; procedural fairness; and a risk management approach to reduce the risks of child exploitation and abuse with aid activities.

---

[2]   HAP joined with Sphere and People in Aid to become part of the Joint Standards Initiative. In December 2014, the Core Humanitarian Standard (CHS) was launched in Copenhagen. In 2015, HAP and People in Aid merged to form the CHS Alliance (Hilhorst et al. 2018, p. 15).

The United States Agency for International Development (USAID) also introduced Child Safeguarding Standards to cover "all activities intended to prevent and respond to abuse, exploitation, or neglect by USAID personnel, contractors, and recipients or as a result of USAID-supported programming" (USAID 2015). The standards complement the USAID Counter Trafficking in Persons Code of Conduct. On an organisational level, policies and standards on child protection/safeguarding, gender equality, and codes of conduct were developed and implemented in many aid organisations to varying degrees.

2.2. New and Emerging Initiatives—Post Oxfam, #MeToo and #AidToo

In February 2018, The Times newspaper published a front-page article headlined 'Top Oxfam staff paid Haiti survivors for sex', which alleged that Oxfam covered up claims that senior staff working in Haiti following the 2010 earthquake used prostitutes, some of whom may have been under 18 (BBC 2018). Around the same time, #MeToo and then #AidToo revelations snowballed.[3] These included accounts of rape, assault, and harassment in the workplace that were seen to be badly handled, denied or concealed by NGOs (Parker 2018b). The parameters of safeguarding in the aid sector thus expanded to include workplace relations and harassment within organisations. The rationale was that both were enabled by power imbalances, especially gender inequality (UK Department for International Development 2018b, p. 15).

In March 2018, the UK Parliamentary International Development Committee launched an inquiry on sexual exploitation and abuse in the aid sector (UK Parliament 2018). In its final report, the committee was highly critical of the failure of the international system to tackle these abuses, and accused the sector generally of "complacency, verging on complicity" (House of Commons, International Development Committee 2018, p. 29). The report made a number of recommendations, largely directed at the UK Department for International Development (DFID), including the creation of an international register of aid workers to function "as one barrier to sexual predators seeking to enter the international aid profession", and the establishment of an independent aid ombudsman "to provide a right to appeal, an avenue through which those who have suffered can seek justice by other means"(House of Commons, International Development Committee 2018, pp. 79, 64). The committee encouraged DFID to use a forthcoming 'Safeguarding Summit' to secure commitments from across the sector to move the measures forward.

The Safeguarding Summit, convened by DFID in October 2018, brought together over 500 delegates including government donors (representing 90 percent of global Official Development Assistance), the UN, international financial institutions, UK NGOs, and UK private sector supply partners (Commitments Made by Donors to Tackle Sexual Exploitation and Abuse and Sexual Harassment in the International Aid Sector). The summit faced some controversy and criticism, including the lack of diversity in the speakers and near absence of voices from the Global South (Donovan 2018; Parker 2018b). At the summit, the UK International Development Secretary launched several initiatives including a DFID scheme to work with Interpol to vet aid workers against criminal records, a Misconduct Disclosure Scheme to allow employers to check for previous misconduct linked to sexual abuse and exploitation, and a Humanitarian Passport Scheme to prove an individual's identity and vetting status (UK Department for International Development 2018a).

Promising commitments were made by all constituencies at the conclusion of the summit. This included pledges by NGOs to address organisational culture and improve existing processes for safeguarding (Bond 2019). Perhaps most significant were the commitments made by 22 donors[4]

---

[3]   The #MeToo movement started over a decade ago in the US as a grassroots effort to show support for survivors of sexual violence, particularly young women of colour from low socio-economic backgrounds, and gained near global prominence from 2017 when the #MeToo hashtag went viral. Women in the international aid sector used the hashtag #AidToo to bring attention to sexual violence within the sector (Gillespie et al. 2019).

[4]   Australia, Austria, Belgium (Ministry of Development Cooperation), Canada, Denmark, Finland, France (Ministry for Europe and Foreign Affairs of France), Germany, Iceland, Ireland, Italy, Japan (Ministry of Foreign Affairs of Japan), Luxembourg (Ministry of Foreign and European Affairs), Mexico (AMEXID), the Netherlands (Ministry for Foreign Trade

designed to bring about four "long-term strategic shifts", namely: (i) ensuring support for survivors, victims and whistle-blowers, enhancing accountability and transparency, strengthening reporting and tackling impunity; (ii) incentivising cultural change through strong leadership, organisational accountability and better human resource processes; (iii) agreeing minimum standards and ensuring donors and their partners meet them; and (iv) strengthening organisational capacity and capability across the international aid sector, including building the capability of implementing partners to meet the minimum standards (Commitments Made by Donors to Tackle Sexual Exploitation and Abuse and Sexual Harassment in the International Aid Sector).

Subsequently, 30 members[5] of the Organisation for Economic Cooperation and Development (OECD) adopted the Development Assistance Committee (DAC) Recommendation on Ending Sexual Exploitation, Abuse, and Harassment in Development Co-operation and Humanitarian Assistance in July 2019 (OECD Development Assistance Committee 2019)[6] This is the first international instrument to address sexual exploitation, abuse, and harassment across the sector. The preamble of the DAC Recommendation recognises the Inter-Agency Standing Committee's Principles and Minimum Operating Standards on Prevention of Sexual Exploitation and Abuse and the Core Humanitarian Standard on Quality and Accountability as essential international standards. The rights and needs of children come out expressly in the preamble of the DAC Recommendation, with the recognition "that child survivors require particular attention to ensure their safety, protection, and well-being". Paragraph 2(d) of the DAC Recommendation also calls for the strengthening of "existing local services and networks and coordination with gender-based violence and child-protection services".

The Dutch Ministry of Foreign Affairs took forward a scoping study to assess whether there is a need for an aid ombudsman and, if so, how it might function and fit with existing governance mechanisms in the sector. The study, published in September 2018, found strong consensus on the need for an ombudsman mechanism in the sector to provide independent recourse for complainants (Hilhorst et al. 2018). While the ombudsman concept has reportedly since been abandoned by the UK Government (Edwards 2019), other initiatives have progressed. For example, the Misconduct Disclosure Scheme to check for previous misconduct linked to sexual exploitation, abuse or harassment is operating. As of October 2019, 10 people have reportedly been prevented from being re-hired (UK Department for International Development 2019, p. 4), and 15 organisations are using the scheme (Steering Committee for Humanitarian Response, *Misconduct Disclosure Scheme*). Some donors are also working with the Core Humanitarian Standards Alliance and Humanitarian Quality Assurance Initiative to strengthen verification options for CHS quality assurance and to develop models that better reflect the needs of organisations (UK Department for International Development 2019, p. 13).

3. International and Regional Child Rights Frameworks to Guide Safeguarding

There are clear intersections between violence against women and violence against children and strong arguments for improved convergence in programming (Guedes et al. 2016). However, there is also a need for a dedicated discussion on the specific rights and needs of children, which has been somewhat diluted in some policy arenas. While the Convention on the Rights of the Child (CRC) is referred to cursorily in the safeguarding discussion as a reference point for guidance and

---

and Development Cooperation), New Zealand (Ministry of Foreign Affairs and Trade), Norway, Spain, Sweden, Switzerland, United Kingdom (including the Scottish Government), and the United States of America (U.S Agency for International Development).

[5] Australia, Austria, Belgium, Canada, Czech Republic, Denmark, Finland, France, Germany, Greece, Hungary, Iceland, Ireland, Italy, Japan, Korea, Luxembourg, Netherlands, New Zealand, Norway, Poland, Portugal, Slovak Republic, Slovenia, Spain, Sweden, Switzerland, United Kingdom, United States and the European Union.

[6] The Recommendation encompasses six pillars: (i) policies, professional conduct standards, organisational change and leadership; (ii) survivor/victim-centred response and support mechanisms; (iii) organisational reporting, response systems and procedures; (iv) training, awareness raising and communication; (v) international coordination; and (vi) monitoring, evaluation, shared learning and reporting.

minimum standards, mentions are largely aspirational and transitory. This section explores how child rights standards and existing monitoring mechanisms for human rights law could support a more sustainable and consistent effort to ensure children's protection in the context of humanitarian and development activity.

3.1. Relevant Treaties and Articles for Safeguarding Children

The CRC is the primary instrument relating to children's right to protection from violence.[7] In the regional context, the African Charter on the Rights and Welfare of the Child (ACRWC) has comparative articles setting out children's rights to protection. The focus on children's rights is important in framing the response to the issue and rejects approaches where children are characterised only as "objects in need of assistance rather than as subjects with rights" (Tobin and Seow 2019, p. 1312). The child rights approach also recognizes that children are human beings in their own right and not 'adults in waiting'.[8]

The monitoring of State party compliance with obligations under the CRC involves external oversight by the Committee on the Rights of the Child (the CRC Committee). African states are also subject to oversight by the African Committee of Experts on the Rights and Welfare of the Child (the African Committee) with regards to compliance with the ACRWC. State parties are required to report periodically to the Committees and Committees thereafter issue Concluding Observations and Recommendations. Although these observations and recommendations impose no legal obligation, they are often an agenda for action and have had an "intensifying or catalyst effect" to support political and legal processes in countries (Sloth-Nielsen 2018, pp. 14–16).

While safeguarding discourse in certain policy arenas has focused on sexual exploitation and abuse, an especially egregious violation of children's rights, a rights-based approach should consider the various intersections between humanitarian and development activity and children's treaty-based rights. This should encompass all risks and harms. By way of example, the 2002 UNHCR and Save the Children report also highlighted other forms of exploitation such as child labour. An adolescent boy in Sierra Leonne is quoted as saying: "I have no father and no mother and there are jobs that I am being made to do like washing underpants in exchange for food which I do because I have no parents. I wish I had my parents because I do not have any support and I am exposed to so much abuse" (United Nations High Commissioner for Refugees & Save the Children UK 2002, p. 43). Issues of safeguarding would fall primarily under the CRC theme (or 'cluster') related to violence against children.[9] The CRC Committee (United Nations Committee on the Rights of the Child 2015, para. 30) explains that this cluster includes abuse and neglect (Article 19),[10] measures to prohibit and eliminate all forms of harmful practices, including, but not limited to, female genital mutilation and early and forced marriages (Article 24), sexual exploitation and sexual abuse (Article 34),[11] the right not to be subjected to torture or other cruel, inhuman, or degrading treatment or punishment, including corporal punishment (Articles 37 (a) and 28), measures to promote the physical and psychological recovery and social reintegration of child victims (Article 39), and the availability of helplines for children. Other forms of exploitation, including child labour, are to be reported under the special protection measures

---

[7] Other international instruments include the Protocol to Prevent, Suppress and Punish Human Trafficking in Persons, especially Women and Children, supplementing the Convention against Transnational Organised Crime, the Convention concerning the Prohibition and Immediate Action for the Elimination of the Worst Forms of Child Labour and the Optional Protocol to the Convention on the Rights of the Child on the Sale of Children, Child Prostitution and Child Pornography. The relationship between the instruments should be understood as complementary (Tobin and Seow 2019, p. 1314).

[8] The authors are grateful to an anonymous reviewer for emphasizing this point.

[9] In 2015, the Committee on the Rights of the Child revised the guidelines for periodic reports to reflect the new cluster on violence against children and to update references to general comments (United Nations Committee on the Rights of the Child 2015).

[10] Article 19 is regarded as "the core provision for discussions and strategies to address and eliminate all forms of violence in the context of the Convention more broadly" ((United Nations Committee on the Rights of the Child 2011, para. 7(a))).

[11] In contrast to Article 19, Article 34 imposts a blanket obligation on states to protect children from sexual abuse and exploitation irrespective of whether they are in the care of their parents (Tobin and Seow 2019, p. 1312).

cluster (United Nations Committee on the Rights of the Child 2015, para. 40). The relevant articles in the ACRWC include Articles 14 (child labour), 16 (child abuse and torture), 21 (harmful social and cultural practices), 22 (armed conflicts) and 27 (sexual exploitation) in particular. In its General Comment No. 5 on State Party Obligations under the African Charter on the Rights and Welfare of the Child (Article 1) and Systems Strengthening for Child Protection, the African Committee elaborates on the measures required to improve implementation of the ACRWC and in particular calls for States to States "to adopt a holistic approach" to realise children's right to survival, development and protection provided by Article 5 of the ACRWC. The African Committee explains that this is enabled by adopting a systems-strengthening approach to child protection (African Committee of Experts on the Rights and Welfare of the Child 2018, p. 12). A systems-strengthening approach would include both formal and informal local contexts around the child (African Committee of Experts on the Rights and Welfare of the Child 2018, p. 33).

3.2. Domestic Implementation and the Role of the International Community

The observations of the CRC Committee are useful to articulate the respective responsibilities of developing vis-à-vis donor countries. The CRC Committee is cognisant of the different starting points of State parties in implementing the CRC and obligations relating to protection of children from violence. The CRC Committee acknowledges that protecting children from all forms of violence is highly challenging in most countries and that States parties are designing and implementing measures from "very different starting points" with respect to existing legal, institutional and service infrastructures, cultural customs and professional competencies, and levels of resources (United Nations Committee on the Rights of the Child 2011, para. 70).

While recognising different starting points, the CRC Committee highlights that the right to protection from all forms of violence outlined in Article 19 is a civil right and freedom. As such, in applying Article 4 of the CRC (taking all appropriate legislative, administrative, and other measures for the implementation of the rights), implementation of Article 19 is "an immediate and unqualified obligation" of States parties (United Nations Committee on the Rights of the Child 2011, para. 65). This means that in spite of economic circumstances, States are required to undertake all possible measures towards the realisation of children's rights, paying special attention to the most disadvantaged and using available resources "to the maximum extent" (United Nations Committee on the Rights of the Child 2011, para. 65). The African Committee likewise emphasises that "whatever their economic circumstances, States Parties are required to undertake all possible positive measures towards the realisation of the rights of the child" and to pay "special attention to the most disadvantaged and marginalised groups" (African Committee of Experts on the Rights and Welfare of the Child 2018, p. 6). On child protection specifically, the African Committee notes "State Party spending on child protection and systems strengthening is far too low, and lacks visibility in government budgets" (African Committee of Experts on the Rights and Welfare of the Child 2018, p. 36).

The CRC Committee is explicit that "resource constraints cannot provide a justification for a State party's failure to take any, or enough, of the measures that are required for child protection" taking into consideration State parties' obligations under Articles 4 and 19 (United Nations Committee on the Rights of the Child 2011, para. 73). While acknowledging fiscal realities in Africa, the African Committee states that the ACRWC standards "were set intentionally" and "do not allow states parties to claim that they do not have any resources for the implementation of social and economic goods for the fulfilment of children's rights" (African Committee of Experts on the Rights and Welfare of the Child 2018, p. 7). Furthermore, the African Committee explains it will "scrutinise diligently claims that non-fulfilment of rights is linked to non-availability of resources" and expects that States parties show "rapid forward progress in extending the reach and impact" of measures to realise children's rights (African Committee of Experts on the Rights and Welfare of the Child 2018, pp. 8–9).

The CRC Committee urges States "to adopt comprehensive, strategic and time-bound coordinating frameworks for child caregiving and protection" (United Nations Committee on the Rights of the Child

2011, para. 73). Similarly, the African Committee calls for "a national policy for children that provides a common, unifying, comprehensive and rights-based framework of action for all role-players", which is costed, has measurable targets and budget allocations (African Committee of Experts on the Rights and Welfare of the Child 2018, p. 35). It is within such frameworks that responsibilities of NGOs in contact with children can be embedded.

In view of "different starting points", and on the understanding that budgets on national and decentralised levels should be the primary source of funds for child protection, the CRC Committee has drawn the attention of States parties to the avenues of international cooperation and assistance outlined in Articles 4 and 45 of the CRC (United Nations Committee on the Rights of the Child 2011, para. 74). The CRC Committee states that implementation of the CRC is "a cooperative exercise for the States of the world" and that the CRC "should form the framework for international development assistance related directly or indirectly to children and that programmes of donor States should be rights-based" (United Nations Committee on the Rights of the Child 2003, paras. 60, 61). The African Committee also encourages State Parties to ensure children's rights are "deliberately reflected and adequately catered for in all donor aid agreements, including with global finance institutions" (African Committee of Experts on the Rights and Welfare of the Child 2018, p. 41). In General Comment No. 13 (2011) on the right of the child to freedom from all forms of violence, the CRC Committee reiterates that child rights-based protection programmes should be one of the main components in assisting sustainable development in countries receiving international assistance (United Nations Committee on the Rights of the Child 2011, para. 74). This is reflected in part in the DAC Recommendation, in which signatories have expressly acknowledged the importance of strengthening child protection services. While forming part of recommendations by UNHCR and Save the Children (United Nations High Commissioner for Refugees & Save the Children UK 2002) and Csáky (Csáky 2008), this important element has not received significant attention in recent safeguarding discussions.

3.3. *Applicability to Non-State Actors*

At the very least, there are 'indirect' children's rights obligations for non-State actors to comply with children's treaty-based rights. In General Comment No. 5 (2003) on General Measures of Implementation, the CRC Committee emphasises that the legal obligation of State parties "to respect and ensure the rights of children as stipulated in the Convention" includes the "obligation to ensure that non-State service providers operate in accordance with its provisions, thus creating indirect obligations on such actors" (United Nations Committee on the Rights of the Child 2003, para. 6).

The CRC Committee further elaborates that child rights responsibilities extend in practice "beyond the State and State-controlled services and institutions to include children, parents and wider families, other adults, and non-State services and organisations" (United Nations Committee on the Rights of the Child 2003, para. 56). The CRC Committee has taken a broad view of NGOs constituting, for example, human rights NGOs, child- and youth-led organisations and youth groups, parent and family groups, faith groups, academic institutions and professional associations (United Nations Committee on the Rights of the Child 2003, para. 58). This broad view is particularly relevant in the African context where most services to children are delivered by civil society organisations (CSOs). These can include NGOs, faith-based organisations, volunteer networks, social enterprises, or philanthropic projects connected to for-profit companies (Parker 2018a, p. 2). Organisations that encounter children are not only those that provide social services such as education, health, nutrition, recreation, alternative care, and protection but also other services, including water and sanitation, infrastructure, as well as humanitarian relief.

The CRC Committee has also expressed its agreement with the Committee on Economic, Social and Cultural Rights in its General Comment No. 14 (2000) of the right to the highest attainable standard of health. Paragraph 42 of the General Comment reiterates that as parties to the Covenant, States are "ultimately accountable for compliance with it" but responsibilities for realisation of the right to health fall to all members of society, including health professionals, families, local communities, intergovernmental and NGOs, CSOs, and the private business sector. States parties are therefore called to "provide an environment which facilitates the discharge of these responsibilities" (United Nations Committee on the Rights of the Child 2003, para. 56).

3.4. Best Interests of the Child

The best interests' principle is fundamental and especially relevant for child safeguarding in the aid sector. Article 3(1) of the CRC provides that the best interests of the child shall be a primary consideration in "all actions concerning children, whether undertaken by public or private social welfare institutions, courts of law, administrative authorities or legislative bodies." Importantly, the CRC Committee elaborates that "public or private social welfare institutions" should not be narrowly construed or limited to strictly social institutions but would apply to "all institutions whose work and decisions impact on children and the realisation of their rights" (United Nations Committee on the Rights of the Child 2013, para. 26).

The CRC Committee notes these would be bodies "not only those related to economic, social and cultural rights (e.g., care, health, environment, education, business, leisure and play, etc.), but also institutions dealing with civil rights and freedoms (e.g., birth registration, protection against violence in all settings, etc.)" (United Nations Committee on the Rights of the Child 2013, para. 26). Private bodies include "either for-profit or non-profit—which play a role in the provision of services that are critical to children's enjoyment of their rights, and which act on behalf of or alongside Government services as an alternative" (United Nations Committee on the Rights of the Child 2013, para. 26). This extension of this obligation to *private* social welfare organisations is quite unusual in an international treaty (Eekelaar and John 2019, p. 80).

The CRC Committee explains that Article 3 has implications for all implementation measures taken by governments, individual decisions made by judicial or administrative authorities or public entities through their agents, decisions made by civil society entities and the private sector, including profit and non-profit organisations, which provide services concerning or impacting on children, and guidelines for actions undertaken by persons working with and for children, including parents and caregivers (United Nations Committee on the Rights of the Child 2013, pt. II). The best interests' principle should therefore be the primary consideration in all actions concerning children undertaken by humanitarian and development organisations. Guidance from the African Committee reinforces the broad application of the best interests' principle. In its General Comment No. 5 on State Party Obligations under the African Charter on the Rights and Welfare of the Child (Article 1) and Systems Strengthening for Child Protection, the African Committee states that Article 4(1) of the ACRWC provides that the best interests of the child shall be the primary consideration and this applies to both private and public institutions (African Committee of Experts on the Rights and Welfare of the Child 2018, p. 11). The African Committee explains it is therefore "the responsibility of the State Party to ensure to the maximum extent possible that private actors, including . . . various non-state actors engaged with children's rights and services, are aware of and apply the best interests of the child in all of their endeavours" (African Committee of Experts on the Rights and Welfare of the Child 2018, p. 11).

Furthermore, Article 3(3) of the CRC provides: "State Parties shall ensure that the institutions, services and facilities responsible for the care or protection of children shall conform with the standards established by competent authorities, particularly in the areas of safety, health, in the number and suitability of their staff, as well as competent supervision." While some doubt was expressed as to the appropriateness of this provision, the legislative history suggests the rationale was to apply the best interests' principle to the very specific area of institutional care and service provision (Office of the United Nations & High Commissioner for Human Rights 2007, pp. 347–48). The application in alternative care settings is also explicit in the commentary of the African Committee (African Committee of Experts on the Rights and Welfare of the Child 2018, p. 12).

There has been little exploration of this article, yet it is highly relevant to safeguarding discourse. In Africa, most institutional care is provided by NGOs and faith-based organisations, many of which are funded by faith communities or individual donors from the Global North, and which often fail to register or comply with relevant government regulations (see for example Munthali 2019, p. 13). In its General Comment No. 5 (2003) on General Measures of Implementation, the CRC Committee emphasises that "enabling the private sector to provide services, run institutions and so on does not in any way lessen the State's obligation to ensure for all children within its jurisdiction the full recognition and realisation of all rights in the Convention." In relation to Article 3 (3), the CRC Committee explains that rigorous inspection is required to ensure compliance and proposes "a permanent monitoring mechanism or process aimed at ensuring that all State and non-State service providers respect the Convention" (United Nations Committee on the Rights of the Child 2003, para. 27).

3.5. Intra-Organisational Processes and Codes of Conduct

In General Comment No. 13 (2011) on the right of the child to freedom from all forms of violence, the CRC Committee explains that administrative measures under Article 19 of the CRC "should reflect governmental obligations to establish policies, programmes, monitoring and oversight systems required to protect the child from all forms of violence" ((United Nations Committee on the Rights of the Child 2011, para. 42(b))). These include the development and implementation "through participatory processes which encourage ownership and sustainability" of intra- and inter-agency child protection policies and professional ethics codes, protocols, memoranda of understanding and standards of care for all childcare services and settings, for all levels of government and civil society institutions. Settings include daycare centres, schools, hospitals, sport clubs and residential institutions ((United Nations Committee on the Rights of the Child 2011, para. 42(b))). The implementation by government and civil society of rights-based child protection policies and procedures and professional ethics codes and standards of care are also mentioned by the CRC Committee in relation to 'prevention measures' (United Nations Committee on the Rights of the Child 2011, para. 47).

The emphasis on ownership and sustainability is important, otherwise there is a risk that the endeavour becomes a 'tick-box' exercise. In other words, if the codes and policies are to impact positively on children's protection, the process will require more than preparing paperwork that is filed and forgotten. There is a need for meaningful consultation among stakeholders, including children and young people themselves, and consideration of how international and regional standards can be implemented in a local context, in the best interests of the child. The values and behaviours elaborated within codes and policies must be owned and championed by organisational leaders and staff, and safeguarding policies and practice continually monitored, assessed and adapted. Pressure to produce a checklist of policies and procedures driven by a compliance imperative is unlikely to lead to change that improves children's protection.

The African Committee has echoed the importance of policies and personnel of NGOs in its recent General Comment No. 5 on State Party Obligations under the African Charter on the Rights and Welfare of the Child (Article 1) and Systems Strengthening for Child Protection. The African Committee requires civil society organisations and international organisations working with children to adopt child safeguarding policies. Furthermore, the Committee suggests persons who have abused children should not be able to work with children, even as volunteers. Importantly, especially for the African context where NGO–government relationships in some countries are "characterised by a large amount of distrust, cooptation, and outright repression"(Gugerty 2010, p. 1090), the African Committee urges "State Parties to review the legislation governing the registration and operation of CSOs to ensure that it does not provide any impediment to their optimal functioning"(African Committee of Experts on the Rights and Welfare of the Child 2018). While there are different legal frameworks and self-regulatory mechanisms for NGOs across the continent (Gugerty 2010), child protection and safeguarding measures are not yet incorporated. Both the CRC and African Committees could raise questions on such standards in its list of issues for State party reports as part of their external oversight role.

4. Key Dilemmas and Challenges for Child Safeguarding

This final section sets out key areas for further consideration and critical debate by practitioners and policymakers in the effort to safeguard children from harm in the context of humanitarian and development activity. Recent developments and commitments are significant and promising. However, to harness the current momentum and ensure initiatives in the Global North positively impact children's safety in the least developed countries, there is arguably scope for a more nuanced and contextualised approach, guided by children's treaty-based rights and the best interests' principle.

Current sectoral efforts appear to largely focus on international NGOs with headquarters in the Global North and the risk of a 'Western' offender harming children in the world's poorest countries. This does not reflect the variety of organisations inhabiting the aid space and in contact with children. The focus on 'Western' staff is arguably disproportionate given that local staff make up the majority of the workforce in the developing world and both local and 'foreign' staff (of all levels) have been implicated in cases of child abuse (Csáky 2008, p. 9). This reality suggests that high-profile initiatives such as the global criminal records register may have a limited impact on the protection of children in the developing world. Firstly, a global criminal records register assumes that the person has already come to the attention of police and justice systems. It is well evidenced that "much abusive behaviour has historically gone unreported" and the majority of "perpetrators detected do not have prior convictions for any form of child maltreatment" (Tilbury 2014, p. 92). Secondly, the register assumes that there are functioning information management systems in the countries in which personnel have resided in order to be able to feed into the global database. This is not the case in most developing countries in Africa.

By way of example, even in one of the most developed countries on the continent, South Africa, implementing a scheme to identify persons unsuitable to work with children has proved largely unsuccessful. South Africa's Children's Act (Act No. 38 of 2005) mandates the Department of Social Development to keep and maintain a Child Protection Register (section 111), which consists of two parts. Part A records all reports of abuse or deliberate neglect of a child and Part B lists persons declared unsuitable to work with children. The Act requires all organisations to assess and verify the suitability of employees and potential employees who will "work with or have access to children" (section 126). As of March 2019, the register has 509 names of persons declared unsuitable to work with children and the department has only received 140,029 suitability check enquiries from employers and individuals. With over 10 million people in South Africa employed in the formal non-agricultural sector (Department of Statistics, South Africa 2019), the small number of suitability checks makes it clear that the register is not functioning optimally. Among other challenges, the register is constrained in that it does not align with the National Register for Sexual Offenders, resulting in critical omissions in the list of crimes that warrant inclusion on the register, such as attempted rape (KPMG 2016, pp. 42–43).

Even high-income countries with functional and routine criminal records checks for determining suitability of working with children are increasingly cognisant of their limitations. In Australia, for example, some commentators suggest the scope of screening regimes risk being "too big and too expensive to be sensible" (Tilbury 2014, p. 92). At worst, an overreliance on such mechanisms can be detrimental to children's safety. The Royal Commission into Institutional Responses to Child Sexual Abuse in Australia—one of the most probing government inquiries to have taken place—found that Australia's Working with Children Checks can provide a "false sense of comfort to parents and communities and may cause organisations to become complacent" due to the mistaken belief that people who have undergone these checks do not pose any risks to children (Australia & Royal Commission into Institutional Responses to Child Sexual Abuse 2015, p. 3).

Screening is only one in a range of strategies needed to make organisations child safe. Rather than a sole focus on trying to identify individuals and prevent them entering organisations, lessons from other jurisdictions emphasise to the need "to modify environments, thereby reducing the likelihood that anyone could engage in abusive behaviour" (Higgins et al. 2016, pp. 54–55). There should also be attention on the structures and opportunities within the sector that enable abuse to occur. Lessons may be drawn from the large body of literature about the role of institutions (both government and non-government) with responsibility for children in preventing and responding to child sexual abuse. The UK Independent Inquiry into Child Sexual Abuse, for example, commissioned a Rapid Evidence Assessment and identified structural and organisational factors shown to facilitate child sexual abuse (Radford et al. 2016). These included privacy and the offender being alone with the child, persons in positions of trust having little supervision or monitoring, lack of safeguarding policies, failure to report or to sanction offenders, a culture where abuse is normalised, hierarchical organisations where it is difficult for junior staff to complain, lack of an adequate complaints system, and a lack of safe space for children who are victimised to tell anyone about the abuse, and to have complaints acted on appropriately (Radford et al. 2016, p. 17). This highlights the limitations of 'tick-box' exercises focused on paperwork and calls for a localised and thorough assessment of how NGOs in the developing world interact with children and what risks these interactions present.

On a larger scale, this also requires the sector to grapple with the inequitable power relations that characterise their interactions with communities and children. In the 2008 Humanitarian Accountability Partnership report of consultations with aid beneficiaries on their perceptions of efforts to prevent and respond to sexual exploitation and abuse, Lattu (Lattu 2008, p. 52) concluded that the single most important reason for the "humanitarian accountability deficit" is the uneven relationship between agencies delivering aid and users of humanitarian assistance which puts the users "at a structural disadvantage in their relationship with humanitarian aid providers." This inequitable relationship is echoed in the voices of children, captured in empirical evidence on the subject. For example, an adolescent girl in Liberia is quoted as saying: "These NGO workers they are clever they use the ration as bait to get you to have sex with them" (United Nations High Commissioner for Refugees & Save the Children UK 2002, p. 44). Similarly, the following quote from an adolescent girl in Cote d'Ivoire, "He's using the girl but without him she won't be able to eat", and an adolescent boy in South Sudan, "People don't report it because they are worried that the agency will stop working here, and we need them" (Csáky 2008, p. 7). This observation is not new, nor limited to children, but it is one that has arguably not yet been adequately addressed. It calls for transformative change in the sector. There are indications of some organisations starting to contend with these entrenched power dynamics.

In addition to inequitable power relations, safeguarding efforts need to pay greater attention to longstanding attitudes and beliefs on child abuse and appropriate responses to it. These social and cultural norms form part of the "very different starting points" in the implementation of children's rights as highlighted by the CRC Committee (United Nations Committee on the Rights of the Child 2011, para. 70). Social and cultural norms relating to children and child abuse may be either protective of children or enhance their vulnerability. These norms need to be considered in safeguarding efforts as they are both risk factors and barriers to help seeking. While not representative across the continent or within countries, the following harmful norms have been identified in the literature: gender norms and gender socialisation including about social roles or expectations that differentiate males and females and place children at increased risk of sexual abuse (Gwirayi 2010; Plummer and Njuguna 2009); patriarchy including male dominance or perceived superiority that can perpetuate abuse, male violence and traditional notions of masculinity and normalisation of inter-personal violence (Gwirayi 2010; Lalor 2004; Petersen et al. 2005; Plummer and Njuguna 2009); a 'culture of silence' relating to sexual matters and discouraging speaking up about sexual violence (Plummer and Njuguna 2009); and sexual norms including sexual initiation rites or harmful practices including female genital mutilation and child marriage (Plummer and Njuguna 2009), and the myth of sexual intercourse with a young child to 'cure' sexually transmitted diseases including HIV/AIDs (Lalor 2004). Many of these norms intersect with norms that enable violence against women but there are also distinct norms relating to children including their low status and socialisation for obedience and acquiescence (Lalor 2004; Plummer and Njuguna 2009). By way of example, the following quote from a South Sudanese girl is illustrative of various attitudes and practices at play that contribute to individual and community responses to abuse: "The father would try to persuade the man to take the girl as a bride and to pay cattle for her.

He would not ask the girl whether she wants this. So really the girl gets no advantage from telling anyone about the abuse" (Csáky 2008, p. 17). Norms on masculinity also contribute to low disclosure rates by boys that experience sexual abuse (Guedes et al. 2016, p. 6). Importantly, those beliefs and norms found on the community level also manifest amongst the local staff of aid organisations as well as the staff and volunteers of their implementing partners (Sloth-Nielsen 2014, p. 957). Additionally, they will be found amongst duty bearers or service providers that will be called upon to respond when allegations of child abuse emerge and are reported.

Closely linked to this point, in most of Africa's least developed countries, the institutional dimensions to address child abuse (such as infrastructure in law enforcement, judiciary, health and social welfare) are constrained. Victim and witness protections are weak and reporting to formal services may put children and communities at further risk. This raises potential ethical dilemmas for reporting abuse. Walker-Simpson argues that "the very act of reporting abuse may actually expose the child to additional risk" in contravention to the 'do no harm' principle (Walker-Simpson 2017, p. 258). Informal community practices are often the prevailing system employed for dealing with child abuse. While these may not always seem to provide adequate protection when "judged through a Western lens", they are "often considered the least stigmatising, most accessible, and most helpful of interventions by communities" (Krueger et al. 2015, p. 22). This highlights the criticality of meaningful consultation and addressing the attitudes and expectations of local people, otherwise "no matter how strong an NGO's internal safeguards, if children and their caregivers are unwilling or unable to report abuse, protection procedures will remain 'fatally flawed'" (Walker-Simpson 2017, p. 259).

The push to establish complaints mechanisms for specific projects or organisations can also be problematic, especially in the absence of a functioning system at local or national level. Parallel systems risk creating perverse situations, where there is a system in place to refer, investigate, report, and act upon cases of violence *only* if it is perpetrated by an aid worker. Violence against children in the context of aid cannot be detached from child protection generally, just as sexual exploitation and abuse by aid workers cannot be detached from gender-based violence generally (Stern 2018). There is a need to "move away from programming silos focussed on perpetrators and their acts", and instead focus "on victims and their harm" (Stern 2018). There is some parallel to efforts to disrupt child sexual abuse and exploitation in the context of tourism, especially in South East Asia, where international advocacy and programmes focused more on the foreign sex offender and less on the underlying and interlinked factors contributing to children's vulnerability (Kaviani Johnson 2014). Similarly, research shows that those children vulnerable to abuse by aid workers are "already vulnerable children" including orphans, children with disabilities, children separated from their parents, children from especially poor families, children who are discriminated and marginalised, children displaced from their home communities, migrant, refugee and asylum-seeking children, and children from families who depend on humanitarian assistance (Csáky 2008, p. 7). The African Committee calls for a systems-strengthening approach to child protection and explains that an issues-based approach has, in the past, "resulted in a fragmented child protection response, marked by numerous inefficiencies and pockets of unmet need" (African Committee of Experts on the Rights and Welfare of the Child 2018, p. 33). It follows that investment in child protection systems strengthening is strongly interlinked with the responsibility of delivering aid in a way that does no harm and would sustain efforts to ensure protection of children in the developing world.

Finally, there are new challenges for children's rights, which arise from development and humanitarian activity in the digital era. The Committee on the Rights of the Child is currently drafting a General Comment on children's rights in relation to the digital environment. One group of rights to be realised in a digital world is the protection of privacy, identity and data processing. This is highly relevant for aid organisations in the developing world. The aid sector uses mobile telecommunications, messaging apps and social media to coordinate their work, communicate with staff and volunteers, and engage with the people they serve ((International Committee of the Red Cross ICRC, p. 11)). Many African countries are also seen as a "testing ground" for technologies produced elsewhere and, as a consequence, the personal data of people on the continent, including children, are increasingly stored in hundreds of databases (Privacy International 2020). This is especially relevant with current digital health surveillance in the response to COVID-19. The way in which data, including children's data, is collected and is used is changing quickly and the ongoing accumulation of data about children throughout their lifetime can create a variety of unforeseen risks and challenges (Viola de Azevedo Cunha 2017). Some children, for example, refugee children, may be particularly vulnerable to invasions of privacy in the form of data surveillance as well as dangers resulting from data-leaks or misuses (Peace Research Institute Oslo 2018). This is an area for further examination and focus for the sector.

5. Conclusions

The increased attention and strong consensus and commitment to address sexual exploitation and abuse in the aid sector is commendable. The suite of standards may coordinate and socialise NGOs in advancing child safeguarding and reducing organisational risk, especially for those NGOs with headquarters—or funded by donors—in the Global North. This is an important endeavor given the fact that, in many of the world's least developed countries, non-State actors deliver the majority of services to children and thus have an important role to play in contributing towards their protection. Furthermore, as discussed, non-State actors have—at the very least—'indirect' obligations to comply with children's treaty-based rights. Going forward, it is suggested that the safeguarding discourse applies a child rights-based approach and considers the various intersections between humanitarian and development activity and children's treaty-based rights. This should encompass all risks and harms, including those emerging in the digital age. Furthermore, given the strong links and dependency between intra-organisational efforts and national systems, there is a need to go beyond intra-organisational policies and self-regulation. NGOs and governments must be jointly and severally responsible for child safeguarding. In the case of national governments, progressive improvement of child protection standards and oversight of non-State actors working with children is required. To do this, national and international investment is needed for strengthening child protection systems on national and local levels in the developing world. To be sustainable and contribute to meaningful change for children, efforts cannot be driven by the latest scandal, but must be motivated by a genuine commitment to children's treaty-based rights. With less than ten years to achieve Agenda 2030 and at a time where the world is battling COVID-19, which rapidly risks becoming a child rights crisis (UNICEF 2020; United Nations Committee on the Rights of the Child 2020), this is more important than ever before.

Author Contributions: A.K.J. drafted the article with conceptual inputs and supervision from J.S.-N. Editing was shared. All authors have read and agreed to the published version of the manuscript.

Funding: This research received no external funding.

Acknowledgments: The authors thank two anonymous reviewers for critically reading the manuscript and providing helpful comments.

Conflicts of Interest: The authors declare no conflict of interest.

References

African Committee of Experts on the Rights and Welfare of the Child. 2018. General Comment No 5 on "State Party Obligations under the African Charter on the Rights and Welfare of the Child (Article 1) and Systems Strengthening for Child Protection.". Available online: https://www.acerwc.africa/wp-content/uploads/2019/09/ACERWC%20General%20Comment%20on%20General%20Measures%20of%20Implementation%20African%20Children\T1\textquoterights%20Charter.pdf (accessed on 16 February 2020).

AusAID. 2013. Child Protection Policy—January 2013—World. ReliefWeb. February 8. Available online: https://reliefweb.int/report/world/child-protection-policy-january-2013 (accessed on 3 March 2020).

Australia & Royal Commission into Institutional Responses to Child Sexual Abuse. 2015. Working with Children Checks Report. Royal Commission into Institutional Responses to Child Sexual Abuse. Available online: http://www.childabuseroyalcommission.gov.au/policy-and-research/working-with-children-checks/working-with-children-checks-report (accessed on 3 March 2020).

BBC. 2018. How the Oxfam Scandal Unfolded. *BBC News.* February 21. Available online: https://www.bbc.com/news/uk-43112200 (accessed on 28 March 2020).

Bond. 2019. Our Commitment to Change in Safeguarding. Available online: https://assets.publishing.service.gov.uk/government/uploads/system/uploads/attachment_data/file/851112/bond-safeguarding-commitments-nov2019.pdf (accessed on 5 March 2020).

Charity Commission for England and Wales. 2019. Inquiry Report, Summary Findings and Conclusions. Available online: https://assets.publishing.service.gov.uk/government/uploads/system/uploads/attachment_data/file/807943/Inquiry_Report_summary_findings_and_conclusions_Oxfam.pdf (accessed on 5 March 2020).

Commitments Made by Donors to Tackle Sexual Exploitation and Abuse and Sexual Harassment in the International Aid Sector. 2018. Available online: https://assets.publishing.service.gov.uk/government/uploads/system/uploads/attachment_data/file/749632/donor-commitments1.pdf (accessed on 15 March 2020).

Core Humanitarian Standard (CHS) Alliance, The Sphere Project, and Groupe URD. 2015. Core Humanitarian Standard Guidance Notes and Indicators. Available online: https://corehumanitarianstandard.org/files/files/CHS_guidance_notes.pdf (accessed on 15 February 2020).

Csáky, Corrina. 2008. *No One to Turn to: The Under-Reporting of Child Sexual Exploitation and Abuse by Aid Workers and Peacekeepers.* London: Save the Children.

Department of Statistics, South Africa. 2019. December 12. 28 000 Jobs Lost in SA Formal Sector Third Quarter of 2019|Statistics South Africa. Statistics South Africa. Available online: http://www.statssa.gov.za/?p=12842 (accessed on 30 March 2020).

Donovan, Paula. 2018. Open Letter to the Rt Hon Penny Mordaunt, MP. October 17. Available online: https://static1.squarespace.com/static/514a0127e4b04d7440e8045d/t/5bc777b99140b756d661e476/1539798969879/2018-10-17%2C+Letter+to+Minister+Mordaunt.pdf (accessed on 14 March 2020).

Edwards, Sophie. 2019. *DFID Gives up on Idea for an International Safeguarding Ombudsman;* Washington: Devex, October 23. Available online: https://www.devex.com/news/dfid-gives-up-on-idea-for-an-international-safeguarding-ombudsman-95886 (accessed on 18 January 2020).

Eekelaar, John, and Tobin John. 2019. Article 3. The Best Interests of the Child. In *The UN Convention on the Rights of the Child: A Commentary.* Oxford: Oxford University Press, pp. 73–107.

Gillespie, Elizabeth, Mirabella Roseanne, and Eikenberry Angela. 2019. #Metoo/#Aidtoo and Creating an Intersectional Feminist NPO/NGO Sector. *Nonprofit Policy Forum* 10. [CrossRef]

Guedes, Alessandra, Sarah Bott, Claudia Garcia-Moreno, and Manuela Colombini. 2016. Bridging the gaps: A global review of intersections of violence against women and violence against children. *Global Health Action* 9: 31516. [CrossRef] [PubMed]

Gugerty, Mary Kay. 2010. The Emergence of Nonprofit Self-Regulation in Africa. *Nonprofit and Voluntary Sector Quarterly* 39: 1087–112. [CrossRef]

Gwirayi, Pesanayi. 2010. The Role of Macro-Systemic Contexts in Understanding the Aetiology and Epidemiology of Child Sexual Abuse in Southern Africa. *Journal of Sustainable Development in Africa* 12: 253–68.

Higgins, Daryl J., Keith Kaufman, and Marcus Erooga. 2016. How can child welfare and youth-serving organisations keep children safe? *Developing Practice* 44: 48.

Hilhorst, Dorothea, Naik Asmita, and Cunningham Andrew. 2018. *International Ombuds for Humanitarian and Development Aid Scoping Study.* The Hague: Netherlands Ministry of Foreign Affairs/Erasmus University—International Institute of Social Studies.

HM Government. 2018. Working Together to Safeguard Children: Statutory Framework: Legislation Relevant to Safeguarding and Promoting the Welfare of Children. p. 13. Available online: https://assets.publishing.service.gov.uk/government/uploads/system/uploads/attachment_data/file/722307/Working_Together_to_Safeguard_Children_Statutory_framework.pdf (accessed on 12 February 2020).

House of Commons, International Development Committee. 2018. Sexual Exploitation and Abuse in the Aid Sector. Eighth Report of Session 2017–19. p. 120. Available online: https://publications.parliament.uk/pa/cm201719/cmselect/cmintdev/840/840.pdf (accessed on 15 February 2020).

Humanitarian Advisory Group. 2018. From an Ombudsman to a Humanitarian Passport: How Should We Be Addressing Abuse in the International Aid Sector? Independent Think Piece. Available online: https://humanitarianadvisorygroup.org/wp-content/uploads/2018/05/HAG-Safeguarding-Thinkpiece-May-2018.pdf (accessed on 7 April 2020).

Inter-Agency Standing Committee. n.d. IASC Products on Protection from Sexual Exploitation and Abuse. Inter-Agency Standing Committee. Available online: https://interagencystandingcommittee.org/resources/iasc-products?f%5B0%5D=product_category%3AProtection%20from%20Sexual%20Exploitation%20and%20Abuse (accessed on 10 April 2020).

International Committee of the Red Cross (ICRC) & Privacy International. 2018. The Humanitarian Metadata Problem: "Doing No Harm in the Digital Era.". Available online: https://privacyinternational.org/sites/default/files/2018-12/The%20Humanitarian%20Metadata%20Problem%20-%20Doing%20No%20Harm%20in%20the%20Digital%20Era.pdf (accessed on 14 February 2020).

Kaviani Johnson, Afrooz. 2014. Protecting Children's Rights in Asian Tourism. *The International Journal of Children's Rights* 22: 581–617. [CrossRef]

Keeping Children Safe. 2014. *Child Safeguarding Standards and How to Implement Them.* Available online: https://resourcecentre.savethechildren.net/library/child-safeguarding-standards-and-how-implement-them (accessed on 16 February 2020).

Keeping Children Safe. n.d. Strategic Plan 2019–2022. Available online: https://www.keepingchildrensafe.global/wp/wp-content/uploads/2019/12/Strategy-Report-191018-singles-2.pdf (accessed on 7 April 2020).

KPMG. 2016. *Report on Diagnostic Review of the State Response to Violence against Women and Children*; Pretoria: Department of Planning, Monitoring and Evaluation, Department of Social Development (South Africa). Available online: https://genderjustice.org.za/wp-content/uploads/2017/12/Report-Diagnostic-Review-State-Response-VAWC.pdf (accessed on 8 February 2020).

Krueger, Alexander, Emma de Vise-Lewis, Guy Thompstone, and Vimala Crispin. 2015. Child protection in development: Evidence-based reflections & questions for practitioners. *Child Abuse & Neglect* 50: 15–25. [CrossRef]

Lalor, Kevin. 2004. Child sexual abuse in sub-Saharan Africa: A literature review. *Child Abuse & Neglect* 28: 439–60. [CrossRef]

Lattu, Kirsti. 2008. *To Complain or Not to Complain: Still the Question*; Geneva: Humanitarian Accountability Partnership, p. 62. Available online: http://www.pseataskforce.org/uploads/tools/tocomplainornottocomplainstillthequestion_hapinternational_english.pdf (accessed on 29 March 2020).

Munthali, Alister C. 2019. *Reintegrating Children from Institutional Care: A Feasibility Study on a Model for Malawi*; Lilongwe: Government of Malawi, Ministry of Gender, Children, Disability and Social Welfare, UNICEF. Available online: https://www.unicef.org/malawi/media/1291/file/UNICEF%20Reintegration%20Children%20Feasibility%20Study.pdf (accessed on 6 April 2020).

OECD Development Assistance Committee. 2019. DAC Recommendation on Ending Sexual Exploitation, Abuse, and Harassment in Development Co-Operation and Humanitarian Assistance: Key Pillars of Prevention and Response. Available online: https://legalinstruments.oecd.org/en/instruments/OECD-LEGAL-5020 (accessed on 18 January 2020).

Office of the United Nations & High Commissioner for Human Rights. 2007. *Legislative History of the Convention on the Rights of the Child, Volume 1* (HR/PUB/07/1); New York and Geneva: United Nations. Available online: https://resourcecentre.savethechildren.net/node/8015/pdf/legislativehistorycrc1en_1.pdf (accessed on 15 March 2020).

Parker, Ben. 2018a. *#MeToo Sex Scandals Spur Interest in Standards for the Aid Sector*; Geneva: The New Humanitarian, May 2. Available online: https://www.thenewhumanitarian.org/analysis/2018/05/02/metoo-sex-scandals-spur-interest-standards-aid-sector (accessed on 14 March 2020).

Parker, Ben. 2018b. *Schemes to Stop Sex Abuse in the Aid Sector off to a Shaky Start*. Geneva: The New Humanitarian, October 18, Available online: https://www.thenewhumanitarian.org/news-feature/2018/10/18/safeguarding-aid-sector-sex-abuse-shaky-start (accessed on 14 March 2020).

Peace Research Institute Oslo. 2018. Smart Phones for Refugees: Tools for Survival, or Surveillance? Available online: https://www.prio.org/utility/DownloadFile.ashx?id=1597&type=publicationfile (accessed on 3 April 2020).

Petersen, Inge, Arvin Bhana, and Mary McKay. 2005. Sexual violence and youth in South Africa: The need for community-based prevention interventions. *Child Abuse & Neglect* 29: 1233–48. [CrossRef]

Plummer, Carol A., and Wambui Njuguna. 2009. Cultural protective and risk factors: Professional perspectives about child sexual abuse in Kenya. *Child Abuse & Neglect* 33: 524–32. [CrossRef]

Privacy International. 2020. *2020 Is a Crucial Year to Fight for Data Protection in Africa*. Privacy International. March 3. Available online: https://privacyinternational.org/long-read/3390/2020-crucial-year-fight-data-protection-africa (accessed on 4 April 2020).

Radford, Lorraine, Helen Richardson Foster, Christine Anne Barter, and Nicky Stanley. 2016. *Rapid Evidence Assessment: What Can Be Learnt from Other Jurisdictions about Preventing and Responding to Child Sexual Abuse, Report for the Independent Inquiry into Child Sexual Abuse*. Lancashire: Connect Centre for International Research on Interpersonal Violence Faculty of Social Work, Care & Community, University of Central Lancashire.

Sandvik, Kristin Bergtora. 2019. 'Safeguarding' as humanitarian buzzword: An initial scoping. *Journal of International Humanitarian Action* 4: 3. [CrossRef]

Sloth-Nielsen, Julia. 2014. Regional Frameworks for Safeguarding Children: The Role of the African Committee of Experts on the Rights and Welfare of the Child. *Social Sciences* 3: 948–61. [CrossRef]

Sloth-Nielsen, Julia. 2018. Monitoring and Implementation of Children's Rights. In *International Human Rights of Children*. Edited by Liefaard Ton and Kilkelly Ursula. Singapore: Springer, pp. 1–35. [CrossRef]

Steering Committee for Humanitarian Response, *Misconduct Disclosure Scheme*. n.d. Steering Committee for Humanitarian Response. Available online: https://www.schr.info/the-misconduct-disclosure-scheme (accessed on 5 April 2020).

Stern, Orly. 2018. *First Person: Two Nearly Identical Cases of Sex Abuse; Two Very Different Responses*; Geneva: The New Humanitarian, June 27. Available online: http://www.thenewhumanitarian.org/opinion/2018/06/27/first-person-two-nearly-identical-cases-sex-abuse-two-very-different-responses (accessed on 29 March 2020).

Tilbury, C. 2014. Working with children checks -time to step back? *Australian Journal of Social Issues* 49: 87–100. [CrossRef]

Tobin, John, and Florence Seow. 2019. Article 34. Protection from Sexual Exploitation and Sexual Abuse. In *The UN Convention on the Rights of the Child: A Commentary*. Oxford: Oxford University Press, pp. 1310–54.

UK Department for International Development. 2018a. *International Development Secretary Penny Mordaunt Gives Key-Note Speech at the Safeguarding Summit 2018*; October 18, GOV.UK. Available online: https://www.gov.uk/government/speeches/international-development-secretary-penny-mordaunt-gives-key-note-speech-at-the-safeguarding-summit-2018 (accessed on 29 March 2020).

UK Department for International Development. 2018b. *Progress Report on Delivering the Donor Commitments from the October 2018 London Safeguarding Summit*; p. 33. Available online: https://assets.publishing.service.gov.uk/government/uploads/system/uploads/attachment_data/file/840067/Progress-report-on-delivering-donor-commitments.pdf (accessed on 5 March 2020).

UK Department for International Development. 2019. *Progress Report—One Year on from the October 2018 London Safeguarding Summit*; London: UK Department for International Development. Available online: https://assets.publishing.service.gov.uk/government/uploads/system/uploads/attachment_data/file/840063/Cross-sector-Safeguarding-Progress-Report-Oct_19.pdf (accessed on 18 January 2020).

UK Parliament. 2018. *Sexual Exploitation and Abuse in the Aid Sector Inquiry Launched—News from Parliament*; London: UK Parliament, March 5. Available online: https://www.parliament.uk/business/committees/committees-a-z/commons-select/international-development-committee/news-parliament-2017/sexual-exploitation-launch-17-19-/ (accessed on 15 February 2020).

UNICEF. 2020. *Don't Let Children Be the Hidden Victims of COVID-19 Pandemic*; New York: UNICEF, April 9. Available online: https://www.unicef.org/press-releases/dont-let-children-be-hidden-victims-covid-19-pandemic (accessed on 10 April 2020).

United Nations Committee on the Rights of the Child. 2003. *General Comment No. 5 (2003), General Measures of Implementation of the Convention on the Rights of the Child (arts. 4, 42 and 44, para. 6)*. 34th Session, adopted 27 November 2003, CRC/GC/2003/5. Available online: https://tbinternet.ohchr.org/_layouts/15/treatybodyexternal/Download.aspx?symbolno=CRC%2fGC%2f2003%2f5&Lang=en (accessed on 22 January 2020).

United Nations Committee on the Rights of the Child. 2011. *General comment No. 13 (2011), The Right of the Child to Freedom from All Forms of Violence*. Adopted 18 April 2011, CRC/C/GC/13. Available online: https://tbinternet.ohchr.org/_layouts/15/treatybodyexternal/Download.aspx?symbolno=CRC%2fC%2fGC%2f13&Lang=en (accessed on 22 January 2020).

United Nations Committee on the Rights of the Child. 2013. *General Comment No. 14 (2013) on the Right of the Child to Have His or Her Best Interests Taken as a Primary Consideration (art 3, para 1)*. 62nd Session, adopted 29 May 2013, CRC/C/GC/14. Available online: https://tbinternet.ohchr.org/_layouts/15/treatybodyexternal/Download.aspx?symbolno=CRC%2fC%2fGC%2f14&Lang=en (accessed on 22 February 2020).

United Nations Committee on the Rights of the Child. 2015. *Treaty-Specific Guidelines Regarding the Form and Content of Periodic Reports to be Submitted by States Parties under Article 44, Paragraph 1 (b), of the Convention on the Rights of the Child*. 55th Session, adopted 25 November 2010, CRC/C/58/Rev.2. Available online: https://tbinternet.ohchr.org/_layouts/15/treatybodyexternal/Download.aspx?symbolno=CRC%2fC%2f58%2fREV.3&Lang=en (accessed on 15 March 2020).

United Nations Committee on the Rights of the Child. 2020. The Committee on the Rights of the Child Warns of the Grave Physical, Emotional and Psychological Effect of the COVID-19 Pandemic on Children and Calls on States to Protect the Rights of Children. Available online: https://tbinternet.ohchr.org/Treaties/CRC/Shared%20Documents/1_Global/INT_CRC_STA_9095_E.pdf (accessed on 11 April 2020).

United Nations General Assembly. 2003. *Investigation into Sexual Exploitation of Refugees by Aid Workers in West Africa, Resolution Adopted by the General Assembly*. New York: UN General Assembly.

United Nations General Assembly. 2015. Transforming Our World: The 2030 Agenda for Sustainable Development, Resolution Adopted by the General Assembly on 25 September 2015. Available online: https://undocs.org/A/RES/70/1 (accessed on 28 March 2020).

United Nations High Commissioner for Refugees & Save the Children UK. 2002. Sexual Violence and Exploitation: The Experience of Refugee Children in Liberia, Guinea and Sierra Leone. Available online: https://www.parliament.uk/documents/commons-committees/international-development/2002-Report-of-sexual-exploitation-and-abuse-Save%20the%20Children.pdf (accessed on 15 February 2020).

United Nations Human Rights Office of the High Commissioner. 2020. *Status of Ratification Interactive Dashboard*; Geneva: United Nations Human Rights Office of the High Commissioner, April 9. Available online: https://indicators.ohchr.org/ (accessed on 10 April 2020).

United Nations Secretariat. 2003. Secretary-General's Bulletin, Special Measures for Protection from Sexual Exploitation and Sexual Abuse. Available online: https://undocs.org/pdf?symbol=en/ST/SGB/2003/13 (accessed on 29 March 2020).

USAID. 2015. Policy/Guidance on the Implementation of USAID Child Safeguarding Standards. Available online: https://www.usaid.gov/sites/default/files/documents/1864/200mbt.pdf (accessed on 3 March 2020).

Viola de Azevedo Cunha, Mario. 2017. *Child Privacy in the Age of Web 2.0 and 3.0: Challenges and Opportunities for Policy*; (No. 2017–03; Innocenti Discussion Paper). Florence: UNICEF Office of Research. Available online: https://www.unicef-irc.org/publications/pdf/Child_privacy_challenges_opportunities.pdf (accessed on 14 February 2020).

Walker-Simpson, Karen. 2017. The Practical Sense of Protection: A Discussion Paper on the Reporting of Child Abuse in Africa and whether International Standards Actually Help Keep Children Safe: The Practical Sense of Protection. *Child Abuse Review* 26: 252–62. [CrossRef]

Zarnegar Deloffre, Maryam. 2016. Global accountability communities: NGO self-regulation in the humanitarian sector. *Review of International Studies* 42: 724–47. [CrossRef]

social sciences

MDPI

Article

Kenya's Over-Reliance on Institutionalization as a Child Care and Child Protection Model: A Root-Cause Approach

Njeri Chege [1,*] and Stephen Ucembe [2]

[1]   Independent Researcher, 1211 Geneva, Switzerland
[2]   Hope and Homes for Children, Nairobi 00200, Kenya; Stephen.Ucembe@hopeandhomes.org
[*]   Correspondence: njeriche@gmail.com

Received: 1 March 2020; Accepted: 17 April 2020; Published: 22 April 2020

Abstract: Institutionalization of children who are deprived of parental care is a thriving phenomenon in the global South, and has generated considerable concern both nationally and internationally, in the last two decades. In Kenya, the number of children growing up in live-in care institutions has been growing ever since the country's early post-independence years. Although legislative and regulatory measures aimed at child protection have been in place for a number of years now, and the national government appears to be standing by the commitment it expressed in recent times to implement care reform which encompasses de-institutionalization, the national child protection system remains very dependent on institutional care. Against the backdrop of a global and national movement towards de-institutionalization of child care and child protection, in this paper we tease out the range of factors reinforcing Kenya's over-reliance on live-in institutions as a child care and child protection model. Numerous factors—structural, political, economic, socio-cultural, and legal—contribute to the complexity of the issue. We highlight this complexity, bringing together different angles, while pointing out the interests of the different stakeholders in reinforcing institutional care. We argue that the sustainability, efficiency and effectiveness of the intended change from institutional care to alternative family-based care requires that a root-cause approach be adopted in addressing the underlying child care and child protection issues.

Keywords: institutionalization of children deprived of parental care; de-institutionalization of child care and child protection; root cause approach; Kenya

---

1. Introduction

In Kenya, despite an increase in national legislative and regulatory measures aimed at child protection over the last three decades, there have been rapid increases in the numbers of institutionalized children, and residential child care facilities[1]. As a result of the observations made, concerns raised and pressure exerted by civil society organizations and international organizations with regard to these rising numbers, and their implications in relation to the welfare, and rights of the concerned children, in November 2017, the Kenyan government announced a moratorium on the registration of new live-in child care facilities. More recently, an active government-led and INGO and civil society-motivated care reform pilot project which encompasses de-institutionalization was launched in mid 2018, in Western Kenya, and is expected to be expanded to other counties countrywide over the next years (Miseki 2018). Yet, the national child care protection system remains very dependent on institutional care.

---

[1]   Throughout this paper, we use the terms residential child care facilities, residential care institutions, live-in care institutions, care institutions and institutions interchangeably.

On the African continent, country specific dynamics and processes related to institutionalization are yet to undergo rigorous examination in existing literature. Hence, as Kenya embarks on a path of care reform, we propose to make a contribution towards this, by focusing on different aspects related to the child care and protection model in Kenya. More specifically we unveil the intertwined range of factors—structural, political, economic, socio-cultural, and legal—that have been reinforcing Kenya's over reliance on institutionalization as a child care and child protection model. We posit that focusing on addressing the root-causes underlying child care and child protection issues in the country is preferable to the current standard approach to child protection—which consists of addressing the visible factors of vulnerability.

While the focus of this paper is on Kenya, child and youth care reform is a crucial issue that is of global relevance, and is one that poses, and encounters particular challenges in global South contexts. Across global South countries, there are particularities, certainly, but also similarities, where issues and challenges related to child protection and care reforms are concerned. Hence, the discussions and insights in this paper are also relevant for readers whose interests may be on other global South countries.

From a methodological perspective, this paper is based on a comprehensive desk research, which included reviews and analyses of published and unpublished peer reviewed works (articles, books, book chapters, theses); grey literature; and press articles, on the thematic fields of child protection, child care, children's rights, institutionalization, de-institutionalization and care reform in Kenya. It is also informed by our professional and personal experiences, personal knowledge, questions and reflections on a range of issues related to the care and protection of children lacking adequate parental care.

We start from the observation that while a lot of knowledge has been generated on family and community-based care in Africa (see for example Isiugo-Abanihe 1985; Foster 2005; Mathambo and Richter 2007; Mushunje 2006, 2014; Hampshire et al. 2015), little is known about residential care institutions as a child protection and care model in African countries (Hermenau et al. 2011). Yet, for over two decades now, the rhetoric of 'Africa's AIDS orphan crisis'[2] has indirectly contributed to perpetuating the idea that on the African continent, institutions are the ideal solution for children deprived of parental care (Richter and Norman 2010; Cheney and Ucembe 2019). This idea has been anchored by, and is evident through the large financial and logistical support, and volunteer or voluntourist labour that 'orphanages' in numerous African countries have continued to receive from individuals, associations, corporates, secular and religious charity organizations locally and more significantly from the global North. This has contributed to the proliferation of residential child care institutions on the continent (Tolfree 1995; Cheney and Ucembe 2019).

2. Background

Evidence from medical and social science research has shown the negative impact institutional up-bringing has on children's physical, cognitive, emotional and social development (Browne et al. 2006; Engle et al. 2011; Beckett et al. 2002; Rutter et al. 1999; O'Connor and Rutter 2000; MacLean 2003; Tolfree 2003). Yet, the upbringing of children in live-in care facilities is still actively practiced in numerous countries around the world.

Over the years, this has become a global preoccupation: concerns have been raised and experiences and practices related to children's institutionalization shared, debated and discussed within, and beyond national borders by child care experts, practitioners and children's rights activists. This, coupled with the human rights revolution, triggered a shift in thinking. Numerous national governments both in the global North and South—but more so in the former—embarked on de-institutionalization, understood as a long haul process through which the national child protection systems are comprehensively

---

[2]   It was driven by UNICEF (2003a) and was taken up and propagated by a range of political and social actors (Governments, INGOs, NGOs and do-it-yourself humanitarians).

The drastic reductions in public spending imposed by the Bretton Woods institutions resulted in the loss of employment for thousands of civil servants, and cuts in public spending on social services. For struggling and poor families, the move from subsidized social services to cost-sharing represented considerable financial burden, and globally aggravated poverty. Alongside parents' struggles with trying to provide their children's most basic needs (food, shelter, clothing), many could no longer access essential services such as health care and education. Parallel to these socio-economic changes, the HIV/AIDS pandemic was raging through the country, resulting among others in deaths, impairment of parents and caregivers' abilities to care for children, shifts in family structure, poverty, and overall family instability (Skovdal and Campbell 2010).

Based on Tolfree's analysis of colonial and post-colonial child protection frameworks and services in former English colonies we can include Kenya in the number of African countries whose post-independence response to the plight of unprotected children was very similar to that of the colonial powers. Kenya's immediate post-colonial and present day legal framework was derived considerably from the 1930s and 1940s English laws governing the protection and care of children. Similar to the latter, the services availed through the post-independence child protection framework reflect a rescue, control (of "deviant" behavior which includes delinquency, vagrancy and prostitution) and train approach. The services, which were characteristically remedial, were comprised of approved schools and other kinds of residential care (Tolfree 1995, p. 39).

The dawn of SAP and consequent privatization policies created a significant space for Non-Governmental Organizations (NGOs) to intervene in providing public goods (Hearn 2002, p. 376). The reduction of public spending resulted in a reduction of the financial burden on the government but also increased humanitarianism through voluntourism and NGOs. This saw the dominance of privately funded child care institutions within a short period. Oversight of these institutions has been significantly wanting (Njoka and Williams 2008, p. 1) resulting in proliferation and all manner of malpractices. This poor oversight could be traced back to the earlier mentioned cuts in public spending through which the government's capacity to provide oversight over NGOs' activities was negatively affected (Hearn 2002, p. 387).

The manufacturing of an 'orphan crisis' by international organizations and individuals is another factor that has contributed to the proliferation of child care institutions. During the 1990s at the height of HIV/AIDS pandemic, the exclusive focus on 'orphans' by international development organizations such as UNICEF (2003a), led to 'misidentification' of children, triggering significant 'save' and 'rescue' interventions among social actors (Cheney and Rotabi 2014; Chege 2018), especially Christian evangelicals from the global North. Apart from the Christian interventions, non-religious groups and individuals ranging from gap year students to do-it yourself humanitarians—through voluntourism—also travelled to the country to offer support (Cheney and Ucembe 2019). The exclusive focus on 'orphans' resulted in an explosive supply of children by both local well-intentioned and unscrupulous organizations, to meet the demand coming from the global North.

Political unrest and armed conflict notably in the early 1990s and in 2007–2008, during former presidents Moi and Kibaki's time in office, respectively, also created conditions that favored the institutionalization of children. Both resulted in loss of lives, displacement and separation of families, more so parent-child separations. The aforementioned socio-economic conditions of the 1990s followed by the political unrest and violence, resulted in the entry and intervention of several NGOs which gradually took over government functions in the social sector, notably in the domain of child protection, care and education.

Alongside, and as a result of these political, economic, and socio-cultural changes, came the disintegration of the kinship care support system, which previously served as a support network that catered for children in need within families and communities (Suda 1997; Mugo 2004). Children who, in the event of their biological parents' deaths or incapacity to care for them, would normally have been cared for by close relatives, ended up on the streets and in charitable children's institutions.

4. Kenya's Current Child Protection and Care Model and Its Problems

For several decades now, the care of children at risk or without parental care is increasingly being assured by secular or faith-based private residential care institutions, which are for the most run by national and international Non Governmental Organizations (NGOs) and/or by individuals. These institutions, officially termed 'Charitable Children's Institutions' (CCI), are recognized by the State, and their roles and legal obligations are outlined in Kenya's Children Act.

4.1. Gaps in Child-Related Statistics

The exact number of children growing up without parental care in Kenya and around the East Africa region today is hard to pin down (Save the Children International 2015). While a common database termed the 'Child Protection Information Management System' exists in Kenya since May 2017 (Mutavi 2017), it has not reached all of the country's counties. By the end of 2017 only 15 counties had been reached, with a plan to roll out the system in the remaining 32 by the end of 2018 (UNICEF 2017, p. 33). To date, this has not been successful.

Such gaps in child-related statistics have resulted in the same or differing figures being recycled in both grey and scholarly literature over a period of years. For instance, in a 2015 study that was part of a UNICEF global initiative, the number of orphans and vulnerable children in Kenya was estimated at 3.6 million, among whom 646,887 were double orphans[6]. It was specified in a footnote that the exact number of orphans and vulnerable children was 3,612,679 (Government of Kenya et al. 2015, p. 6). This figure was sourced from the Kenya Social Protection Sector Report published by the Ministry for Planning, National Development and Vision 2030, in June 2012, where it also appears to have been sourced from an earlier publication.

Comparatively, a study conducted in 2014 using data from the 2012 Kenya AIDS Indicator Survey (KAIS)[7], estimated the number of orphans and vulnerable children in the country at 2.6 million, with orphans estimated at 1.8 million (among whom 15 percent or 270,000 were double orphans) and vulnerable children at 750,000 (Lee et al. 2014).

The aforementioned collaborative Government of Kenya, UNICEF and Global Affairs Canada study estimated charitable children's institutions in Kenya in 2015 at over 830 (Government of Kenya et al. 2015, p. 8). According to the study, an estimated 40,000 to 42,000 children lacking parental care were living in CCIs (Government of Kenya et al. 2015, p. 8)[8]. It is also estimated that over 80% of children in institutional care have one or both living parents. As with the national statistics on children living without parental care, these figures have been quoted and re-quoted over a period of several years, and it is often difficult to find the source of the estimates, which at best, are guesstimates.

4.2. National Laws Skewed to Care in CCIs

The Kenyan government is considered to be among the 'most child-friendly' on the African continent (African Child Policy Forum ACPF, p. 6). Kenyan legislation related to children has often been referred to as progressive to the extent that the country was ranked first by the African Child Policy Forum (ACPF), in relation to its efforts to put in place an appropriate legal and policy framework for the protection of children (African Child Policy Forum ACPF, pp. 49–51). The country is a signatory to the UN Convention on the Rights of the Child, the Hague Convention on Protection of Children and Co-operation in Respect of Inter-country Adoption, the African Charter on the Rights and Welfare of the Child, and the UN Convention on the Rights of Persons with Disabilities. However, Kenya's adherence

---

[6] According to UNICEF's broadened definition of orphan, a 'double orphan' is a child whose both parents have died, while a 'single orphan' has one living parent (UNICEF 2003a).

[7] For the 2012 Kenya AIDS Indicator Survey (KAIS) see National AIDS and STI Control Programme .

[8] The uncertainty surrounding these figures and the caution with which one needs to consider them is clearly reflected in the large bracket.

to these international legal conventions has not resulted in the successful protection of vulnerable children in the country. As Cooper rightly puts it, 'the existence of laws and protocols cannot be trusted as indicators of success in protecting vulnerable children' (Cooper 2012, p. 495). Although the country led in policy and legal frameworks with regard to child protection, the African Child Policy Forum in the aforementioned report shows that Kenya was ranked 20 (out of 52) in terms of the government's budgetary commitment to provide for children's basic needs and ensure their well-being (African Child Policy Forum ACPF, p. 64). The restrictive allocation of financial resources to child protection and care by the national government has been possible because it both passively and actively outsources child protection and care to the third sector (Ucembe 2015b; Chege 2018). Subsequently, a 'not our money, not our problem' mentality has characterized the last three post-independence governments' work related to child protection and care.

The progress made in legal frameworks cannot avoid being faulted for the many defects of the care reform. The current Children Act has paid more attention to elaborating institutional care than other family and community-based care options (Ucembe 2015a). For instance, while the Act in Part 5 has 15 sections and 55 mentions, kinship care is not mentioned, foster care has 8 sections and is not clearly defined to enable proper practice. The Act's third schedule is particularly problematic in that it stipulates that in order to receive registration approval, an institution, 'must accommodate or have capacity to accommodate at least twenty children'. This has led to many CCIs going out in search of children in families and communities so as to fill the required 20 children bed capacity. The government also came up with the National Standards for Best Practices in Charitable Children's Institutions (Government of Kenya 2013), and although well intended, in doing so, it furthered the narrative that serves to promote these institutions. The aforementioned third schedule clearly shows that certain legal provisions, if not critically examined, can hinder progress or change.

4.3. Fragmented National Framework and Absence of Coordination in Child Protection Policy

In 2011 Kenya defined a national framework for child protection system. However, the framework in question is quite fragmented. As was defined by the National Council for Children's Services (2011) it is weighed down by governmental ministries (nine) and state services, and not much place, if any, is accorded to communities and parents as stakeholders. A key consequence of such fragmentation has been the absence of coordination in policy development, implementation, and enforcement which has in turn been contributing to reinforcing the institutionalization of children. This can be seen, first, in the absence of coordination related to cash transfer programmes put in place by the national government. While traditionally in Kenya the care of children who were deprived of parental care was assured by kin, over the years, this changed following the socio-economic upheavals (discussed in the previous section), which resulted in deepening poverty and social inequality across the country[9]. This contributed to the disintegration of families and weakening of the extended family networks, which motivated the initiation of Cash Transfer Programmes in 2004, which included the Orphans and Vulnerable Children Cash Transfer (OVC-CT); Cash Transfer for Persons with Severe Disabilities; Cash Transfer for the Elderly, and the Hunger Safety Net Programme.

Since the introduction of these programmes, the country experienced a three-fold increase in public funding between 2010 and 2014 (Wanyama and McCord 2017, p. 11). However, these cash transfer programmes were, and are still not interweaved with alternative care, which would prioritize prevention and reinforce family-based care. This is despite the availability of evidence indicating the benefits of such an approach. A report that was officially launched and released in Nairobi by Family for Every Child (Roelen 2016), and which was based on a study conducted in three African countries (Ghana, Rwanda and South Africa), showed that cash transfers can among others 'prevent family

---

[9] It is important to note that little effort was made to monitor these dynamics, and to institute social protection measures to protect against family disintegration.

separation and increase reintegration of children' and can 'enable families to care for children who are not their own' (Roelen 2016, p. 9).

The absence of coordination in policy development, implementation and enforcement can also be seen in the enormous time lapses between the periods when evidence of impediments to child protection is provided by official bodies within the country, and the national government's lagged response to the problems. From as early as November 2008, the Department of Children's Services under the Ministry of Gender, Children and Social Development on assessing the legal provisions and practices of guardianship, foster care and adoption of children in Kenya, observed that the proliferation and mal-practices of CCIs stood as an impediment to the development of alternative family care solutions. Therefore, the Ministry recommended that a moratorium on the establishment and registration of CCIs be pronounced and enforced. However, it was not until November 2017 that the government pronounced a ban on the registration of new CCIs[10]. This ban, and a related earlier one pronounced against intercountry adoption in November 2014 (discussed further on) revealed that Charitable Children's Institutions had become pathways of child trafficking[11].

It is important to note the connection between the institutionalization model and the growth of inter-country adoption. Since the late 1990s, there has been a decrease in the availability of adoptable children in the former source countries, namely Russia, China and Korea (Selman 2009). Consequently, over the last three decades, the African continent as a source for adoptable children, has increasingly attracted the attention of prospective adoptive parents and adoption agencies in the global North (Mezmur 2010; African Child Policy Forum ACPF; Cheney 2014). In Kenya, CCIs are a gateway to adoption, since officially, children have to go through an institution in order to be adopted, as provided in the Children Act (Laws of Kenya 2001). The combination of demand for adoptable children through inter-county adoption[12] and inter-country adoption being a money spinner, has resulted in a process whereby more adoptable children, in this case young children, have to be produced and admitted to institutions for inter-country adoption purposes, thus resulting in commodification.

In Kenya, pervasive inter-country adoption malpractices by institutions led to a countrywide ban pronounced by the national government in 2014[13]. A government commissioned study showed unusually high rates of inter-country adoption relative to domestic adoptions: between 2003 and 2008, the latter amounted to approximately 62 percent of total adoptions, against 38 percent in inter-country adoption (Njoka and Williams 2008, pp. vi, 16, 17). These statistics were considered unnecessarily high as the number of children being placed for inter-country adoptions is expected to have been significantly lower. This is so since the Hague Convention on the Protection of Children and Co-operation in Respect of Inter-Country Adoption—of which Kenya is a signatory—underscores the principle of subsidiarity (Dambach 2019, pp. 6, 7), which means that priority is unquestionably accorded to local adoptions.

Another consequence of fragmentation of the framework can be seen in the absence of preventive action that the national ministries would be expected to undertake. It has now been several years since social scientists, INGOs and Intragovernmental organizations begun drawing attention to the practice of orphanage tourism and orphanage voluntourism in the global South and their detrimental effects on children and their families (cf Guiney 2012, Save the Children[14], UNICEF[15]). Voluntourism

---

[10] See: https://www.bettercarenetwork.nl/nw-17382-7-3673126/nieuws/kenia_schort_de_registratie_van_nieuwe_kinderhuizen_op.html (accessed on 15 December 2018).
[11] See Mathenge and Otieno (2014), https://www.standardmedia.co.ke/article/2000142876/kenyan-government-bans-adoption-of-children-by-foreigners (accessed on 15 July 2018).
[12] See Ochieng (2018b), https://www.nation.co.ke/news/How-children-are-sold-to-highest-bidder-in-name-of-adoption/1056-4640320-x1fce6/index.html (accessed on 15 July 2018).
[13] See Ochieng (2018a), https://www.nation.co.ke/news/Experts-want-tough-laws-on-adoption/1056-4772800-or9q5jz/index.html (accessed on 1 October 2018).
[14] https://blogs.savethechildren.org.uk/2016/05/why-we-dont-support-orphanage-volunteering/ (accessed on 31 May 2019).
[15] https://www.unicef.org.au/blog/news-and-insights/august-2016/travel-tips-avoid-orphanage-tourism (accessed on 30 May 2019); https://blogs.unicef.org/east-asia-pacific/children-not-tourist-attractions-keeping-families-together-in-myanmar/ (accessed on 30 May 2019).

and orphanage tourism are widespread in Kenya, more so in its touristic coastal region. Yet, to date, no efforts in the form of national or transnational sensitization campaigns have been made towards sensitizing international tourists, students and schools to the need to stop establishing or supporting the establishment of children's homes (and rather support efforts geared towards de-institutionalization notably by supporting initiatives that focus on strengthening families and communities).

Similarly, there have been no official campaigns geared towards deconstructing local attitudes through which institutions have come to be considered good solutions for children from poor families, in particular within communities situated in regions where the presence of numerous foreign sponsored residential child-care facilities are functioning as pull factors for parents who are struggling to provide for their children's most basic needs.

5. Addressing the Root Causes

The problem with institutional care in Kenya and elsewhere is not just the earlier mentioned socio-emotional, physical and cognitive challenges it engenders for the children, and the adults that they later become. It is also the fact that institutionalization of children by itself never addresses the underlying issues and is often a reactive model in many instances.

Currently, with on-going care reform efforts, the Kenya government has accepted that the model is harmful, unsustainable and significantly misused. However, there are complexities and challenges in how the issue of children without adequate parental care is addressed in the country. Some of the institutional care actors have argued that they are responding to poverty; their intervention thus involves addressing issues related to the provision of education, food, health, shelter, protection from abuse and neglect, which are mostly visible factors or symptoms of vulnerability. While treating these symptoms is essential, addressing the underlying issues is fundamental. We argue that the standard approach to child protection—which consists of addressing the symptoms—is inadequate at best and counter-productive at worst.

For example, *the issue of street connected children* has reinforced the relevance and maintenance of institutions with many of their administrators arguing that they are a lesser evil, compared to having children growing up on the streets. This is a very narrow, yet widely held view. Section 5 of the World Report on Violence against Children, decries the use of institutional care for these children and urges governments to look into alternatives because of their harmful nature (Pinheiro 2006). Despite the country having over 200 institutions focusing on street connected children, the number of children on the streets keeps growing (Onyiko and Pechacova 2015, p. 161). This is evidence indicating that institutions are not a panacea. It also underscores the fact that expecting different results while continuing to use the same approach is at best illogical.

In the case of street connected children, institutional care is not only harmful but fundamentally ignores the root causes of their presence on the streets. Research has shown that most children who are to be found living on the streets are predominantly there as a result of poverty (Onyiko and Pechacova 2015), and poverty-related issues that would include violence, abuse, neglect, and abandonment by their families or displacement during armed conflict (Suda 1997; Cottrell-Boyce 2010). Subsequently many of them end up in institutions. It is worth noting that the 2015 case study conducted under UNICEF, in collaboration with the Government of Kenya and Global Affairs Canada showed that over 76 percent of children in Kenya had experienced a form of violence—sexual, physical, and emotional (Government of Kenya et al. 2015). It is these plights—violence, negligence, exploitation, and which are intricately connected to poverty in families—that often drive many to seek salvation on the streets (Suda 1997; Cottrell-Boyce 2010). While a sizeable number of these children find their way to the streets, and subsequently end up in institutions, some are 'rescued' from their malfunctioning families; they are withdrawn from their homes and taken to residential child care institutions. Indeed, it seems that it would make more sense if organizations galvanized themselves in prevention, since the current approach is often cyclical, and organizations only end up addressing the symptoms.

Although *discrimination against children living with HIV/AIDS and those with disabilities* has reduced over the years, children in these situations still continue to face stigma and discrimination in families and communities. They have often been condemned to upbringing in institutions, which claim to respond to their needs. However, relegating these children to institutional life often reinforces *othering*, which subsequently widens the gap between them and their healthier and non-disabled peers, and society at large, hence reinforcing stigma and discrimination. Intensive efforts to create awareness and to bring resources closer to communities would be sensible in reducing such inequalities as well as the stigma and discrimination. For such children to develop and attain their full potential like all other children, their upbringing in loving and accepting families and communities is essential.

Retrogressive cultural practices such as genital cutting and early marriages for girls have also been a major concern in several parts of the country (UNICEF 2018a). Official reports show that although there has been a general national decrease in prevalence of female genital cutting[16], it is still highly prevalent in certain communities[17] (National Council for Population and Development 2013; Kenya National Bureau of Statistics et al. 2015, p. 333; UNICEF 2018a, p. 94). Similarly, early/child marriages are also rampant in Kenya, due to social economic factors, which include poverty, low education and the view that girls are economic assets (UNICEF 2018a, p. 96), with one in six teenagers aged 15–19 years being reported to be pregnant or a mother[18]. Girls who want to avoid undergoing genital cutting and early marriages often seek shelter in 'rescue centers'. These children tend to spend long periods of time in such institutions, and are generally entirely separated from their families and communities because of fear of discrimination or punishment.

Research has shown that millions of households are living in *extreme poverty*[19]. In these conditions, care givers—including biological parents who have little or no support—sometimes become desperate enough to let their children go to residential care institutions whose representatives sometimes come knocking at their doors (Ucembe 2015c, p. 22). Furthermore, there is evidence showing that some institutions see children as commodities, and as bait for funding at best (Njoka and Williams 2008, p. 20). Additionally, many consider that having high numbers of children in their institutions is viewed more favourably by donors who consider institutionalization as assisting children (Cheney and Ucembe 2019, p. 41). This preoccupation with numbers and orphans has significantly resulted in children being separated from their families and communities and labelled as 'orphans'. Many refer to their facilities as 'orphanages'" having realized that individuals and charitable organizations in North America and Europe are willing to financially and materially support 'orphans' in 'orphanages' in African countries.

These and other unscrupulous people have tapped into this model, as it *lacks adequate oversight by the national and county governments*. This absence of proper oversight comes with drastic repercussions for the concerned children and young people. Indeed, the accounts of some young Kenyans with care experiences have shown that it is not unusual for children to be moved back to their families by the owners of institutions, when the latter decide to pursue business opportunities with the available infrastructure, material and financial resources (Ucembe 2015c, p. 33). Such malpractices are often possible when the care institutions are unregistered and unregulated. In addition, the absence of regulations obliging the administrative actors of all CCIs to declare their funding sources and to formally account for the use of their funding and resources, also contributes to such gross misconduct. Evidently, such a lucrative model—one that allows people to acquire property and infrastructure and that brings in easy money—becomes increasingly difficult to abandon and to dismantle.

---

[16] According to the 2014 Kenya Demographic and Health Survey, 21 percent of women aged 15–49 had undergone genital cutting, which is a drop from 27 percent in 2008–2009 and 32 percent in 2003 (Kenya National Bureau of Statistics et al. 2015, p. 333).

[17] It is worth noting that genital cutting for girls/women is not a generalized practice among all Kenyan ethnic communities; it is present in some and absent in others.

[18] See Otieno (2018), https://www.nation.co.ke/newsplex/earlymarriage/2718262-4876266-41d2rb/index.html# (accessed on 10 December 2019).

[19] See Government of Kenya (2012); https://www.unicef.org/kenya/social-inclusion (accessed on 10 December 2019).

6. Concluding Discussion

Research based evidence about and around institutional care stretches back almost eighty years. Yet, in Kenya, the child protection system has failed to take an evidence-based approach. Some stakeholders, notably those running residential care facilities, have argued that since the research on children and institutional care is predominantly eurocentric, the findings do not apply to the Kenyan context. Although there is a dearth of research on institutional care in Kenya, this argument is undoubtedly narrow because the residential child care model in Kenya has characteristics that are similar to those previously found in western institutional care models, and from which it has 'inherited', imported or replicated.

The denial or ignorance of evidence has opened up grounds for charity. However, acts of 'doing good' which are not based on evidence have proved to be detrimental to child protection efforts and to children's well-being. Well-intentioned religious groups or individuals and other philanthropists from the global North often fall prey to sensationalized poverty and are generally made to believe that institutions can offer the concerned children a haven. This, coupled with an unregulated child protection system leads to the proliferation of residential care institutions, contributing to the country's reliance on institutionalization as a child protection model.

A major limitation of the national government's decision to leave care and protection in the hands of the third sector, has been that charity has replaced the idea of rights and social justice, and oversight of the child protection system has also been weakened (Ucembe 2015b, p. 3). There is a need to resist child protection that is grounded on a mentality and approach that commodifies children and child protection, as it encourages situations whereby desperate care givers feel obligated and constrained to give up their child or children in exchange for support that would be provided to the child within a certain space that is neither the caregivers' nor the child's home. Such approaches are not beneficial to the children, but rather are detrimental to their well-being.

Indeed, the concerned children are rarely the main beneficiaries of Kenya's institution-weighted child protection and care system; quite the contrary. Evidence shows that those who benefit the most are not the children, but rather owners of residential care facilities, their employees, tourists and volunteers, and the state. In numerous cases, it is not the local actors who determine how to support children, but owners of the facilities, who also double as fundraisers or donors. For example, it is the owner-fundraisers/owner-donors—not child protection 'professionals'—who decide whether or not a child should go home to their family. Their decision is often based on their perception of what constitutes a family and a good family environment. Often, the village life that is the lived reality of many children and their families does not match these perceptions, and some facility owners argue that taking a child (back) to a village amounts to taking her/him to poverty, and that the child is better off within their facilities.

Such approaches also put children at risk of *institutional abuse* (Tolfree 1995, p. 107; 2003, p. 5) defined as 'any system, programme, policy, procedure or individual interaction with a child in placement that abuses, neglects, or is detrimental to the child's health, safety, or emotional and physical well-being, or in any way exploits or violates the child's basic rights' (Cashmore et al. 1994, p. 10). In the country, there have been several cases of sexual abuse in residential care facilities, perpetrated by both local and foreign persons. Since background checks are rarely conducted, known pedophiles and other unidentified sexual offenders generally have easy access to children, and are sometimes the very persons who establish and run the care facilities, or are employed within them (See Scolforo 2019 for sexual and psychological abuses perpetrated by a 'missionary' founder). Other sexual offenders gain access to the children through the funds, material donations or the volunteer services they offer, often using an overt 'missionary' identity or prestigious occupations to gain the trust of children and their adult care-givers (see Wright and Allen 2013; Ferrigno 2017 for sexual abuses and psychological abuses perpetrated by a young 'missionary' and an airline pilot).

It is worth noting that during interventions, solutions which focus on removing children from their families are also rooted on an exclusive focus on children, that is, children are viewed in isolation, with little or no consideration given to the role of their environments and their primary care givers in assuring their consistent care, protection and overall well-being. In a way, the emphasis and focus on 'orphans' legitimizes this approach. From the preceding, it is evident that the sustainability of the intended change from institutional care to alternative family care requires that a root-cause approach be adopted in addressing the underlying child care and child protection issues. For instance, research clearly indicates that child protection efforts need to be combined with income-generating and poverty-reduction projects, as this would help curb child abuse and neglect (Lachman et al. 2002) and would thus reduce the pressure to relinquish children experienced by financially and subsequently emotionally struggling parents. Therefore, it is necessary that policy and legal frameworks that strengthen and develop alternatives to institutional care be established and enhanced. In parting, let us consider some evidence from the African continent that indicates government-led root cause approaches to child protection are more effective and sustainable compared to institutionalization. In 2013 the government of Rwanda in collaboration with UNICEF launched *Tubarerere Mu Muryango* (TMM—Let's Raise Children in Families)—a care reform programme that seeks to accomplish change from an institutional model of care to a family and community-based model. In 2017 the project's first phase was evaluated and showed a dramatic decrease in the number of children and young adults living in institutions: out of a total of 3323 children and youth, 2388 had been reintegrated into families and communities, which resulted in improvements in different aspects of their and their families' well-being (National Commission for Children et al. 2019, pp. 14–15).

Although the government of Rwanda still needs to do more, it has sustainably increased funding for social protection which is key in addressing poverty and its related issues. A national survey of children in institutions in Rwanda showed that one of the major reasons of institutionalization was poverty (Government of Rwanda and Hope and Homes for Children 2012, p. 9). A 2018/2019 social protection budget report prepared by UNICEF shows that over a period of 5 years, government spending in the social protection sector rose from FRW 73.1 billion in 2014/15 to FRW 138.3 billion in 2018/19, representing an increase of 89.3 percent (UNICEF 2018b, p. 9). The country's social protection sector has a number of core and complementary social protection programmes (involving services and cash transfers) which support families and different categories of vulnerable and marginalized citizens (children, orphans, elderly and disabled, low-income earners); they cover livelihood, shelter assistance, finance, health and education. The same report also shows a rise from FRW 6.4 billion to FRW 22.9 between 2017 and 2018 and 2018 and 2019 in the budget allocated to child-centered social protection (nutrition and child protection).

Alongside budgetary measures, the government has also invested in strengthening the performance of its larger child protection system through the training and recruitment of a social work force (social workers and psychologists) and governmental oversight and monitoring. It has established and strengthened responsive community structures with 29,764 community volunteers (local), whose roles include identifying needy families and linking them to support, responding to issues of violence, and monitoring the well-being of children (National Commission for Children et al. 2019). Through a sensitization and training programme, it has established foster care on a large scale, and has also undertaken awareness raising in communities to curb discrimination against children with disabilities. Additionally, it has embarked on constructing and supporting sustainable community centers to respond to the needs of the poor with regard to livelihoods, respite care, schooling and early childhood development.

Today, no new institutions can be established in the country and children can no longer be placed in institutions. The country is currently reported to be on track to be the first country in Africa to be orphanage-free by 2022[20].

---

[20] See Graham (2018), https://apolitical.co/en/solution_article/rwanda-wants-to-become-africas-first-orphanage-free-country-heres-how (accessed on 4 April 2020).

Transforming Kenya's child protection and care approach is a long-haul process within a complex social system. As the experiences of other countries show, it will take considerable time, effort, financial and human resources, and will necessitate sacrifices and trade-offs in the short-term. It requires political and public will, inclusive and collective action at all levels, coordinated commitment as well as governmental ownership of the process.

Author Contributions: Both authors contributed equally to this paper and have read and agreed to the published version of the manuscript.

Funding: This research received no external funding.

Conflicts of Interest: The authors declare no conflict of interest.

References

African Child Policy Forum (ACPF). 2008. How Child-Friendly Are African Governments? Addis Ababa. Available online: https://resourcecentre.savethechildren.net/node/1250/pdf/1250.pdf (accessed on 28 February 2020).

African Child Policy Forum (ACPF). 2012. *Africa: The New Frontier for Intercountry Adoption*. Addis Ababa: ACPF.

Beckett, Celia, Diana Bredenkamp, Jenny Castle, Christine Groothues, Thomas G. O'connor, and Michael Rutter. 2002. English and Romanian Adoptees (ERA) Study Team. Behavior patterns associated with institutional deprivation: A study of children adopted from Romania. *Journal of Developmental and Behavioral Pediatrics* 23: 297–303. [CrossRef] [PubMed]

Better Care Network. 2017. Deinstitutionalisation of Europe's Children. Opening Doors for Europe's Children. Available online: https://bettercarenetwork.org/sites/default/files/OD_DI_QA_07122017.pdf (accessed on 10 October 2019).

Browne, Kevin, Catherine Hamilton-Giachritsis, Rebecca Johnson, and Mikael Ostergren. 2006. Overuse of institutional care of children in Europe. *BMJ* 332: 485–87. [CrossRef] [PubMed]

Cashmore, Judy, Robin Dolby, and Deborah Brennan. 1994. *Systems Abuse: Problems and Solutions*; Sydney: NSW Child Protection Council.

Chege, Njeri. 2018. Children's Personal Data: Discursive Legitimation Strategies of Private Residential Care Institutions on the Kenyan Coast. *Social Sciences* 7: 114. [CrossRef]

Cheney, Kristen E. 2014. Giving Children a Better Life? Reconsidering Social Reproduction, Humanitarianism and Development in Intercountry Adoption. *European Journal of Development Research* 26: 247–63. [CrossRef]

Cheney, Kristen E., and Karen Smith Rotabi. 2014. Addicted to Orphans: How the Global Orphan Industrial Complex Jeopardizes Local Child Protection Systems. In *Conflict, Violence and Peace, Geographies of Children and Young People*. Edited by Christopher Harker, Kathrin Hörschelman and Tracey Skelton. Singapore: Springer, vol. 11.

Cheney, Kristen E., and Stephen Ucembe. 2019. The Orphan Industrial Complex: The Charitable Commodification of Children and Its Consequences for Child Protection. In *Disadvantaged Childhoods and Humanitarian Intervention. Palgrave Studies on Children and Development*. Edited by Kristen Cheney and Aviva Sinervo. Basingstoke: Palgrave Macmillan.

Cooper, Elizabeth. 2012. Following the law, but losing the spirit of child protection in Kenya. *Development in Practice* 22: 486–97. [CrossRef]

Cottrell-Boyce, Joseph. 2010. The Role of Solvents in the Lives of Kenyan Street Children: An Ethnographic Perspective. *African Journal of Drug & Alcohol Studies* 9. [CrossRef]

Dambach, Mia. 2019. *Principle of Subsidiarity*. ISS/IRC Comparative Working Paper 1: Spotlight on Solutions. Geneva: International Social Service, Available online: https://www.iss-ssi.org/images/Publications_ISS/ENG/PRINCIPLE_SUBSDIARITY_ANG.pdf (accessed on 13 February 2019).

Engle, Patrice L., Gary Nelson Gamer, and Emily Vargas-Barón. 2011. *Early Childhood Development What Parliamentarians Need to Know and Do*. Geneva: UNICEF Regional Office for Central and Eastern Europe and The Commonwealth of Independent States.

Ferrigno, Lorenzo. 2017. Missionary Sentenced to 40 Years for Sexually Assaulting Children in Kenya. *CNN*. February 23. Available online: https://edition.cnn.com/2016/03/07/us/missionary-sexual-assault-kenya-children/index.html (accessed on 14 December 2019).

Foster, Geoff. 2005. *Under the Radar-Community Safety Nets for Children Affected by HIV/AIDS in Poor Households in Sub-Saharan Africa.* Zimbabwe: United Nations Research Institute for Social Development (UNRISD).

Government of Kenya. 2012. Kenya Social Protection Sector Review. Ministry for Planning, National Development and Vision 2030, June 2012. Available online: https://www.unicef.org/evaldatabase/files/Kenya_Social_Protection_Sector_Review.pdf (accessed on 10 October 2019).

Government of Kenya. 2013. National Standards for Best Practices in Charitable Children's Institutions. Ministry of Gender, Children and Social Development. Available online: https://bettercarenetwork.org/sites/default/files/National%20Standards%20for%20Best%20Practices%20in%20Charitable%20Children%27s%20Institutions.pdf (accessed on 18 November 2018).

Government of Kenya, UNICEF, and Global Affairs Canada. 2015. Taking Child Protection to the Next Level in Kenya. Available online: https://www.unicef.org/protection/files/Kenya_CP_system_case_study.pdf (accessed on 13 October 2019).

Government of Rwanda and Hope and Homes for Children. 2012. National Survey of Institutions for Children in Rwanda. Available online: http://www.socialserviceworkforce.org/system/files/resource/files/NATIONAL%20SURVEY%20OF%20INSTITUTIONS%20FOR%20CHILDREN%20IN%20RWANDA_FINAL.pdf (accessed on 4 October 2019).

Graham, Jack. 2018. Rwanda Wants to Become Africa's First Orphanage-free Country—Here's How. May 24. Available online: https://apolitical.co/en/solution_article/rwanda-wants-to-become-africas-first-orphanage-free-country-heres-how (accessed on 4 April 2020).

Guiney, Tess. 2012. 'Orphanage tourism' in Cambodia: When residential care centres become tourist attractions'. *Pacific News*. N° 38 (July/August). Available online: https://bettercarenetwork.org/sites/default/files/Orphanage%20Tourism%20in%20Cambodia%20-%20When%20Residential%20Care%20Centres%20Become%20Tourist%20Attractions.pdf (accessed on 16 December 2019).

Hampshire, Kate, Gina Porter, Samuel Agblorti, Elsbeth Robson, Alister Munthali, and Albert Abane. 2015. Context Matters: Fostering, Orphanhood And Schooling in Sub-Saharan Africa. *Journal of Biosocial Science* 47: 141–64. [CrossRef]

Hearn, Julie. 2002. The 'invisible' NGO: US evangelical missions in Kenya. *Journal of Religion in Africa* 32: 32–60. [CrossRef]

Hermenau, Katharin, Tobias Hecker, Martina Ruf, Elisabeth Schauer, Thomas Elbert, and Maggie Schauer. 2011. Childhood adversity, mental ill-health and aggressive behavior in an African orphanage: Changes in response to trauma-focused therapy and the implementation of a new instructional system. *Child and Adolescent Psychiatry and Mental Health* 5: 29. Available online: http://www.capmh.com/content/5/1/29 (accessed on 10 October 2019). [CrossRef]

Isiugo-Abanihe, Uche C. 1985. Child fosterage in West Africa. *Population and Development Review* 11: 53–73. [CrossRef]

Kenya National Bureau of Statistics, Ministry of Health, the National AIDS Control Council (NACC), the National Council for Population and Development (NCPD), and the Kenya Medical Research Institute (KEMRI). 2015. Kenya Demographic and Health Survey 2014. Available online: https://dhsprogram.com/pubs/pdf/fr308/fr308.pdf (accessed on 22 November 2019).

Khamisi, Joe. 2016. *The Wretched Africans: A Study of Rabai and Freretown Slave Settlements.* Plano: Jodey.

Lachman, Peter, Ximena Poblete, Peter O Ebigbo, Sally Nyandiya-Bundy, Robert P Bundy, Bev Killian, and Jaap Doek. 2002. Challenges facing child protection. *Child Abuse & Neglect* 26: 587–617.

Laws of Kenya. 2001. *Children Act, Chapter 141, Revised Edition 2010 (2007).* Nairobi: The National Council for Law Reporting/Kenya Law, Available online: https://bettercarenetwork.org/sites/default/files/The%20Children%27s%20Act%2C%20Kenya_0.pdf (accessed on 4 August 2019).

Lee, Veronica, Patrick Muriithi, Ulrike Gilbert-Nandra, Andrea Kim, Mary Schmitz, James Odek, Rose Mokaya, Jennifer Galbraith, and KAIS Study Group. 2014. Orphans and vulnerable children in Kenya: Results from a nationally representative population-based survey. *Journal of Acquired Immune Deficiency Syndromes* 66: S89–S97. [CrossRef] [PubMed]

MacLean, Kim. 2003. The impact of institutionalization on child development. *Development and Psychopathology* 15: 853–84. [CrossRef] [PubMed]

Mathambo, Vuyiswa, and Linda Richter. 2007. *"We Are Volunteering": Endogenous Community-based Responses to the Needs of Children Made Vulnerable by HIV and AID*. Cape Town: HSRC, Available online: http://www.hsrc.ac.za/en/research-data/view/3381 (accessed on 9 October 2019).

Mathenge, Thiong'o, and Rawlings Otieno. 2014. Kenyan Government Bans Adoption of Children by Foreigners. *The Standard Digital*. November 29. Available online: https://www.standardmedia.co.ke/article/2000142876/kenyan-government-bans-adoption-of-children-by-foreigners (accessed on 15 July 2018).

Mbotela, James. 1934. *Uhuru wa watumwa (The Freeing of Slaves)*. London: Sheldon Press.

Mezmur, D. Benyam. 2010. "The Sins of The 'Saviours'": Child Trafficking in The Context of Intercountry Adoption in Africa. Information Document N° 2 for the attention of the Special Commission of June 2010 on the practical operation of the Hague Convention of 29 May 1993 on Protection of Children and Co-operation in Respect of Intercountry Adoption. Available online: https://assets.hcch.net/upload/wop/adop2010id02e.pdf (accessed on 11 February 2018).

Miseki, Risa. 2018. Deinstitutionalization of Children in Kenya: Exploring Tensions in the Policy Shift from Dependence on Institutional Care to Family—Based Care. Master's thesis, ISS, The Hague, The Netherlands.

Morton, Fred. 2009. Small Change: Children in the Nineteenth-Century East African Slave Trade. In *Children in Slavery through the Ages*. Edited by Gwyn Campbell, Suzanne Miers and Joseph C. Miller. Athens: Ohio University Press, pp. 55–70. Available online: http://www.jstor.org/stable/j.ctt1j7x8dd.6 (accessed on 12 October 2019).

Mugo, John Kabutha. 2004. *Rehabilitation of Street Children in Kenya*. London: IKO, Verlag für Kulturelle Kommunikation.

Mushunje, Mildred T. 2006. Child protection in Zimbabwe: Yesterday, today and tomorrow. *Journal of Social Development in Africa* 21: 12–34.

Mushunje, Mildred T. 2014. Interrogating the relevance of the extended family as a social safety net for vulnerable children in Zimbabwe. *AJSW* 4: 78–110.

Mutavi, Lilian. 2017. Portal on child protection launched. *The Daily Nation*. May 9. Available online: https://www.nation.co.ke/news/Portal-on-child-protection-launched/1056-3920600-vvww1no/index.html (accessed on 2 October 2018).

National Academies of Sciences, Engineering, and Medicine. 2016. *Reaching and Investing in Children at the Margins: Summary of a Joint Workshop by the National Academies of Sciences, Engineering, and Medicine; Open Society Foundations; and the International Step by Step Association (ISSA)*. Washington: The National Academies Press. [CrossRef]

National AIDS and STI Control Programme (NASCOP). 2014. *Kenya AIDS Indicator Survey 2012: Final Report*. Nairobi: National AIDS and STI Control Programme (NASCOP), Available online: http://nacc.or.ke/wp-content/uploads/2015/10/KAIS-2012.pdf (accessed on 13 October 2019).

National Commission for Children, Rwanda, and UNICEF. 2019. Evaluation of Tubarerere Mu Muryango (Let's Raise Children in Families) Programme in Rwanda, Phase 1: Summary. Available online: https://www.unicef.org/rwanda/media/1641/file/TMM%20Summary%20Evaluation%20Phase%20I.pdf (accessed on 4 April 2020).

National Council for Children's Services. 2011. The Framework for the National Child Protection System for Kenya. Available online: https://resourcecentre.savethechildren.net/sites/default/files/documents/5429.pdf (accessed on 21 April 2019).

National Council for Population and Development. 2013. Ending Female Genital Mutilation: Laws Are Just the First Step. Policy Brief, N° 32, June 2013. Available online: https://www.ncpd.go.ke/wp-content/uploads/2016/11/Policy-Brief-32-Ending-Female-Genital-Mutilation-F-1.pdf (accessed on 21 November 2019).

Njoka, John, and John Parry Williams. 2008. *A Technical Assessment of the Legal Provisions and Practices of Guaradinship, Foster Care and Adoption of Children in Kenya.* Nairobi: Department of Children's Services Ministry of Gender, Children and Social Development with the Support of UNICEF, Available online: https://resourcecentre.savethechildren.net/sites/default/files/documents/6399.pdf (accessed on 13 April 2018).

O'Connor, Thomas G., and Michael Rutter. 2000. Attachment disorder behavior following early severe deprivation: Extension and longitudinal follow-up. English and Romanian Adoptees Study Team. *Journal of the American Academy of Child and Adolescent Psychiatry* 39: 703–12. [CrossRef]

Ochieng, Abiud. 2018a. Experts want tough laws on lucrative adoption business. *Daily Nation.* September 23. Available online: https://www.nation.co.ke/news/Experts-want-tough-laws-on-adoption/1056-4772800-or9q5jz/index.html (accessed on 1 October 2018).

Ochieng, Abiud. 2018b. Traffickers on the loose: How children are sold to highest bidder in name of adoption. *Daily Nation.* July 1. Available online: https://www.nation.co.ke/news/How-children-are-sold-to-highest-bidder-in-name-of-adoption/1056-4640320-x1fce6/index.html (accessed on 15 July 2018).

Onyiko, Kennedy Karani, and Daria Kimuli Pechacova. 2015. The Impact of Institutionalization of Street children: A Case Study of Nairobi County. *Research on Humanities and Social Sciences* 5: 160–81. Available online: http://www.iiste.org/Journals/index.php/RHSS/article/view/21957 (accessed on 12 October 2019).

Opening Doors. 2012. *Deinstitutionalisation and Quality Alternative Care for Children in Europe: Lessons Learned and the Way Forward. Eurochild Working Paper.* Brussels: Opening Doors.

Otieno, Dorothy. 2018. Child marriage costs Africa trillions of shillings, World Bank warns. *Daily Nation.* December 3. Available online: https://www.nation.co.ke/newsplex/earlymarriage/2718262-4876266-41d2rb/index.html# (accessed on 10 December 2019).

Parsons, Timothy. 1999. *The African Rank-and-file: Social Implications of Colonial Military Service in the King's African Rifles, 1902–1964.* Portsmouth: Heinemann.

Pinheiro, Paulo Sérgio. 2006. World Report on Violence Against Children. *United Nations.* Available online: https://www.unicef.org/violencestudy/I.%20World%20Report%20on%20Violence%20against%20Children.pdf (accessed on 12 February 2018).

Richter, Linda M., and Amy Norman. 2010. AIDS orphan tourism: A threat to young children in residential care. *Vulnerable Children and Youth Studies* 5: 217–29. [CrossRef]

Roelen, Keetie. 2016. *Cash for Care: Making Social Protection Work for Children's Care and Well-Being.* London: Family for Every Child.

Rutter, Michael, Lucie Andersen-Wood, Celia Beckett, Danie Bredenkamp, Jenny Castle, Christine Groothues, Jana Kreppner, Lisa Keaveney, Catherine Lord, and Thomas G. O'Connor. 1999. Quasi-autistic patterns following severe early global privation. English and Romanian Adoptees (ERA) Study Team. *Journal of Child Psychology and Psychiatry* 40: 537–49. [CrossRef]

Save the Children International. 2015. *A Sense of Belonging: Understanding and Improving Informal Alternative Care Mechanisms to Increase the Care and Protection of Children, with a Focus on Kinship Care in East Africa.* Nairobi: Save the Children, Available online: https://resourcecentre.savethechildren.net/node/9081/pdf/final_regional_report_updated_21052015.pdf (accessed on 10 October 2019).

Scolforo, Mark. 2019. US Man Accused of Sex Abuse at Kenyan Orphanage He Founded. *AP News.* July 12. Available online: https://apnews.com/bcbb3814448c430490dcedfc10848277 (accessed on 14 December 2019).

Selman, Peter. 2009. The rise and fall of intercountry adoption in the 21st century. *International Social Work* 52: 575–94. [CrossRef]

Skovdal, Morten, and Catherine Campbell. 2010. Orphan competent communities: A framework for community analysis and action. *Vulnerable Children and Youth Studies* 5: 19–30. [CrossRef]

Suda, Collette A. 1997. Street Children in Nairobi and the African cultural ideology of kin-based support system. *Child Abuse Review* 6: 199–217. [CrossRef]

Tolfree, David. 1995. *Roofs and Roots: The Care of Separated Children in the Developing World.* London: Save the Children Fund, Farnham: Arena/Ashgate Publishing.

Tolfree, David. 2003. *Community Based Care for Separated Children.* Stockholm: Save the Children.

Ucembe, Stephen. 2015a. Charitable Children Institutions in Kenya: Factors Influencing Institutionalization of Children. Available online: https://www.academia.edu/15586601/Factors_Influencing_Institutionalization_of_Children_in_Kenya (accessed on 4 April 2018).

Ucembe, Stephen. 2015b. Institutionalization of Children in Kenya: Does Institutionalization of Children in Kenya Neglect a Child Rights Based Approach. Available online: https://bettercarenetwork.org/sites/default/files/Institutionalization%20of%20Children%20in%20Kenya%20-%20A%20Child%20Rights%20Perspective.pdf (accessed on 4 April 2018).

Ucembe, Stephen. 2015c. Exploring the Nexus between Social Capital and Individual Biographies of "Care leavers" in Nairobi, Kenya: A Life Course Perspective. *Social Policy for Development (SPD)*. Available online: http://hdl.handle.net/2105/33427 (accessed on 4 January 2019).

Ucembe, Stephen. 2016. Institutional care for children in Kenya. In *Residential Child and Youth Care in a Developing World: Global Perspectives*. Edited by Islam Tuhinul and Leon Fulcher. Cape Town: Pretext/CYC-Net.

UNICEF. 2003a. *Africa's Orphaned Generations*. New York: UNICEF/UNAIDS.

UNICEF. 2003b. *Children in Institutions: The Beginning of The End? The Cases of Italy, Spain, Argentina, Chile and Uruguay*. Florence: Innocenti Research Centre.

UNICEF. 2017. UNICEF Annual Report Kenya. Available online: https://www.unicef.org/about/annualreport/files/Kenya__2017_COAR.pdf (accessed on 6 October 2019).

UNICEF. 2018a. *Situation Analysis of Children and Women in Kenya 2017*. Nairobi: UNICEF.

UNICEF. 2018b. *Social Protection Budget Brief: Investing in Inclusiveness in Rwanda*. Rwanda: United Nations Children's Fund (UNICEF), Available online: https://www.unicef.org/esaro/UNICEF-Rwanda-2018-Social-Protection-Budget-Brief.pdf (accessed on 4 April 2020).

Wanyama, Frederick O., and Anna G. McCord. 2017. *The Politics of Scaling Up Social Protection in Kenya*. ESID Working Paper No. 87. Manchester: The University of Manchester.

White, Luise. 1990. Separating the men from the boys: Constructions of gender, sexuality, and terrorism in Central Kenya, 1939–1959. *International Journal of African Historical Studies* 23: 1–25. [CrossRef]

Wright, Stephen, and Vanessa Allen. 2013. Pilot abused his position at British Airways to molest hundreds of girls at African orphanages while claiming he was doing charity work. *Daily Mail*. September 5. Available online: https://www.dailymail.co.uk/news/article-2408557/British-Airways-pilot-Simon-Wood-abused-position-molest-hundreds-girls-orphanages-Africa.html (accessed on 14 December 2019).

social sciences

MDPI

Article

Algorithmic Justice in Child Protection: Statistical Fairness, Social Justice and the Implications for Practice

Emily Keddell

Social and Community Work Programme, School of Social Science, University of Otago, Dunedin 9054, Aotearoa, New Zealand; emily.keddell@otago.ac.nz

Received: 5 August 2019; Accepted: 26 September 2019; Published: 8 October 2019

Abstract: Algorithmic tools are increasingly used in child protection decision-making. Fairness considerations of algorithmic tools usually focus on statistical fairness, but there are broader justice implications relating to the data used to construct source databases, and how algorithms are incorporated into complex sociotechnical decision-making contexts. This article explores how data that inform child protection algorithms are produced and relates this production to both traditional notions of statistical fairness and broader justice concepts. Predictive tools have a number of challenging problems in the child protection context, as the data that predictive tools draw on do not represent child abuse incidence across the population and child abuse itself is difficult to define, making key decisions that become data variable and subjective. Algorithms using these data have distorted feedback loops and can contain inequalities and biases. The challenge to justice concepts is that individual and group rights to non-discrimination become threatened as the algorithm itself becomes skewed, leading to inaccurate risk predictions drawing on spurious correlations. The right to be treated as an individual is threatened when statistical risk is based on a group categorisation, and the rights of families to understand and participate in the decisions made about them is difficult when they have not consented to data linkage, and the function of the algorithm is obscured by its complexity. The use of uninterpretable algorithmic tools may create 'moral crumple zones', where practitioners are held responsible for decisions even when they are partially determined by an algorithm. Many of these criticisms can also be levelled at human decision makers in the child protection system, but the reification of these processes within algorithms render their articulation even more difficult, and can diminish other important relational and ethical aims of social work practice.

Keywords: child protection; predictive analytics; rights; social justice; algorithms; decision making

1. Introduction

This article takes a critical perspective on the debates occurring in many nations in relation to the use of algorithms to assist with risk judgements in child protection contexts. Fundamental to discussions about the use of large, linked datasets to construct algorithms in this domain are the key ethical issues of fairness, transparency and accountability. Given recent developments, some scholars suggest this framework does not go far enough: that justice and rights are more effective concepts to analyse predictive tools, as they go beyond technical solutions, to consider broader social justice consequences (Gurses et al. 2019; Naranayan 2018). These debates should be of much interest to social work, given the professional commitment to social justice ideals in social work as a discipline, and the sharp uptake of predictive tools in child protection contexts where many social workers practice. This article discusses how the data used to create algorithmic tools affect their usefulness and create important justice issues for both the families child protection systems work with and the social workers charged with their use. Justice issues are discussed with reference to statistical data fairness aspects such as the sample frame, the malleability of data points, and the feedback loop. Justice concepts are examined by connecting the potential for bias in algorithms with wider debates around rights for families in contact with child protection systems. Implications for transparency and implementation within the special context of the child protection system are discussed.

2. Setting the Scene: Algorithms in Context

The use of algorithms in child protection systems is expanding rapidly in the US and UK as well as other jurisdictions (Dencik et al. 2018; Whittaker et al. 2018). Alongside these technical expansions are important ethical and political discussions regarding their use in this context (Keddell 2015b; Dare and Gambrill 2016; Eubanks 2017). The child protection context is one already highly contested in terms of its aims, ideological underpinnings and institutional mechanisms. Whether a child protection system is based on a child protection-, child welfare- or child-focussed policy orientation, for example, will shape its philosophical basis, broad institutional structures, preferred priorities and methods of social work practice (Gilbert et al. 2011). In turn, these broad policy patterns intersect with political and economic structures, with a 'child protection' orientation finding an easy alliance with a neoliberal individualised approach to social problems and a residual state role (Keddell 2015a). Notions of rights are also contested in child protection, as the rights of children and parents have areas of convergence, as well as divergence. Consensus about the point at which they should diverge is often not clear in practice, as many studies of child protection decision making show (Benbenishty et al. 2016). Injecting algorithmic forms of decision making into this context adds a further dimension of complexity when considering justice and rights within a child protection system. As Veale and Brass (2019) note, the use of algorithms in public sector domains can brush over important political debates and the contested nature of policy aims. They note that "the literature on the governance of sociotechnical problems has similarly emphasised the intractability of 'unstructured' or 'semi-structured' problems where there is a lack of consensus around appropriate means and/or ends, and how participatory processes that open up rather than close down are required to socially reach more navigable issues" (p. 5). It would be difficult to find a social policy area with less consensus than child protection, where competing ideologies relating to the proper role of the state in family life, cultural considerations, and children's rights, needs and 'best interests' concepts are diverse and contested (Keddell 2017; Gilbert et al. 2011).

Implications for justice are made even more complex by the socio-technical context of use of algorithmic tools (Green and Chen 2019). There is not a single type of use, a single type of algorithm, uniform types of data, nor a single end user impacted by the use of algorithmic risk prediction tools in child protection. In terms of type of use, algorithmic tools can be used either to distribute preventive family support services, in child protection screening decision making, or in risk terrain profiling to predict spatially where child abuse reports might occur (Cuccaro-Alamin et al. 2017; Daley et al. 2016; van der Put et al. 2017). The type of algorithm selected categorises data in algorithm-specific ways to generate graded recommendations or binary flags and can include decision trees or regression methods amongst others, with varying levels of transparency or opacity. Data provenance or sources are from varied places depending on the national and local context, and have differing levels of representativeness, consent for use, ability for accurate linkage, biases, and 'explainability'. Children and parents involved in the child protection system have a set of complex and at times divergent rights and needs, complicating just who is considered the 'end user' and therefore who the algorithmic tool should be fair to. Finally, how an algorithm intersects with the multi-faceted social negotiations already underway in the child protection decision-making environment is important. How an algorithm is used determines its impact within the socio-technical institutional context that is a child protection organisation, yet discussions often focus on accuracy comparisons at the expense of considering the interacting nature of humans, social and institutional contexts, and algorithmic tools (Green and Chen 2019). Tools are seldom used to automate decisions, but more usually are as an aid to human decisions, and can be made available to all or only some decision makers along the child protection decision making continuum (Allegheny County Department of Human Services 2017; Baumann et al. 2013).

Views on the use of algorithms in child protection can be polarised. As with any new technology or practice, there are important roles for both promoters and sceptics in the development of the debates. On the one hand, some argue predictive tools can contribute to the prevention of child abuse and neglect by efficient prediction of future service contact, substantiation or placement, through the triage of large linked datasets, drawing on more data than a human could rapidly and accurately appraise, and can select predictor variables based on predictive power in real-time (Cuccaro-Alamin et al. 2017). Particularly at system intake, when human decision-makers have limited information and time (particularly poor conditions for optimum decision-making), algorithms can quickly compute risks of future system contact (Cuccaro-Alamin et al. 2017). On the other hand, issues relating to class and ethnic biases in the data used, other sources of variability in the decisions used as data, data privacy implications, the issue of false positives, limited service user consultation and the lack of transparency of algorithmic processes are cited as serious challenges to the use of algorithmic tools in child protection, particularly where the recipients of services experience high levels of social inequalities, marginalisation, and lack of power in the state–family relationship (Keddell 2014, 2015a, 2016; Munro 2019; Eubanks 2017; Dencik et al. 2018).

While some tool developers have made inroads into responding to some of these criticisms, several issues remain unresolved (Chouldechova et al. 2018; Gurses et al. 2019). As Gurses et al. (2019) note, "addressing societal problems embedded in such computing systems may require more holistic approaches … and they appeal to diverse theories, frameworks, and histories that challenge and expand the scope of FAT* studies" (Fairness, accountability and transparency). In what follows, I will discuss several aspects of these unresolved debates, specifically, the nature of the data used to construct such algorithms, the feedback loops algorithms rely on, and the contextual justice issues these create for both social workers and service users.

3. Predictive Tool Development

The use of number-based assessment tools in child protection contexts is not new. For some 30 years, various actuarial tools (that are in fact simple algorithms) have been used in child protection practice. The key aims were to establish consistency and the correct inclusion and weighting of specific risk factors, derived either from research or professional consensus (Gambrill 2005; Shlonsky and Wagner 2005). Actuarial tools have been the subject of debate. Key criticisms are that child abuse and neglect is inherently uncertain and is not directly amenable to prediction either by humans or statistically, as identified risk factors are neither necessary nor sufficient to predict abuse (Munro et al. 2014). Further critiques note that actuarial tools tend to reduce the professional discretion of social workers and do not include either the perspectives or cultural context of parents or children, nor the interpretive, social and relational elements of decision making (Gillingham 2011; Goddard et al. 1999; Munro et al. 2014). However, their accuracy in some studies are better than clinical prediction, while meta-studies show the majority are more accurate, though not all (Bartelink et al. 2015; van der Put et al. 2017).

Algorithmic predictive tools build on the actuarial tradition, arguing that they can improve on actuarial tools in several ways. They are able to draw on more variables derived from large administrative datasets, and weight them directly in relation to the outcome of interest. They can be updated with data in real-time or near real-time; they do not rely on a human to input data; and derive the predictive variables from the data itself, rather than relying on research or professional consensus to identify them (Cuccaro-Alamin et al. 2017). They can then be used to both direct limited resources to the most needy/risky families, or triage notifications to child protection services, serving utilitarian ideals of both demand management in a context of limited resources, and distribute fairly based on need rather than more arbitrary methods of referral or child protection worker decision maker. Based on these logics, tools have been developed and are in use in numerous child protection contexts. One strand of development used linked administrative data to attempt to predict children at risk of future substantiation in the child protection system, originally for the purposes of selection for preventive, in-home visiting services in New Zealand (Vaithianathan 2012; Vaithianathan et al. 2013; Wilson et al. 2015). A later study in the same country trialled a similar tool at the intake centre of the national child protection service and compared the tool's accuracy to human decision makers—social workers—in that context (Rea and Erasmus 2017). Further research used a predictive tool to determine whether the predictions based on the child protection system data could also predict increased risk for hospital admissions and death by maltreatment (Vaithianathan et al. 2018). In the US, Allegheny county in Pennsylvania introduced a predictive tool in child protection screening—the Allegheny Family Safety tool (AFST)—to triage referrals at the point of notification to the child protection system (Vaithianathan et al. 2017). In Florida, tools were introduced by Eckerd Connect and its for-profit partner, Mindshare Technology, to predict child abuse harm, which was then adopted in Connecticut, Louisiana, Maine, Oklahoma and Tennessee and Chicago. Eckerd's tool, the 'rapid feedback safety program' tool was axed after a short time due to its inaccurate predictions. This latter tool rated children's risk of being killed or severely injured in the following two years, but the system was swamped with high-risk scores, including 4000 children deemed at 90% or higher of serious injury or death, while children who did experience serious harm were missed (Jackson and Marx 2017). In the UK, companies such as Xantura and others have been working with at least five local authorities to develop predictive tools to identify families likely to access services with preventive services before they present as high need (McIntyre and Pegg 2018).

In each instance, there have been concerns raised regarding issues such as data accuracy, the accuracy of the tool's predictions, profiling, stigma and data privacy, with varying levels of transparency regarding the tools from their progenitors. For example, a Freedom of Information Act request regarding the predictor variables of Xantura's tool was largely declined due to commercial sensitivity concerns (Sheridan 2018). The Allegheny tool has had much more transparency than others and considerable community involvement, a public technical report, and ethical and impact evaluations, but when asked to report the weighting of the actual variables used, Allegheny Department of Human Services declined to make this or the positive predictive accuracy of the tool—what percentage of those it accurately identifies at different risk levels—public (Eubanks 2018). In Aotearoa New Zealand, political concerns regarding the development of predictive tools in child welfare stopped further research on the tool's use and implementation due to concern about the experimental design (Kirk 2016). Concerns about the ethical issues associated with these tools have also been examined (Keddell 2015a, 2016; Dare and Gambrill 2016), yet there have been few examinations of algorithm use in child protection from the perspective of the growing movement on fairness, transparency and accountability, nor a consideration of the limits of technical solutions to the important justice issues they evoke (Chouldechova 2017).

What are the outstanding challenges to fairness, and the justice and rights issues they raise, when considering predictive algorithms in child protection? Key statistical biases in the data used to create child protection predictive models are as follows. Firstly, the lack of representativeness of the data sample frame, challenging the right to non-discrimination. The social malleability of the outcome an algorithmic tool is trained on, and the fundamental problems with how the algorithm 'learns' via its feedback loop both challenge the right to non-discrimination and equality of treatment, as they can result in people not being treated in a 'like for like' manner. They may also, through inequalities in the training data, reinforce classed and racialized inequity that is not reflective of actual differences in incidence. These claims are now examined.

4. Statistical Fairness and Social Justice

The concept of fairness has multiple definitions when used to analyse algorithms (Naranayan 2018). Definitions relate broadly to statistical fairness and social fairness or justice—but they are interrelated as discussed below. Statistical fairness issues include the sample frame (the boundaries defining the data sample), how feedback loops are constructed, and differences in predictive parity (how accurate the algorithm is for different groups). Social definitions of fairness are much broader, relating directly to social justice and rights. Moral conceptualisations of rights are relatively broad, while legal rights are more restricted and clearly defined. Rights-based definitions of fairness generally describe the right to equality of access, treatment and outcomes and the right to non-discrimination—that is, to not be unfairly targeted for restriction of rights. If rights are restricted, this should be proportionate to a person's harm or risk of harm, and non-arbitrary. Social definitions of fairness also encompass the right to due process—that is, the individual right to equality of treatment under the law and law-like systems, which is what the child protection system is. These are key aspects to consider when an algorithmic tool is used to define risk, as the potential for false positives within an algorithmic construction of risk (and other accuracy issues discussed below) can unfairly discriminate, and result in either an arbitrary or dis-proportionate response to the perceived level of risk. It can also challenge one's right to due process by resting on a risk of future harm potential and similarity to a group, rather than current individual behaviour (Hughes 2017). These processes therefore can create what McQuillan (2015) calls 'states of exception' when it comes to rights, with those calculated as high risk essentially losing rights claims due to their perceived 'high-risk' status (Keddell 2015b). Eubanks (2017) argues that in the child protection system due to the profound inequalities in the populations in system contact (often highly classed and raced), that algorithmic tools are more likely to be used because it is a 'low rights' environment to begin with, where few end 'users' have the power or resources to challenge tool use.

Finally, a social justice definition of fairness expects an algorithm not to reproduce or exacerbate social inequalities relating to group rights, such as those related to race, class or gender, a key claim of critics of algorithmic use in public services (Lepri Letouze et al. 2017; Barocas et al. 2017; Eubanks 2017; Keddell 2015b). In child protection systems, the rights of parents and children are both affected by algorithm use. Parents rights in particular are affected, and the emotive aim of protecting children from harm is often used to justify both data use without consent and the inevitable false positives (Dare 2013). Whether the child protection system is considered benign or punitive also affects views of rights considerations in child protection (Dare and Gambrill 2016). To be offered a voluntary, in-home support service or better housing has different ramifications than being investigated for child abuse. There are national differences in how child protection systems are constructed that shape the service offered in response. However, critical perspectives of child protection systems point out that in most Anglophone countries they operate as a key site of the reproduction of social inequalities, have both care and control functions and, while offering protection, can also promote normative parenting ideals mired in cultural and class specificities (Edwards and Gillies 2015). Furthermore, the mixed outcomes of child protection intervention for both children and their families point to the less positive implications of protection-oriented systems that rely on legal intervention within a broader residualist or neoliberal political and economic system (Gilbert et al. 2011; Featherstone et al. 2014).

5. Statistical Fairness and the Sample Frame

The first element of statistical fairness that relates to justice considered here centres on the sample frame, as this should capture the whole population it is attempting to predict an event within, or be a randomly selected, large subsample of that population. Without this, the algorithm "diverges from the population it attempts to represent" (Lepri Letouze et al. 2017, p. 7; Sloane 2018). This basic statistical principle ensures that predictions reflect accurate incidence base rates across an entire population and subpopulation groups. Without representational data of a phenomenon, an algorithm's predictions will become skewed, as it does not have an accurate picture of incidence, so it cannot find the predictor variables related directly to the phenomenon of interest (the outcome variable) (Barocas et al. 2017). As it chooses predictor variables from the data it is provided with, skewed datasets may pick up confounding variables that predict the outcome it is trained on, but neither the outcome, nor the relationships between the predictors and the outcome of actual interest may be reliable.

This is especially pertinent in the child protection context, where proxies for child abuse in the child protection data algorithms are trained on may be only weakly related to abuse incidence across the population (Keddell 2016). This is because the sample frame is not representative of child abuse incidence, but instead reflects reported abuse. Much child abuse and neglect are never reported, and many families that are reported may be subject to both surveillance and personal biases. Via these processes, the sample frame available in data generated by child protection systems is not representative of the prevalence of child abuse across a population (Keddell 2015b, 2016; Daro 2009; McDonell et al. 2015; Swahn et al. 2006). For example, a study of a cohort of New Zealand children born in 1998 found that 10% were substantiated for child abuse within the child protection system, but a more representative longitudinal study in the same country found that while 10% of children had 'definitely' been abused, a further 27% 'probably had'. Even if only half of the 'probably had' group had been, that would be 23%, showing the higher rates of self-reported abuse compared to child protection system data (Danese et al. 2009; Rouland and Vaithianathan 2018).

In another example, a study examining the assumed intergenerational transmission of child abuse found that the greatest influence on the reported levels of intergenerational transmission was the role of detection bias as expressed in Child Protection Service reports (Widom et al. 2015). The extent of the intergenerational transmission of abuse and neglect as recorded in the system contact data "depended in large part on the source of the information used. Individuals with histories of childhood abuse and neglect have higher rates of being reported to child protection services (CPS)for child maltreatment but do not self-report more physical and sexual abuse than matched comparisons" (Widom et al. 2015, p. 1480). The way earlier reports to child protection systems affect later reports is another way in which child protection system data can become skewed. While an algorithm is likely to find earlier reports highly predictive of later reports, (see Wilson et al. 2015), the contribution of greater surveillance of families who have been reported before is not accounted for, and is unlikely to be acknowledged in an unthinking algorithmic process unable to understand these confounds (Keddell 2016). An algorithm views re-reports as unconnected by surveillance mechanisms.

If under-reported abuse was evenly spread across the population, there would be less concern about using child protection system data in predictive tools, as while some people would be missed, those identified would be an evenly spread subset of incidence. But there are substantial inequalities built into child protection system data that may not evenly reflect under-reporting (Bywaters 2015). For example, Swahn et al. (2006) compared self-reported abuse amongst detained youths with their child protection records. They found that official data generally "seriously underestimated the prevalence of maltreatment" (p. 415). Importantly, they also found that abused African Americans and girls were both more likely to have court records of abuse compared to Whites/Hispanics, and boys respectively. For example, 86% of White youths self-reported abuse, but only 12% had court records of abuse, 79% of Hispanics self-reported abuse, while just 7% had a court record. For African Americans, 83% self-reported abuse, while 19% had a court record. When converted to a ratio of self-report to court records, this ratio differed between groups, with 1:7 for whites, 1:11 for Hispanics, and 1:4 for African Americans, suggesting that African Americans are more likely to be reported for abuse than other groups, despite very similar self-reported rates of abuse. Inconsistencies between self-reported child abuse or incidence studies, and child protection system contact profoundly affect the ability of predictive tools to accurately identify those at risk of abuse, and lends weight to claims of racial and class-based discrimination built into such tools, as it may lead to some groups (for example, African-Americans) to be considered high risk by a predictive tool, and other ethnic groups to be calculated as low risk, when true incidence across these groups may be more similar than CPS reports suggest.

6. Issues in Predictive Parity between Racialized Groups—How Should Fairness Be Evaluated with a View to Justice?

Algorithmic prediction tools are used to generate risk scores, and at each risk level, the accuracy rates change—that is, the rates of positive predictive accuracy: what % of those identified have the outcome, as well as other indicators such as false positives, and true and false negatives (Chouldechova et al. 2018). One definition of statistical fairness in the use of predictive analytics is ensuring that the rates of true positives are equal between population groups, although this 'predictive parity' may change the risk level at which intervention of some kind occurs for each group, or change the rates of false negatives between groups (For example, the COMPAS debate over racial bias embedded in criminal justice tools was essentially over predictive parity (Whittaker et al. 2018)). Reducing one type of statistical bias may increase another. This means trade-offs are inevitable but, as discussed below, this is even more complex in child protection, as what is considered a true or false positive is mired in the social contexts they are interpreted in, producing many further confounding variables (Chouldechova et al. 2018; Whittaker et al. 2018). Further, the use of algorithmic tools takes place in a complex institutional and human environment where many factors contribute to decision outcomes, not the tool alone.

One important factor to know in order to judge the trade-offs between competing fairness criteria is the basic positive predictive accuracy of the model (the proportion of those identified as high risk that have the outcome of interest), together with what cut-off point recommendations will be generated at, and comparing them to what currently happens in a given context. It is only by knowing both predictive accuracy and comparing that to current practice that the inevitable 'weighing up' of harms and benefits can be done. The accuracy of algorithms in child protection is often reported as an 'area under the curve', instead of the more everyday understanding of positive predictive values. The few times positive predictive values are given in reports, they tend to be low. For example, one study shows 25% of those categorised in the top 10% of risk were true positives when measured over time (Wilson et al. 2015). A study of human decision-makers at the intake service of a child protection agency found that they were 60% accurate in their estimations of future harm, although the algorithmic tool used was 66% accurate (Rea and Erasmus 2017). Bartelink et al. (2015) in a meta-analysis of studies of decision-making tools in child protection found that the relative improvement of actuarial tools is around 10% improvement in accuracy (Bartelink et al. 2015). Their study also shows that the context of decision-making is important: in some studies, actuarial or predictive models are more accurate, in others clinical and predictive tools are about equal, and in a few, humans are more accurate, especially in complex decision contexts (Bartelink et al. 2015). These varied findings show the importance of actual comparisons with humans in context, rather than vague claims based on non-comparable research that 'algorithms are better'.

As mentioned, comparative accuracy studies or evaluations are rare. This because they are difficult to conduct, can be controlled by commercial interests, and are sensitive to public critique. One of the few to conduct a substantial independent evaluation of a child protection prediction tool and make it public, compared accuracy rates before and after implementation of the Allegheny Family Safety tool (AFST) (Goldhaber-Fiebert and Prince 2019). The tool does not mandate decisions but is used in conjunction with human decision makers as a decision support tool at the point of notification. The tool scores notifications from 0–20, and those scoring highly must be discussed with a supervisor. The case is then screened in or out. The evaluation was premised on a subsequent 'case open' decision by a case worker to judge whether the screen-in decision had been correct, and on a time limited re-referral rate to see if screen outs had improved. A caseworker is likely to have collected much more depth and quality of information and can weigh up the complex ethical issues at stake, so their judgement for these reasons are a good way to evaluate whether the algorithm-assisted decision was correct (Bartelink et al. 2015). On the other hand, the potential for bias still remains in the human decision and, as discussed below, particularly when considering racial equity, relying on a potentially biased human decision to test the accuracy of a potentially biased algorithmic one appears tautological. A recent study, for example, found that humans using an algorithm to inform their decision still showed bias when combining it with their own judgement process (Green and Chen 2019).

Nevertheless, overall, the evaluation found an improvement of those children 'screened in' who then had a case opened, of 2.9%, from 43.7% to 46.6%. Of interest is that the improvement is small, (as were all changes) and that even with the tool, 53% of screen-ins are still considered false positives. The evaluation also showed the tool led to a small decrease in the accuracy of screen outs, down to 72.3% from 73.9% (based on those re-referred within a 6 month period), showing that those who were 'screened out' using the tool had a higher chance of re-referral, than before its introduction. On the one hand, it could be argued that the conclusion the tool reduced screen out accuracy is somewhat simplistic, as many community factors can affect rates of re-referral: policy changes, changes to the provision of preventive services, changes in poverty levels, and changes in social cohesion (Klein and Merritt 2014). On the other hand, a key claim of algorithmic tools is that they are able to reflect these rapidly changing social and organisational conditions in order to make predictions. This issue points to the difficulties of evaluating predictive tools in context, when so many confounding factors affect both algorithmic and human decision-making, as well as highlighting the limits of the data to begin with: without all relevant data, the tool cannot account for it in its computations.

The evaluation also measured the effect of the AFST on racial disparities. The evaluation shows that for those children screened out, the tool had no effect on the chances of re-referral for either Black or White children (p. 21). For those screened in, the percentage of Black children who were first screened in and then had a 'case opened' on them remained the same before and after the tool's introduction, at 47%, while the percentage of White children with a case opened increased from 39% to 46%. So while disparities between the groups of what could be considered 'true positives' reduced, this was because of a moderate increase of 7% in the perceived accuracy of White child screen-ins, not an improvement in the accuracy of Black child screen-ins, (who are in this case the protected class), nor of a decrease in the disproportionality of Black children (that is, the comparison to their population rate). As mentioned, this method of measuring accuracy relies on a human decision that could be subject to bias—that is, to 'open the case'. This is circuitous reasoning, as the tool's introduction is premised on its unbiased accuracy, yet a human, potentially biased, decision to open the case is used to judge it. While the case worker is not supplied with the score as a way to reduce the confirmation bias aspect of this process, nevertheless, the case worker knows that the case was screened in, in order for them to now be investigating it. This is an issue for the use of subsequent 'case opens' for all findings of the evaluation, but particularly so for evaluating changes in racial disparities.

Is there a more objective measure to add to this 'case open' measure in order to evaluate the claim that the tool 'reduces racial disparities'? An objective measure required to assess racial disparities is any change to the proportion of Black and White children notified, who were then screened in. This did not appear to be reported in the evaluation. This objective metric—how did the tool affect the proportion of screen-ins, by race—was absent. This example highlights the many nuanced issues of comparing racial groups when evaluating algorithmic tools, and in particular, what counts as equality of outcome.

The tool's evaluation raises the question: how should 'true positives' be measured when considering racial justice questions? If a subsequent 'case opening' is equated with a 'true positive', then the AFST tool reduces racial disparities by improving the accuracy of white child 'case openings'. But if equality is reducing the disproportionality of Black children being screened in compared to their population share, or disparities between White and Black children's rates of screen in, then this tool's effect is not known. But nor could either of these measures be taken solely as evidence of success—in order to consider that reduction successful, one needs to know the incidence of abuse across the population (see above). Reducing protection for Black children is an equally poor outcome, and changes in screen-ins could reflect increasing community need/incidence or bias in referrers. However, as above, algorithmic tools claim to be able to account for all these factors despite the limits of the data used. How an algorithm crystallises and reproduces disproportionality remains an enduring issue, reproducing the disparities already within the wider interlocking child welfare systems, obscuring the ways they may be shaped by bias, and providing them with a veneer of objectivity. Interrogating these assumptions highlights not the creation of inequalities in child protection systems by algorithmic tools, but the reproduction and reification of existing ones.

7. The Social Production of Data and the Feedback Loop

In addition to the lack of representativeness of the sample, other data problems can also introduce bias and arbitrariness into predictive tools, challenging rights to equality of treatment. The outcome variables that tools are trained on are usually one of various decision points on the decision-making continuum (Baumann et al. 2013). These include decisions to refer, made by various people outside of child protection systems; decisions to substantiate abuse, made by child protection workers within child protection systems; decisions to remove children, usually made by a judge after a social work recommendation (Chouldechova 2017; Keddell 2016). Each of these decisions can be affected by factors other than the direct abuse or risk of abuse of a child that spring from the social context in which they are made, creating variability in responses to children in similar circumstances, and therefore the data recorded about them (Baumann et al. 2013; Keddell 2014).

For example, a recent study in England found that there were significant regional variations in care proceedings in the court system, suggesting different courts have different practices and thresholds for removal (Harwin et al. 2018). A study in New Zealand found that the site office of the national child protection service was the fourth most predictive variable out of 15 for abuse substantiation, even after other variables had been controlled for, suggesting something about the site office culture itself is at play (Wilson et al. 2015). Another UK study found that an 'inverse intervention law' seemed to be operating, where poor children in neighbourhoods surrounded by a larger less deprived neighbourhood were much more likely to have contact with the child protection system than equally deprived children surrounded by a highly deprived neighbourhood (Bywaters et al. 2015). Others point out that decisions to notify, substantiate and investigate child abuse can be shaped by multiple factors such as the values and beliefs of the social worker, experience, role type, perceptions of risk, available resources and professional or institutional cultures (Bywaters et al. 2018; Davidson-Arad and Benbenishty 2016; Fallon et al. 2013; Fleming et al. 2014; Fluke et al. 2016; Keddell 2014, 2016). Variations in specific ethnic groups' contact rates can be particularly affected by both bias and service factors. Indigenous children's system contact in Canada was more related to the variable provision of local culturally appropriate prevention services, than differences in case characteristics (Fluke et al. 2010). Māori children in New Zealand were perceived by social workers as more risky than non-Maori children in the same situation (Keddell and Hyslop 2019). A Spanish study found no bias related to ethnic group or socio-economic status (SES) in caseworkers, but in students about to become social workers, physical abuse in low SES families was perceived as more severe than in mid SES families, suggesting experience may influence bias in caseworkers (Arruabarrena et al. 2017). In each of these examples, statistical prediction tools that use decision points from the child protection system as the outcome the tool is trained on will reflect, and lend reification to, the many elements that contribute to system contact that have little to do with child abuse, and more to do with inequalities, individual practitioner values, location, decision-making variability and service supply and demand factors (Keddell 2014; McLaughlin and Jonson-Reid 2017).

Importantly, in none of the examples given did system contact reflect only the case characteristics of the actual families involved—all were shaped by other factors. These factors mean that hardly any of the decisions that become data points in predictive tools in the child protection context reflect objective outcomes or, rather, outcomes that represent what is assumed about them. Is a child protection office in a particular location more likely to substantiate cases of domestic violence (DV) as child abuse than another? That means that data derived from that office are likely to assign a higher risk score to children witnessing DV from that area in the future, and not those in the same situation in other areas. Is there classed or racial bias in the populations notified and/or investigated for child abuse? Then the use of, for example, parental contact with child protection systems (the third most predictive variable in one study) (Wilson et al. 2015), or parental contact with the criminal justice system, is just as likely to reinforce existing ethnic inequalities in the system rather than reduce them, as it will erroneously identify ethnic or indigenous minorities as high risk compared to people from other groups.

In Aotearoa New Zealand, when the adults today were children, a ministerial inquiry found that the cause of ethnic disproportionality in New Zealand's child welfare system was due to "forms of cultural racism ... that result in the values and lifestyle of the dominant group being regarded as superior to those of other groups, especially Māori" (p. 9). Many US and UK examples are similar. Certainly, there is evidence of continuing bias that affects who is investigated and how similar parenting behaviours are viewed depending on the parent's socioeconomic and ethnic status (Roberts and Sangoi 2018; Wexler 2018). These processes show the embedded nature of ethnic or racial bias in the data algorithmic tools tend to draw on. As Whittaker et al. (2018) point out in the criminal justice context, "most assessment systems include several risk factors that function as proxies for race. One risk factor that is often used is "parental criminality" which, given the long and well-documented history of racial bias in law enforcement, including the over-policing of communities of color, can easily skew "high risk" ratings on the basis of a proxy for race." (p. 13). These same issues are pertinent to child protection data.

These data issues can skew an algorithm not only when it is created, but over time as data are fed back into it. If those data are inaccurate, then the algorithm's opportunity to correct itself is lost. Chouldechova notes that "A key challenge is that we do not get to observe placement outcomes for a large fraction of cases that are screened out. This makes it difficult to assess the accuracy of the models on the full set of referrals, not just those that were screened in" (Chouldechova et al. 2018, p. 12). Where cases are screened out, but abuse occurs again and is not re-reported, the algorithm learns it is correct, even though it was not. It adjusts its predictor variables accordingly. Likewise, other types of data that could significantly change a child's risk levels are not captured in administrative data, such as improved or decreased levels of informal social support—a key factor in child abuse development (Rostad et al. 2017). A parent might seek formal help from private providers for something that directly affects the likelihood of abuse, yet those data would not be included in the algorithm, nor will changed living arrangements or household membership, all of which could affect true risk (Eubanks 2017). Aradau and Blake note this, commenting that "Debates about big data problematize exactly the limitations of traditional statistical procedures, which ... do not capture the detailed relationships between individuals and groups as they exist and change in particular situations" (Aradau and Blanke 2017, p. 378).

It is these subtle ways that both bias and arbitrariness—equally destructive to notions of fairness—become 'baked in' to administrative data that predictor and outcome variables, and feedback loops over time, are drawn from. This results in consistently over-assigning risk to some people while understating it for others in algorithmic computations in child protection and assigning risks to individuals that may have little to do with their individual true 'risk' level. As Boyd states "Racism, sexism, and other forms of bigotry and prejudice are still pervasive in contemporary society, but new technologies have a tendency to obscure the ways in which societal biases are baked into algorithmic decision making" (Boyd 2014, p. 56).

This lends weight to claims that predictive tools result in the 'poverty profiling' of individuals that could impact negatively on their rights to fair treatment, especially given the marked socioeconomic inequities in child protection system contact (Eubanks 2017, 2018). The child protection context is not a benign one—while protecting children from abuse, unwarranted investigations are experienced by families as stressful, intrusive and stigmatising, while in colonial contexts, they operate as a key site of the ongoing reproduction of inequalities for Indigenous peoples (Healy et al. 2011; Keddell and Hyslop 2019). Choate and Lindstrom (2017), for example, examine the use of parenting capacity assessments that contribute to legal intervention in child protection systems. They find that these assessments rest on euro-centric definitions of family, have not been normed on Indigenous populations, and do not take into account the poverty, poor service access and intergenerational trauma that frame the socio-political contexts of many first nations families. In light of how negative perceptions of Indigenous people can get into data that is then used as the basis of state intervention, there are many movements by Indigenous people that aim to reclaim data sovereignty, arguing that data about Indigenous people should be controlled by them, not the state (see the US Indigenous Data Network https://usindigenousdata.arizona.edu/about-us-0 or Te Mana Raraunga https://www.temanararaunga.maori.nz for examples).

Of increasing interest is who is missing altogether from data sources used to train algorithms. When there are groups who have hardly any contact with administrative systems, the ledger becomes even more unbalanced. The resulting algorithm will not only over-identify poorer and Indigenous or ethnic minority people but will miss risk amongst more affluent populations (Eubanks 2017). The relative intrusion this disparity creates in the lives of those least able to seek redress compared to the escape from scrutiny of wealthier populations challenges rights to non-discrimination, as some people are ascribed high-risk status while others escape surveillance altogether. Big administrative datasets essentially 'go easier' on some people compared to others. These examples highlight the problems in the sample frames used to generate data, and the potential for feedback loops to exacerbate this over time.

8. Consistently Biased?

Others argue that despite all this, the sheer amount of data allow for more consistent predictions and are more accurate as the algorithm self-selects the predictor variables—that is, which variables predict the outcome. Cuccaro-Alamin et al. (2017), for example, argue that "PRM (predictive risk modelling) as an approach is inherently more consistent than other risk assessment procedures. Variable selection, although limited by available data, is mathematical and there is no arbitrary selection of predictors ... they are learning models that continually adjust to new relationships inherent in the data" (p. 293, brackets mine). There are benefits to this, as theoretically speaking, unknown influences, if able to be captured in the data, could be identified by this process that may not be discernible to a human. Yet the limits of the available data are marked as the discussion above shows. Without accurate incidence, and other biases and non-relevant influences on data points, an algorithm's self-selection of variables can result in spurious associations and predictions that reflect bias of some kind, as in the example of parent's contact with child protection systems as a child discussed above. While an algorithm may indeed be a more consistent decision maker, consistently biased or skewed recommendations remain problematic. The algorithm self-selecting predictor variable means errors are also difficult to track, leading to reduced transparency.

Some argue that a predictive tool's function is only to predict, not suggest causes. What does it matter if it is predicting based on unknown associations? When the data are so varied (as above) and the associations generated unknown, the function of the algorithm may be calculating quite spurious associations and replicating 'ecological fallacies'. The invisibility of the function requires examination, including the underpinning assumptions that imply causality (Rowe 2019). A predictive tool may not *claim* causality, yet it is used in child protection as if it does imply causality, because high-risk scores generate information about specific families that can lead to intervention on those families (Pearl and Mckenzie 2018). This means that the use of an algorithm can identify families whose risk of child protection system contact may have little to do with their specific family relationships or behaviour, but results in an individualistic response that assumes there is something deterministic about them. As Mittelstadt et al. (2016) note: "Causality is not established prior to acting upon the evidence produced by the algorithm ... Acting on correlations can be doubly problematic ... Spurious correlations may be discovered rather than genuine causal knowledge ... Even if strong correlations or causal knowledge are found, this knowledge may only concern populations while actions are directed towards individuals" (p. 5).

Where data expected to affect predictions do not, this should cause developers to ask more holistic questions about why this is the case. For example, health data were included in one study, but as they did not increase accuracy, were withdrawn from the model (Wilson et al. 2015). This could have indicated that the predictive tool was reproducing child protection system surveillance patterns (or something else), rather than predicting abuse across the population, as parental and child health issues (prematurity, poor mental health, substance abuse), are well known predictors of child abuse in the research literature (Munro 2002). Chouldechova et al. (2018) note this problem, stating that when considering why certain variables are highly predictive of the outcome variable in child protection algorithms, we "may nevertheless fail to offer a satisfactory answer to why more penetrating than that the particular values of input variables combined to produce a high-risk prediction. One may be able to understand the risk factors involved and how they combine in the model, but the models have no claim to being causal. The overall utility of such an understanding may be quite limited" (p. 11).

9. Improving the Feedback Loop or Reducing Justice?

This discussion so far explores statistical issues relating to fairness, highlighting the technical complexities of data production and evaluating tools, but as many authors highlight, broader discussions of justice must consider algorithmic use against a wider set of ethical and political concerns (Dencik et al. 2018; McQuillan 2015). Naranayan (2018) argues we need more focus on "connecting technical issues with theories of justice". When an algorithm has low accuracy related to problems with feedback, the technical solution focusses on improving the range of data (also called 'tech solutionism' (Gurses et al. 2019)). The larger justice issues around improving the data in the child protection context are not discussed. For example, after the cancellation of the Eckerd tool in Chicago child protection which overestimated risk, one of the solutions proposed was to reverse the current practice of expunging unsubstantiated cases from official records (and data) (Jackson and Marx 2017).

From a technical perspective, removing unsubstantiated cases introduced statistical bias into the data by excluding cases that were investigated, abuse was not found, but nevertheless may have had other similar characteristics as those that were. Their exclusion damaged the learning ability of the algorithm, as it reduced its ability to make fine-grained, more accurate differentiations between different cases. The fix proposed was to reverse expungement. But in some states, expungement exists to protect people's right to future due process, so that an earlier child abuse investigation does not taint future notifications and judgements. This method is used in some states to reduce racial and legal biases (Jackson and Marx 2017). Without data on unsubstantiated cases, an algorithm cannot learn whether it was correct in its earlier prediction, but to seek increasing amounts of unsubstantiated cases included in data could exacerbate the very biases predictive tools claim to reduce, by reproducing the racial and classed biases in referrals, even though they may be unfounded (Boyd 2014). This important justice issue should not be subsumed by the need to increase the accuracy of an algorithm.

This issue reflects the incidence issue described above. For those cases never notified to child protection services or notified but not investigated, neither of these situations means abuse has not occurred, just that no one saw and reported it. It is for these reasons that the 'moneyball' analogy often used to describe algorithmic tools in child protection is a bad one (Riley 2018). In baseball, all outcomes are easily observable and categorically definite. Player x scored a home run, and everybody saw it. When it comes to child abuse, neither the action itself is easily defined, nor who sees it. A child left in a bath slips and hits their head getting out. The parent was distracted by another child. Is this neglect? And what if no one saw it and reported it? Did it happen? Not in the data it did not. And what about if this situation occurred in a poor neighbourhood as opposed to a wealthy whiter one? Will it be viewed differently, and hence get into the data differently? Attempts to improve data lead to increasingly intrusive surveillance and challenges to legal equity. This means that while some claim a predictive model helps track and correct error rates, in fact error rates in real incidence are fundamentally unknown (see Dare and Gambrill 2016).

As is described above, attention to precisely what feedback the model is referring to in its selected outcome is important and challenges the ability of the model to learn accurately. It not only does not 'see' some abuse, the lack of consensus of the definition of abuse creates further distorted data, as decisions to investigate or substantiate abuse can be highly variable (Doherty 2016; Munro 2002). In the classic Dawes et al. (1989) study of predictive abilities, the three outcomes they used to compare human and actuarial predictions were: major mental illness, the detection of brain damage, and the prediction of survival times relating to illness. All three, or at least the last two, are objective, concrete outcomes unaffected by earlier predictions about them occurring. Neither of these criteria apply to the child protection context, where the outcome is ill-defined and earlier decisions may affect later ones, as earlier substantiations may lead to greater surveillance, further interventions, and a greater likelihood of substantiating further referrals (Keddell 2016). This means that the future recurrence of the outcome required to 'train' the algorithm so it can improve on its predictive accuracy is sullied in the child protection context—it is trying to predict an outcome that is socially malleable and affected by the system that is at once intervening on it and recording data about it, creating confounding variables.

These inaccuracies in the feedback loop make it difficult for a predictive tool to become more accurate over time. As Gambrill and Schlonsky note in regards to actuarial tools: "The actual risk of recurrence cannot be explored in the absence of intervention by child protective service agencies. Given these limitations, obtaining an accurate base rate of maltreatment is probably impossible ... Further, discovering the false positive rate is almost impossible. Once the risk has been responded to (i.e., child welfare services are provided) the likelihood of recurrence of abuse in the absence of intervention cannot be determined." (Gambrill and Shlonsky 2000, p. 823).

The damaging nature of the effects of poor feedback can be understood as an accuracy effect, and a justice effect. The distorted exposure to referrers of some groups of people relative to others, and other distortions in incidence reduces the effectiveness of the feedback loop by feeding back into the algorithm those cases that are likely to be a small proportion of child abuse cases across a population, and a skewed proportion of those total cases, overestimating the predictive power of factors such as low income, race and previous service involvement. Presented with only a proportion of future events as feedback, the algorithm then will correct its weighting of predictor variables, and this may reinforce not only inaccurate predictions, but may reproduce, not reduce, the biases within child protection systems. In conclusion, the poor sample frame and feedback issues create significant problems for the use of predictive tools in child protection. Now, I will turn to the implications for social workers using these tools and comment on rights implications.

10. Implications for Practice: Social Worker Responsibility and Family Participation

The use of predictive tools presents a number of implementation issues affecting both social workers and the 'users' of child protection services. One implementation issue for social work practice is the relative responsibility of the social worker for the decision made. Social workers have responsibilities to ethical principles and codes that assume they are solely responsible for the decisions they make, and they may also hold legal, statutorily defined responsibilities within child protection practice. For example, it is a 'social worker' in the Aotearoa New Zealand legislation who must 'form a belief' that a child is in need of 'care and protection' before legal proceedings can be undertaken (s14, New Zealand Government 1989), and decisions should uphold social justice and human rights obligations (International Federation of Social Work 2014). At the same time, within child protection there are numerous examples of social workers attracting blame, particularly for child deaths, even when there are extensive wider system failings (Lees et al. 2011; Munro 2011). The importation of new public management methods, within neoliberal economic and public service environments, heightens this individualising of blame, as notions of individual responsibility combine with an emphasis on audit and accountability, leaving social workers vulnerable to high levels of personal responsibility (Healy 2009).

In the context of algorithmic tools that may contribute to or even mandate decisions, a social worker who relies on such a tool, but cannot explain, nor understand its inner 'black box' workings, is vulnerable to approbation from professional regulators, managers within the system and families they are working with. They may be construed as the 'human in the loop' essential to limit the unrestrained governance by the algorithm or retain human oversight. But in a high stakes environment and high blame environment, the opposite could also occur—the human actor may defer to the algorithm (Rahwan 2018). In practice, this can leave a social worker vulnerable to either excessive blame if they did not follow the risk score, or captured in a 'moral crumple zone' if they do. Elish (2019) describes a moral crumple zone as "how responsibility for an action may be misattributed to a human actor who had limited control over the behavior of an automated or autonomous system. Just as the crumple zone in a car is designed to absorb the force of impact in a crash, the human in a highly complex and automated system may become simply a component—accidentally or intentionally—that bears the brunt of the moral and legal responsibilities when the overall system malfunctions" (p. 20).

Studies of child protection workers' reactions to algorithmic tools illustrate some of these issues. While most practitioners surveyed as part of an Aotearoa New Zealand trial of a tool at intake were open to the predictive tool being used, a significant minority viewed the tool as a labelling device too focussed on risk while minimising protective factors. They were concerned that the data used did not contain accurate information, pointing out that "some information is not able to be put into the model even though it may include the most accurate information about a child or young person (and) some information is reported in the CYF database without being verified" (Rea and Erasmus 2017, p. 83). These concerns echo the more abstract concerns about data discussed above. In the Allegheny county trial, a quarter of practitioners using the tool chose to override its recommendations, suggesting some level of discomfort with the tool's scoring function, but also suggesting workers may not feel as pressured by the tool as I have suggested above (Chouldechova et al. 2018). The latter evaluation also showed that the tool did not improve consistency between case workers, suggesting many exercised discretion over how much they used the tool's recommendation. In a study by Bosk (2018) child welfare workers felt that the tendency of statistical tools to operate on the basis of the presence or absence of risk factors without an understanding of how they interacted in the lives of specific individuals led to an overestimation of risk in unfair ways, penalising people for demographic factors such as having more than three children, or children born close together. Thus, some frontline practitioners who often have the best 'practice-near' experience of the system, have reservations about data quality, and how the data shapes practice decisions (White et al. 2009). An ability to critically reflect on the tool may protect against the possibility of a tool becoming too powerful, and is a reminder that practitioners often utilise discretion even in highly constrained systems. How tools are implemented and managed are crucial to assisting workers to maintain ultimate control for decisions made.

There are also ethical issues of predictive tool use relating to families involved in the child protection system. Families should be able to expect decisions to be explained to them and have input into decision-making processes. Diminished input into decisions challenges many best practice and legal requirements to consider parent and child perspectives and include them in decision making (Healy and Darlington 2009). This lack of explainability affects social worker's ethical mandates. Where social workers themselves are unable to explain decisions to families, this lack of transparency may cause a sense of moral injury: where social workers know that transparency around decisions, and the implied ability for parents to contribute to and participate in decisions that affect them, is important, but are unable to implement this in their practice (Fenton and Kelly 2017). The marked lack of family involvement as stakeholders in tool development is also a justice issue. There is a call for citizens' councils or panels as ways to include a citizen voice when algorithmic tools are being developed in public service contexts. Yet the position of parents particularly as potential 'abusers of children' is a powerful unspoken reason for their rights as mandated 'users' to be diminished in both data consent and participation discussions. As people involved with child protection services come from the most marginalised populations, and due to the mandated nature of the 'service', the need for this inclusion is arguably even stronger than for other public service users (McQuillan 2018).

11. Human Rights and the Individual—The Right to Reasonable Inference, Consent and Relational Practice

Social work remains committed to respect for persons and human rights, as well as humane and relationship-based approaches to practice (International Federation of Social Work 2014). How are these aims affected by the limits of the data as described above? Algorithms rely on a process of grouping people according to their statistical similarities to others across a population, based on available data. Most legal conceptualisations of human rights, however, are intimately tied to the individual, and most nation states have undertaken international covenants to protect the rights of individuals. It is clear from the limits of the data in the child protection context that this right requires special protection in the context of the known biases in the child protection data algorithms draw on; the distal and incomplete nature of available data to accurately depict and predict human behaviour; and the 'networked' nature of biases in the data. Other adults in a household in addition to parents may also be risk scored in the prediction process. This can also exacerbate racialised bias, as people's personal networks are likely to reflect histories of racialized disadvantage and poverty, leading to 'networked bias', where parents may be considered high risk due to family members, neighbours or community location (Madden et al. 2017).

The conflation of personal with group risk challenges one's right to be treated as an individual in legal and law-like systems, where due process relies on individual consideration before the law (Barocas and Selbst 2016). This challenges the right to non-discrimination for individuals, as they are judged based essentially on their statistical similarities to others. While the General Data Protection Regulation (EUGDPR EU General Data Protection) enshrines the right to an explanation of algorithmic decisions, Wachter and Mittelstadt (2019) propose an alternative—a right to reasonable inference when using algorithmic scores. It is clear that given the problems with data in the child protection context, anything beyond the most tentative inference is highly contestable, and the 'inference' of high risk may be patently unreasonable. Given the power differential between the child protection system and many people coming into contact with it, their general observation may be exacerbated: "individuals are granted little control and oversight over how their personal data is used to draw inferences about them" (p. 3).

This control is heightened in contexts where there has been no or little consent to the use of data for this purpose. Some ethicists argue that the imperative to protect children from harm should attenuate data privacy concerns, especially when data or information is already shared without consent after a notification has been made to CPS. The highly emotive nature of the politics of child protection encourages this logic. However, the risk of extreme harm is very small, and false positives are high, while the size of the data net is vast, capturing many people for whom no harm will ever be found (the majority of reports in most countries). In this context, families have a right to know at least how their risk score has been interpreted, and the right to challenge it if they feel it is inaccurate. As Drefuss and Chang (2019) provocatively argue, in a 'no consent' or forced consent (to data sharing) environment, the right to challenge and correct is heightened. But whose knowledge is deemed 'correct' in such circumstances, and who controls perceptions of accuracy? The hierarchies of knowledge implicit in algorithmically produced forms of knowledge is that they are objectively correct and uncontestable, while service users' own views about their lives derived from lived experience is relegated to a lesser value, as are any other risk/protective factors not available in the data, nor social worker's own 'guilty knowledge' (that related to values, relationships, emotion and care) (McQuillan 2017; Weick 1999). This 'machinic neoplatonism' can evade due process considerations due to the opacity of algorithmic functions, and "appears to reveal a hidden mathematical order in the world that is superior to our direct experience" (McQuillan 2017, p. 1).

Along with knowledge, relationships themselves are also affected by the 'thoughtlessness' of algorithmic tools. The use of algorithmic tools adds a mechanistic and distant tone to practice relationships and prioritises the task of predicting future harm. In child protection, however, the prediction of future harm is only one of a variety of aims. To actually address the risk of harm, rather than assess it, an engaged and collaborative relationship based on genuineness and trust is needed (Cameron et al. 2013; Spratt and Callan 2004). If people are aware that they have been identified as 'high risk' via predictive tools, perceptions of judgement and stigma may damage the quality of this necessary relationship (Spratt and Callan 2004).

12. Considering the Counter-Argument: Problems in Human Child Protection Decision Making

It is important, however, to note the mirroring of many algorithmic problems in human decisions in the child protection context. Many system inequalities reflect wider socio-structural conditions. Human decisions can also be arbitrary, biased and subject to institutional processes that lead to variations and inequities in decision outcomes (Keddell 2014). Humans can also rely on invisible heuristics and pattern matching that can lead to decisions based on a cognitive categorisation process, rather than a humane, relational approach that considers each individual person (Vedder 1999). Heuristics can become similarly biased when based on experiences that reflect a 'skewed sample' of particular kinds of cases compared to the general population. Other types of discretion-based assessment tools can be introduced to practice with little or no user involvement, direct the focus of practice in perverse or unintended ways dominated by risk, and can lack participatory processes for adults or children. Nor can Social Work claim that social work practice always embodies relationship-based ideals imbued with care, emotion and justice—social work's history is of both care and control, operationalizing many oppressive state agendas (Margolin 1997). The issue with algorithms is that due to the issues above, they replicate these problems, and through the appearance of objective 'science' and the difficulties in explaining them, add another layer of mechanisms that exacerbate rather than address these known injustices.

This leads to a consideration as to whether data can be developed to a point where at least the sampling issues could be corrected. In order to provide incidence data, an extreme level of surveillance would be required, as most abuse takes place in the home. Efforts to create large-scale population-wide databases of children have failed on this point. For example, the 'contact point' database in the UK was established in 2004 in the wake of the Victoria Climbie tragedy (a child who was killed despite many professionals being aware of her ongoing injuries and abuse) and aimed to contain information about all children in the UK. It was set up to try and improve data sharing but was shut down in 2010 due to concerns about both parents and children's rights to privacy, the increase in family surveillance and functionality of the database. The example of contact point highlights issues of class and surveillance more generally. The level of surveillance, data linking and targeting that results from these tools only gain traction because they initially affect people from low socioeconomic backgrounds in 'low rights' environments. When they are applied to middle class people via 'whole of population' approaches, there is often outcry (Eubanks 2017).

Another idea for improving data is to focus on more objective outcomes than those found in child protection agency data, such as child injury hospitalizations (see Vaithianathan et al. 2018). This removes the subjective nature of the outcome variable, and health data are becoming more complete in relation to the whole population, at least in countries where there is a national health system (as opposed to private providers who do not share data (see Eubanks 2017). While some have suggested child deaths, these are often in such small numbers that prediction is not possible, and to combine them with hospitalization data muddies the waters (Vaithianathan et al. 2013). Nevertheless, a focus on hospitalisations may correct the sample frame, improve feedback loops, and reduce some exposure surveillance effects, although the 'spurious correlations' issue discussed above still remain. Another way to consider research development is to focus on the counterfactual, for example focusing on predictive models trained on 'unsubstantiation' as Rodriguez et al. (2019) did, in order to see if protective factors could predict it. While they found accuracy was similar to other tools, they also found that system- and definitional-related factors—rather than family-related factors—were most predictive (such as abuse type, number of days between notification and investigation and if the child was already in foster care). This suggests that the issue remains that some factors unrelated to real harm to children skew the data in significant ways.

13. Conclusions

Evaluating algorithmic tools in child protection by combining technical conceptualisations of fairness with social justice perspectives leads to a number of troubling conclusions. Without a database that reflects incidence, the racial and class disproportionalities within child protection system contact are likely to reproduce inequities that relate as much to surveillance biases as they do to differences in true incidence. Poor and ethnic minority families will therefore be subjected to higher rates of state intervention than real disparities in rates, while other children at risk may be incorrectly assumed to be low risk. Other elements of variability relating to poor outcome definition, and the inevitably messy context of decisions that become data points in databases may heighten inaccuracies and biases. Algorithmic tools can produce ecological fallacies, leading to spurious variable selection and prediction that reflect system factors rather than actual incidence risk. Statistical scores relating to group similarities are used to inform an individually focussed decision that may not reflect that specific person's risk level, but population level risk. As the child protection system is a law-like process with significant implications for people's lives, people should instead have the right to be treated as an individual and have decisions made about their lives that they are able to participate in and understand. Tool evaluations show very small changes to decision-making patterns compared to prior to tool introduction, suggesting the reproduction of existing decision patterns. Because the feedback loop requires information that is fundamentally not known, distortions in data may be exacerbated over time. Remedies to the feedback loop may also contain threats to justice, such as the retaining of unsubstantiated cases within highly racialized contexts. The broader justice implications for replicating, rather than remedying, both social inequities and the known problems with child protection decisions in child protection system data are only just beginning to be fully understood. The implications of algorithm tool use for both families and social workers require careful consideration, as the 'reasonable inference' services users have a right to, may be remarkably tentative in child protection. Social workers occupy a difficult position where they are responsible for upholding ethical codes and principles that may be challenged by using an algorithmic score. Further applied research on the ways social workers, families and algorithms interact as part of complex sociotechnical systems in child protection is needed, as well as ongoing interrogation of the sources and functions of data.

Funding: This research received no external funding.

Conflicts of Interest: The authors declare no conflict of interest.

References

Allegheny County Department of Human Services. 2017. *Developing Predictive Risk Models to Support Child Maltreatment Hotline Screening Decisions.* Allegheny County: Allegheny County Department of Human Services.

Aradau, Claudia, and Tobias Blanke. 2017. Politics of prediction: Security and the time/space of governmentality in the age of big data. *European Journal of Social Theory* 20: 373–91. [CrossRef]

Arruabarrena, Ignacia, Joaquín de Paúl, Silvia Indias, and Mikel García. 2017. Racial/ethnic and socio-economic biases in child maltreatment severity assessment in Spanish child protection services caseworkers. *Child & Family Social Work* 22: 575–86.

Barocas, Solon, and Andrew Selbst. 2016. Big Data's Disparate Impact. *California Law Review* 671: 62. Available online: https://ssrn.com/abstract=2477899 (accessed on 1 March 2019). [CrossRef]

Barocas, Solon, Elizabeth Bradley, Vasant Honavar, and Foster Provost. 2017. Big Data, Data Science, and Civil Rights. Computing Consortium White Paper. Available online: https://arxiv.org/abs/1706.03102 (accessed on 9 August 2018).

Bartelink, Cora, Tom A. van Yperen, and Ingrid J. ten Berge. 2015. Deciding on child maltreatment: A literature review on methods that improve decision-making. *Child Abuse & Neglect* 49: 142–53. [CrossRef]

Baumann, D., Jon Fluke, L. Dalgleish, and H. Kern. 2013. The decision-making ecology. In *From Evidence to Outcomes in Child Welfare: An International Reader*. Edited by Aron Shlonsky and Rami Benbenishty. New York: Oxford University Press, pp. 24–38.

Benbenishty, Rami, Bilha Davidson-Arad, Mónica López, John Devaney, Trevor Spratt, Carien Koopmans, Erik J. Knorth, Cilia LM Witteman, Jorge F. Del Valle, and David Hayes. 2016. Decision making in child protection: An international comparative study on maltreatment substantiation, risk assessment and interventions recommendations, and the role of professionals' child welfare attitudes. *Child Abuse and Neglect* 49: 63–75. [CrossRef] [PubMed]

Bosk, Emily Adlin. 2018. What counts? Quantification, worker judgment, and divergence in child welfare decision-making. *Human Service Organizations: Management, Leadership & Governance*. [CrossRef]

Boyd, Reiko. 2014. African American disproportionality and disparity in child welfare: Toward a comprehensive conceptual framework. *Children and Youth Services Review* 37: 15–27. [CrossRef]

Bywaters, Paul. 2015. Inequalities in child welfare: Towards a new policy, research and action agenda. *British Journal of Social Work* 45: 6–23. [CrossRef]

Bywaters, Paul, Geraldine Brady, Tim Sparks, Elizabeth Bos, Lisa Bunting, Brigid Daniel, Brid Featherstone, Kate Morris, and Jonathan Scourfield. 2015. Exploring inequities in child welfare and child protection services: Explaining the 'inverse intervention law'. *Children and Youth Services Review* 57: 98–105. [CrossRef]

Bywaters, Paul, Geraldine Brady, Lisa Bunting, Brigid Daniel, Brid Featherstone, Chantel Jones, Kate Morris, Jonathan Scourfield, Tim Sparks, and Calum Webb. 2018. Inequalities in English child protection practice under austerity: A universal challenge? *Child & Family Social Work* 23: 1365–2206. [CrossRef]

Cameron, Gary, Marshall Fine, Sarah Maiter, Karen Frensch, and Nancy Freymond. 2013. *Creating Positive Systems of Child and Family Welfare: Congruence with the Everyday Lives of Children and Parents*. Toronto: University of Toronto Press.

Choate, Peter, and G. Lindstrom. 2017. Parenting capacity assessment as a colonial strategy. *Canadian Family Law Quarterly* 37: 41–56.

Chouldechova, Alexandra. 2017. Fair Prediction with Disparate Impact: A Study of Bias in Recidivism Prediction Instruments. *Big Data* 5: 153–63. [CrossRef] [PubMed]

Chouldechova, Alexandra, Emily Putnam-Hornstein, Diana Benavides-Prado, Oleksandr Fialko, and Rhema Vaithianathan. 2018. A case study of algorithm-assisted decision making in child maltreatment hotline screening decisions. *Proceedings of Machine Learning Research* 81: 1–15.

Cuccaro-Alamin, Stephanie, Regan Foust, Rhema Vaithianathan, and Emily Putnam-Hornstein. 2017. Risk assessment and decision making in child protective services: Predictive risk modeling in context. *Children and Youth Services Review* 79: 291–98. [CrossRef]

Daley, Dyann, Michael Bachmann, Brittany A. Bachmann, Christian Pedigo, Minh-Thuy Bui, and Jamye Coffman. 2016. Risk terrain modeling predicts child maltreatment. *Child Abuse & Neglect* 62: 29–38. [CrossRef]

Danese, Andrea, Terrie E. Moffitt, HonaLee Harrington, Barry J. Milne, Guilherme Polanczyk, Carmine M. Pariante, Richie Poulton, and Avshalom Caspi. 2009. Adverse childhood experiences and adult risk factors for age-related disease: Depression, inflammation, and clustering of metabolic risk markers. *Archives of Pediatrics and Adolescent Medicine* 163: 1135–43. [CrossRef] [PubMed]

Dare, Tim. 2013. Predictive risk modelling and child maltreatment: Ethical challenges. In *Children in Crisis*. Hamilton: University of Waikato.

Dare, Tim, and Eileen Gambrill. 2016. *Ethical Analysis: Predictive Risk Models at Call Screening for Allegheny County*. Pittsburgh: Allegheny County Department of Human Services.

Daro, Deborah. 2009. The history of science and child abuse prevention: A reciprocal relationship. In *Preventing Child Maltreatment: Community Approaches*. Edited by Kenneth Dodge and Doriane Coleman. New York: The Guildford Press.

Davidson-Arad, Bilha, and Rami Benbenishty. 2016. Child Welfare Attitudes, Risk Assessments and Intervention Recommendations: The Role of Professional Expertise. *British Journal of Social Work* 46: 186–203. [CrossRef]

Dawes, Robyn M., David Faust, and Paul E. Meehl. 1989. Clinical versus actuarial judgment. *Science* 243: 1668–74. [CrossRef] [PubMed]

Dencik, Lina, Arne Hintz, Joanna Redden, and Harry Warne. 2018. *Data Scores as Governance: Investigating Uses of Citizen Scoring in Public Services*. Cardiff: Cardiff University.

Doherty, Paula. 2016. Child protection threshold talk and ambivalent case formulations in 'borderline' care proceedings cases. *Qualitative Social Work* 16: 698–716. [CrossRef]

Drefuss, Suelette, and Shanton Chang. 2019. Uber surveillance in consumer markets. Paper presented at the Digital Citizen's Conference, University of Melbourne, Melbourne, Australia, July 24–26.

Edwards, Ros, and Val Gillies. 2015. Brain science and early years policy: Hopeful ethos or 'cruel optimism'? *Critical Social Policy* 35: 167–87. [CrossRef]

Elish, Madeleine Claire. 2019. Moral crumple zones: Cautionary tales in human-robot interaction. *Science, Technology, and Society* 5: 40–60. [CrossRef]

Eubanks, Virginia. 2017. *Automating Inequality: How High-Tech Tools Profile, Police and Punish the Poor*. New York: St. Martin's Press.

Eubanks, Virginia. 2018. A response to Allegheny County DHS. Available online: https://virginia-eubanks.com/2018/02/16/a-response-to-allegheny-county-dhs/ (accessed on 28 March 2019).

EUGDPR (EU General Data Protection). 2019. General Data Protection Regulation. EU. Available online: https://eugdpr.org (accessed on 2 October 2018).

Fallon, Barbara, Martin Chabot, John Fluke, Cindy Blackstock, Bruce MacLaurin, and Lil Tonmyr. 2013. Placement decisions and disparities among Aboriginal children: Further analysis of the Canadian incidence study of reported child abuse and neglect part A: Comparisons of the 1998 and 2003 surveys. *Child Abuse & Neglect* 37: 47–60. [CrossRef]

Featherstone, Brid, Kate Morris, and Sue White. 2014. *Re-Imagining Child Protection: Towards Humane Social Work with Families*. Bristol: Policy Press.

Fenton, Jane, and Timothy Kelly. 2017. 'Risk is King and Needs to take a Backseat!' Can social workers' experiences of moral injury strengthen practice? *Journal of Social Work Practice* 31: 461–75. [CrossRef]

Fleming, Piers, Laura Biggart, and Chris Beckett. 2014. Effects of Professional Experience on Child Maltreatment Risk Assessments: A Comparison of Students and Qualified Social Workers. *British Journal of Social Work* 45: 2298–316. [CrossRef]

Fluke, John D., Martin Chabot, Barbara Fallon, Bruce MacLaurin, and Cindy Blackstock. 2010. Placement decisions and disparities among aboriginal groups: An application of the decision making ecology through multi-level analysis. *Child Abuse & Neglect* 34: 57–69. [CrossRef]

Fluke, John D., Tyler W. Corwin, Dana M. Hollinshead, and Erin J. Maher. 2016. Family preservation or child safety? Associations between child welfare workers' experience, position, and perspectives. *Children and Youth Services Review* 69: 210–18. [CrossRef]

Gambrill, Eileen. 2005. Decision making in child welfare: Errors and their context. *Children and Youth Services Review* 27: 347–52. [CrossRef]

Gambrill, Eileen, and Aron Shlonsky. 2000. Risk assessment in context. *Children and Youth Services Review* 22: 813–37. [CrossRef]

Gilbert, Neil, Nigel Parton, and Marit Skivenes. 2011. *Child Protection Systems: International Trends and Orientations*. Oxford: Oxford University Press.

Gillingham, Phillip. 2011. Decision-making tools and the development of expertise in child protection practitioners: Are we 'just breeding workers who are good at ticking boxes'? *Child & Family Social Work* 16: 412–21. [CrossRef]

Goddard, Chris R., Bernadette J. Saunders, Janet R. Stanley, and Joe Tucci. 1999. Structured risk assessment procedures: Instruments of abuse? *Child Abuse Review* 8: 251–63. [CrossRef]

Goldhaber-Fiebert, Jeremy, and Lea Prince. 2019. *Impact Evaluation of a Predictive Risk Modeling Tool for Allegheny County's Child Welfare Office*. Pittsburgh: Allegheny County.

Green, Ben, and Yiling Chen. 2019. The principles and limits of algorithm-in-the-loop decision-making. *Proceedings of the ACM on Human-Computer Interaction* 3: 50–74.

Gurses, Seeda, Sita Gangadharan, and Suresh Venkatasubramanian. 2019. Critiquing and Rethinking Accountability, Fairness, and Transparency. *Our Data Bodies Project US: Our Data Bodies Project*. Available online: https://www.odbproject.org/2019/07/15/critiquing-and-rethinking-fairness-accountability-and-transparency/ (accessed on 30 July 2019).

Harwin, Judith, B. Alrouh, S. Bedson, and Karen Broadhurst. 2018. *Care Demand and Regional Variability in England: 2010/11 to 2016/17*. Lancaster: Lancaster University.

Healy, Karen. 2009. A case of mistaken identity: The social welfare professions and New Public Management. *Journal of Sociology* 45: 401–18. [CrossRef]

Healy, Karen, and Yvonne Darlington. 2009. Service user participation in diverse child protection contexts: Principles for practice. *Child and Family Social Work* 14: 420–30. [CrossRef]

Healy, Karen, Yvonne Darlington, and Judith A. Feeney. 2011. Parents' participation in child protection practice: Toward respect and inclusion. *Families in Society: The Journal of Contemporary Social Services* 92: 282–88. [CrossRef]

Hughes, Tim. 2017. Prediction and Social Investment. In *Social Investment: A New Zealand Policy Experiment*. Edited by Jonathan Boston and David Gill. Wellington: Bridget Williams Books, pp. 179–202.

International Federation of Social Work. 2014. Global Definition of Social Work. IFSW. Available online: https://www.ifsw.org/what-is-social-work/global-definition-of-social-work/ (accessed on 1 August 2019).

Jackson, David, and Gary Marx. 2017. Data Mining Program Designed to Predict Child Abuse Proves Unreliable, DCFS Says. Chicago Tribune. December 6. Available online: http://www.chicagotribune.com/news/watchdog/ct-dcfs-eckerd-met-20171206-story.html (accessed on 22 February 2018).

Keddell, Emily. 2014. Current debates on variability in child welfare decision-making: A selected literature review. *Social Sciences* 3: 916–40. [CrossRef]

Keddell, Emily. 2015a. The ethics of predictive risk modelling in the Aotearoa/New Zealand child welfare context: Child abuse prevention or neo-liberal tool? *Critical Social Policy* 35: 69–88. [CrossRef]

Keddell, Emily. 2015b. Predictive Risk Modelling: On Data, Rights and Politics. Reimagining Social Work. Available online: http://www.reimaginingsocialwork.nz/2015/06/predictive-risk-modelling-on-rights-data-and-politics/ (accessed on 6 October 2019).

Keddell, Emily. 2016. Substantiation, decision-making and risk prediction in child protection systems. *Policy Quarterly* 12: 46–59. [CrossRef]

Keddell, Emily. 2017. Interpreting children's best interests: Needs, attachment and decision-making. *Journal of Social Work* 17: 324–42. [CrossRef]

Keddell, Emily, and Ian Hyslop. 2019. Ethnic inequalities in child welfare: The role of practitioner risk perceptions. *Child & Family Social Work*, 1–12. [CrossRef]

Kirk, Shelley. 2016. Children 'not lab-rats'—Anne Tolley intervenes in child abuse experiment. *Stuff*, July 30.

Klein, Sacha, and Darcey Merritt. 2014. Neighborhood racial & ethnic diversity as a predictor of child welfare system involvement. *Children and Youth Services Review* 41: 95–105.

Lees, Amanda, Edgar Meyer, and Jackie Rafferty. 2011. From Menzies Lyth to Munro: The Problem of Managerialism. *British Journal of Social Work* 43: 542–58. [CrossRef]

Lepri Letouze, Bruno, Jacopo Staiano, David Sangokoya, Emmanuel Letouzé, and Nuria Oliver. 2017. The Tyranny of Data? The Bright and Dark Sides of Data-Driven Decision-Making for Social Good. In *Transparent Data Mining for Big and Small Data, Studies in Big Data Series*. Springer: Cham, Switzerland.

Madden, M., M. Gilman, K. Levy, and A. Marwick. 2017. Privacy, Poverty, and Big Data: A Matrix of Vulnerabilities for Poor Americans. *Washington University Law Review* 95: 53–125.

Margolin, L. 1997. *Under the Cover of Kindness: The Invention of Social Work*. Charlottesville and London: University Press of Virginia.

McDonell, J. R., A. Ben-Arieh, and G. B. Melton. 2015. Strong Communities for Children: Results of a Multi-Year Community-Based Initiative to Protect Children from Harm. *Child Abuse & Neglect* 41: 79–96.

McIntyre, N., and D. Pegg. 2018. Councils use 377,000 people's data in efforts to predict child abuse. *The Guardian*, September 16.

McLaughlin, Michael, and Melissa Jonson-Reid. 2017. The relationship between child welfare financing, screening, and substantiation. *Children and Youth Services Review* 82: 407–12. [CrossRef]

McQuillan, Dan. 2015. Algorithmic states of exception. *European Journal of Cultural Studies* 18: 564–76. [CrossRef]

McQuillan, Dan. 2017. Data Science as Machinic Neoplatonism. *Philosophy & Technology* 31: 253–72. [CrossRef]

McQuillan, Dan. 2018. People's Councils for Ethical Machine Learning. *Social Media + Society* 4. [CrossRef]

Mittelstadt, Brent Daniel, Patrick Allo, Mariarosaria Taddeo, Sandra Wachter, and Luciano Floridi. 2016. The ethics of algorithms: Mapping the debate. *Big Data & Society* 3: 2053951716679679.

Munro, Eileen. 2002. *Effective Child Protection*. London: Sage.

Munro, Eileen. 2011. *The Munro Review of Child Protection: Final Report, a Child-Centred System*. London: The Stationary Office Limited.

Munro, Eileen. 2019. *Predictive Analytics in Child Protection*. CHESS Working Paper No. 2019-03. Knowledge for use (K4U) Project. Durham, UK: Durham University.

Munro, Eileen, Julie Taylor, and Caroline Bradbury-Jones. 2014. Understanding the Causal Pathways to Child Maltreatment: Implications for Health and Social Care Policy and Practice. *Child Abuse Review* 23: 61–74. [CrossRef]

Naranayan, Arvind. 2018. *21 Fairness Definitions and Their Politics*. Youtube: Arvind Naranayan, Available online: https://www.youtube.com/watch?v=jIXIuYdnyyk (accessed on 1 August 2019).

New Zealand Government. 1989. *Oranga Tamariki Act*; Wellington: New Zealand Government. Available online: http://www.legislation.govt.nz/act/public/1989/0024/latest/whole.html (accessed on 1 August 2019).

Pearl, Judea, and Dana Mckenzie. 2018. *The Book of Why: The New Science of Cause and Effect*. New York: Basic Books.

Rahwan, Iyad. 2018. Society-in-the-loop: Programming the algorithmic social contract. *Ethics and Information Technology* 20: 5–14. [CrossRef]

Rea, David, and Robert Erasmus. 2017. *Report of the Enhancing Decision-Making Project*; Wellington: Ministry of Social Development. Available online: https://mvcot.govt.nz/assets/Uploads/OIA-responses/Report-of-the-Enhancing-Intake-Decision-Making-Project.pdf (accessed on 15 September 2017).

Riley, Naomi. 2018. *Can Big Data Help Save Abused Kids?* Washington, DC: American Enterprise Institute, Available online: https://reason.com/2018/01/22/can-big-data-help-save-abused/ (accessed on 1 August 2019).

Roberts, Dorothy, and Lisa Sangoi. 2018. Black Families Matter: How the Child Welfare System Punishes Poor Families of Color. *Injustice Today*. March 26. Available online: https://theappeal.org/black-families-matter-how-the-child-welfare-system-punishes-poor-families-of-color-33ad20e2882e/ (accessed on 1 August 2019).

Rodriguez, Maria, Diane DePanfilis, and Paul Lanier. 2019. Bridging the Gap: Social Work Insights for Ethical Algorithmic Decision-Making in Human Services. *IBM Journal of Research and Development*, 1. [CrossRef]

Rostad, Whitney L., Tia McGill Rogers, and Mark J. Chaffin. 2017. The influence of concrete support on child welfare program engagement, progress, and recurrence. *Children and Youth Services Review* 72: 26–33. [CrossRef] [PubMed]

Rouland, Bénédicte, and Rhema Vaithianathan. 2018. Cumulative Prevalence of Maltreatment among New Zealand Children, 1998–2015. *American Journal of Public Health* 108: 511–13. [CrossRef] [PubMed]

Rowe, Michael. 2019. Shaping Our Algorithms Before They Shape Us. In *Artificial Intelligence and Inclusive Education: Speculative Futures and Emerging Practices*. Edited by Jeremy Knox, Yuchen Wang and Michael Gallagher. Singapore: Springer Singapore, pp. 151–63.

Sheridan, Ed. 2018. *Hackney Council Pays £360k to Data Firm Whose Software Profiles Troubled Families*. London: Hackney Citizen.

Shlonsky, Aron, and David Wagner. 2005. The next step: Integrating actuarial risk assessment and clinical judgment into an evidence-based practice framework in CPS case management. *Children and Youth Services Review* 27: 409–27. [CrossRef]

Sloane, Mona. 2018. *Making Artificial Intelligence Socially Just: Why the Current Focus on Ethics Is Not Enough*. London: London School of Economics., Available online: http://blogs.lse.ac.uk/politicsandpolicy/artificial-intelligence-and-society-ethics/ (accessed on 1 August 2019).

Spratt, Trevor, and J. Callan. 2004. Parents' Views on Social Work Interventions in Child Welfare Cases. *British Journal of Social Work* 34: 199–224. [CrossRef]

Swahn, Monica H., Daniel J. Whitaker, Courtney B. Pippen, Rebecca T. Leeb, Linda A. Teplin, Karen M. Abram, and Gary M. McClelland. 2006. Concordance between Self-Reported Maltreatment and Court Records of Abuse or Neglect among High-Risk Youths. *American Journal of Public Health* 96: 1849–53. [CrossRef] [PubMed]

Vaithianathan, Rhema. 2012. *Can Administrative Data Be Used to Identify Children at Risk of Adverse Outcomes?* Auckland: The University of Auckland.

Vaithianathan, Rhema, Tim Maloney, Emily Putnam-Hornstein, and Nan Jiang. 2013. Children in the Public Benefit System at Risk of Maltreatment: Identification via Predictive Modeling. *American Journal of Preventive Medicine* 45: 354–59. [CrossRef] [PubMed]

Vaithianathan, Rhema Nan Jiang, Tim Maloney, and Emily Putnam-Hornstein. 2017. Developing Predictive Risk Models to Support Child Maltreatment Hotline Screening Decisions: Allegheny County Methodology and Implementation. In *Center for Social Data Analytics*. Auckland: Auckland University of Technology.

Vaithianathan, Rhema, Bénédicte Rouland, and Emily Putnam-Hornstein. 2018. Injury and Mortality Among Children Identified as at High Risk of Maltreatment. *Pediatrics* 141. [CrossRef] [PubMed]

van der Put, Claudia E., Merian B. R. Bouwmeester-Landweer, Eleonore A. Landsmeer-Beker, Jan M. Wit, Friedo W. Dekker, N. Pieter J. Kousemaker, and Herman E. M. Baartman. 2017. Screening for potential child maltreatment in parents of a newborn baby: The predictive validity of an Instrument for early identification of Parents at Risk for child Abuse and Neglect (IPARAN). *Child Abuse & Neglect* 70: 160–68. [CrossRef]

Veale, Michael, and Irina Brass. 2019. Administration by Algorithm? Public Management meets Public Sector Machine Learning. In *Algorithmic Regulation*. Edited by Karen Yeung and Martin Lodge. Oxford: Oxford University Press.

Vedder, Anton. 1999. KDD: The challenge to individualism. *Ethics and Information Technology* 1: 275–81. [CrossRef]

Wachter, Sandra, and Brett Mittelstadt. 2019. A Right to Reasonable Inferences: Re-Thinking Data Protection Law in the Age of Big Data and AI. *Columbia Business Law Review* 2: 1–84.

Weick, Ann. 1999. Guilty knowledge. *Families in Society* 80: 327–32. [CrossRef]

Wexler, Richard. 2018. Poor Kids End Up in Foster Care Because Parents Don't Get Margin of Error Rich Do. *Youth Today*, March 16.

White, Sue, Karen Broadhurst, David Wastell, Sue Peckover, Chris Hall, and Andy Pithouse. 2009. Whither practice-near research in the modernization programme? Policy blunders in children's services. *Journal of Social Work Practice* 23: 401–11. [CrossRef]

Whittaker, Meredith, Kate Crawford, Roel Dobbe, Genevieve Fried, Elizabeth Kaziunas, Varoon Mathur, Sarah Myers West, Rashida Richardson, Jason Schultz, and Oscar Schwartz. 2018. *AI Now Report 2018*. New York: AI Now Institute.

Widom, Cathy Spatz, Sally J. Czaja, and Kimberly A. DuMont. 2015. Intergenerational transmission of child abuse and neglect: Real or detection bias? *Science* 347: 1480–85. [CrossRef] [PubMed]

Wilson, Moira L., Sarah Tumen, Rissa Ota, and Anthony G. Simmers. 2015. Predictive Modeling: Potential Application in Prevention Services. *American Journal of Preventive Medicine* 48: 509–19. [CrossRef] [PubMed]

social sciences

MDPI

Article

Professional Values Challenged by Case Management—Theorizing Practice in Child Protection with Reflexive Practitioners

Edgar Marthinsen [1],*, Graham Clifford [1], Halvor Fauske [2] and Willy Lichtwarck [1]

[1] Department of Social Work, Norwegian University of Science and Technology (NTNU), 7491 Trondheim, Norway; gcmclc47@gmail.com (G.C.); willy.lichtwarck@ntnu.no (W.L.)
[2] Department of Social Work, Inland Norway University of Applied Sciences, Postboks 400, 2418 Elverum, Norway; Halvor.Fauske@inn.no
* Correspondence: edgar.marthinsen@ntnu.no

Received: 28 February 2020; Accepted: 2 April 2020; Published: 8 April 2020

Abstract: In this article, we theorize and reflect based on former research into professional practice and discretion as well as use some results from working together with practitioners in child protection services to explore the phenomenon of non-performing. Regulation lies at the heart of the contemporary child protection discourse. On the one hand we have seen a trend towards systematization of assessment content and procedures, on the other hand it is assumed that rational management approaches can secure consistency of performance. Social workers may be weary of the constraints all this imposes, but seem generally content to comply. Our reasoning was that social workers in child protection should be helped to get to grips with modifications to practice so that multi-challenged families could be accorded priority. These changes would include a reframing of assessment to take account of family needs as well as the needs of children. Follow-up would also require much more attention. Additionally, the choice of help provided for children and families would have to come into better focus, despite the limitations often experienced in practice. The question we asked was whether these types of reframing could be fostered within local child welfare units. We conducted a field trial in which child protection units were encouraged to reframe their practices, with the support of an expert group. The idea was to enhance and enable innovation through the combination of a more thorough dialogue with the families involved, as well as critical reflection based on available knowledge related to the identified challenges. We do a critical discussion of the work and the results from this in order to enhance knowledge on innovation in child protection.

Keywords: child protection; social work; complexity theory

When discretionary power is delegated,

the presumption is that the entrusted

actor is capable of performing the

involved tasks and will do so judiciously.

Molander (2016, p. 4)

1. Introduction

While carrying out research as well as examining researching practices and the world of social work for more than three decades, the authors have experienced the influx of neoliberal reasoning, especially involving an increased focus on metrics and performance in welfare services. This development has adversely affected social work service development in many ways, does not explain why social work often disapproved of by the clients who rely on it. Very often, we have seen qualified social workers who have clear ideas of the needs of clients and value the cooperation and responsibility that lies at the heart of social work as being relevant to people's lives and wellbeing, but in a reflexive mode must acknowledge their failure in practicing their professional values. In this article, we theorize and reflect based on former research into professional practice and discretion. We also use some results from working together with practitioners to explore the phenomenon of non-performing.

Regulation lies at the heart of the contemporary child protection discourse. On the one hand we have seen a trend toward systematization of assessment content and procedures, on the other hand it is assumed that rational management approaches can secure consistency of performance. Social workers may be weary of the constraints all this imposes, but seem generally content to comply (Fauske et al. 2009; Marthinsen and Lichtwarck 2013; Clifford et al. 2015). Research in the *New Child Welfare* (NCW) found that efforts to develop a knowledge-based practice in Norwegian child protection with considerable attention paid to management have not resulted in a service with clear or even defensible priorities. The most marginalized and deprived children and families were those who received the least help designed to improve the care of their children. Parents were critical of the fragmented nature of the help they were provided with, and what they perceived to be inadequate follow-up and assistance provided.

On this basis we proposed an innovation project, which was accepted and financed by the Norwegian Research Council. During the years 2013 through 2016, we carried out the project "Innovative Approaches to Work with Neglected Families: Targeted intervention and support for high-risk families in Child Welfare". This project was part of the Program for Practice-based RandD for Health and Welfare Services (PraksisVEL).

Our reasoning was that social workers in child protection should be helped to get to grips with modifications to practice so that multi-challenged families could be accorded priority. These changes would include a reframing of assessments to take account of family needs as well as the needs of children. Follow-up would also require much more attention. Also, the choice of help provided for children and families would have to come into better focus, despite the limitations often experienced in practice. The question we asked was whether these kinds of reframing could be fostered within local child welfare units. The offices and their managers included in the trial took the normative position of acknowledging that work could and should be improved in order to deliver sustainable services to multi-challenged families and their children. Innovative actions would be supported from the outset. We conducted a field trial in which child protection units were encouraged to reframe their practices, with the support of a group of experts in child protection assessment and treatment that should act as a discussion partner in order to enhance critical reflection. The group was not to act as supervisors but should discuss challenges on a general level—not work with the families and children as such. The idea was to enhance and enable innovation through a combination of a more thorough dialogue with the families involved, as well as critical reflection based on available knowledge related to the identified challenges. Innovation here would mean developing actions to broaden the scope of investments in families with multiple challenges, and following up and evaluating how these innovations could be adapted to use when facing similar challenges with other families in need.

Another line of reasoning was that social workers in child protection by virtue of their training are unfamiliar with the mindset and skills that can support low-level innovation of the kind envisaged here. The university set up a trial master-level course designed to develop innovation skills. This was offered to social workers drawn from the municipalities participating in the field trial. These offices had taken part in the research program "the new child protection" where the lack of investment in multi-challenged families were documented from researching a representative part of their clients (>700).

New families with the same characteristics as the challenged families were identified to be followed up in the coming two years, and those in charge in four offices were offered the master course. The course proved successful and led to the initiation of a European project "Learning to Innovate with Families" (LIFE) funded by the Erasmus + program.

Innovation in practical settings, however, proved to be very difficult. The main reasons for this were not hard to detect. In the four municipalities that took part in the trial, major reorganizations of the child protection service began early in the trial period.

These changes were relatively drastic; one municipality dispensed with a considerable portion of its middle management to cut expenditure, another had a breakdown due to infringements of regulations and embarked on a lengthy reorganization and rehabilitation process under new leadership. Two municipalities had difficulty in meeting deadlines for assessments after referral. One of the municipalities abandoned a purchaser-provider model for organizing its service, while another adopted the same model. There were other signs of retrenchment due to cost pressures, with child welfare units removing vulnerable families from their caseloads. All the child protection units that took part in the trial experienced severe pressure and had great difficulty in complying with the trial design, which required that 12–20 families with multiple and complex problems be selected for a reframing of assessment and follow-up.

The field trial and the master's degree course did however provide much interesting material that enabled us to trace some of the phenomena which played out in the organizations that could explain why families were not followed up with and the lack of innovation. Our article is based on our experience of organizational conditions that may preclude or hinder innovation in child protection and some examples of how innovation is viewed by the social workers themselves. We explore dilemmas that arise in giving priority to clients' needs in settings where managerial demands prevail and regulate social work. To support this discussion, we draw from the two-weeks-home-based exam papers and two days of structured discussions reflecting with the social workers/students upon their first year of experiences trying to innovate when working with challenged families.

We interviewed some of the chosen families for these services; these interviews are not presented here, but they do confirm stories or descriptions given by some of the social workers. We do not discuss other ways of working with families, such as projects based on emancipatory, feminist or critical social work. This research is to some extent focusing on how disciplinary traits in social work settings is acted out, without regarding or working with resistance.

2. Research and Theory Background

In child protection, discourses of management and of professional concern have been divergent for some time. Policy makers have increasingly favored approaches that are research-based and there is a pressure for innovation and accountability in practice (Parton et al. 1997; Gray et al. 2009).

Research on child protection practices based on information from clients as well as social workers has shown increasing conflict around assessing needs, responding to them and problems of handling caseloads under new public management regimes. Much social work literature points to how new public management and the neoliberal ethos challenges social work values and client focused practices (Lorenz 2005; Ferguson 2007; Garrett 2009; Featherstone et al. 2016). Social workers report a lack of time and resources while clients often express frustration about the lack of adequate response, fragmented services and lack of respect for their expressed needs. Juhasz and Skivenes (2016, p. 1) have studied care order preparation in several countries—including Norway—and they find that "roughly two out of three workers say they would experience obstacles, and the main obstacle by far is related to time and/or large caseloads. Lack of organizational structures or poor management is the second major obstacle, followed by collaborative problems with external partners and challenges related to providing evidence. Only a few workers mention individual factors".

Government papers as well as reviews and inspection reports point to high workforce turnover, lack of competence and the need for reorganization and stricter management. The discourse on child protection practice and its expansion reveals disagreement about possible solutions. These solutions range from demands for better management and stricter regulation to specific competence-building strategies and yet further toward enhanced reflexivity and more expertise in coping respectfully with uncertainty. Enhancing or promoting innovative practices has over the years surfaced as one way of coping with the increasing complexity.

If one particular discourse becomes hegemonic in a field, there are likely to be reasons for this. The dilemmas that arise from the coexistence of, and possible conflict between different value hierarchies will have to be negotiated (Garrett 2009; Rugowski 2010). Decisions have to be justified as social workers get on with their everyday tasks. Concern about accountability, threatening to overbalance into a moralizing culture of blame, permeates public service organizations nowadays. Parton et al.'s (1997) breakthrough contribution Child protection, Risk and the Moral Order was an early empirically based contribution questioning the development of a child protection that embodied social and cultural biases. A Bourdeuasian analysis of child protection in Norway (Marthinsen 2003) using the notion of accumulation of symbolic burdens among clients deployed a wholly different approach but drew a similar picture. Munro's report on child protection in the UK averred that instead of *"doing things right" (i.e., following procedures) the system needed to be focused on doing the right thing (i.e., checking whether children and young people are being helped)* (Department of Education 2011).

However, developments in Norway since 1990, in the child protection field, cannot be seen simply as a process in which tension between managers and professionals has escalated. The service can be seen as an example of a mixed knowledge regime (Sørhaug 2004). When knowledge is the organization's capital, knowledge, power and authority are also bound together, and as Sørhaug points out, different knowledge domains (or regimes) are involved. These include the organizational hierarchy (line management) the collegium (its interaction based on continual discussion) and the network in which personal alliances, reciprocity, antagonisms and trust are articulated. These knowledge regimes infiltrate one another. An analysis based on dichotomization of management and professional interests may be blind to important coalitions of interest that bring management and social workers together at particular junctures or even over longer periods.

Some earlier theorizing and research about this problem area will be explored here, as well as social workers' need to cope with questions of accountability and discretion. We must emphasize that the shortcomings of child protection services are interesting and relevant in terms of theory and formulation of research questions and approaches. But they are scarcely abstract. Our own research based on client's narratives concerning experiences with child protection services revealed frequencies of service-family contact that were very low, fragmented service provision from a range of services involved, high levels of turnover among caseworkers, a lack of continuity on the part of responsible social workers, frequent cancelling of appointments and promises not being kept (Clifford et al. 2015).

Our approach has applied complexity theory and critical social theory based on Bourdieu's 'toolbox'. We use the concept of bifurcation point (explained below) to illustrate how managerial values may challenge social work priorities regarding families in need. We found that this helped us to get a better grasp of the practices involved and could help the participating social workers to reflect upon why they were not able to give priority to the chosen multi-challenged families involved and thus why little innovation evolved.

Child protection and welfare services have been expanding in Norway as in many western countries, with an increasing emphasis on child protection as opposed to more general child welfare work (Lonne et al. 2008; Gilbert et al. 2011; Parton 2014; Christiansen and Kojan 2016). In Norway, the growth in volume of service as measured by numbers of children referred and children and families provided with services, has been considerably greater than the growth in numbers of staff employed in the services Clifford et al. 2015. As a result, there are more tasks for each worker than there were before. As services expanded (from 12,000 children in 1982 to more than 50,000 receiving services in 2010) workers and management found it difficult to maintain an effective overview of which children and families became clients and why did they come into contact with the service. Statistics have been vague and not able to count for the increase enabling the services to develop good strategies to cope (Marthinsen and Lichtwarck 2013). The services have become dependent upon databases to access information about their work and their users. The tools adopted have focused on client flow related to certain tasks from intake to output (controlling time limits for reports, assessments and actions), rather than the content of the operations carried out during working hours. Research carried out after the introduction of the new Children Act in 1991, which set up a system of time limits and deadlines for assessments, showed an emerging pattern in which the office became the prime site for social work, the child care workers made home visits and visited other contacts much less frequently (Clifford et al. 1996). The research revealed a lack of focus on some of the more time-consuming activities involved in social work, especially those tasks related to follow-up and practical work with families and children. The monitored tasks were mistaken as being the most time-consuming ones, while the routine follow ups that were not monitored were the real time consumer (Clifford et al. 1996). The data recorded in computerized monitoring systems as they have evolved since the mid 1990's mainly does not concern direct client-related work, but rather task completions related to deadlines, legal grounds for intervention and reasons for intake and allocation of services. Databases regulate much of the working day and draw attention to the measured activities. When set goals or time limits are not fulfilled, these are often flagged and reported to management as flaws that have to be corrected, since much of this is later reported to the inspectorate and may lead to fines and criticism. Social work with families, follow-ups and responses to developing needs are seldom measured. Social workers have reported deficits of working time available for core client-related activities. Gautun (2010) found that 87% of municipal child protection workers claimed that there were serious bureaucratic constraints on their working practices. The same research indicated that four out of ten complained of a lack of necessary resources to practice early intervention, 34% said there was no opportunity to improve their own competence and more than half reported resorting to non-optimal handling of cases within the previous year.

Tension between managerial and professional interests has been a long-standing issue in social work, certainly predating the advent of New Public Management. Howe (1991) turned the awareness on the ongoing shift of power from the practitioner to the manager. Evans and Harris (2004) discussed the impact of managerialism and how it influenced and possibly reduced social workers' discretion. Norwegian social work has very similar development to that of the Anglophone world. Christiansen (1977) in a seminal article on "administration or treatment" showed how encroaching bureaucracy and older practices of management dating back to the days of the poor legal administration still haunted social services that were being increasingly professionalized with the employment of trained social workers. These professionalizing changings included working with people to enhance personal development, to facilitate social change and to engage in community work, but ended up with the administration of applications for social security benefits. She outlined the conflicts between professionals and the bureaucracy by pointing to the values of social work; promoting active involvement by the client, their right to influence decisions and the need for trust in relationships: This in contrast to the conditional management of economic support that often disempowered clients.

Billingsley's early work on the challenges facing most social workers operating within bureaucratic organizations is also of interest in this connection (Billingsley 1964). He discussed how social workers approach their work in terms of role orientation or attitudes towards the job. He also uses the notion of orientation patterns. This may be compared to Bourdieu's (1999) later concept of habitus within social fields that allows for value and identity distinctions to have different impacts within hierarchies of distinct groups. Within bureaucracies, professional workers seem to become *"socialized according to a set of values that differ from those inherent in their professional calling"* (Billingsley 1964). Social workers operate within *"subsystems of society made up by social units with distinctive boundaries and patterns of interaction that are oriented toward rules"* (op.cit 401). For social workers Billingsley used the notion of subsystems: the profession, the agency, the clients and the community. All these imply different obligations and make demands on their role orientation. The different systems may refer to or enhance different values, which we here have chosen to categorize as distinctions and attractors. Billingsley's work concluded that the clients and the community had less influence than the profession and agency on social workers' orientation at work. This state of affairs was quite general in spite of the social workers' intellectual and emotional commitment to meeting the needs of their clients' (ibid). He also found that social workers were more oriented to carrying out agency policies and procedures than toward carrying out their professional commitments, when these were in conflict. Billingsley developed Riesman's (1949) idea of role conceptions in his analysis, and created four orientation categories that seemed to be in operation. The first category, termed 'professionals' included those who tended to give primary allegiance to professional standards and who regarded their job as a setting to do their professional practice, and feeling free to leave or change jobs if their values and professional aims were challenged. The second category, 'bureaucrats' were primarily oriented towards carrying out agency policies and procedures. This group was more loyal towards their agency. These two are the roles dichotomized by Christiansen (1977) although her article is not based on research but is rather part of a debate on social work and its challenges in the evolving welfare state. Billingsley's third category is the 'conformists' with a relatively high commitment to conform to the expectations of both agency policies and professional standards. He compares this group to Riesman's 'service bureaucrats'. The last group is the 'innovators' who show low commitment to both agency policies and professional standards, and have a willingness to challenge or violate agency as well as professional standards in order to meet the needs of clients. This group is also more responsive to the community. Although this research dates back to the 1960s, it identifies some important patterns that are probably still in play in organizations today. As we came across this after our project was finished, we were not able to reproduce Billingsley's work, but it has certainly made us aware of these tensions appearing in our empirical data.

3. The Question of Discretion

The Oxford Handbook of Public Accountability (Bovens et al. 2014) operates with several prerequisites for accountability when viewed as a social as well as political mechanism; accountability is fundamental in influencing the extent and character of discretion. In an account-giving discussion, the actor must inform about the conduct performed, its tasks, outcomes and procedures. Explanations and justifications become important—especially in case of failure. Secondly, it must be possible to question the actor about the legitimacy and the adequacy of the explanation given. Accountability relates to answerability, that is, specific questions and the feasibility of providing an answer to them. Lastly, we must be able to pass judgement on the conduct of the actor to facilitate reward as well as criticism (Bovens et al. 2014).

Evans (2016) has an interesting analysis of the influence of new management structures and on the continuing relevance of Lipsky's street level bureaucrat theory. Evans´s point is that new public management has given senior management greater influence in the sense of governing the room for discretion among those who work with clients (street level bureaucrats). Their working conditions are increasingly restrained by resource shortages and policy confusion as well as having to live with a political concern with the avoidance of blame and culpability (Evans 2016, p. 603). Evans shows that two strategies may be in use in order to manage risk. One is proceduralist; guidelines and detailed specification of procedures are used to achieve control. This is reminiscent of Munro's (Department of Education 2011) dictum about doing things right, but not caring about the right things. The other strategy Evans points to is 'service abandonment' which in child protection means that one closes a case and cannot be blamed, or one refers it to someone else. This may be done by using tools to assess needs and allocate services, and interpreting and applying them in ways that reduce demand for example through 'nudging' in certain directions by politicians and management (Thaler and Sunstein 2008). Høybye-Mortensen's (2015) study of decision-making tools in social work seems to indicate that in spite of the increasing use of such tools, discretion seems to still rest on the workers ability to maneuver inside or outside the services available, and that the real challenge is when clients present needs which are not included in the available 'service package', for instance to cope with loneliness or have more frequent contact with their family than time allows. Lorenz (2005, quoted in Spolander et al. 2016, p. 644) suggests that *"social workers often withdraw to privatisation and therapeutic approaches or accept dictates of New Public Management without opposition"*. This may explain why social workers do not usually show open opposition towards management or policies that may inhibit efforts to improve the lives of clients or oppressed or marginalized groups. In the light of the older research referred to earlier about social workers' mode of operation or orientation patterns, Lorenz's expectations directed at social workers as political actors in everyday life may of course be unrealistic.

Professional social work has to relate to the need for legitimacy of public or private services and has to comply with rules that regulate discretion and accountability. Its role conceptions have to evolve within this context. Molander (2016) discusses the anatomy of discretion in relation to the welfare state. He refers to Rawls (1993), who provides a list of six points describing non-eliminable hazards that influence both theoretical and practical reasoning involved in coping with the burdens of judgement (Molander 2016, p. 39):

(a) Relevant facts in a case can be complex, contradictory and difficult to assess because they point in different directions.
(b) Even if there is agreement about which considerations are relevant in a case, there can be disagreement about their weight, and therefore, different conclusions can be drawn.
(c) All concepts are to a certain degree indeterminate and vulnerable to hard cases. The use of concepts must therefore be based on judgements and interpretation, wherein reasonable persons can disagree.
(d) The experiences that one has had during one's life shape how one selects facts and how one weighs moral and political values.
(e) Most often there are normative considerations with different forces on all sides of a case; hence, an overall assessment of these considerations can be difficult.
(f) One cannot realize all possible values simultaneously. For this reason, one must range values that per se can be equally good.

However, there is mostly a lack of clear and uncontroversial criteria for such rankings. To explain how people may cope with this Molander discusses heuristics, which is a form of reasoning that may remind us of populism (Müller 2016). These simple procedures for answering difficult questions allow us to replace complexity with simple questions and answers about what is, and why and how. Compared to more thorough reflexive reasoning in which we take precautions based on insecurity and lack of knowledge, heuristics may allow us to make (even if maybe false) conclusions about futures, for example. This fits well with the kind of discretion necessary in child and family work with families with children at risk. Heuristics may be a type of warrant or inference rules that bridge the gap between data and conclusions (Molander 2016, p. 41). For instance, this way of reasoning may explain why a social worker chose to cancel an appointment with a mother for follow up work with the family and give priority to bureaucratic work on the computer to meet deadlines for reporting to avoid sanction from superiors and inspectors. Usually nothing critical happens, but it might be that something really bad could have been avoided had she/he kept that appointment. Then she/he would have to be accountable for the exercise of discretion and the manager would have to account for this incident. This is what would be called a bifurcation point where different attractors/distinctions (symbolic capital) would be at stake, as demonstrated in the analysis we provide below. Clifford et al. (2015) see child protection as an organization on alert that always has to be prepared to intervene in its everyday practice to avoid and prevent public and political criticism directed at presumed mismanagement. This results in a strong, even exaggerated focus on assessment, categorization and goal attainment, quality assurance systems and fast track thinking regarding the seriousness/gravity of maltreatment or abuse, all conducted at the same time in an at times bewildering complex of case trajectories. We have seen this in these services elsewhere, not least in the UK over the same period of time (Garrett 2009, Department of Education 2011). As such, this notion of organizations on alert seems to correspond to Evans's point about service abandonment.

4. Theorizing Practice in Everyday Life

Complexity theory operates with a nonlinear logic. It allows us to observe how certain decisions transpire based on judgement in everyday work. When do choices turn up and what choice is made in certain situations? A situation may escalate to what can be characterized as chaos. We experience dissipative structures and may reach a bifurcation point where several options may apply, or else someone will have to innovate. The choices made may be regarded as more or less attractive depending on the future they may contribute to within the organization and in relation to service for families (Stevens and Hassett 2007; Stevens and Cox 2008). The main questions involving making these choices are: Can we manage the situation, can we afford these changes, what kind of knowledge may support our decision—are there time and resources available, etc.?

We have chosen to combine complexity theory with Bourdieu's (1999) concepts of habitus, social fields and symbolic power or capital. The dissipative structures operate within social fields with kinds of habitus that may not be stable over time. What are at stake are attractors or distinctions that may represent different kinds of symbolic capital to agents within the social fields in operation. If management promotes change and innovative work, it also has to support and enhance the allocation of resources such as time, competence and funding to these activities. If not, then management is not in effect promoting the distinctions or the symbolic capital at stake that are about meeting needs and coping with fears about the future among those involved. At the bifurcation point, the dissipative structures (habitus with a certain hierarchy of distinctions defended) lead to a choice among attractors that will lead in certain directions—confirming the value positioning of the agents involved.

How is a situation perceived, what is the importance of certain actions available and what kind of futures are at stake? A constructed example based on non- linear logic could be:

There is a telephone call from a mother about her concern for her child due to her new fiancé's interest in her teenage daughter. This call may result in an agreement to see whether her new boyfriend is on a register or has been convicted of any previous maltreatment or assaults. The check may result in two outcomes, either he has been convicted, or not. If the answer were "no", then the social worker might choose to leave the case for now, and give priority to other cases. A risk is of course that sexually abusing this girl might be his first offence of this kind. The criminal record versus no criminal record may be regarded as a bifurcation point, which imposes a certain action where risk has been operationalized to be equivalent to what is recorded. The social worker has chosen to believe that this man does have good intentions, wants to be a decent stepfather and so does not move on towards suspecting him of ill intention. The mother is thus regarded as too concerned and no action taken. The good/bad thinking is an attractor that weights the decision in certain directions. Of course, this may also be regarded as a risk assessment, but the decision is not based on linear cause-effect thinking. It is more about understanding processes that are in train in which prediction is not based on elaborate thinking—what is described here might well be thought of as a routine procedure.

5. Materials and Methods

Starting in 2007, we developed a research program aiming at expanding our knowledge about clients in Norwegian and later Swedish Child Protection services (Fauske et al. 2009; Marthinsen and Lichtwarck 2013; Clifford et al. 2015). The initial survey of a representative selection of children (N = 715) and families was followed by a longitudinal study based on 96 of these families. These families were selected as multi-challenged households based on interviews assessing the children and parents scores on certain psychosocial stressors. We used the concept of families with complex needs based on high scores on at least three of these variables reflecting different life areas. The conclusion was that the needs of these families were poorly met by services. We developed a research project based on this knowledge where four of the services that took part in earlier research were offered two kinds of support in order to facilitate innovation working with this group. One was a team of experts who could be used as discussion partners in working with these families, though not as supervisors. The services were supposed to develop their own actions in cooperation with the clients. The other resource was a master level year course focusing on innovation in child protection working with families with complex needs. The innovation team was offered only to Norwegian participants from four service units, but the master-course (20ect) included social workers from eight service units in Sweden. The Swedish social workers came from services who had been involved in a replication of the Norwegian survey and a comparative follow up (Davidson and Bredmar 2012). In each office, the system of selection developed earlier was applied to identify new families with complex needs. Each service unit was asked to appoint participants to the innovation course based on the premise that these participants should be in charge of the selected families, and were given the task of innovating in dialogue with the families and the innovation-team. The 16 students (1 male) attending the course were social workers, except for one occupational therapist. All of these students had more than five years of experience in child protection work, with ages between 30 and 50 years old. The course included theories and experiences of innovation, the setting of knowledge production, some relevant theory of science and the possible impact of neoliberal policies and management. Much of the teaching was focused on recent knowledge developments in working with challenged families and their children and the team of experts did some of this teaching.

Specific theorizing of the conflicting or competing values of management versus social work using research like Billingsley's were not presented during the course. This was immediate and evident in their everyday experiences and discussed as challenges in practice. Critical reflection was the mode for teaching, much like in the UK's Making Research Count projects and the Critical reflective practice forum (personal visit by authors 2020). The learning was shared among the researchers and students, more than being socialized into a certain way of thinking. The teaching during the course was very much focused on active student learning through presentations in groups and individually based on material chosen by students themselves, as well as active discussions in class and during meetings in setting at work and in gatherings and meetings related to the research project in practice.

The idea of using complexity theory came among the researchers during the course, and the referred article by Stevens and Cox (2008) was enclosed in the home exam as an analytic tool. Part of the home exam was to discuss what may support and what may restrict innovation in social work practices.

At the end of the course, two days included discussions with four of the researchers/teachers concerning the possible explanations and reasons for challenges met during the innovation project. This setting was similar to a focus group session with researchers taking notes during discussion. The number of participants attending classes varied due to turnover but 14 completed the examination. The exams used in this article was an essay written during a full week, based on applying theories and research presented during the course to their own experiences and ideas about how to enhance innovation, as well as what may restrict it. All students gave consent to the use of the examination material for research purposes.

The main project these social workers were a part of was a trial, and not an experiment or a variant of action research, since there was no feedback other than the communication facilitated during the master course. Our design was more user-focused, and included an initial interview with the families selected that contained a life history interview and survey data on living conditions, as well as health and psychosocial functioning and burdens for parents and children. These families were supposed to be interviewed again after two years, but due to the fact that many never received any follow up or cases were closed, we only managed to interview a couple for the second time. There were little traces of social work to look for, and we also lost contact with many of the participants. The motive for this article is to discuss some of the phenomena playing itself out that may explain why innovation in the sense intended did not succeed. We do not intend to present to what degree innovation practices have evolved in such a way that clients experience change but concentrates upon managerial issues evolving in relation to the realization of the project. Whereas the master-level course provided learning opportunities that were highly valued by the participants, our efforts to promote innovation opportunities in child protection units were much less successful. Access to the innovation team had little impact upon fieldwork and focus interviews with the innovation team confirmed this—their expertise might as well be used to comment on other challenges rather than the involved families. The discussion that follows is mainly based upon the discussions from the two days reflecting with the course participants and their exams where they elaborate upon their experiences with the project to enable learning. We do not think the setting of an exam is greatly influenced by the researchers/teachers based on looking at the experiences. The influence may be the tools they were able to incorporate in their thinking and the way experiences and context are theorized and discussed.

We did not regard these students' work as being representative of social workers in child protection in general, but we did see them as experienced (not experts in Dreyfus' terms) in situations where research and knowledge in general could be applied in a test to develop and implement innovative practices. They were strategic informants chosen for their particular experience, situational perception and professional backgrounds. Their experiences can provide a description of what happens in these organizations when change is at stake or made possible. There may be biases in their accounts and perceptions, but these are unlikely to have been systematic or be artefacts.

Rather than general knowledge, working with these social workers allowed for sharing of typical experiences in practice, especially with the intention to innovate and use and produce knowledge in their own organizations. The reflexive analysis and theorizing enabled by this cooperation provided an opportunity for developing a more thorough understanding of the possible relationship between social work and management.

6. Practicing Discretion

The examples cited below were drawn from examination papers and researchers written notes from the discussions focusing on recording the arguments presented, the challenges met and how they were interpreted and eventually shared among participants. The notes and the exam scripts were analyzed using concepts central to complexity theory, by identifying attractors in play as well as analyzing reasons for action. The arguments participants presented and the attractors were also analyzed in the light of professional versus managerial values. Junctures when discretion was exercised were identified as bifurcation points—they had to choose between at least two options, where one would regard the follow up of families, while the other is a managerial task. This is primarily what we mean by a 'dilemma' between managerial and professional interests.

6.1. Examples of Attractors—Distinctions at Play in Our Empirical Data

The list below is a selection of some of the arguments interpreted as representing attractors or symbolic capital. We choose not to comment on every one of these and rather present the data as examples of the points we want to make here. The different attractors may be discussed as values within certain social fields, but we want to present them as options rather than preferred directions of good practices. In the real world, the decision to move in a certain direction has to be seen and understood in relation to the whole context of the decision. While reading the extracts, one should bear in mind the six points referred to above as non-eliminable hazards. Students emphasized issues such as:

- Time to do follow up with a few cases versus handling a large case load and box ticking
- Looking at parenting skills rather than poverty
- Risk assessment versus engaging with families expressing fear and concern of undesirable futures
- Use of manuals (Kvello in Norway and BBiC in Sweden) versus listening to parents and children's own accounts of their needs
- Enhancing user involvement and 'letting go' of certain routines and established ways of moving forward—relinquishing managerial control
- Focusing on learning and evaluation rather than experiencing lack of success as a failure
- Focus on cost of provisions/investments rather than families and children's needs

- Evidence based practices hampered by costly learning and skills improving programs with certification
- Reduction of compensating provisions (risk reduction and proactive actions), which suffer because priority is given to short term change investments
- Retreat to a belief in resilience rather than taking responsibility for risk reduction
- Class based, culturalized sets of thinking that involve treating the precariat in different ways to middle class families.

Høybye-Mortensen's (2015) point about moving outside the available service package may also be relevant here, as well as in the examples of bifurcation points provided below (This analysis does not take into account any actions or opinions of families, since this may be discussed elsewhere. The interviews with some of the families involved show some of the same as previous research—that many social workers often cancel appointments, there is a high turnover of workers, it is hard to build trustful relationships and not much new is tried—things may start or be discussed, but not followed by new case workers.).

6.2. Examples of Bifurcation Points

The following extracts are presented not as interpretations but as direct quotations from the texts analyzed. One should have in mind that there are reflections made after the social workers looked back and discussed what may have influenced them at different bifurcation points to the extent that the service discarded the family rather than choosing to follow up with them more closely. This included for families where no harm or injury threatened the safeguarding of the children. What the service did not manage was supporting needs and develop new resources (symbolic capital) to increase the life chances and access to symbolic capital for children and adults. The headings are our interpretation of what is at stake.

6.3. Strict Routines and Guidelines Versus Individually Crafted Social Work

At what point during the assessment do we start to consider a family as a complex problem as opposed to an easy one—a problem that is suitable for standard procedures and actions?

A family included in the project may have complex needs, but these needs may not lead to any action, since there is no immediate threat to the child or the situation. Identifying a problem that has a known solution may simplify work with a child in a family with complex needs, without regarding the whole situation in all its complexity. But complexity does not necessarily result in complications.

6.4. Management Trumping Professional Judgement and Other Constraints

Based on my own experience, I wonder if we ever will have access to resources that may help the most complex families. Even if they were within reach, we are hampered by individual factors, framing by the organization and management as well as the culture at work. Resources seem to be regarded as the usually accessible routine solutions rather than as solutions that could be deployed to support innovative practices.

When you face resistance, regard it as being energy in play rather than undesirable and as a personal failure.

When a social worker sees matters in this way, it may lead them towards innovation in terms of assessment as well as in addressing questions as to what help a child and family may need. This may affect other decisions and their attitude to discretion in general.

Do we need to move some of the social work out of the bureaucratic child protection service to other parts of the organization?

This question arose partly on the basis of experience from a Swedish project in which a team was established to work only with families with complex needs, a unit to a considerable extent being allowed to dispense with the strictures enforced in the rest of the service. The reorganization here is becoming a bifurcation point.

6.5. Transcending Organizational and Professional Constraints

- Do we need to acknowledge the lack of knowledge about children at risk, and families with complex needs and start using scientific work in a more elaborate sense—to research our practices?
- If love and good intentions are virtues in social work practice, how is it possible to not give priority to children and families in need—and how do we organize the work?
- Do we need to look at more interprofessional and systems interplay—and how might this improve our ability to provide appropriate responses?

These last points comply in a certain degree with the challenges presented in Rawls' list on non-eliminable hazards that influence reasoning. A reductionism related to ideas of practical reason is also found in Bourdieu (1999).

A case presented by a student concerned a mother who confesses to a serious long-lasting drug problem. Her children are not removed, but her network and family are activated as supporting resources while she is undergoing treatment. This work goes on for months without any set goals besides working with the recognized problem—an approach that later is regarded as a decisive resource to stabilize the situation. The mother is also diagnosed with a neuropsychiatric problem; the family will be in need of assistance as long as the children are involved and probably even longer. This is not efficient problem solving, it involves allocating resources to a chronic situation—but placing the children in an adoptive situation would have been even more expensive, so it is defended as economically sustainable, and might leave the mother and the child happier for a while? Who knows if the child someday might sue the municipality for not removing him or her to provide better life chances in a more stable family?

The kind of work carried out in services seems to be of great interest for many, and several of the social workers talked about turnover as a result of personal interest in what kind of professional work they preferred. Those who moved into a 'task force' for families with complex needs valued their work as interesting and challenging in positive terms, while regretting the time they earlier had to spend on management of heavy caseloads. In complexity theory terms, a more professional focus on a few families as an attractor and the establishment of a new team in the service making this possible, became a bifurcation point where personal preferences influenced their decisions. In social theory, this is also a preference for a certain symbolic capital where values and professional interest can be identified as distinctions defining a social field. Those who worked in this 'family task force' team made up their own social field where there were integrated professional activities and processes of change rather than set goals that they worked to attain. User involvement and recognition were also central values in this field—values that may be part of the rhetoric in the system as such but could in this situation be realized with closer and more continuous involvement on the social workers' part.

An interesting comment made was that in order to apply new knowledge, take part in research and give recognition to others' knowledge, the service or organization has to be open to innovative practices and experiments. This corresponds to Eräsaari's (2003) idea of open rather than closed expertise as Karvinen Niinikoski has discussed:

> The position of scientists and professionals as experts and knowledge creators is re-constructed in relation to the expertise contained in the personal experience of practitioners and citizens, the users and providers of human services in our case. The new ideas of expertise and knowledge emphasize new kinds of negotiations, co-operational and networking environments in the processes of learning and of knowledge production. Expertise and knowledge are understood as more open and dialogical and even conditional for negotiation. They are seen to be context-dependent (Nowotny 2000), the context being an important source for generation and validation of knowledge. Additionally, the knowledge of street level professionals and the lay-expertise of service-users are seen as necessary parts

in the dialogue. There is a need for new kinds of mechanisms of innovative knowledge production, forums for dialogue in promoting knowledge creation and an epistemic pluralism (e.g., Nonaka et al. 2000; Nowotny et al. 2004). *All this sounds familiar from the angle of social work and could be called reflexive expertise.*

(Karvinen-Niinikoski 2005, p. 264)

7. Discussion

According to Molander (2016), discretion involves possessing negative liberty that provides the actor with an area for choice and action consisting of those options that are neither forbidden nor prescribed (Molander 2016, p. 9). The involved 'risk assessments' may include both a possible client orientation as well as an agency orientation with different attractors involved. Since the managerial distinctions related to the symbolic capital identified by the checklists and monitored deadlines and actions so easily may backfire if not complied with, the non-feedback system from doing good social work with clients is left in a black box only partly known to families and children and the social worker involved. Based on the discussions in sessions with our students as well as the exam papers analyzed, the point of departure is an acknowledgement of the failure to meet needs for families and in general the time needed to do long term follow up of many kinds of problems that users may present. This is not in line with ideas of professional standards or best practices. These social workers looked for ways of coping and ways of overcoming the resistance they faced in wanting to promote change. The exam papers as well as the discussions had a strong focus on available time as a major deficiency in the services. Lack of knowledge does not seem to be regarded as a major obstacle, since it may be met by reviewing accessible knowledge and by supervision as well as practice research. Enhancing user involvement may also increase the ability to meet needs in better and more efficient ways. The social workers also looked at ways of reducing bureaucracy for social workers by using assistants in recording and reporting. There also seems to be some disagreement about why everybody within an organization should necessarily have to take part in innovations—why is it not sufficient to engage only those involved and management. It is argued that this may reduce tensions and resistance, since many do not want to rearrange their priorities (distinctions and different attractors).

It has to be pointed out that the social workers in our study are not representative of the child protection field in general, as they have seen a good deal of research involvement in their local practices over many years. On the other hand, the knowledge developed among staff members, and especially those attending the master course, may have enhanced their ability to identify and describe situations and settings. Another problem may be the fact that we have not tested where they have their loyalty according to Billingsley's concepts. This might have indicated problems and challenges that we do not have any knowledge about. Our data does not allow for any categorization of role conceptions such as professionals, bureaucrats, conformists and innovators, which may have been useful. Some workers seemed to fit into some category that may seem relevant or belonged to two, but we did not use Billingsley´s categorization.

Supplementing complexity theory with culture sociology (in particular Bourdieu's symbolic capital concepts) one can regard management's focus on goal attainment, certain ideas of efficiency related to quality and work within limited timeframes that result in desired change as distinctions counting as symbolic capital within the social field of management and in the interface with politics. Social workers who find themselves at these bifurcation points seem to be exposed to some kind of leverage where professional values related to individual needs that families have presented have to be put on hold or ignored in order to avoid criticism that may ensue from breaching efficiency standards. This seems to be one of the factors influencing the fact that families with complex needs are not given priority.

Innovative practices could in time lead to better social work, but taking risks with improvisation to devise new ways of being in dialogue with families may also lead to unwanted or unforeseen negative results, such as increased risk of domestic violence, child abuse or maltreatment. This would invite even more criticism and perhaps sanction directed at the service and the social workers involved. At such bifurcation points, it seems the system prefers safety rather than innovation.

Social workers describe what we have dubbed the 'vicious circle': they have a heavy workload, they end up falling behind in their work and risk getting behind, leading to criticism from the inspectorate. They see their workplaces as understaffed, leading to sick leave being taken and burnout. Research may offer some possible strategies to avoid this. One is to develop more precision and efficiency in getting on with cases and obtaining more effective outcomes. A second strategy is more elaborate and involves better prevention and early intervention. The problem with the latter is the extra resources needed in order to do good social work and also have a health promotion strategy, work inclusion, etc. This may require changes to society that might be thought unlikely under prevailing neo-liberal conditions (Garrett 2009; Featherstone et al. 2016).

Our experience is that one may move towards innovation and change during a project, but the system reverts to 'normal' or the status quo after some time due to a lack of integration of changes in the total infrastructure of the organization. Change thus becomes dependent on knowledge management, action learning as well as devoted and competent workers and the available resources to continue at a higher level of intervention. Discretion may also imply actual disobedience when work and practices run against a professional interpretation of the client's rights and legitimate demands in respect of services, but this requires the will to oppose management or institutional policies (Kadish and Kadish 2010, in Evans 2016). Turnover, organizational change and continuous increasing pressure due to unrelenting reporting of new cases seem to force systems back to a restart. Processes of change may thus have to be regarded as the modus operandi, and in order to secure some impact from applied social and other research, the system will have to include research as an integral part of the organization—a complex practice with an interplay between child protection work, innovative research, evaluation and a management that has the resources to support both long term development and everyday priorities. A relevant question is how likely it may be that a focus on knowledge development and professional value based needs-orientations can be maintained in a situation where management seems to be ever more constrained by the downward pressure imposed by policy: the desired policy results being all the time operationalized in detail via computer systems that do not reflect the way that needs will have to be met in the 'real' world encountered in social work with children and families.

Author Contributions: The text is produced in cooperation between all authors based on research by the same, E.M. rewriting the final text after supplements from all authors. All authors have read and agreed to the published version of the manuscript.

Funding: The research is primarily funded by the Norwegian University of Science and Technology and Inland Norway University of Applied Sciences, in addition to a three year grant from the Norwegian Research Board (NFR).

Conflicts of Interest: The authors declare no conflict of interest.

References

Billingsley, Andrew. 1964. Bureaucratic and Professional Orientation Patterns in Social Casework. *Social Service Review* 38: 400–7. Available online: http://www.jstor.org/stable/30017112 (accessed on 26 October 2016). [CrossRef]

Bourdieu, Pierre. 1999. *Praktisk Förnuft*. London: Daidalos.

Bovens, Mark, Robert E. Goodin, and Thomas Schillemans. 2014. *The Oxford Handbook of Public Accountability*. Oxford: Oxford University Press.

Christiansen, Kikkan U. 1977. Forvaltning eller behandling. *Sosionomen* 9: 400–10.

Christiansen, Øivin, and Bente Heggem Kojan. 2016. *Beslutninger i Barnevernet*. Oslo: Universitetsforlaget.

Clifford, Graham, Edgar Marthinsen, and Anne Sofie Samuelsen. 1996. *Hjelpetenesten, en virksomhetsanalyse av Nardo distrikt i Trondheim. Rapport nr. 42*. Trondheim: NOSEB.

Clifford, Graham, Willy Lichtwarck, Halvor Fauske, and Edgar Marthinsen. 2015. Minst hjelp til dem som trenger det mest? Sluttrapport fra forsknings- og utviklingsprosjektet «Det nye barnevernet». NF-rapport 6/2015. Available online: http://www.nordlandsforskning.no/getfile.php/138752-1445428350/Dokumenter/Rapporter/2015/Rapport_06_2015.pdf (accessed on 7 April 2020).

Davidson, Bo, and Margareta Bredmar. 2012. *Familjer i Socialtjänsten—Levnadsvillkor, Livssituation och Erfarenheter av Socialtjänsten Slutrapport.* Linköping: FoU Centrum för vård, Available online: http://www.diva-portal.org/smash/get/diva2:528193/FULLTEXT02.pdf (accessed on 7 April 2020).

Department of Education. 2011. *The Munro Review of Child Protection: Final Report. A Child-Centered System;* London: Secretary of State for Education, p. 171.

Eräsaari, Risto. 2003. Open-Context Expertise. In *Yearbook 2003 of the Institute for Advanced Studies on Science, Technology and Society.* Edited by Günter Getzinger. München/Wien: Profil, pp. 31–65.

Evans, Tony. 2016. Street-level bureaucracy, management and the corrupted wold of service. *European Journal of Social Work* 19: 602–15. [CrossRef]

Evans, Tony, and John Harris. 2004. Street-Level Bureaucracy, Social Work and the (Exaggerated) Death of Discretion. *British Journal of Social Work* 34: 871–895. [CrossRef]

Fauske, Halvor, Willy Lichtwarck, Edgar Marthinsen, Elisabeth Willumsen, Graham Clifford, and Bente Heggem Kojan. 2009. *Barnevernet på ny kurs? Rapport nr. 8/2009.* Bodø: Nordlandsforskning.

Featherstone, Brid, Anne Gupta, Kate M. Morris, and Joanne Warner. 2016. Let's Stop Feeding the Risk Monster: Towards a Social Model of 'Child Protection'. *Families Relationships and Societies.* Available online: http://eprints.Whiterose.ac.uk/98016/ (accessed on 16 February 2016). [CrossRef]

Ferguson, Iain. 2007. *Reclaiming Social Work: Challenging Neo-liberalism and Promoting Social Justice.* London: Sage.

Garrett, Paul Michael. 2009. *'Transforming' Childrens Services? Social Work, Neoliberalism and the 'Modern' World.* Berkshire: Mc Graw Hill.

Gautun, Heidi. 2010. *Det nye barnevernbyråkratiet II. En kartlegging av samarbeid mellom kommune og stat innen barnevernet.* Oslo: FAFO.

Gilbert, Niel, Nigel Parton, and Marit Skivenes. 2011. *Child Protection Systems: International Trends and Emerging Orientations.* Oxford: Oxford University Press.

Gray, Mel, Debbie Plath, and Stephen Webb. 2009. *Evidence-based Social Work: A Critical Stance.* London: Routledge.

Howe, David. 1991. Knowledge, power and the shape of social work practice. In *The Sociology of Social Work.* Edited by Martin Davies. London: Routledge.

Høybye-Mortensen, Matilde. 2015. Decision-Making Tools and Their Influence on Caseworkers' Room for Discretion. *British Journal of Social Work* 45: 600–15. [CrossRef]

Juhasz, Ida Benedicte, and Marit Skivenes. 2016. The population's confidence in the child protection system - A survey study of England, Finland, Norway and the United States (California). *Social Policy & Administration* 51: 1330–47.

Kadish, Mortimer, and Sanford Kadish. 2010. *Discretion to Disobey.* New Orleans: Quid Pro Law Books.

Karvinen-Niinikoski, Synnöve. 2005. Research orientation and expertise in social work/challenges for social work education. *European Journal of Social Work* 8: 259–71. [CrossRef]

Lonne, Bob, Nigel Parton, Jane Thomson, and Maria Harries. 2008. *Reforming Child Protection.* London: Routledge.

Lorenz, W. 2005. Social work and a new social order: Challenging new liberalism's erosion of solidarity. *Social Work and Society* 3: 93–101.

Marthinsen, Edgar. 2003. Sosialt arbeid og symbolsk kapital i et senmoderne barnevern. Ph.D. thesis, Norwegian University of Science and Technology, Trondheim, Norway.

Marthinsen, Edgar, and Willy Lichtwarck. 2013. *Det nye barnevernet.* Oslo: Universitetsforlaget.

Molander, Anders. 2016. *Discretion in the Welfare State: Social Rights and Professional Judgment.* London: Routledge.

Müller, Jan-Werner. 2016. *Hvad er Populisme?* London: Daidalos.

Nonaka, Ikujiro, Ryoko Toyama, and Noboru Konno. 2000. SECI, Ba and Leadership: A Unified Model of Dynamic Knowledge Creation. *Long Range Planning:* 33: 5–34. [CrossRef]

Nowotny, Helga. 2000. Transgressive competence. The narrative of expertise. *European Journal of Social Theory* 3: 5–21. [CrossRef]

Nowotny, Helga, Peter Scott, and Michael Gibbons. 2004. *Re-Thinking Science. Knowledge and the Public in the Age of Uncertainty.* Cambridge: Polity Press.

Parton, Nigel. 2014. *The Politics of Child Protection: Contemporary Developments and Future Directions*. London: Palgrave Macmillan.

Parton, Nigel, David H. Thorpe, and Corinne Wattam. 1997. *Child Protection: Risk and the Moral Order*. Basingstoke: Macmillan.

Rawls, John. 1993. *Political Liberalism*. New York: Columbia University Press.

Riesman, Leonard. 1949. A Study of Role Conceptions in Bureaucracy. *Social Forces* XXV: 305–10. [CrossRef]

Rugowski, Steve. 2010. *Social Work. The Rise and Fall of a Profession?* Bristol: Policy Press.

Sørhaug, Tian. 2004. *Managementalitet og Autoritetens Forvandling*. Bergen: Fagbokforlaget.

Spolander, Gary, Lambert Engelbrecht, and Annie Pullen Sansfaçon. 2016. Social work and macro-economic neoliberalism: Beyond the social justice rhetoric. *European Journal of Social Work* 19: 634–49. [CrossRef]

Stevens, Irene, and Pat Cox. 2008. Complexity Theory: Developing New Understandings of Child Protection in Field Settings and in Residential Child Care. *British Journal of Social Work* 38: 1320–36. [CrossRef]

Stevens, Irene, and Peter Hassett. 2007. Applying Complexity Theory to Risk in Child Protection Practice. *Childhood* 14: 128. [CrossRef]

Thaler, Richard H., and Cass R. Sunstein. 2008. *Nudge: Improving Decisions about Health, Wealth, and Happiness*. London: Penguin Books.

social sciences

MDPI

Article

Watching over or Working with? Understanding Social Work Innovation in Response to Extra-Familial Harm

Lauren Elizabeth Wroe * and Jenny Lloyd

Institute of Applied Social Research, University of Bedfordshire, Room F303, Park Square, Luton LU1 3JU, UK;
jenny.lloyd@beds.ac.uk
* Correspondence: lauren.wroe@beds.ac.uk

Received: 27 February 2020; Accepted: 26 March 2020; Published: 1 April 2020

Abstract: This paper critically reflects on the role of surveillance and trusted relationships in social work in England and Wales. It explores the characteristics of relationships of trust and relationships of surveillance and asks how these approaches apply to emerging policy and practices responses to extra-familial forms of harm (EFH). Five bodies of research that explore safeguarding responses across a range of public bodies are drawn on to present an analytical framework that explores elements of safeguarding responses, constituting relationships of trust or relationships of surveillance and control. This analytic framework is applied to two case studies, each of which detail a recent practice innovation in response to EFH studied by the authors, as part of a larger body of work under the Contextual Safeguarding programme. The application of this framework signals a number of critical issues related to the focus/rationale, methods and impact of interventions into EFH that should be considered in future work to address EFH, to ensure young people's rights to privacy and participation are upheld.

Keywords: care; child protection; contextual safeguarding; control; extra-familial harm; surveillance

1. Introduction

Since the first social services departments in England and Wales in 1971 were established, social work has seen a seismic shift in its scope and remit, placing increased demands on social workers and, arguably, increased surveillance on a broader population of children and families (Parton 2019). The increased bureaucratization of social work appears alongside the encroachment of neoliberal values into social welfare systems (Eubanks 2018), where families become problems to be managed. One feature of this bureaucratization is the use of surveillance (through data collection, monitoring and risk assessment) to assess, prevent and monitor social harms, and the subjects of social welfare. This has been subject to significant academic (Penna 2005; Edwards 2016; White and Wastell 2017) and sector debate (Shabde and Craft 1999; Mellon 2017). Yet, alongside what some (McKendrick and Finch 2017) term the 'securitization' of social welfare, and social work specifically, the importance of relationships and relational ways of working has remained intact (Bryan et al. 2016; Care Crisis Review 2018).

Working with families has been positioned as dichotomous to 'watching over' (surveillance from the French: 'sur'—'over' and 'veiller'—watch), highlighting contradictions in surveillance and relationship centred social work (Parton 2011). A body of literature details the detrimental impact of over-surveillance on relationships between young people and statutory bodies (Fine et al. 2003; Williams 2018). Relational ways of working and the participation of young people and families in social work have been championed as promoting not only effective social work practice but the rights of children and families that should underpin any such intervention (Cossar et al. 2016).

Within ostensibly incompatible paradigms, social work is tasked with responding to ever-changing forms of harm. While child protection in England and Wales has historically focused on the risks that children face within their families, there is increasing awareness of harm happening outside the home (Firmin 2017; Department for Education 2018b). Abuse such as child sexual exploitation (CSE), serious youth violence and child criminal exploitation (CCE) are often forms of extra-familial harm (EFH) occurring in social settings beyond the home. As such, policy and practice across England and Wales are placing greater requirements on multi-agency partnerships to respond to contexts where harm occurs, most recently through the inclusion of Contextual Safeguarding in safeguarding guidance (Llywodraeth Cymru 2019; Firmin 2017; Department for Education 2018b). Working Together (Department for Education 2018b) notes that social workers should "understand the level of need and risk in, or faced by, a family from the child's perspective" (p. 28) and "interventions should focus on addressing wider environmental factors" (p. 22). The recognition of EFH as a form of child abuse has been welcomed by many working within child protection to address the system challenges practitioners face when responding to harm outside the home (ADCS 2017; Department for Education 2018a).

The broadening of child protection frameworks to the harm faced by, as well as within, families, places new demand on children's services: how to respond effectively to EFH within child protection legislative frameworks, with questions around thresholds, partnerships and interventions currently unanswered. These are not simply technical or operational questions; the expansion of the child protection lens to new arenas of private and public life poses ethical questions around which social work values, theory and practices will drive innovation in the area of EFH. If current child protection practice is experienced as adversarial and punitive (Morris 2012) and young people report distrust and isolation in response to surveillance in their families, schools and communities (Fine et al. 2003; Williams 2018), how can new practice responses to EFH learn from decades of debates and scholarship in social work to inform effective and ethical interventions? This article explores these questions in further detail, drawing upon two current practice responses to EFH that use a Contextual Safeguarding Framework, to evaluate the extent to which the interventions represent an extension of welfare-driven and care-led responses to child abuse, or further the encroachment of punitive forms of state surveillance into the lives of young people and their families.

2. Interventions into Extra Familial Harm

Children subject to child protection interventions have steadily increased in England and Wales since the 1990s (Department for Education 2019). In 2017, the number of children in care was its highest since the Children Act 1989 (Care Crisis Review 2018). James Munby named this a 'crisis' in child welfare and a 2018 Family Rights Group report, aimed at addressing the crisis, concluded that cultures of blame "led to an environment that is increasingly mistrusting and risk averse and prompts individuals to seek refuge in procedural processes" (Care Crisis Review 2018, p. 5). Whereas child protection interventions have traditionally focused on harm in the family, increasing focus on EFH arguably broadens the child protection lens. In 2019, the Children's Commissioner reported increasing numbers of young people aged 12 or more entering care for the first time, often as a result of EFH (Stability Index 2019).

Yet, growing awareness and high-profile cases of EFH, such as CSE (Jay 2014), have raised questions about the efficacy of child protection services to respond to the harm children face externally to their families (Munro 2011; Lloyd and Firmin 2019). In response, a number of practice and policy frameworks are emerging. Contextual Safeguarding is one approach, seeking to expand the reach of child protection systems into a range of social contexts beyond families such as peer groups, schools and neighbourhoods (Firmin 2017). Despite the inclusion of Contextual Safeguarding in statutory guidance, there are few practical suggestions as to how to do so. As such, agencies are developing their own practice frameworks, either through specific reference to Contextual Safeguarding or emphasis on community-based or location-specific practices. For example, through the use of peer group mapping (to identify children's peer relationships) and safety mapping (by exploring young people's experiences of safety and risk in their neighbourhoods) (ALDCS 2018).

Responses to EFH require child protection systems to respond to forms of harm that had previously been criminalized or understood as outside the remit of child safeguarding. These include forms of youth exploitation and violence; from CSE, to serious youth violence and more recently the exploitation of children to distribute drugs via 'county lines'. Whilst increased sector attention to these forms of harm (and recognition they are forms of child abuse) are welcomed, responses to EFH are ubiquitously accompanied by increases in surveillance practices and technologies. From the monitoring of young people's social media accounts by schools and social workers (Shade and Singh 2016; Montgomery 2015), to mandatory reporting by civic institutions of children at risk of 'radicalization' (McKendrick and Finch 2017; Stanley et al. 2018), or serious youth violence (Community Practitioner 2019), the use of multi-agency risk panels and databases to record, share and monitor 'at risk' young people (Williams and Clarke 2016), the use of child Covert Human Intelligence Sources to investigate child exploitation (Twite 2018) and the increased use in managed moves and secure accommodation (Stability Index 2019). Whilst these interventions are justified by a need to safeguard children and young people, they present significant challenges to rights-based approaches grounded in participatory and relational ways of working. Wrennall (2010) describes these kinds of child protection interventions as a 'Trojan horse', via which extensive surveillance practices are justified with often competing or contradictory policing or other social, political or economic goals.

Extra-Familial Harm and Surveillance Approaches

The recognition of EFH as child abuse impacts both the scope and remit of child protection and the subsequent interventions. A major outcome of the Care Crisis Review, which sought to address the rising number of young people entering care, was recognition of professionals' desire to 'work with' rather than 'do to' families, and similarly families and young people expressed a 'strong desire' (Care Crisis Review 2018, p. 5) to work with services to improve systems for protecting children. Partnership with children and families is a founding principle of the Children Act 1989, and is enshrined in international rights treaties (UNCRC 1989, Article 12) and supported by a vast academic and practice research (see van Bijleveld et al. 2013; Cossar et al. 2016). As the Care Crisis Review summarized:

> There was consensus that relationship building has been and is at the heart of good practice.
> The challenge for all of us is how to create the conditions within children's social care and
> family justice that allow good relationships to flourish everywhere, within and between
> agencies, within families, and between families and practitioners. (Care Crisis Review 2018,
> p. 4)

Yet, for some, relational forms of practice are under threat from institutions tasked with protecting children and young people. Hingley-Jones and Ruch (2016) draw on Parton's (2000) conceptualization of the social worker as inhabiting the 'social' space between the individual and the state. They position relational social work, where the social worker positions themself alongside families to find "solutions to problems in living" (Hingley-Jones and Ruch 2016, p. 240), as increasingly restricted. They ask, what role can the social worker play in mediating between the individual and a state that does not listen to the needs of young people and families, instead subjecting them to discipline and management approaches? Such approaches are documented as increasingly targeting children and families through relationships of control and surveillance (Edwards 2016; White and Wastell 2017).

The negative impact of experiences of surveillance on trusted relationships with young people is well documented, particularly where this intersects with class and race. A 2003 study exploring the surveillance experiences of young people in urban public places in New York concluded:

urban youth, overall, express a strong sense of betrayal by adults and report feeling mistrusted by adults, with young men of color most likely to report these perceptions. (Fine et al. 2003, p. 142)

Fine et al. (2003) propose that youth perceptions of authority surveillance undermine trust and may have "adverse developmental and also democratic consequences of society as a whole" (Fine et al. 2003, p. 143). Similarly, O'Neill and Loftus (2013) detail how intensive information gathering, within unreflexive and loose information sharing arrangements, disproportionately impacts already marginalized individuals, families and communities. Recent research into the monitoring of young people on the London 'Gangs Matrix', as a means of addressing serious youth violence and 'gang' association, similarly demonstrates the lasting impact of surveillance activity. An Amnesty (2018) report into the Gangs Matrix highlighted significant and lasting impacts to education and employment opportunities for young people.

3. Analytical Framework

The impacts of surveillance as a form of 'watching over' rather than 'working with' are further amplified when EFH and adolescence are considered. In light of this need, and the changing landscape of child protection in response to EFH, we develop an analytical framework to explore how contemporary approaches to EFH fare in way of these debates. Drawing upon five bodies of research, individually exploring safeguarding responses across a range of public bodies, we present an analytical framework that explores elements of safeguarding responses, constituting relationships of trust (Bryan et al. 2016) or relationships of surveillance and control (Fernandez and Huey 2009). A focused literature review was conducted. Academic and grey literature was searched using focused search terms. English language returns were reviewed in the period 2000–2020 to capture debates emerging in the last two decades on control/surveillance and trusted relationships in social care and to capture the period that the issue of child exploitation and EFH entered child protection practice and policy discourse. Five papers were selected that effectively distilled or exemplified themes emerging in the broader search. The five studies underpinning this framework consider the role of statutory agencies in the lives of young people and families and have been selected on the basis that they tackle the dynamics of trust and surveillance in such interventions. O'Neill and Loftus (2013) (article one) detail how social policy focused on crime control contributes to accelerating surveillance processes, which target 'problematic' individuals through detailed data sharing across public sector bodies. Focusing on the policing of adolescents, Fine et al. (2003) (article two) consider the process of alienation young people feel through increasingly punitive police practices. For Wrennall (2010) (article three), the rhetoric of child protection is seen to be a 'Trojan horse', whereby the seemingly innocuous aim of protecting children justifies and normalizes the encroachment of expansive and powerful legislation and techniques which disguise the surveillance of young people for the economic, political and commercial interests of the state and other parties. The Care Crisis Review (2018) (article four) includes a rapid academic review resulting in 20 recommendations for change, based on a consensus that relationship building is 'at the heart of good practice', despite current cultures of blame, anxiety, mistrust and distance between professionals and families. Similarly, Hingley-Jones and Ruch (2016) (article five) locate professional anxiety in the context of neoliberalism and austerity as a barrier to relational ways of working. Using a psychoanalytical and structural framework, the authors argue 'life begins with relationships' but that financially austere socio-political climates create a 'relational austerity' (2016, p. 237), where practice is authoritative and combative rather than assertive and compassionate.

Creating an Analytic Framework

Drawing on these studies, we present an analytical framework which explores the components of systems constituting welfare and participatory approaches based on relationships of trust with young people, or systems and interventions where relationships between services and young people are characterized by surveillance and monitoring.

Table 1 distils the learning from the articles detailed above across three areas:

- Focus/rationale: Who or what is the focus of the intervention and what is the legal/moral justification?
- Method: How does the system or intervention pursue its aim and through which methods?
- Impact: What is the impact on those subject to interventions?

Table 1. Key components of five studies (numbers indicate article).

	Relationships of Trust	Relationships of Surveillance
Focus/rationale	<ul><li>Rights-based and operates within a moral framework</li><li>Focus on populations rather than individuals[1]</li><li>Risk-sensible[4]</li><li>Focus on current needs and wishes of families and young people[4,5]</li><li>Recognises citizens' right to privacy</li><li>Targets structural causes of poverty and disadvantage[4]</li><li>Working with[5]</li></ul>	<ul><li>Legal basis is the prevention of antisocial behaviour or crime and disorder[1] bypassing civil liberties, data protection and human rights legislation[3]</li><li>Disproportionally targets marginalised groups or areas across racialised, gendered and classed lines[1,2,3,5]</li><li>Focus on future threats and risks[1]</li><li>Rhetoric of child protection misused to legitimise expansive focus of child protection to populations 'at risk'[3]</li><li>Focus on individual harms detached from wider socio-economic causes[5]</li><li>Doing to[5]</li></ul>
Method	<ul><li>Intelligent use of data shared for intended purposes with informed consent is proportional and considered[5]</li><li>Formal and transparent partnership arrangements and secure sharing, with systems in place to hold individuals to account</li><li>'Felt thoughtfulness'—feelings matter. Principles of humanity, kindness and warmth are emphasised[4]</li><li>Focus on capabilities and prioritises resources that support families, drawing on relationships and restorative practice</li><li>Relationships with families and communities and meaningful contact is at the heart of practice[5,4]</li><li>Practice is confident, strengths-based, authoritative and has humility. Systems are open to uncertainty, complexity, irrationality and subjectivity. The limits and impact of interventions are recognised[4]</li></ul>	<ul><li>Large amount of personal and intrusive data are gathered and shared across vast electronic systems. This is unquestioned by professionals and used for purposes beyond those originally intended[1,3]</li><li>Relatively open partnership arrangements encourage informal sharing and communication. Individuals unaware of sharing or options to opt-out[1]</li><li>Lack of reciprocity/ listening and empathy from adults to young people[2]</li><li>Assessment and monitoring outweighs provision and support provided. Protective interventions (such as section 47 inquiries, case conferences and child protection plans) are prioritised[3,5]</li><li>Disciplines and manages through adversarial relationships[4,5]</li><li>Relies on notions of certainty, simplicity, risk aversion[5]; is rational, objective, outcome driven and techno-bureaucratic[4]</li></ul>
Impact	<ul><li>Families are supported to understand professional concerns and draw upon their own strengths and networks to make safe plans for their child[5]</li><li>Results in building, strengthening and repairing relationships as the key to long-term stability and security for children[5]</li><li>Enables young people to develop trust and build healthy relationships with professionals[5]</li><li>Increases feelings of safety for young people</li><li>Eases stress, dispels families' fears and does not reinforce shame and suffering[5]</li><li>Maintains the 'no order' principle underpinning the Children Act 1989—no order is made in relation to a child unless doing so would be better for the child than making no order at all [5]</li></ul>	<ul><li>Individuals provided with welfare rather than rights through 'coercive paternalism'[4,3]</li><li>Negative impact on individuals for housing, education and employment prospects and criminalisation[1,3]</li><li>Results in youth alienation and disengagement from adult society, resulting in likelihood of seeking help/disclosing[2]</li><li>Reduces feeling of safety in some places, moving youth populations from public space to marginal spaces[2]</li><li>Normalises punitive policing and sanction-based approaches, such as stop and search and increasing securitisation[2]</li><li>Financially benefits particular industries including IT, adoption and foster care companies and care home companies[3]</li></ul>

Table 1 condenses this to capture the core components of each pillar.

Employing this framework, we consider where developments in child protection work, tackling EFH, fall across this relational scale, using findings from the two studies detailed below.

4. Methodology

The findings presented here are taken from work undertaken as part of the Contextual Safeguarding programme (Firmin 2017). Since 2011, this programme of work has been concerned with understanding and advancing the efficacy of child protection systems to respond to EFH.

This article presents data from two studies. Both were chosen, and are analysed in tandem, as the interventions they focus on were unique and/or innovative in the way they sought to address a form of EFH. The project under analysis in study 1 innovated by coordinating a regional approach to EFH, bringing together policing, social services and the voluntary sector. The project under analysis in study 2 engaged a contextual assessment and intervention. To ensure anonymity and confidentiality, some details of the projects have been amended.

Ethical approval was granted for all studies from a University of Bedfordshire ethics committee, and in study 1 the participating local authorities ethics board and the Director of Children and Families. In study 2, additional ethical approval was granted by participating local authorities. Ethics considered research and participant welfare, referral process, confidentiality and consent and the ethical analysis and dissemination of the data.

4.1. Study 1: A Regionally Coordinated Cross-Sector Response to Child Exploitation

From January 2019, researchers from the Contextual Safeguarding team at the University of Bedfordshire were embedded within a regionally coordinated, cross-sector project, that aimed to understand and tackle the exploitation of children and young people from a particular form of EFH. The project was innovative, in that it brought together statutory and voluntary sector organizations, and analytic work with the provision of direct support. The project identified a cohort of young people impacted by this form of EFH across the region through the analysis of police data, and coordinated referrals from across the region to a central system. The project notified local areas about young people deemed to be 'at risk' and if there was no local provision for support, a referral was made for specialist case work from the commissioned voluntary and community sector organizations. The one-year study of this project utilized a range of research methods, including statutory and voluntary sector case file reviews (n = 38), embedded observations of analysts and statutory multi-agency meetings (n = 18) and semi-structured interviews with statutory and voluntary sector workers (n = 39).

Case Study 1: Identification, Mapping and Network Analysis

The project aimed to coordinate responses to young people subject to EFH across the statutory and voluntary sector and policing, and to support the identification of young people 'at risk' through the use of police data and network mapping and analysis. The analysis of police data established a very large cohort of individuals involved in this form of EFH, six times larger than those who were referred to the project for support. The VCS organizations used a one-to-one case work model to work with young people on education, employment and training, awareness raising, and confidence building, as well as family work and advocacy around criminal justice interventions, and in response to school exclusions.

Individuals associated with child exploitation (as victims and perpetrators) were identified by project staff from police data (i.e., arrest reports) and from project referrals. The names, gender, ethnicity, address, 'gang' affiliation, locations frequented and police intelligence linking the individual to this form of EFH were recorded on a spreadsheet held by the project, and uploaded to police systems. The names of the young people on the spreadsheet up to the age of 25 were shared with local authority safeguarding leads and multi-agency safeguarding hubs. The full list of names (including young people and adults) from the police data and the project referrals were added to police systems.

For those who were identified as in need of support (and where there was no local support provision available), the project referred the young person to the specially commissioned voluntary sector service for one-to-one case work.

Mapping work was carried out by the project team to support multi-agency risk panels, to identify young people and locations at risk. Information was gathered by the project analysts during multi-agency panels (such as names of young people and their friends) and then expanded using police data and the project referral data. The mapping depicted the names and ages of young people discussed in the panel, plus additional young people identified as associates or young people at risk, through police data and the project referral data (i.e., the names of siblings/family members or friends). The mapping established connections between young people and addresses/locations of harm or frequently occurring locations (e.g., schools) and 'gang' affiliation/association. The mapping also noted whether police data could evidence that the young person was subject to exploitation. This data was then shared with the regional police and a sanitized version without police data (other than that originally shared in the panel) was shared with the local authority via the multi-agency risk panel.

4.2. Study 2: Developing and Embedding a Whole Systems Approach to Extra-Familial Harm

From May 2017 to May 2019, researchers from the Contextual Safeguarding programme were embedded within one statutory child protection team in England to work with a project team (formed of social and youth work practitioners), to create and embed a Contextual Safeguarding approach to EFH. This action research study utilised a range of research methods, including observations of strategic and operational multi-agency meetings (n = 12), meeting participation (n = 16), reflective meetings (n = 7), weekly team and project meetings across two years, case file review (n = 43), practitioner interviews (n = 7), observations of practice and analysis of five context assessments, a school assessment (n = 1), neighbourhood assessments (n = 2) and peer group assessment (n = 3).

Case Study 2: Context Assessments

In study 2, the local authority piloted context assessments to engage with young people's experiences of EFH. Context assessments follow statutory child protection frameworks, but rather than assessing and intervening with individual children or families, do so with contexts. This work is developing nationally, and so far, has been trialled within schools, housing estates, restaurants, shopping centres and with peer groups. Here, a neighbourhood assessment was piloted in a small urban area, which encompassed a community centre, park, youth club, shops, and one primary school. The assessment was instigated following two incidents between January and March 2018 (the separate sexual and physical assault of young people). Further incidents and data prompted the authority to choose this location as the test site for a location assessment, including; data from an Integrated Gangs Unit (IGU) and recent crime data captured by the local authority data analyst. The assessment was led by two social workers, two youth work practitioners and a participation officer over 6 weeks, and involved a number of assessment activities, including:

- Forming a youth panel of 10 young people engaged weekly
- Five focus groups with young people from the youth club and school
- Young person engagement at the local youth club
- Business surveys with local businesses
- Review local regeneration board minutes
- A member of the assessment team located weekly in the community centre
- A weekend local community event to engage local residents and young people

The assessment concluded that the location "is a context in which young people may experience significant harm" (assessment report). The risks included "exposure to substance misuse, child and adult exploitation (sexual and criminal), harmful attitudes and violence, lack of resources and the normalization of these factors in this context" (assessment report). Following analysis, a context conference was convened, chaired by an independent reviewing officer and attended by ward councillors, the local youth service, substance misuse team, community safety, the IGU, community resilience partnership, anti-social behaviour team, housing and local businesses. No names or details were provided relating to individual young people or families, as it was the neighbourhood, not individuals, that were under assessment. At the context conference assessment, the findings were presented, and a plan was developed. The plan included a range of activities, including; alcohol and drugs outreach; community safety patrols; identification of community guardians and a single point of contact for local residents; training to businesses and options to indicate businesses as safe places for young people; detached youth work hired by local young people, and restorative interventions for young people that were identified during the neighbourhood assessment.

5. Findings

Both projects studied sought ways to respond to EFH. In doing so, they raise ethical questions about the rationale, methods and impact. Below, we critically analyse both studies using the framework developed in this article (Figure 1).

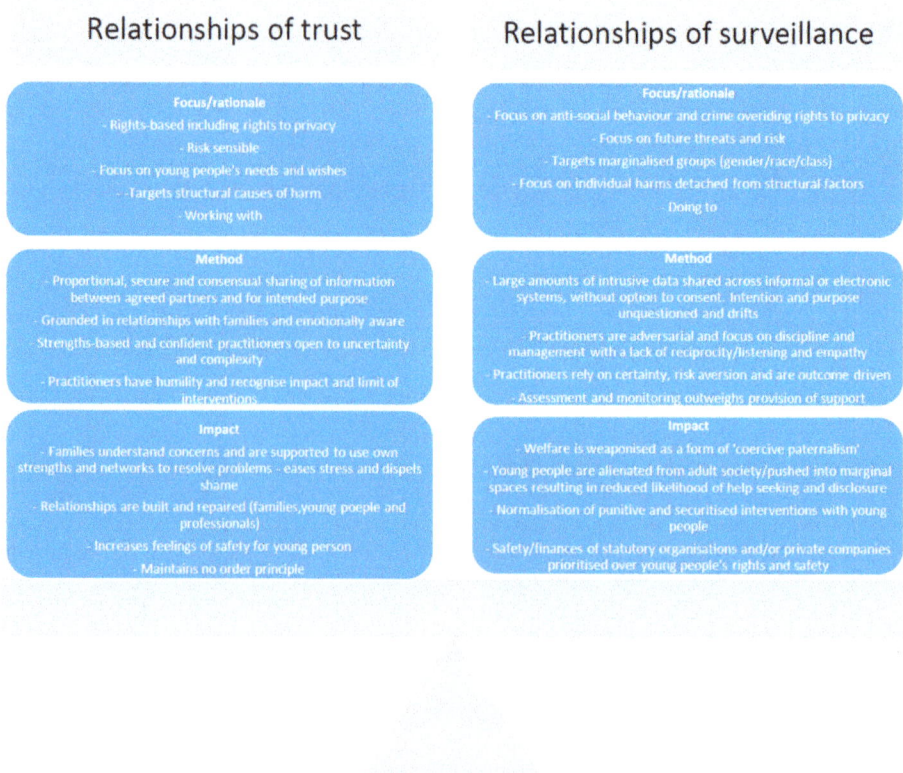

Relationships of trust

Focus/rationale
- Rights-based including rights to privacy
- Risk sensible
- Focus on young people's needs and wishes
- Targets structural causes of harm
- Working with

Method
- Proportional, secure and consensual sharing of information between agreed partners and for intended purpose
- Grounded in relationships with families and emotionally aware
- Strengths-based and confident practitioners open to uncertainty and complexity
- Practitioners have humility and recognise impact and limit of interventions

Impact
- Families understand concerns and are supported to use own strengths and networks to resolve problems - eases stress and dispels shame
- Relationships are built and repaired (families, young poeple and professionals)
- Increases feelings of safety for young person
- Maintains no order principle

Relationships of surveillance

Focus/rationale
- Focus on anti-social behaviour and crime overriding rights to privacy
- Focus on future threats and risk
- Targets marginalised groups (gender/race/class)
- Focus on individual harms detached from structural factors
- Doing to

Method
- Large amounts of intrusive data shared across informal or electronic systems, without option to consent. Intention and purpose unquestioned and drifts
- Practitioners are adversarial and focus on discipline and management with a lack of reciprocity/listening and empathy
- Practitioners rely on certainty, risk aversion and are outcome driven
- Assessment and monitoring outweighs provision of support

Impact
- Welfare is weaponised as a form of 'coercive paternalism'
- Young people are alienated from adult society/pushed into marginal spaces resulting in reduced likelihood of help seeking and disclosure
- Normalisation of punitive and securitised interventions with young people
- Safety/finances of statutory organisations and/or private companies prioritised over young people's rights and safety

Figure 1. Relationships of trust or relationships of surveillance.

5.1. Focus/Rationale

Both projects sought, in different ways, opportunities to respond to young people's experiences of EFH through multi-agency working around a specific form or location of harm. Project 1 was motivated by a concern about the unknown reach and impact of a particular form of child exploitation in a geographical region of the UK. Whilst the focus was child safeguarding, the project was funded via policing and crime funds. The project aimed to combine intelligence gathering and sharing across the region, with the provision of specialist direct support for young people. It aimed to ensure young people most at risk, or on the cusp of exploitation, were known to services and a support service could be offered. An additional objective was ensuring those who perpetrate harm against young people could be brought to justice. The rationale for the project was that the issue of child exploitation, via this particular crime type, was little understood and that coordination was required at a regional level to tackle the issue. The project therefore had a dual rationale and focus: the prevention of crime and the safeguarding of children and young people. This is not unusual for multi-agency safeguarding partnerships where disruption and protection operate alongside each other, however, the at times competing and conflicting methods and impacts of these kinds of interventions require critical consideration (discussed below).

For project 2, the overwhelming rationale for the neighbourhood assessment was the recognition that young people had locally experienced physical and sexual harm, contributing to concerns that young people in the area were at risk of further harm. The project sought to conduct a neighbourhood assessment, develop a plan and intervene in the location. In some senses, the use of crime data and information from the IGU, contributed to the rationale underpinning the assessment—the reduction of future threats and risks, including the prevention of crime. However, by locating the assessment within children's social care, led by social workers and youth work practitioners, the team sought to root the assessment from a child welfare, as opposed to crime reduction, perspective.

Project 1 aimed to identify young people who were potential victims of exploitation. The project aims were then ostensibly aligned to the rights of children and young people to live lives free from abuse, to ensure their welfare is paramount and their best interests are protected. Despite this, an overwhelming majority of young people identified and documented through the project as at risk were identified through police data collected with a crime prevention priority. Police data are not an accurate reflection of crime or vulnerability, but in this instance were stored and shared across a range of agencies, using safeguarding and crime prevention legislation to override GDPR or data protection considerations, for example where information from referrals identifying young people at risk was shared with police partners and uploaded to police systems. The project was both motivated by present and future risk to young people. The collating and sharing of policing data that indicated involvement in this form of EFH (i.e., arrest data/stop and search reports) were legitimised by the project as allowing partners to identify young people not yet known to services (although many were) as 'at risk' of this particular form of child exploitation. The use of police data to identify young people at risk came with a number of inherent biases. Police data are only accurate representations of policing, not of crime, and it is well established that certain demographics of young people are policed at a higher rate than their peers (Lammy 2017). The project disproportionately collated and shared data in multi-agency settings about young people from Black, Asian and ethnic minority backgrounds and almost 60% of young people identified were already open to children's services.

In study 2, the distinction between focusing predominantly on children's rights and welfare, as opposed to crime reduction, was more evident. Most strongly through the emphasis on working with members of the community within the location area, such as local residents, local businesses and schools and health services, and particularly through the early engagement of young people in order to focus on their needs and wishes (discussed below). Yet, in other ways, the trigger and focus for the assessment as 'working with' young people were less clear. As location assessments were not part of the everyday practice of this social care department, the referral route was atypical to how a child and family may enter the child protection system—via screening and threshold decisions based on level of harm (as opposed to crime) at the front door. As such, the authority determined the assessment location, based on data from a range of sources. Social workers in the team, and youth workers that sat on the project advisory board, were keen to choose a location based on reports from young people that they had experienced harm or felt unsafe in the area. However, the project's analyst and community safety partners promoted a location based predominantly on the combination of police crime data and information from social care referrals. Ultimately, the location was expanded to include a combination of both.

The issue of 'working with' or 'watching over' was complicated in project 1. Whilst young people did not know, and therefore could not consent, to their information being collated and shared between policing and child welfare agencies, their consent was sought for a referral to one of the voluntary sector support services commissioned by the project. At this point young people's needs and wishes were taken into account and support services were responsive to these needs; supporting young people with education, employment and training, advocating around school exclusions, and ensuring National Referral Mechanism referrals were made and young people were supported in court. Although young people and families consented to take part in the intervention, the vast data gathering and sharing leading up to this point were conducted without their knowledge or consent.

Project 2 strongly promoted working with young people, but despite this, a number of challenges were raised. As in study 1, relying on police data provides only a partial representation of harm—which is likely to disproportionally target marginalized groups—or areas. Furthermore, the analyst and policing community safety colleagues were sceptical of relying on young people's 'anecdotal' experiences of safety. This can be seen to contribute to a hierarchy of experiences, where young people's experiences are subjugated, despite the fact low reporting rates mean that we already know very little about young people's experiences of crime (Beckett and Warrington 2015). In some respects, the focus on locations rather than individual children and family reduced the ability to intrude on individual rights to privacy, but in other ways the intervention could be seen to expand the role and remit of child protection, subjecting a greater number of young people (and the neighbourhood in which they live) to surveillance and monitoring, through a focus on places not people.

Both projects sought, in varying ways, to consider locational, if not structural, forms of harm. For example, project 2 aimed to address the impacts of ongoing regeneration and gentrification for young people from the area. Furthermore, interventions sought to question and raise the issues of gender and race, which underpinned some of their experiences of harm. For example, sessions with the youth group discussed the impact of policing and experiences of sexism. In study 1, caseworkers helped young people to navigate a range of structural factors that create the conditions for, and vulnerability to, child exploitation. For example, young people were supported to find means of earning money safely and legally, mediating poverty as a push factor into precarious and exploitative 'work'. However, these are individualized responses to structural factors; could efforts have been made to address structural harms to young people in the area, such as high levels of child poverty and school exclusions, both identified as drivers of this particular form of child exploitation?

5.2. Methods

The use of data in child welfare interventions featured heavily in the analytical framework. Both projects relied on a range of data sources to determine who and what was the focus and the rationale for the intervention. For project 1, the threshold for a young person being identified as at risk or on the cusp of exploitation was determined via two data sources: police crime data and referral data provided by multi-agency partners. The project shared this information between the project and its partners (including police and social care), without the consent of young people and families. Information was shared via usual multi-agency processes, such as verbally and in document form in multi-agency risk panels, through referrals to the Multi-agency Safeguarding Hub and directly to safeguarding teams and via mapping and network analysis documents to strategic panels. The information was shared securely and in sanitized form where required (i.e., removing policing data from information shared in non-police settings). The extent to which data were shared proportionally was tied to the proposed level of risk the young people were in/posed to others, and whether or not information sharing increased their safety. As the project data were shared across policing and child welfare spaces without consistent follow-up (as to how the data were used) it is difficult to establish if the information sharing was either proportionate or effective. In some cases, managers in the VCS organizations redacted referral information provided by the project, as it was felt that having too much information about a young person impacted on the ability to form trusted relationships and exacerbated existing power imbalances.

In project 2, information was not shared about individual children and families. Consent was an on-going process and raised a number of ethical questions. For elements where people were engaged directly, for example the youth participation groups, focus groups' and business surveys' consent was sought from individuals. Information from these sources was recorded by social workers and shared with other agencies anonymously. For other forms of data, for example that shared by the police and intelligence unit, existing information sharing and confidentiality agreements were used. While information relating to individuals was never shared, it was evident that some information was sourced from social media platforms and open source sites. While the focus was a location and not individuals, the project does, however, raise a number of questions about the scope and remit of assessments of this nature. Individuals, unless they were directly contacted, did not consent and were unaware of this process. Furthermore, practitioners within the project raised, on a number of occasions, issues around how the location assessment would be linked to children and families already known to their service. For example, how would plans developed for the area, or concerns raised, link to individual plans for children locally. Information was shared to the individual social workers of these families, but did not form part of the location assessment.

Practitioners in project 1 delivered support services in a relational way with young people and their families, drawing on empathy, lived experience and access to resources to form and maintain relationships with young people, that were flexible and patient in response to inconsistent attendance/engagement. The project recorded fairly rigid outcomes, such as a pre-specified number of young people it aimed to engage, and measures such as 'reduction in offending', which are not accurate indications of reduced vulnerability or increased safety. There were six times as many individuals deemed via police data to be involved in this form of child exploitation, whose data were collected, collated and shared, than those identified and referred to the project by agencies in the region. Of those referred to the projects support service (7% of the total number of young people identified by the project), half were successfully engaged and just over half of those reported a reduction in involvement. The assessment and monitoring of the harm outweighed the provision of support.

Methods employed in study 2 varied significantly from study 1, most clearly, through the participation of young people and families within assessment. The project's assessment in study 2 was grounded in relationships with families. Throughout the project, one practitioner from the assessment team was located weekly in the local community centre within the assessment area. This allowed them to engage with local residents, businesses and services in the area and develop relationships forming the basis of the assessment, information captured and focus of interventions. Secondly, this same practitioner and the participatory lead formed, and met weekly, with a group of young people in the area. The information from these sessions guided the assessment and methods used, allowing practitioners to learn from the young people, to understand their experiences, develop strength-based interventions and be transparent about when and how information was used and shared.

5.3. Impact

Young people and families engaged through project 1 were supported in a relational and strengths-based way, and emotional and material support was provided to protect young people from criminalization and ensure their safety. However, the impact of the project went beyond the one-to-one case work delivered to young people, and although welfare was not used in a coercive manner by the case workers (i.e., young people's support was not contingent on their engagement or performance), the issue of child welfare provided the rationale for an extensive data collation and sharing exercise, that went beyond those young people who were at risk or deemed by child welfare agencies as being at risk of significant harm. Whilst locally, young people were engaged by caseworkers who could support them to participate in and gain access to support in their local communities, the broader remit of the project and the reported disproportionality raises questions about the impact of extensive data collecting and sharing on community/service relations, for those young people and families who already feel over-policed and over-intervened. The project promoted safeguarding responses to young people and the case work provided had a focus on welfare and de-criminalization, however the information collated and shared about young people, which detailed crime data and association with a particular crime type (sometimes as both perpetrator and victim), has unknown consequences for young people's futures. Finally, the engagement of a private company to work alongside the project to monitor patterns and trends on open source platforms again removed the assessment of risk and vulnerability away from young people and those that have trusted relationships with them.

The true extent of the impact of the assessment and subsequent intervention carried in project 2 is difficult to determine. In particular, it is hard to consider the extent that interventions can increase the safety of young people living locally. While this is certainly an aim, evidencing this proves difficult, for a number of reasons. Firstly, re-engaging those who were part of the first assessment would be challenging. Secondly, the catalyst for assessment was a number of sexual and physically violent incidents in the area, including the influence of criminal exploitation. Successful interventions for such harm are not clear-cut or easily available. Thirdly, the area was part of one of many locations undergoing significant amounts of regeneration. The assessment was used to inform elements of this, but it was clear it was not always the views and needs of families who shaped this agenda. Fourthly, while the assessment and interventions developed sought to work with families and children locally, such approaches run counter to other approaches locally—such as stop and search and cuts to essential services and welfare provision. It is within these wider contexts that the impact of interventions must be reviewed.

6. Discussion and Conclusions

The framework presented here provided a lens to examine emerging responses to EFH against long-standing debates in child and family social work, on the ethics of surveillance and relational approaches when working with families and communities. Core to the definition of three major forms of extra-familial harm (CSE, CCE and trafficking) are power, consent and exchange (Firmin et al. 2019). Often forms of EFH manipulate imbalances of power and the right to consent; grooming often masks exploitation as mutually beneficial. Service developments to EFH therefore need to repair, rather than replicate, the erosion of trust and consent that exploitation can instil in young people's early relational experiences (Warrington et al. 2017). This article proposes that there is a danger in advancing uncritically into the area of EFH, without considering significant ethical and practice issues emerging from more traditional forms of child protection interventions. Application of the analytic framework to emerging responses to EFH highlights a number of crucial practice issues.

6.1. Focus/Rationale

Firstly, the focus and rationale of interventions must be transparent and reflexive. Collating and sharing information in multi-agency partnerships is not in itself benign and can have multiple unknown consequences for young people (as discussed above). This is particularly pertinent when we consider the complex ways EFH often manifests (i.e., through peer-to-peer 'recruitment', often involving 'offending' behaviour), and the environments where young people make decisions and act. This troubles dichotomous understandings of 'victim' and 'perpetrator'. Our analysis indicates that not only do interventions need to be clearly defined and transparent, but must actively, reflexively, and critically consider whether the safety of young people remains in focus and is protected in a context of competing service, and indeed political and economic, objectives.

Secondly, whilst the sharing of locational data moves away from individual level surveillance and intervention, it simultaneously opens possibilities for surveillance of broader populations of young people (and indeed anyone) using and moving through spaces. Location mapping can, then, impact civil liberties and be skewed with the same biases as person-level mapping. It should not be considered a loophole out of data protection and privacy considerations.

Finally, interventions to address EFH will inevitably encounter structures and systems that drive inter-personal harm and create vulnerable conditions for young people (i.e., poverty/lack of resources). Location-based or contextual approaches seek to move away from, or enhance, casework approaches, by targeting the conditions of abuse that create vulnerabilities for young people. The contexts of children's lives are broader than their friendship circles, schools and neighbourhoods, and location-based approaches could be further enhanced through the consideration of poverty-aware (Featherstone et al. 2018) or de-colonial (Harden et al. 2014) models of intervention. This not only ensures that interventions move beyond individualized responses to structural forms of harm, but also provides critical frameworks to monitor the extent to which interventions contribute to or exacerbate harmful and oppressive systems.

6.2. Method

Both projects raised questions about the boundaries and nature of information gathering and sharing, leading us to consider the question 'how much information is too much information?' Learning from project 1 centred a practical question: what information needs to be shared and why? There was also an ethical question: should we share information just because we can? Broadening the remit of safeguarding simultaneously broadens the occasions on which it is conceivable to share information in line with Working Together 2018 or the Crime and Disorder Act 1998, subjugating GDPR considerations. Just because the information is already available, or is publicly available, should it be used for this purpose and at this time? When do we need to seek, or re-seek consent? There is a danger that trust and relationships with young people become the collateral damage of loose and invasive information sharing arrangements.

How and when young people experiencing EFH are engaged requires further examination. It is well established that participation and trusted relationships are key to effective practice. Both projects raise questions about partnerships with young people. Do we consult young people during planning and implementation (as in project 2)? Or do we only engage young people at the point of service delivery (as in project 1)? In an era of advancing technology and automation, safeguarding partnerships increasingly rely on data-driven and algorithmic forms of problem detection (Carlo and Krueckeberg 2018). Arguably, such technologies can wedge a relational and spatial distance between young people, the problems they face and our understanding of them. Such approaches are burdened with bias, and simultaneously do not have the capacity to reflexively engage with that bias; an approach that we propose is critical for professionals engaging in interventions into EFH.

6.3. Impact

Interventions into EFH are only as good as their impact, which ultimately is the extent to which they create safety in young people's lives. Applying our analytical framework points us to a more nuanced understanding of 'impact'. Contextual approaches require a consideration of both contextual and individual outcomes, moving us away from individualized outcomes (as in project 2) that leave unsafe locations wide open to other young people. However, where do we draw the line at evaluating impact? If 20 young people are safer due to locational intervention requiring intrusive data collection and sharing without consent, what of the 150 other young people (and indeed adults) who were subject to monitoring without consent? Or for whom the profiling might have adverse future consequences? Is this a utilitarian question of greater good, or an indication that the impact has not been sufficiently examined and developed to consider the best interests of all? This raises our final question, can we evaluate impact without informing young people of the extent of intervention, asking them if they feel safer as a result? This is a question that some have begun to ask of more traditional forms of child protection intervention (Dillon et al. 2019) and should be central to the emerging scholarship and evaluation of approaches to EFH.

We propose a framework for evaluating interventions into EFH and suggest that its application guides the sector, as it navigates new forms of harm and a responsibility to respond. If the objective of interventions is creating safety in young people's lives, we must be transparent in the focus and rationale of interventions, consider whether the methods we adopt promote relationships of trust, or relationships of control, and establish the impact of our work, by including the feedback of young people, whilst looking beyond individual outcomes to establish the broader ethical and societal impact of child protection interventions.

We welcome the enthusiastic uptake of Contextual Safeguarding practices nationally. Contextual Safeguarding is shaped through collaboration with practitioners and in this sense is not prescriptive. We are seeing the practice develop in new and exciting ways. Yet, alongside innovation, we are also faced with practice developments that, while not aligning to the principles of Contextual Safeguarding, are presented under its banner. It is not possible to be attuned to all of these practices. In presenting this article, we caution against Contextual Safeguarding becoming the next 'Trojan horse' of child protection, facilitating the expansion and intrusion of surveillance into the lives of children and families. In presenting the analytical framework, we seek to provide practitioners, and indeed researchers, with a tool to critically reflect on interventions into EFH.

Author Contributions: Conceptualization, L.E.W. and J.L.; methodology, L.E.W. and J.L.; formal analysis, L.E.W. and J.L.; writing—original draft preparation, L.E.W. and J.L.; writing—review and editing, L.E.W. and J.L.; visualization, L.E.W. and J.L.; funding acquisition, Contextual Safeguarding team. All authors have read and agreed to the published version of the manuscript.

Funding: This projects under investigation in this research were funded by a range of sources which are withheld here for project anonymity.

Acknowledgments: The authors would like to thank all individuals and agencies that have facilitated our embedded research.

Conflicts of Interest: The authors declare no conflict of interest. The funders of the projects under investigation had no role in the design of the study; in the collection, analyses, or interpretation of data; in the writing of the manuscript, or in the decision to publish the results.

References

ADCS. 2017. ADCS Response to Working Together to Safeguard Children: Changes to Statutory Guidance. Available online: https://adcs.org.uk/assets/documentation/ADCS_response_Working_Together_FINAL_20_December_2017.pdf (accessed on 17 September 2019).

ALDCS. 2018. The Response of London Children's Services to Serious Youth Violence and Knife Crime—May 2018. Available online: https://www.londoncouncils.gov.uk/node/34040 (accessed on 6 January 2019).

Amnesty. 2018. Trapped in the Gangs Matrix. Available online: https://yjlc.uk/child-spies-being-used-to-gather-intelligence/ (accessed on 24 February 2020).

Beckett, Helen, and Camille Warrington. 2015. *Making Justice Work: Experiences of Criminal Justice for Children and Young People Affected by Sexual Exploitation as Victims and Witnesses.* Luton: University of Bedfordshire.

Bryan, Agnes, Helen Hingley-Jones, and Gillian Ruch. 2016. Relationship Based Practice Revisited. *Journal of Social Work Practice* 30: 229–33. [CrossRef]

Care Crisis Review. 2018. *Care Crisis Review: Options for Change.* London: Family Rights Group.

Carlo, Silkie, and Jennifer Krueckeberg. 2018. The State of Surveillance in 2018. Available online: https://bigbrotherwatch.org.uk/wp-content/uploads/2018/09/The-State-of-Surveillance-in-2018.pdf (accessed on 27 February 2020).

Community Practitioner. 2019. Knife Crime: Where's the Public Health Approach? Available online: https://www.communitypractitioner.co.uk/sites/default/files/media/document/2019/news_big_story_community_practitioner_julyaugust_2019_community_practitioner_magazine.pdf (accessed on 24 February 2020).

Cossar, Jeanette, Marian Brandon, and Peter Jordan. 2016. 'You've got to trust her and she's got to trust you': Children's views on participation in the child protection system. *Child & Family Social Work* 21: 103–12.

Department for Education. 2018a. *Keeping Children Safe in Education Staturotry Guidance for Schools and Colleges.* London: Crown Copyright.

Department for Education. 2018b. *Working Together to Safeguard Children.* London: Author.

Department for Education. 2019. Characteristics of Children in Need: 2018 to 2019. Available online: https://assets.publishing.service.gov.uk/government/uploads/system/uploads/attachment_data/file/843046/Characteristics_of_children_in_need_2018_to_2019_main_text.pdf (accessed on 25 February 2020).

Dillon, Jo, Daz Greenop, and Mel Hills. 2019. Participation in Child Protection; A small-scale qualitative study. *Qualitative Social Work* 15: 70–85. [CrossRef]

Edwards, Frank. 2016. Saving Children, Controlling Families: Punishment, Redistribution, and Child Protection. *American Sociological Review* 81: 575–95. [CrossRef]

Eubanks, Virginia. 2018. *Automating Inequality: How High Tech Tools Profile, Police and Punish the Poor.* New York: St Martins Press.

Featherstone, Brid, Anna Gupta, Kate Morris, and Sue White. 2018. *Protecting Children: A Social Model.* Bristol: Policy Press.

Fernandez, Luis A., and Laura Huey. 2009. Is resistance futile? Some thoughts on resisting surveillance. *Surveillance & Society* 6: 198–202.

Fine, Michelle, Nick Freudenberg, Yasser Payne, Tiffany Perkins, Kersha Smith, and Katya Wanzer. 2003. "Anything can happen with police around": Urban youth evaluate strategies of surveillance in public places. *Journal of Social Issues* 59: 141–58. [CrossRef]

Firmin, Carlene. 2017. *Abuse between Young People: A Contextual Account.* Oxon: Routledge.

Firmin, Carlene, Lauren Wroe, and Jenny Lloyd. 2019. *Safeguarding and Exploitation—Complex, Contextual and Holistic Approaches.* Strategic Briefing. Darlington: Research in Practice.

Harden, Troy, Thomas Kenemore, Kimberley Mann, Michael Edwards, Christine List, and Karen Jean Martinson. 2014. The truth 'n' trauma project: Addressing community violence through a youth-led, trauma-informed and restorative framework. *Child and Adolescent Social Work Journal* 32: 65–70. [CrossRef]

Hingley-Jones, Helen, and Gillian Ruch. 2016. 'Stumbling through'? Relationships-based social work practice in austere times. *Journal of Social Work Practice* 30: 235–48. [CrossRef]

Jay, Alexis. 2014. *Independent Inquiry into Child Sexual Exploitation in Rotherham: 1997–2013*; Rotherham: Rotherham Metropolitan Borough Council.

Lammy, David. 2017. The Lammy Review: An Independent Review into the Treatment of, and Outcomes for, Black, Asian and Minority Ethnic Individuals in the Criminal Justice System. Available online: https://assets.publishing.service.gov.uk/government/uploads/system/uploads/attachment_data/file/643001/lammy-review-final-report.pdf (accessed on 24 February 2020).

Lloyd, Jenny, and Carlene Firmin. 2019. No Further Action: Contextualising Social Care Decisions for Children Victimised in Extra-Familial Settings. *Youth Justice.* ahead-of-print. [CrossRef]

Llywodraeth Cymru. 2019. Safeguarding children from Child Sexual Exploitation (CSE). Available online: https://gov.wales/safeguarding-children-child-sexual-exploitation (accessed on 24 February 2020).

McKendrick, David, and Jo Finch. 2017. 'Under heavy manners?': Social work, radicalisation, troubled families and non-linear war. *British Journal of Social Work* 47: 308–24. [CrossRef]

Mellon, Maggie. 2017. Child Protection: Listening and Learning from Parents. Available online: https://www.iriss.org.uk/resources/insights/child-protection-listening-and-learning-parents (accessed on 24 February 2020).

Montgomery, Kathryn C. 2015. Youth and surveillance in the Facebook era: Policy interventions and social implications. *Telecommunications Policy* 39: 771–86. [CrossRef]

Morris, Kate. 2012. Troubled families: Vulnerable families experiences of multiple service use. *Child and Family Social Work* 18: 198–206. [CrossRef]

Munro, Eileen. 2011. *The Munro Review of Child Protection: Final Report, a Child-Centred System.* London: The Stationery Office, vol. 8062.

O'Neill, Megan, and Bethan Loftus. 2013. Policing and the surveillance of the marginal: Everyday contexts of social control. *Theoretical Criminology* 17: 437–54. [CrossRef]

Parton, Nigel. 2000. Some thoughts on the relationship between theory & practice in and for social work. *British Journal of Social Work* 30: 449–63.

Parton, Nigel. 2011. Child protection and safeguarding in England: Changing and competing notions of risk and their implications for social work. *British Journal of Social Work* 41: 845–75. [CrossRef]

Parton, Nigel. 2019. Changing and competing conceptions of risk and their implications for public health approaches to child protection. In *Re-Visioning Public Health Approaches for Protecting Children*. Edited by Bob Lonne, Deb Scott, Daryl Higgins and Todd Herrenkohl. Basel: Springer, chp. 5, pp. 65–78. ISBN 978-83-030-05857-9.

Penna, Sue. 2005. The Children Act 2004: Child Protection and Social Surveillance. *Journal of Social Welfare and Family Law* 27: 143–57. [CrossRef]

Shabde, Neela, and Alan W. Craft. 1999. Covert video surveillance: An important investigative tool or a breach of trust? *Archives of Disease in Childhood* 81: 291–94. [CrossRef]

Shade, Leslie Regan, and Rianka Singh. 2016. "Honestly we're not spying on kids": School surveillance of young people's social media. *Social Media and Society* 2: 1–12. [CrossRef]

Stability Index. 2019. Available online: https://childrenscommissioner.github.io/stabilityindex2019/ (accessed on 27 February 2020).

Stanley, Tony, Surinder Guru, and Anna Gupta. 2018. Working with PREVENT: Social work options for cases of 'radicalisation risk'. *Practice: Social Work in Action* 30: 131–46. [CrossRef]

Twite, Jennifer. 2018. Child Spies Being Used to Gather Intelligence on County Lines Gangs. Available online: https://yjlc.uk/child-spies-being-used-to-gather-intelligence/ (accessed on 24 February 2020).

United Nations Convention on the Rights of the Child. 1989. United Nations, Treaty Series; New York: United Nations, vol. 1577, p. 3.

van Bijleveld, Ganna G., Christine W. M. Dedding, and Joske F. G. Bunders-Aelen. 2013. Children's and young people's participation within child welfare and child protection services: A state-of-the-art review. *Child and Family Social Work* 20: 129–38. [CrossRef]

Warrington, Camille, Elizabeth Ackerley, Helen Beckett, Megan Walker, and Debbie Allnock. 2017. *Making Noise: Children's Voices for Positive Change after Sexual Abuse*. Luton: University of Bedfordshire/Office of Children's Commissioner.

White, Sue, and David Wastell. 2017. The rise and rise of prevention science in UK family welfare: Surveillance gets under the skin. *Families, Relationships and Societies* 6: 427–45. [CrossRef]

Williams, Patrick. 2018. *Being Matrixed: The (Over)Policing of Gang Suspects in London*. London: StopWatch, Available online: www.stop-watch.org/uploads/documents/Being_Matrixed.pdf (accessed on 28 February 2020).

Williams, Patrick, and Becky Clarke. 2016. Dangerous Associations: Joint Enterprise, Gangs and Racism: An Analysis of the Processes of Criminalisation of Black, Asian and Minority Ethnic Individuals. Centre for Crime and Justice Studies. Available online: https://www.crimeandjustice.org.uk/sites/crimeandjustice.org.uk/files/Dangerous%20assocations%20Joint%20Enterprise%20gangs%20and%20racism.pdf (accessed on 24 February 2020).

Wrennall, Lynne. 2010. Surveillance and child protection: De-mystifying the Trojan Horse. *Surveillance & Society* 7: 304–24.

![social sciences logo] *social sciences*

MDPI

Article

Participation of Children and Parents in the Swiss Child Protection System in the Past and Present: An Interdisciplinary Perspective

Aline Schoch [1,*], Gaëlle Aeby [2,*], Brigitte Müller [1], Michelle Cottier [2], Loretta Seglias [3], Kay Biesel [1], Gaëlle Sauthier [4] and Stefan Schnurr [1]

[1]   Institute for Studies in Children and Youth Services, School of Social Work, University of Applied Sciences Northwestern Switzerland FHNW, 4132 Muttenz, Switzerland; brigitte.mueller@fhnw.ch (B.M.); kay.biesel@fhnw.ch (K.B.); stefan.schnurr@fhnw.ch (S.S.)
[2]   Centre for Evaluation and Legislative Studies, Faculty of Law, University of Geneva, 1211 Geneva, Switzerland; michelle.cottier@unige.ch
[3]   Independent researcher, 8820 Wädenswil, Switzerland; l.seglias@unitone.ch
[4]   Centre for Children's Rights Studies, University of Geneva, 1950 Sion, Switzerland; gaelle.sauthier@unige.ch
*   Correspondence: aline.schoch@fhnw.ch (A.S.); Gaelle.Aeby@unige.ch (G.A.)

Received: 6 July 2020; Accepted: 12 August 2020; Published: 18 August 2020

Abstract: As in other European countries, the Swiss child protection system has gone through substantial changes in the course of the 20th century up to today. Increasingly, the needs as well as the participation of children and parents affected by child protection interventions have become a central concern. In Switzerland, critical debates around care-related detention of children and adults until 1981 have led to the launch of the National Research Program 'Welfare and Coercion—Past, Present and Future' (NRP 76), with the aim of understanding past and current welfare practices. This paper is based on our research project, which is part of this national program. We first discuss three overarching concepts—integrity, autonomy and participation—at the heart of a theoretical framework in order to understand the position of parents and children in child protection proceedings. Secondly, we critically analyze the historical and legal development of the child protection system in Switzerland and its effects on children and parents from 1912 until today. Thirdly, we give an insight into the current Swiss child protection system, with an investigation of hearings of parents and children conducted by the Child and Adult Protection Authorities (CAPA) based on participant observations. In particular, we show the importance of information exchanges and of signs of mutual recognition. Finally, in light of our findings, we discuss the interplay between socio-historical and legal developments in child protection and their consequences for the integrity, autonomy and participation of the people involved.

Keywords: child protection; child protection system; participation; integrity; autonomy; historical analysis; legal analysis; participant observation; human rights; children's rights; Switzerland

---

1. Introduction

Since the 1970s, the legal status of children and the question of the best interest of the child have been given greater relevance in Swiss child protection. This has led to several legislative reforms that aimed to emphasize the personal fundamental rights and opportunities for children and parents and facilitated their participation in child protection proceedings. On one hand, these legislative reforms were initiated as a response to the European Convention on Human Rights, which Switzerland ratified in 1974. They also responded to problematic welfare policies and practices in the past, in which persons concerned were not informed, heard or given the opportunity to participate systematically in legal decisions and were placed against their will. On the other hand, the reforms were fueled by changing social awareness of the rights and needs of children as well as the growing importance of the UN Convention on the Rights of the Child, which came into force in 1989 and was ratified by Switzerland in 1997. Nevertheless, currently, little is known about the effects of these reforms, how they strengthened the autonomy of children, parents and families and to what extent they promote their integrity and their participation in child protection procedures. Empirical knowledge is lacking regarding the impact of the modified provisions on care-related detention in 1981, which set an end to placements ordered without granting due process of law (so called "administrative detention"). Furthermore, little empirical knowledge is available on the new Child and Adult Protection Authorities (CAPA), which have been in operation since 2013 and have replaced the former layperson-based Guardianship Authorities (Müller et al. 2020).

In view of this fact, in 2017, the Swiss National Science Foundation (SNSF) was commissioned to deepen scientific knowledge of compulsory social measures and placements (coercive welfare measures) in different contexts in Switzerland, following the recognition of harm caused up until the 1980s by the disregard of the fundamental rights of the persons concerned. In order to do so, the National Research Program "Welfare and Coercion—Past, Present and Future" (NRP 76) was launched. The aim of the NRP 76 is to analyze the mechanisms, modes and features of Swiss welfare policy and practice in the past and present. The program has the objective of identifying causes of welfare practices that damaged or restored the integrity of persons concerned. Furthermore, it is a designated goal to explore the effects of welfare practices on persons affected. A total number of 27 research projects have been funded by the SNSF, one of which is our research project, "Intapart: Integrity, Autonomy and Participation: How do children and parents experience child protection?"[1] (Swiss National Science Foundation (SNSF) 2020).

"Intapart" addresses the objectives of the NRP 76 by exploring the perceptions of persons subject to compulsory social measures in the past and the present. It researches the subjective experiences of individuals within the child protection system regarding their integrity. The interdisciplinary research design aims to investigate the question of how children and parents understand, experience and respond to what happens to them during child protection proceedings. It includes a historical and legal analysis as well as an empirical study. The historical analysis highlights how children and parents experienced encounters with the child protection system between 1940 and 2012. The legal analysis researches how children's and parents' procedural rights have developed from 1912 to 2012, with a focus on the right to be heard in child protection proceedings. It also tackles the question of how the existing law addresses perceived violations of the integrity, autonomy and participation rights of children and parents. The research questions of the empirical study focus on how children and parents perceive and react to the interventions of CAPA in the current child protection system. It explores what actions the authorities take to protect children from abuse and neglect and to strengthen the rights, legal position and participation of children and parents in child protection proceedings.

In this paper, we start with a theoretical discussion of the overarching concepts of integrity, autonomy and participation and show how closely these concepts are related to one another. We then analyze how the Swiss child protection system has developed from the implementation of the new civil code of 1912 until today. In this context, we focus on the ways in which the rights and needs of children and parents have been considered and describe dramatic state interventions associated with them. We then give an insight into the CAPA's current practice by sharing initial findings of participant observation of interactions with children and parents. Finally, we debate how the child protection system and its stakeholders could ensure that children and parents receive sustainable help, respecting their integrity, autonomy and participation in child protection proceedings.

---

[1] For more details about the project, see: http://www.nfp76.ch/en/projects/interventions-and-pathways-in-life/project-cottier.

2. Theoretical Reflections on the Nexus of Integrity, Autonomy and Participation

Children and parents are at the center of child protection and should thus be considered as active social actors with agency, embedded in complex power relations and as part of dynamic family configurations. Agency describes the capacity to act autonomously and intentionally within a certain social structure and has to be understood as a varying restricting or enabling context (cf. Duncan 2019; Raithelhuber and Schröer 2018, p. 50; for more general critical discussions on the agency of children, see Esser et al. 2016). Social scientists have long overlooked children as active and independent social actors and have considered them rather as objects in need of protection (Bühler-Niederberger 2010; Wolff et al. 2016). In order not to reproduce this blind spot, we suggest considering children as active social actors in line with the "sociology of childhood" (Alanen 1988; Ambert 1986; Corsaro 1997; Qvortrup 1987). Nevertheless, a child-centered perspective also holds the potential of losing sight of the social embeddedness of the child and the existing power relations within and outside the family system. Children in particular are in a structurally weaker position in relation to adults (parents and professionals)—as are parents in relation to child protection professionals (Duncan 2019; Graham and Fitzgerald 2010). Hence, children as well as parents may feel powerless in child protection proceedings, that they are not being heard or listened to or that they are not being recognized (Biesel 2016; Cossar et al. 2016; Dillon 2018; Dillon et al. 2016; Duerr Berrick 2018; Duncan 2019; Husby et al. 2018; Tisdall 2016; Wolff et al. 2016). In order to understand the child protection system and how cases of child abuse and neglect are dealt with, it is therefore necessary to think of integrity, autonomy and participation together as a nexus and a focal point.

2.1. Integrity

Within this context, integrity can be defined as a state of soundness and functionality of physical and mental health as well as the opportunity and capability to achieve self-set goals. Autonomy is needed in order to have the capacity to do so (Becker-Lenz and Müller-Hermann 2013, p. 212). Axel Honneth's theory of recognition (Honneth 1995) can be an inspiring approach to define and establish integrity in social interactions.

The theory of recognition refers to three axes of mutual recognition: (1) love linked to self-confidence, (2) rights in the legal sphere linked to self-respect and (3) solidarity linked to self-esteem. The experience of love in close relationships, such as among family members or friends, creates self-confidence. Violence would be at the opposite end and shows disrespect for recognition. Recognition in the legal sphere can be realized in the form of having rights and in the equal treatment of all individuals, which promotes self-respect. The opposite would be exclusion from certain rights. Recognition in the form of solidarity and esteem means being respectful of other people's opinions, attitudes, skills and roles or status and leads to self-esteem. The opposite of this is experiencing shame, the loss of honor or denigration. The experience of disrespect on one axis or multiple axes of recognition can lead to social resistance, conflict and the struggle for recognition of disrespected individuals. By struggling for recognition, an individual tries to re-establish lost dignity. When children are asked about what they consider important about participation, they refer quite directly to these axes of recognition (Graham and Fitzgerald 2010).

Disrespecting social recognition in Honneth's understanding can be seen as the violation of a person's integrity, since experiencing curtailed integrity, e.g., not being listened to, can lead to self-set goals neither being defined nor achieved. Whenever children or parents experience violence in the child protection system, if their legal rights are not respected or if they feel ashamed, they might perceive this as a violation of their integrity. A lack of mutual recognition leads to being held back from achieving (or even formulating) self-set goals, i.e., to preserve integrity. If children or parents resist child protection interventions, it might be that they are trying to restore their recognition by opposing them. It is thus crucial to build up a respectful and trustful relationship between child protection professionals and all family members in order to prevent negative experiences (Husby et al. 2018; Duerr Berrick 2018, p. 38; Husby et al. 2019; Cossar et al. 2016, p. 106f.).

2.2. Autonomy

Autonomy is strongly connected to the conceptualization of integrity defined above and closely related to participation. The concept of autonomy is often associated with that of independence, but it has a broader scope as it also encompasses subjective dimensions (De Singly 2000). Autonomy can be defined as "as an acquired set of capacities to lead one's own life", including "the capacity to develop and pursue one's own conception of a worthwhile life" (Anderson and Honneth 2005, pp. 127, 130) or, in other words, freedom of choice (Join-Lambert Milova 2006). Autonomy can further be understood as the opportunity to live a life in which "reasonable" decisions can be made, and actions can be taken according to these decisions (Becker-Lenz and Müller-Hermann 2013). Duncan (2019, p. 129) suggests questioning critically the notion that families involved in child protection have sufficient agency to make such decisions. She argues that developed agency can be assessed if a decision is based on rational and logical reasons as well as if there is an understanding of the consequences of a certain decision by the persons concerned.

According to Anderson and Honneth, individuals' autonomy is restricted if social relationships of respect, care and esteem are damaged. Being able to re-establish or maintain relationships of mutual recognition is hence a condition for leading an autonomous life (Anderson and Honneth 2005, pp. 127, 131–32). Families involved with the child protection system are often in challenging situations and their autonomy is strained in two ways, as their scope of decision and their scope of action to lead a self-determined life are limited, on one hand, with regard to their personal life, which is often a "highly constrained context", and on the other hand, by state interventions in the form of child protection measures (Tisdall 2016, p. 5). Under such circumstances of potentially damaged (relationships of) recognition—for instance, in the context of social isolation—it can be difficult to take action and make "reasonable" decisions or to express agency (ibid.; Anderson and Honneth 2005). However, according to Beate Rössler (2017), it is possible to live an autonomous and self-determined life under challenging social or biographical conditions—for instance, when facing economic deprivation. Autonomy does not exclude experiencing ambivalent conflicts, emotions and decisions, since wishes and the conditions of their realization are often incompatible. Autonomy should therefore be understood as the reasonable management of such ambivalence (ibid., pp. 393, 395). The crucial condition, however, is that an autonomous person can develop, decide for and stand behind their own undertakings by striving for a self-determined and worthwhile life (Rössler 2017, pp. 394–96). The "social context" in which autonomy can be built must thus—from a perspective of justice—be protected or restored for deprived individuals or groups (Anderson and Honneth 2005, p. 137).

2.3. Participation

At the core of theorizing child protection and thinking of integrity, autonomy and participation as a nexus is the capacity to make decisions. Indeed, participation has been recognized as a key concept in child protection (Lansdown 2010; Svevo-Cianci et al. 2011). Developing one's own opinion, achieving self-determined goals (integrity), making self-determined choices and pursuing one's own undertakings (autonomy) require knowledge.

Regarding participation, it is fundamental for children and parents to receive sufficient information on the child protection proceedings and on the child protection system itself, in order to understand and make sense of their situation. Information is a prerequisite to having the capacity to develop, advocate and reflect on a self-determined life and to making "reasonable" decisions (cf. for example, Duncan 2019, p. 135, referring to Giddens' structuration theory). Information is hence central to the concept of autonomy and integrity, as well as to participation (for the relevance of information to participation, see Bouma et al. 2018). Receiving information and understanding the child protection proceedings is also part of the procedural "right to be heard", laid down in the Swiss Federal Constitution (Art. 29 FC). It includes the right to be informed of decisions, to express oneself, to comment on the issues concerning the case and to participate in the process of decision-making. The overarching goal of the "right to be heard" is "effective participation" (Steinmann 2014, p. 661, Eng. translation by the authors). In their model of participation, Bouma et al. (2018) include three dimensions: informing, hearing, involving.

Duncan (2019, pp. 141–48) also emphasizes information and a trustful relationship between children and child protection professionals as key factors with regard to children's participation in child protection and has developed an interesting typology of participation, ranging from active participation (congenial participation) to skeptical participation, up to withdrawing (disaffected participation). Specific institutional patterns of information, communication and power structures within organizations are thus a prerequisite to realizing congenial or full participation (Hillmann 1994, pp. 654–55). Dumbrill's study (Dumbrill 2006, pp. 30–33) showed that, when parents perceived child protection professionals as using power "over" them as a form of control, they were more likely to either openly oppose them or to simulate co-operation. When parents felt that power was used "with" them, they tended to collaborate. It is therefore a fundamental need with regard to participation that child protection professionals share power and information with children and parents (Duerr Berrick 2018, p. 38; Husby et al. 2018, p. 444). Holding back information from children and parents can be understood as restricting their power because they are being held in inferior positions compared to the professionals and are hindered in reaching their goals and participating fully (Duerr Berrick 2018, p. 38). To establish a relationship of trust and respect, a certain amount of support as well as clear information and communication is crucial to enable children and parents to participate in decision-making processes (Graham and Fitzgerald 2010; Husby et al. 2018).

In summary, we propose to conceptualize full participation by integrating aspects of the above-mentioned nexus of integrity, autonomy and participation. Participation thus includes aspects of integrity such as receiving recognition by experiencing a trustful and respectful relationship between family members and child protection professionals and by having one's rights and opinions respected as a basis for achieving self-set goals. The precondition for this is the soundness of physical and mental integrity and the opportunity to live autonomously, i.e., to have the capacity to develop and pursue one's own conception of a worthwhile life. To achieve this, families in the child protection system need to have sufficient information to understand the child protection proceedings, implying and understanding of child protection professionals' concerns about problematic parenting practices (Healy and Darlington 2009, pp. 427–28). Information is also crucial in order to anticipate the potential consequences of decisions and hence to get involved, i.e., to fully participate. By these means of full participation, children and parents are given the structural conditions to regain or enhance their agency in a context in which their autonomy is restricted by often highly-constrained social (family) situations and by state intrusion in the form of child protection measures.

3. The Evolution of the Legal and Institutional Framework of Swiss Child Protection in the 20th Century

The legal and institutional framework is a crucial factor for the opportunity to substantiate the integrity, autonomy and participation of parents and children in any child protection system. In Switzerland, this framework evolved greatly throughout the 20th century. A structural characteristic that changed only marginally over that time was the high degree of federalism and the principle of subsidiarity. Switzerland is a confederation of 26 cantons, which are rather small units (16,000 to 1.5 million inhabitants) but have considerably more autonomy and competencies against the federal level than constituent states in other federal systems usually do. Instead of a homogenized system consisting of uniform institutions, in many aspects, child protection in Switzerland resembles a patchwork of 26 regimes, which can be understood as the result of interactions between federal legislation, cantonal legislation (the reach and regulations of which also varies) and cantonal as well as local patterns of institutionalization and implementation (Schnurr 2017). In order to understand the current state of the Swiss child protection system and its most recent reform in 2013, it is necessary to study its development over time, taking a legal-historical approach. We start with the first nationwide set of regulations that went beyond cantonal legislation on the poor (poverty laws), the federal Swiss

Civil Code (SCC) of 1912. We analyze the most important changes in the legal and institutional framework throughout the 20th century. While we paint the evolution in broad strokes, our project aims to produce an even more detailed analysis of the experiences of dis-/respect of integrity, autonomy and participation rights of parents and children affected by an intervention of the former Guardianship Authorities between 1978 and 2012 (historical analysis) as well as of the opportunities the law provided between 1912 and 2012 to address perceived violations of these rights (legal analysis).

3.1. Systematic Disregard for Integrity, Autonomy and Participation in the First Half of the 20th Century

While private law, including family law, was the responsibility of the cantons in the 19th century, the first federal Swiss Civil Code (SCC) of 1912 codified parental duties at a federal level for the first time and thus acknowledged the state's responsibility for children. The Guardianship Authorities were henceforth legitimated to remove a child from his or her parents if they did not meet their obligations to care for him or her (Häsler 2008). As the focus changed from substantiated neglect and the misery of children to a broader notion of risk and prevention of endangerment, the new law entitled authorities to also remove children on the grounds of suspected or probable neglect (Seglias 2013). This approach to placements was reflected in the "child protection articles" (Art. 283–285 SCC). They introduced the possibility of placing children not only if their families depended on welfare benefits (under poverty laws) but also on the basis of the mere assumption that a family was unable to care for a child, e.g., if the family was seen as "work-shy" or "slovenly" or if the "moral neglect" of a child was claimed (Ramsauer 2000; Leuenberger and Seglias 2015, pp. 232–49). The cantons did not only have the competence to implement these measures under federal law but, until 1981, additionally retained the authority to legislate on the internment of persons, based on the public interest. Thus, cantonal laws aimed to protect the public interest and public order (namely the management of poverty and attendant symptoms), whereas the federal civil law, the SCC, pursued the protection of minors and vulnerable adults. The preventive rationale of this combined federal and cantonal approach to the regulation of childhood created a very broad scope of action for the decision-making authorities and facilitated arbitrariness in sanctioning lifestyles and behaviors judged as deviant (ibid.; Furrer et al. 2014).

The SCC delegated to the authority the responsibility to define the structures and proceedings of the child and adult protection field to the cantons. This concerned the organization of the Guardianship Authorities and the application of the law. Parallel structures were established for the above-mentioned restrictions to a person's freedom and civil rights for reasons such as public order, prevention of poverty, public health, "social prevention", etc. under cantonal public law (Independent Expert Commission (IEC) on Administrative (2019)). The system was predominantly lay-based: the Guardianship Authorities were subdivisions of the elected bodies of municipalities and therefore lay bodies (in most German-speaking cantons) or magistrates (justice of the peace) in the French-speaking part of Switzerland, who had considerable discretion to handle child protection cases (Schnyder et al. 1995, pp. 26–28; Affolter 2013, p. 11). In addition, under cantonal "detention laws", the cantonal welfare authorities were entitled to separate families and place persons, including adolescents, in workhouses for re-education, mental institutions, homes for "fallen women" or even prisons, without court proceedings or court rulings (ibid.). The resulting practice of "administrative detention" led to an estimated tens of thousands of individuals becoming subject to coercive placements over the course of the 20th century up to 1981 (Guggisberg and Molin 2019)[2]. Moreover, the federalist division

---

[2] However, many authors (e.g., Leuenberger and Seglias 2015; Guggisberg and Molin 2019; Schnurr 2017) problematize the general lack of reliable statistics on family or institutional placements, since Switzerland did not and still does not collect them systematically. The Independent Expert Commission (IEC) on Administrative Detention estimates that 40,000 to 60,000 individuals were subject to administrative detention between 1930 and 1980 (Guggisberg and Molin 2019). Leuenberger and Seglias (2015) estimate that 6–10% of children in the second half of the 20th century (or hundreds of thousands of children in the 19th and 20th centuries) were affected by such forms of family placements ("indentured child laborers").

of public tasks implied that regulations and norms for child removal differed considerably between cantons and regions.

With regard to the placement of children, the cantonal introductory acts concerning the application of the SCC were intended to regulate the supervision and inspection of the placements, but, in fact, it took several more decades to put this in place (Leuenberger et al. 2011; Seglias 2013, p. 60). Altogether, this constituted a system of child protection characterized by a multitude of federal and cantonal regulations and proceedings with only marginal mechanisms of control and considerable discretion for stakeholders and persons in charge—a system that facilitated arbitrary decisions (Akermann et al. 2012; Seglias 2013). Although the legal framework of the SCC represented the rule of law, the street-level practice implied violations of the principle of legal equality (ibid.).

The description of legal and institutional frameworks and placement practices shows that children were removed from their families for two main reasons: the alleviation and management of poverty (Seglias 2013; Furrer et al. 2014) and the imposing of social norms and discipline (Bütow et al. 2014; Guggisberg 2014; Thieme 2013). Placements and coercive welfare measures did not imply that persons concerned by state intervention in their civil rights had the opportunity to participate or be heard in legal decisions. This holds true for children in particular, who, for the greater part of the 20th century, were seen as immature, whose status was completely different from the present and who were stigmatized for being raised by "degenerate" or otherwise incapable families (Mazza Muschietti 2016). In this context, children's participation in the decision-making process was not even considered an issue. It was uncommon to announce a placement to the children involved, to mention reasons or give further information about the location or duration of it (ibid.). Moreover, given the absence (or weakness) of the state's supervisory function, a common consequence of coercive measures taken to "protect" children was that the placed children were left completely at the mercy of their carers (Leuenberger et al. 2011). The analysis shows that the personal and procedural rights of the persons concerned were practically non-existent for a long time and, although several legal and medical professionals were critical of this lack of protection, there was no public awareness of this systematic violation of their integrity, autonomy and participation.

3.2. The Road to Change: Legal Developments and Changing Placement Practices after the Mid-20th Century

Already at the end of the 19th century, and throughout the 20th century, there was criticism regarding some of the methods and approaches practiced in child and youth welfare, residential facilities and the placing of children as farmhands in families ("indentured child laborers") (Seglias 2013). Although there were selective efforts to improve placement settings and to introduce quality standards, a broad discussion of the practices of placements and coercive welfare measures carried out by the state did not arise (ibid.).

The shift in social values in the 1960s and 1970s contributed to a range of legal changes which had an impact on the legal foundation of child protection measures such as removals and placements (Seglias 2013). Reforms of the SCC in the 1970s, e.g., in family law, were concerned with the legal status of children. Legitimate and illegitimate children were given equal status and the best interest of the child was introduced as an important reference point in decisions that concerned him or her (ibid.). The ratification of the European Convention on Human Rights (ECHR) was an important milestone which led to a major reform of the law in 1981. The conditions for the deprivation of liberty defined in the ECHR (Art. 5) were henceforth imperative and Swiss law had to be adapted accordingly (Rietmann 2012; Independent Expert Commission (IEC) on Administrative 2019). These developments led to plans for a more thorough reform of the SCC with regard to the articles on child and adult protection. The reform process started in 1993 but the new law, introducing the new multi-professional Child and Adult Protection Authorities (CAPAs), did not enter into force before 2013 (Müller et al. 2020). The ratification of the UN Convention on the Rights of the Child in 1997 intensified the discourse on children's rights and the question of how to include children's perspectives in legal proceedings (ibid.). A reform of the divorce law in the year 2000 substantiated this question by giving the child the opportunity to be heard in family law, including child protection proceedings, which defined the child as a subject of the law (Cottier 2008).

Concerning the experiences of children placed in care, a range of biographical reports and studies in the 1970s and 1980s shed light on the living circumstances and perspectives of these children (summarized in Nett and Trevor 2012; Müller et al. 2020). After 2005, a number of studies analyzed Switzerland's detention practices during the 20th century (e.g., Leuenberger and Seglias 2008; Freisler-Mühlemann 2011; Ries and Beck 2013). However, despite these developments, which changed the way in which placements in the past were accounted for, research and activities to commemorate the experiences of formerly placed children organized by user/survivor organizations remained poorly funded up to around 2010, when the efforts made to obtain official recognition from the Swiss government were successful. An official apology and commemoration for all surviving victims of coercive welfare measures followed, and reparation payments were made in 2013 (Müller et al. 2020; Independent Expert Commission (IEC) on Administrative 2019). In the context of the political process, several research programs were initiated and funded (ibid.; NRP 76) which, together with the findings of earlier research, drew a more accurate picture of the Swiss welfare system and its practices in the 20th century. It became clear that these practices and experiences of abuse led to considerable health and psychological problems and prolonged socio-economic disadvantages for the children, youth and adults who were subjected to coercive welfare measures of several kinds (Independent Expert Commission (IEC) on Administrative 2019; Freisler-Mühlemann 2011; Akermann et al. 2012; Kuhlman et al. 2013; summarized in Schoch and Müller 2020). A further crucial finding of these studies was that the placed children experienced the disregard for their integrity and the denial of an opportunity to participate and be heard in decision-making as similarly traumatic to the original abuse and neglect which they had suffered in foster families and residential care facilities (Wohlwend and Honegger 2004; Freisler-Mühlemann 2011; Akermann et al. 2012; Leuenberger and Seglias 2008, 2015; Leuenberger et al. 2011).

3.3. Reorganization and Professionalization of Child Protection: The Turning Point in 2013

Due to the latest reform of child and adult protection, which was initiated in 1993 and implemented in 2013, the former layperson-based Guardianship Authority was replaced by the Child and Adult Protection Authorities (CAPAs). Child Protection Authorities became multi-professional decision-making bodies responsible for statutory child protection decisions.

The main results of the 2013 reform were the professionalization of decision-making in the Swiss child protection system and the reduction of the number of authorities from 1414 to 148. The legislator pursued the idea of a collegial body whose members apply expert knowledge from different fields and disciplines (such as law, social work, psychology, accounting and medicine) to meet the substantially diverse characteristics and requirements of complex cases (Cottier and Steck 2012; Schnurr 2017, pp. 125–27). Consequently, the law stipulates that the decisions of a CAPA must in principle be made by a quorum of three members. According to a recent evaluation survey, 93% of the CAPAs have multi-professional decision-making bodies, with law and social work being the most frequent combination (Rieder et al. 2016, p. 40). The CAPAs—unlike in other countries—are responsible for child as well as adult protection. It is at the discretion of the cantonal law makers whether CAPAs are administrative authorities or judicial authorities (courts). In addition, they can be cantonal, municipal or intercommunal/regional authorities. The population served by a CAPA varies from 2700 to 485,000 inhabitants, with the majority of CAPAs serving a population of more than 50,000 (KOKES 2017; Rieder et al. 2016, p. 9). Hence, there is diversity in the child protection regimes across the cantons.

As a general rule, the CAPA is obliged to hear a person affected by a decision "in person" (Art. 447 SCC)—an expression of the fundamental "right to be heard", as laid out in the Swiss Federal Constitution (Art. 29, 30 FC). Moreover, with respect to child protection proceedings, the SCC stipulates that "the child is heard in person in an appropriate manner by the child protection authority or by a third party appointed for this purpose, unless this is inadvisable due to the child's age or other good cause" (Art. 314a SCC). The explicit obligation to hear the child, introduced in 2000 in the context of the divorce law reform and strengthened by the reform of 2013, reflects the implementation of Art. 12 UN-CRC in the federal law on child protection. The Federal Supreme Court stipulates the right of a child to a hearing from six years old onward and indicates a (flexible) threshold of around 12 years for the acquisition of the capacity for judgement in family law matters, meaning that the child's view has more weight from this age on (Cottier 2017).

Besides the CAPA, which represents the statutory arm of the Swiss child protection system, there are social agencies (social services or children's services in a number of cantons) which are often referred to as "voluntary" child protection (Rosch and Hauri 2016). They bear responsibility for (1) facilitating access to non-statutory services for children and families and (2) decision-making on the non-statutory removal of children to alternative care. In addition, these agencies are often commissioned by the CAPAs to carry out assessments of the well-being of a child.

There is still considerable heterogeneity in the organization and form of the CAPAs, due to the federalist structure and the principle of subsidiarity, which regulate the competencies between the confederation, cantons and municipalities (Fassbind 2013, p. 15). As a consequence of the reform of 2013, a completely new administrative structure had to be established and new procedures and different forms of cooperation with relevant stakeholders needed to be developed (Fassbind 2013). Even though formal rights such as hearing the child's wishes, interests and views have been strengthened in child protection proceedings, there is still little knowledge available on the ways in which they are put into practice (Hitz Quenon et al. 2014; Hitz Quenon and Matthey 2017).

The reform of 2013 also triggered considerable criticism by the media, who worried that the new system would bring bureaucratization and overly intrusive interventions in families. The media also scandalized some problematic child protection cases and fueled the discussion on deficiencies in Swiss child protection (e.g., the case of Flaach: Direktion der Justiz und des Inneren 2016). A national report by the Federal Council attested to the CAPAs an appropriate standard of work and showed that the numbers of statutory measures in child and adult protection had not risen since the reform (Bundesrat 2017, p. 29). Nevertheless, the report recommended the development of appropriate standards—for instance, concerning the assessment of a child's needs and of the risks to his or her well-being.

4. A Look Inside the CAPA: Interactions and Communication between Children, Parents and CAPA Members

As stated earlier, little empirical knowledge is available on the current everyday practices of the Swiss Child and Adult Protection Authorities (CAPAs) or how individuals experience encounters with them. Our research project "Intapart: Integrity, Autonomy and Participation: How do children and parents experience child protection?" aims at closing this research gap. The following section gives insight into the findings of an in-depth investigation of children's and parents' interactions and communication with Swiss CAPAs, obtained through the analysis of participant observations of hearings. We first start with a description of our data and analysis methodology. We then focus on two fundamentally relevant themes discovered in the data: information exchange and interactions of recognition between CAPA members and individuals concerned. These two thematic complexes are central, since both information as well as interactions of recognition are seen as prerequisites for full participation as they extend and amplify opportunities to influence the outcome of the proceedings (agency). Further steps in our project will include qualitative interviews, questionnaires and focus groups.

4.1. Methodological Approach

We used participant observation as a method for qualitative data collection. Our main epistemological interest for the participant observations was to identify typical interactions and communications between CAPA members and parents and children. In line with Garfinkel's understanding of ethnomethodology, the aim was to grasp the production of "social reality of everyday activities". The stance of our observing researchers can be described as "passive participation", naively documenting the unknown (Spradley 1980; Pollner and Emerson 2001, pp. 121–25). The observed hearings were documented on the spot in the form of handwritten field notes (observation protocols). The field notes were taken in a structured manner, guided by an observation grid to augment verification and replication and to reduce researchers' bias (Angrosino and Perez 2000; Kawulich 2005). The common criteria for reliable and ethically sound field notes were followed with the observation grid (DeWalt and DeWalt 1998; Kawulich 2005; Merriam 1988; Olivier de Sardan 2008; Schensul et al. 1999). The mere and exact description of interactions in the order in which they occurred, including the exact time, were made. The participants present, a description of them, a spatial map indicating where individuals were seated, the physical surrounding and setting, informal exchanges and the researchers' personal feelings were noted too.

The participant observation was conducted by one or two experienced researchers over a period of eight months in 2019. Altogether, the sample consists of 24 hearings in 19 different cases in four CAPAs, covering a high degree of diversity in potential child endangerment situations, varying in intensity and severity. It is worth mentioning that we found that the four CAPAs varied in their degree of formality and structuring of the hearings and also differed in their organizational procedures.

Data were systematically coded using QDA software. For the analysis of the participant observations, we followed propositions of thematic analyses (Braun and Clarke 2006), with the aim of identifying themes in the data which are important in relation to the research question. Given the nexus of integrity, autonomy and participation as our focal point, we were interested in identifying themes relating to these three key concepts ("keyness" being a guiding principle to build codes and detect themes) (Braun and Clarke 2006, p. 82). We followed an "inductive development" of codes directly derived from the data; at the same time, our work was theoretically informed (ibid., p. 83). We focused on a "latent level" to identify relevant codes and themes, following a "constructionist perspective" to analyze the social production and structural conditions of the observed interactions (ibid., pp. 84–85).

Using a thematic analysis-inspired approach to analyze our data, two researchers worked as a team to elaborate thematic codes by coding the field notes of 24 hearings in 19 different cases in four CAPAs. Each code contained an "interesting aspect" and consisted of a thorough definition and coding rule, stemming from the data (Braun and Clarke 2006, p. 89). Based on the created codes, "themes" were identified which formed a "repeated pattern" and summarized interrelated sub-code-sets ("sub-themes") (ibid., pp. 89, 90). Working as a team during the coding development stage is a well-known strategy to ensure the reliability of the coding system (Armstrong et al. 1997). Within recurrent feedback loops with other researchers from the project team, the coding system was validated, refined and eventually regrouped into main themes. In fact, minor adjustments within the coding system were made throughout the whole coding process, to ensure that we grasped all important aspects contained in the data. Hence, we carried out the coding in an "ongoing organic" and "recursive process" (Braun and Clarke 2006, pp. 86, 91). This first analysis stage resulted in a coding system with ten main "themes" consisting of the following sub-code-sets: power dynamics, signs of recognition, expression of emotions, cooperation behaviors, negotiations around the problem definition, life domains, characteristics of the proceedings, definition of roles and perception of child protection.

4.2. Results: "Information Exchange" and "Signs of Recognition" during the Hearings of Parents and Children

As previously stated, the CAPA is the decision-making body for statutory child protection measures. The CAPA members make decisions on the basis of the assessment report (which is often produced by an external social service agency) and of the hearing with the concerned persons. Overall, our observations strongly support conceptualizations of decision-making in child protection, which emphasizes the procedural nature of such decisions (Bastian 2019; Forkby and Höjer 2011; Helm and Roesch-Marsh 2016; Pomey 2017).

Based on the analysis of participant observations of hearings, we highlight two crucial themes which are highly relevant in order to understand interactions in terms of their potential to facilitate participation: information exchange and signs of recognition. Information exchange encompasses all exchanges between parents and children and CAPA members related to the child protection proceedings. Signs of recognition are organized into three groups—those related to legal rights, those related to love and those related to solidarity. We show how these were displayed by the authorities and responded to by the persons concerned and discuss their overall impact on participation.

Regarding information exchange, findings show that key information was systematically given orally by the CAPA to parents and children, mostly at the beginning of hearings but also frequently in interactions during the conversation. Information on the following issues was identified: the CAPA's tasks and organization; potential child protection measures; stages of the decision-making process; child protection procedure in general; legal rights and duties. This information exchange could be observed in all cases.

In only one observed case was printed information in the form of an information brochure handed out to parents at the hearing[3]. Information on the aspects mentioned was not only given to parents and children by the CAPA members but sometimes the individuals concerned also actively asked for it. A broad range of ways in which parents and children acted out their agency was observed, ranging from parents requesting an additional hearing in order to influence the intended decision to parents who remained more passive and did not take any anticipatory actions. In one case with two young parents-to-be, this exploration of their scope of action was very marked, since they actively and variously asked for the concrete consequences if they would not comply or would only partly comply with the CAPA. The CAPA members used this situation to repeatedly underline that, if at all possible, they would clearly aim for consensual agreements with the parents, but they also mentioned that they had the authority to make non-consensual decisions. We also observed wide variation in parents' and children's understanding of the child protection proceedings. Given the complexity of the child protection system and time constraints, we could document that misunderstandings happen at various stages of the hearing. While some misunderstandings were acknowledged by the CAPA members and resolved, others remained unnoticed. A commonly observed confusion was regarding the question of whether decisions had already been made or if the negotiation of the decision was still ongoing. We observed that the CAPA members tried to clarify this point, either by bringing it up by themselves or in reaction to parents explicitly expressing confusion over the stages of the decision-making process.

The analysis of information exchange leads us to the issue of the explicit recognition of legal rights. It is important to recall that the Child and Adult Protection Authority is structurally positioned within the family law system and is entitled to make statutory child protection decisions. The persons present at the hearings have thus been guaranteed the formal legal "right to be heard" by the CAPA. We repeatedly observed CAPA members referring to or explaining the legal framework to parents and children—for example, by informing them of their right to appeal against the decision or that the decision can only be taken by a quorum of three CAPA members, not merely by one. In Honneth's understanding (Honneth 1995), this can be read as a sign of recognition in the sphere of "rights", which encompasses the equality of people in terms of rights and fosters self-respect. We did not observe open exclusion of individuals from their rights, but we noticed some practices which could potentially lead to more subtle forms of denial. A quite commonly observed example of this could be seen when the CAPA requested parents to release professionals from their obligation to maintain confidentiality so that they could contact them regarding the child protection proceedings. In formal legal terms, it is correct to ask the parents to give their consent to release professionals from their obligation to maintain confidentiality. Interestingly, consent is usually reached quite incidentally, which, in one case

---

[3]   In this analysis, we did not include written communication such as the CAPA's invitation letter to the parents, which probably already contains information on the child protection proceedings.

(second hearing), led to open criticism by a mother who felt that she had lost control over her personal information and felt passed over. The CAPA member tried to restore the mother's lost confidence in the CAPA by giving her further information on her right to define the exact scope of application which the release of obligation to maintain confidentiality encompasses.

Displaying legal authority by the CAPA can translate into signs of a lack of recognition and put a strain on the relationship. For instance, we observed that parents and children could perceive CAPA members mentioning legal obligations (such as the legal duty of parents to cooperate in the child protection proceedings) or describing possible legal consequences (such as mandated child protection measures against the will of the parents) as a threat that undermined their participatory agency. Hence, the recognition of parents and children on a legal level seems to be a sensitive issue. We also identified situations in which parents and children actively requested information on the legal framework of child protection proceedings. For example, a 14-year-old girl asked if her parents were allowed to decide against her will that she could not move out of the family home.

Apart from information exchange and the recognition of rights, two other forms of recognition proved to be critical to understanding the dynamics of hearings: recognition in terms of "love" and recognition in terms of "solidarity" (Honneth 1995). As delineated in the theoretical reflections, we conceptualize recognition as an integral part of integrity.

In the context of child protection, love is close to empathy and is an expression of a respectful and trusting relationship between the authorities and the persons concerned. Empathy was shown at different levels during hearings. Different behaviors expressed by CAPA members were indicators of such recognition: thanking parents and children for their presence; looking out for their physical well-being by offering them a glass of water; acknowledging signs of distress when someone was overcome by emotions. Even if parents and children are invited to a hearing by the CAPA, the observed practice of thanking parents and children for their attendance (instead of just greeting them) is a way to acknowledge them as individuals and to somewhat reduce the distance between persons concerned and the authorities. These behaviors seemed to have a positive impact on the interactions, helping to release tension and improve open communication. In contrast, ignoring tears or statements about not feeling well, interrupting explanations or correcting language errors had a negative impact. For instance, some CAPA members reformulated statements for the minute-taker (e.g., translating common terms to adequate legal terms, translating spoken terms to more formal written terms). This practice was perceived as unsettling by some parents who were interrupted and lost the train of their thoughts. Recognition of love/empathy is directly linked to people's self-confidence, and self-confidence increased or decreased as a result.

The third group of signs of recognition is related to solidarity, which encompassed being respectful of other people's opinions, attitudes, skills and roles or status. Parents and children were very sensitive to their views being understood and respected by the CAPA members. Interestingly, it seemed that obtaining the CAPA's approval was not the crucial point but rather listening attentively and acknowledging their perspective. Very simple and clear sentences like "I understand" and "Yes, it is difficult" seemed to foster feelings of recognition and enhance self-esteem. For instance, acknowledgments of the challenges of being a parent were met with relief by distressed parents who could more easily disclose their problems as a result. Solidarity was also shown the other way around when parents recognized that they had a need for support or agreed with an offer of support made by the authorities. CAPA members seemed to feel encouraged to have a supportive attitude and enhance cooperation as opposed to exerting power strategies. Moreover, we noticed that the most participative way to negotiate potential measures with parents or children was enhanced by formulations such as "what kind of support would you need?" rather than already suggesting a concrete measure. Indeed, this allows for a common definition of needs and potential solutions. In this regard, such open formulations are a recognition of the opinions of the persons concerned.

The opposite of solidarity was likely to happen in hearings with signs of disapproval, when parents' opinions were dismissed, delegitimized or contradicted. CAPA members would sometimes feel the need to correct or rectify parents' statements with the aim of fact-checking, establishing the truth or on moral grounds. Interestingly, however, it is possible to acknowledge a different opinion without approving it, as this may be enough to create a feeling of recognition and self-esteem. In one case, parents were expressing their disapproval of homosexuality based on their religious values. Two CAPA members challenged their view on two dimensions: human rights and a different interpretation of religious beliefs. The debate was heated and heading nowhere. A third CAPA member eventually stepped in and stated their respect for the parents' different views on this matter and then suggested focusing on the child's well-being and school achievement for the time being. This statement of recognition was enough to move the discussion forward and then to allow the parents to accept a child protection measure.

5. Discussion

The analysis indicates that there is a lack of information on the side of parents and children even in cases where CAPA members seem to follow the relevant organizational standard procedures to provide such information: for children and parents, it is often not clear what exactly the CAPA does, which stage of the decision-making process they are at, which measures the CAPA can take and what they potentially entail. In addition, the emotional dimension may make children and parents less able to process crucial information and to reflect rationally on their options. Subsequently, a full understanding of the child protection proceedings might be lacking in many cases. The hearing consequently must be understood as a situation where parents receive and have to process new information. The hearing can therefore be seen as a constitutive moment for parents and children as they make sense of their situation and the child protection proceedings and form their opinion. This adds to the original objective of hearings: giving the opportunity to bring in the perspective of the individuals concerned, their opinions and wishes and to discuss and negotiate the action to be taken. Not only are parents expected to give an account of their point of view but at the same time they have to explore the limitations of the context and their possible range of action by asking questions.

The hearing has the function of the legal instruction of the persons concerned on their rights and duties, which clarifies legal boundaries and opportunities for possible actions. As in the example mentioned, we observed that clarification of legal rights was often made in reaction to a comment or a question by parents or children but not systematically, since it is considered impossible to inform them about all their rights. It further remains unclear how well parents and children are informed in respect to their legal rights and duties, as the responsibility to make sure all individuals are equally informed of their rights and guaranteed the same rights is left fully to the CAPA. This may reproduce (or create) inequalities in understanding the child protection proceedings between individuals who are able and dare to actively seek information and less proactive individuals.

These results illustrate why being informed and understanding is such a crucial point for participation in child protection proceedings: as long as parents and children do not fully understand and are not well informed about the proceedings, their rights and duties, potential measures and their consequences or the CAPA's tasks, it is hard for them to know their scope of action (autonomy within the proceedings) and hence to fully participate. In addition, it is problematic if parents and children do not know which stage of the decision-making process they are at, since they do not recognize when they are at a crucial point at which they can influence the decision. Consequently, their agency can be considered restricted.

Overall, we observed signs of recognition in all cases but also signs of a lack of recognition in hearings. This might reflect the seemingly contradictory mission of the CAPA of protecting children and intervening in the family sphere if the child's well-being is endangered. They can, or sometimes have to, use their legal authority to impose constraining measures if individuals do not comply to ensure the child's well-being. Hence, the CAPA members are challenged to ensure parents' and children's participation by allowing a relationship of recognition (integrity) and providing a high level of information.

As in any qualitative study based on participant observation, the generalization of our results has some limitations. We have observed sequences of the everyday practice of four CAPAs located in two different language regions in Switzerland, in rural and urban settings. Even if our research sites have contrasting differences in relevant dimensions, the generalizability of the results presented above is limited. The "Intapart" research project will move on to explore in depth what children and parents experienced as supporting or hampering their integrity, autonomy and participation in their contact with the CAPA with qualitative interviews and focus groups and, later on, with a quantitative survey using questionnaires.

6. Conclusions

From the adoption of the Swiss civil code in 1912 to the reform of 2013, the Swiss child protection system has gone through tremendous changes, from systematic disregard for the integrity, autonomy and participation of parents and children in the past, towards an orientation that puts the persons concerned more and more at its heart. We propose a legally and historically informed perspective on child protection that builds the foundation for critical reflection and an analysis of current welfare practices and policies. It thereby aims to raise the awareness of child protection professionals regarding the conditions and settings that encourage and support the full participation of children and parents. This perspective further underlines the need for empirical knowledge on people's perspectives as the basis for the development of effective and sustainable practices in child protection proceedings, which secure the integrity, autonomy and participation of children and parents.

As our empirical analysis of the current practices of hearings at the Child and Adult Protection Authorities (CAPAs) in Switzerland shows, many parents and children entering the hearing do not seem to be well-enough informed. Collecting, processing and using information to identify one's scope of action within the child protection proceedings seems to be a central issue during hearings. Hearings should therefore be understood as situations of information exchange at multiple levels: informing parents and children about the child protection proceedings, the CAPA's tasks and potential measures, rights and duties and clarifying the stage within the decision-making process. Being informed and understanding the situation and one's rights and duties is crucial, since it is a prerequisite to forming and express one's opinion (acting autonomously) and to participating within a given structure. If parents and children experience recognition in the form of empathic and respectful interactions with the CAPA (integrity), they seem more likely to be at ease and able to participate. This means that CAPA members find themselves in very demanding situations when they interact with parents and children: they need to be highly sensitive to signs of misunderstanding, lack of information or discomfort and should be able to establish a relationship of recognition, i.e., to guarantee their interlocutors' integrity. Furthermore, when parents and children experience recognition through the assistance that child protection provides them in (re-)establishing supporting relationships, they are likely to be empowered to take "reasonable" decisions to live a self-determined life without state intrusion (autonomy).

Fostering participation in child protection proceedings should further be characterized by a power-sensitive approach, facilitating dialogical work with the concerned children and parents. Indeed, the establishment of a dialogic form of conversation can be a helpful starting point to establish full participation and a foundation for a relationship of recognition (Husby et al. 2019). Dialog can be understood as the production of shared meaning, not merely the understanding of one another's standpoint within a conversation. Hence, dialogic conversation suggests questioning existing assumptions, understandings and prejudices and shifts the perspective towards change (Graham and Fitzgerald 2010; Biesel et al. 2017). This aligns well with Habermas' concept of deliberation (Habermas 1981) and the basic idea "that in order to make legitimate decisions, one has to engage the people affected by these decisions in deliberating on what ought to be done" (Willumsen and Skivenes 2005, p. 198). Also referring to Habermas, Duncan sees the communication between children and professionals in child protection as systematically distorted by the power asymmetry between adults and children—for instance, by adults' power to judge what children say. A less distorted situation of communication could be achieved if everyone had the "same opportunity to talk and listen" and the same "right to question and answer". This would also limit the risk of trying to persuade others but instead facilitate the convincing of others of a better argument (Duncan 2019, p. 147).

With our study, we hope to contribute to the development of sustainable child protection proceedings that provide effective support for children and parents, guaranteeing their integrity by allowing for the interaction of mutual recognition and making sufficient information available to the persons concerned for full participation in the child protection system.

Author Contributions: Conceptualization, A.S., G.A., B.M., K.B. and S.S.; methodology, A.S., G.A., B.M., L.S., K.B., M.C., G.S. and S.S.; formal analysis, A.S., G.A., B.M., L.S. and G.S.; investigation, A.S., G.A., B.M., L.S. and G.S.; writing original draft preparation, A.S., G.A., B.M., L.S., K.B., M.C., G.S. and S.S.; writing—review and editing, A.S., G.A., B.M., L.S., K.B., M.C., G.S. and S.S.; project administration, M.C., K.B. and S.S.; funding acquisition, M.C., K.B. and S.S. All authors have read and agreed to the published version of the manuscript.

Funding: This research was funded by the Swiss National Science Foundation (SNSF) grant number 407640_177445.

Acknowledgments: We first would like to thank all participants and partners for their engagement to realize this research project. We are also thankful for the support and commitment of the interns Aude Saugy and Mathilde Etienne and would like to thank Margaret Oertig for proofreading.

Conflicts of Interest: The authors declare no conflict of interest.

References

Affolter, Kurt. 2013. Die Totalrevision des Vormundschaftsrechts [The complete revision of the guardianship law]. *SozialAktuell* 45: 10–14.

Akermann, Martina, Markus Furrer, and Sabine Jenzer. 2012. *Bericht Kinderheime im Kanton Luzern im Zeitraum von 1930–1970 [Report Children's homes in the canton of Lucerne in the period 1930–1970]*. Luzern: Gesundheits- und Sozialdepartement des Kantons Luzern.

Alanen, Leena. 1988. Rethinking childhood. *Acta Sociologica* 31: 53–67. [CrossRef]

Ambert, Anne-Marie. 1986. Sociology of Sociology: The Place of Children in North American Sociology. *Sociological Studies of Child Development* 1: 11–31.

Anderson, Joel H., and Axel Honneth. 2005. Autonomy, Vulnerability, Recognition, and Justice. In *Autonomy and the Challenges to Liberalism: New Essays*. Edited by John Christman and Joel H. Anderson. New York: Cambridge University Press, pp. 127–49. Available online: http://dspace.library.uu.nl/handle/1874/20309 (accessed on 6 January 2020).

Angrosino, Michael V., and Kimberly A. Mays de Perez. 2000. Rethinking observation: From method to context. In *Handbook of Qualitative Research*, 2nd ed. Edited by Norman K. Denzin and Yvonna S. Lincoln. Thousand Oaks: Sage Publications, pp. 673–702.

Armstrong, David, Ann Gosling, John Weinman, and Theresa Marteau. 1997. The Place of Inter-Rater Reliability in Qualitative Research: An Empirical Study. *Sociology* 31: 597–606. [CrossRef]

Bastian, Pascal. 2019. *Sozialpädagogische Entscheidungen [Decison-Making in Social-Pedagogy]*. Opladen and Toronto: Barbara Budrich.

Becker-Lenz, Roland, and Silke Müller-Hermann. 2013. Die Notwendigkeit von wissenschaftlichem Wissen und die Bedeutung eines professionellen Habitus für die Berufspraxis der Sozialen Arbeit [The need for scientific knowledge and the importance of a professional habitus for the professional practice of social work.]. In *Professionalität in der Sozialen Arbeit [Professionalism in Social Work]*. Edited by Roland Becker-Lenz, Stefan Busse, Gudrun Ehlert and Silke Müller-Hermann. Wiesbaden: VS Verlag für Sozialwissenschaften, pp. 203–29. [CrossRef]

Biesel, Kay, Lukas Fellmann, Brigitte Müller, Clarissa Schär, and Stefan Schnurr. 2017. *Prozessmanual: Dialogisch-Systemische Kindeswohlabklärung [Process Manual: Dialogic-Systemic Assessment of the Well-Being of the Child]*. Bern: Haupt Verlag.

Biesel, Kay. 2016. Chancen und Risiken von Kinderrechten im Kinderschutz [Opportunities and risks of children's rights in child protection]. In *Kinderrechte als Fixstern Moderner Pädagogik? Grundlagen, Praxis, Perspektiven [Children's Rights as a Fixed Star of Modern Pedagogy? Basics, Practice, Perspectives]*. Edited by Luise Hartwig, Gerald Mennen and Christian Schrapper. Weinheim Basel: Beltz Juventa, pp. 241–49.

Bouma, Helen, Mónica López López, Erik J. Knorth, and Hans Grietens. 2018. Meaningful participation for children in the Dutch child protection system: A critical analysis of relevant provisions in policy documents. *Child Abuse & Neglect* 79: 279–92. [CrossRef]

Braun, Virginia, and Victoria Clarke. 2006. Using Thematic Analysis in Psychology. *Qualitative Research in Psychology* 3: 77–101. [CrossRef]

Bühler-Niederberger, Doris. 2010. Introduction: Childhood Sociology—Defining the State of the Art and Ensuring Reflection. *Current Sociology* 58: 155–64. [CrossRef]

Bundesrat. 2017. *Erste Erfahrungen mit dem Neuen Kindes- und Erwachsenenschutzrecht: Bericht des Bundesrates in Erfüllung der Postulate 14.3776, 14.3891, 14.4113 und 15.3614 [Initial Experiences with the New Law in Child and Adult Protection: Report of the Federal Council Answering the Parliamentary Postulates 14.3776, 14.3891, 14.4113 und 15.3614].* Bern: Schweizerische Eidgenossenschaft.

Bütow, Birgit, Marion Pomey, Myriam Rutschmann, Clarissa Schär, and Tobias Studer, eds. 2014. *Sozialpädagogik Zwischen Staat und Familie. Alte und Neue Politiken des Eingreifens [Social Pedagogy between State and Families. Old and New Policies of Intervention].* Wiesbaden: VS Verlag für Sozialwissenschaften.

Corsaro, William A. 1997. *The Sociology of Childhood.* Thousand Oaks: Pine Forge Press.

Cossar, Jeanette, Marian Brandon, and Peter Jordan. 2016. 'You've got to trust her and she's got to trust you': Children's views on participation in the child protection system. *Child & Family Social Work* 21: 103–12. [CrossRef]

Cottier, Michelle, and Daniel Steck. 2012. Das Verfahren vor der Kindes- und Erwachsenenschutzbehörde [Procedures before the Child and Adult Protection Authority]. *Praxis des Familienrechts* 13: 981–1000.

Cottier, Michelle. 2008. Verfahrensvertretung des Kindes im Familienrecht der Schweiz: aktuelle Rechtslage und Reformbedarf [Legal representation of the child in Swiss family law: Current legal situation and need for reform]. In *Anwalt des Kindes. Ein Europäischer Vergleich zum Recht des Kindes auf Eigene Vertretung in Behördlichen und Gerichtlichen Verfahren [Advocate for the Child. A European Comparison on the Right of the Child to be Represented in Administrative and Judicial Proceedings].* Edited by Stefan Blum, Michelle Cottier and Daniela Migliazza. Bern: Stämpfli, pp. 125–52.

Cottier, Michelle. 2017. L'enfant sujet de droit: bilan mitigé de la jurisprudence récente du Tribunal fédéral suisse [The child as a subject of law: a mixed record of the recent jurisprudence of the Swiss Federal Court]. In *Le Droit en Question [The Law in Question].* Edited by Audrey Leuba, Marie-Laure Papaux Van Delden and Bénédict Foëx. Geneva: Schulthess éd. Romandes, pp. 81–100. Available online: https://archive-ouverte.unige.ch/unige:92956 (accessed on 6 January 2020).

De Singly, François. 2000. Penser autrement la jeunesse [Thinking differently about youth]. *Lien Social et Politiques* 43: 9–21.

DeWalt, Kathleen M., and Billie R. DeWalt. 1998. Participant observation. In *Handbook of Methods in Cultural Anthropology.* Edited by H. Russell Bernard. Walnut Creek: AltaMira Press, pp. 259–300.

Dillon, Jo, Daz Greenop, and Mel Hills. 2016. Participation in child protection: A small-scale qualitative study. *Qualitative Social Work: Research and Practice* 15: 70–85. [CrossRef]

Dillon, Jo. 2018. 'Revolutionizing' Participation in Child Protection Proceedings. Ph.D. dissertation, Liverpool John Moores University, Liverpool, UK, December. Available online: https://pdfs.semanticscholar.org/efb5/0af382519e9861072fb10cf3d9fdc8b76960.pdf (accessed on 9 March 2020).

Direktion der Justiz und des Inneren. 2016. *Aufsichtsrechtliche Würdigung der Handlungsweise der KESB Winterthur-Andelfingen im Fall Flaach [Regulatory appraisal of the CAPA's conduct in the Flaach Case].* Zürich: Kanton Zürich, Direktion der Justiz und des Inneren als Aufsichtsbehörde im Kindes- und Erwachsenenschutz.

Duerr Berrick, Jill. 2018. *The Impossible Imperative. Navigating the Competing Principles of Child Protection.* Oxford: Oxford University Press.

Dumbrill, Gary C. 2006. Parental experience of child protection intervention: A qualitative study. *Child Abuse & Neglect* 30: 27–37. [CrossRef]

Duncan, Mandy. 2019. *Participation in Child Protection. Theorizing Children's Perspectives.* Basingstoke: Palgrave Macmillan.

Esser, Florian, Meike S. Baader, Tanja Betz, and Beatrice Hungerland. 2016. *Reconceptualising Agency and Childhood: New Perspectives in Childhood Studies.* London: Routledge.

Fassbind, Patrick. 2013. Kantonale und innerkantonale Buntheit—Die Organisation der Kindes- und Erwachsenenschutzbehörden in der Schweiz [Cantonal and inner-cantonal colorfulness—The organization of child and adult protection authorities in Switzerland]. *SozialAktuell* 45: 15–17.

Forkby, Torbjörn, and Staffan Höjer. 2011. Navigations between regulations and gut instinct: the unveiling of collective memory in decision-making processes where teenagers are placed in residential care. *Child & Family Social Work* 16: 159–68. [CrossRef]

Freisler-Mühlemann, Daniela. 2011. *Verdingkinder—Ein Leben auf der Suche nach Normalität [Indentured Child Laborers—A Life in Search of Normality].* Bern: HEP.

Furrer, Markus, Kevin Heiniger, Thomas Huonker, Sabine Jenzer, and Anne-Françoise Praz. 2014. Einleitung [Introduction]. In *Fürsorge und Zwang: Fremdplatzierung von Kindern und Jugendlichen in der Schweiz 1850–1980 [Welfare and Coercion: Placing Children in Care in Switzerland 1850–1980].* Edited by Markus Furrer, Kevin Heiniger, Thomas Huonker, Sabine Jenzer and Anne-Françoise Praz. Basel: Schwabe, pp. 7–23.

Graham, Anne, and Robyn Fitzgerald. 2010. Progressing children's participation: Exploring the potential of a dialogical turn. *Childhood* 17: 343–59. [CrossRef]

Guggisberg, Ernst, and Marco Dal Molin. 2019. *Zehntausende. Zahlen zur Administrativen Versorgung und zur Anstaltslandschaft ["Tens of Thousands". Figures on Administrative Detention and on the Institutional Care Landscape].* Chronos Verlag, Éditions Alphil, Edizioni Casagrande. Zürich, Neuchâtel and Bellinzona: Independent Expert Commission (IEC) on Administrative Detention, vol. 6.

Guggisberg, Ernst. 2014. 'Brauchbare Glieder der Volksgemeinschaft'. Rezeption vereinsgetragener Fremdplatzierung anhand der Solothurner Armenerziehungsvereine, 1880–1930 ['Useful members of society'. Reception of placements conducted by charity associations using the example of the 'associations for the education of the poor' in the canton of Solothurn, 1880–1930]. In *Fürsorge und Zwang: Fremdplatzierung von Kindern und Jugendlichen in der Schweiz 1850–1980 [Welfare and Coercion: Placing Children in Care in Switzerland 1850–1980].* Edited by Markus Furrer, Kevin Heiniger, Thomas Huonker, Sabine Jenzer and Anne-Françoise Praz. Basel: Schwabe, pp. 181–92.

Habermas, Jürgen. 1981. *Theorie des Kommunikativen Handelns. [Theory of Communicative Action].* Frankfurt: Suhrkamp.

Häsler, Mirjam. 2008. *In Fremden Händen: Die Lebensumstände von Kost- und Pflegekindern in Basel vom Mittelalter bis heute [In the Hands of Strangers: The Living Condition of Placed Children in Basel from the Medieval Times to the Present].* Basel: Schwabe.

Healy, Karen, and Yvonne Darlington. 2009. Service user participation in diverse child protection contexts: Principles for practice. *Child & Family Social Work* 14: 420–30. [CrossRef]

Helm, Duncan, and Autumn Roesch-Marsh. 2016. The Ecology of Judgement: A Model for Understanding and Improving Social Work Judgements. *The British Journal of Social Work* 47: 1361–76. [CrossRef]

Hillmann, Karl-Heinz. 1994. *Wörterbuch der Soziologie [Dictionary of Sociology],* 4th ed. Stuttgart: Alfred Kröner Verlag.

Hitz Quenon, Nicole, and Fanny Matthey. 2017. *Une Justice Adaptée aux Enfants. L'audition lors d'un Placement en Droit Civil et Lors du Renvoi d'un Parent en Droit des étrangers [Child-Friendly Justice. The Hearing in Case of a Placement under Civil Law and Due to the Expulsion of a Parent under Migration Law].* Bern: Schweizerisches Kompetenzzentrum für Menschenrechte.

Hitz Quenon, Nicole, Eric Paulus, and Laure Luchetta Myit. 2014. *Le Droit de Protection de l'enfant. Les Premiers Effets de la Mise en Oeuvre dans les Cantons de Genève, Vaud et Zurich [Child Protection Law. First Effects in the Cantons Geneva, Vaud and Zurich].* Bern: Swiss Centre of Expertise in Human Rights (SCHR), Available online: http://www.skmr.ch/cms/upload/pdf/150409_Studie_Kindesschutzrecht.pdf (accessed on 9 March 2020).

Honneth, Axel. 1995. *The Struggle for Recognition: The Moral Grammar of Social Conflicts.* Cambridge: MIT Press.

Husby, Inger Sofie Dahlø, Riina Kiik, and Randi Juul. 2019. Children's encounters with professionals—Recognition and respect during collaboration. *European Journal of Social Work* 22: 987–98. [CrossRef]

Husby, Inger Sofie Dahlø, Tor Slettebø, and Randi Juul. 2018. Partnerships with children in child welfare: The importance of trust and pedagogical support. *Child & Family Social Work* 23: 443–50. [CrossRef]

Independent Expert Commission (IEC) on Administrative, Detention, ed. 2019. *Organisierte Willkür. Administrative Versorgungen in der Schweiz 1930–1981 (V. 10) [Organized arbitrariness. Administrative detention in Switzerland 1930–1981].* Zürich, Neuenburg and Lumino: Chronos Verlag, Éditions Alphil, Edizioni Casagrande.

Join-Lambert Milova, Hélène. 2006. Autonomie et participation d'adolescents placés en foyer (France, Allemagne, Russie) [Autonomy and participation of adolescents in residential care (France, Germany, Russia)]. *Sociétés et Jeunesses en Difficulté.* Available online: http://sejed.revues.org/index188.html (accessed on 9 March 2020).

Kawulich, Barbara B. 2005. Participant Observation as a Data Collection Method. *Forum: Qualitative Social Research* 6. [CrossRef]

KOKES Konferenz für Kindes- und Erwachsenenschutz. 2017. *KESB: Organisation in den Kantonen [CAPA: Organization in the Cantons].* (Stand 01.01.2017). Available online: https://www.kokes.ch/application/files/5214/9027/3916/KOKES_KESB_Organisation_Kantone_ZKE_1-2017.pdf (accessed on 9 March 2020).

Kuhlman, Kate Ryan, Andreas Maercker, Rahel Bachem, Keti Simmen, and Andrea Burri. 2013. Developmental and Contextual Factors in the Role of Severe Childhood Trauma in Geriatric Depression: The Sample Case of Former Indentured Child Laborers. *Child Abuse & Neglect* 37: 969–78. [CrossRef]

Lansdown, Gerison. 2010. The realisation of children's participation rights: Critical reflections. In *A Handbook of Children and Young People's Participation.* Edited by Barry Percy-Smith and Nigel Thomas. London and New York: Routledge, pp. 11–23.

Leuenberger, Marco, and Loretta Seglias. 2008. *Versorgt und Vergessen. Ehemalige Verdingkinder Erzählen [Placed and Forgotten. Former Indentured Child Laborers Tell Their Stories].* Zürich: Rotpunktverlag.

Leuenberger, Marco, and Loretta Seglias. 2015. *Geprägt fürs Leben. Lebenswelten Fremdplatzierter Kinder in der Schweiz im 20. Jahrhundert [Marked for Life. The Lives and Experiences of Placed Children in Switzerland in the 20th Century].* Zürich: Chronos.

Leuenberger, Marco, Lea Mani, Simone Rudin, and Loretta Seglias. 2011. *'Die Behörde Beschliesst'—Zum Wohl des Kindes? Fremdplatzierte Kinder im Kanton Bern 1912–1987 ['The Authority Decides'—For the Well-Being of the Child? Children Placed in Care in the Canton of Berne 1912–1978].* Baden: hier + jetzt.

Mazza Muschietti, Eva. 2016. *Lebensbewältigung nach Zwangsmassnahmen und Fremdplatzierungen. Eine Vergleichende Analyse Ausgewählter Autobiographien von Betroffenen im Lichte der Resilienzforschung [Coping with Life after Coercive Welfare Measures and Placements. A Comparative Analysis of Selected Autobiographies in the Perspective of Research on Resilience].* Lausanne: IDHEAP Institut de Hautes études en Administration Publique, Université de Lausanne.

Merriam, Sharan B. 1988. *Case Study Research in Education: A Qualitative Approach.* San Francisco: Jossey-Bass Publishers.

Müller, Brigitte, Kay Biesel, and Clarissa Schär. 2020. Errors and Mistakes in Child Protection in Switzerland: A Missed Opportunity of Reflection? In *Errors and Mistakes in Child Protection. International Discourses, Approaches and Strategies.* Edited by Kay Biesel, Judith Masson, Nigel Parton and Tarja Pösö. Bristol: Policy Press, pp. 153–72. [CrossRef]

Nett, Jachen, and Spratt Trevor, eds. 2012. *An International Study Comparing Child Protection Systems from Five Countries (Australia, Finland, Germany, Sweden, United Kingdom) That Provides Scientifically Founded Recommendations for Improving Child Protection in Switzerland.* Bern: Programme National Pour la Protection de l'Enfant.

Olivier de Sardan, Jean-Pierre. 2008. *La Rigueur du Qualitatif: Les Contraintes Empiriques de l'interprétation Socio-Anthropologique [The Rigor of the Qualitative: The Empirical Constraints of Socio-Anthropological Interpretation].* Anthropologie Prospective 3. Louvain-la-Neuve: Academia-Bruylant.

Pollner, Melvin, and Robert M. Emerson. 2001. Ethnomethodology and Ethnography. In *Handbook of Ethnography.* Edited by Paul Atkinson, Amanda Coffey, Sara Delamont, John Lofland and Lyn Lofland. London: Sage Publications, pp. 118–35. [CrossRef]

Pomey, Marion. 2017. *Vulnerabilität und Fremdunterbringung. Eine Studie zur Entscheidungspraxis bei Kindeswohlgefährdung [Vulnerability and Placement in Care. A Study on Decisional Practice in Cases of Children at Risk].* Weinheim and Basel: Beltz Juventa.

Qvortrup, Jens. 1987. Introduction to Sociology of Childhood. *International Journal of Sociology* 17: 3–37. [CrossRef]

Raithelhuber, Eberhard, and Wolfgang Schröer. 2018. Agency [Agency]. In *Handbuch Soziale Arbeit [Handbook of Social Work].* Edited by Hans-Uwe Otto, Hans Thiersch, Rainer Treptow and Holger Ziegler. München: Ernst Reinhardt Verlag, pp. 49–58.

Ramsauer, Nadja. 2000. *'Verwahrlost': Kindswegnahmen und die Entstehung der Jugendfürsorge im Schweizerischen Sozialstaat 1900–1945 ['Neglected': Child Removals and the Development of Child and Youth Welfare in the Swiss Welfare State 1900–1945].* Zürich: Chronos.

Rieder, Stefan, Oliver Bieri, Christoph Schwenkel, Vera Hertig, and Helen Amberg. 2016. *Evaluation Kindes- und Erwachsenenschutzrecht. Analyse der Organisatorischen Umsetzung und Kennzahlen zu Leistungen und Kosten [Evaluation of the Child and Adult Protection Law. Analysis of the Organisational Implementation and Key Figures on Services and Costs].* Luzern: Interface Politikstudien Forschung Beratung, Available online: https://www.bj.admin.ch/bj/de/home/publiservice/publikationen/externe/2016-04-05.html (accessed on 9 March 2020).

Ries, Markus, and Valentin Beck. 2013. *Hinter Mauern. Fürsorge und Gewalt in Kirchlich Geführten Erziehungsanstalten im Kanton Luzern [Behind Walls. Welfare and Violence in Church-Run Reformatories in the Canton of Lucerne].* Zürich: Theologischer Verlag Zürich.

Rietmann, Tanja. 2012. *'Liederlich' und 'Arbeitsscheu'. Die Administrative Anstaltsversorgung im Kanton Bern, 1884–1981* [*'Slovenly' and 'Work-Shy'. Administrative Detention in the Canton of Bern, 1884–1981*]. Zürich: Chronos.

Rosch, Daniel, and Andrea Hauri. 2016. *Begriff und Arten des Kindesschutzes. [Child Protection—Terms and Types]* In *Handbuch Kindes- und Erwachsenenschutz. Recht und Methodik für Fachleute [Handbook on Child and Adult Protection. Law and Methodology for Professionals]*. Edited by Daniel Rosch, Christiana Fountoulakis and Christoph Heck. Bern: Haupt, pp. 406–9.

Rössler, Beate. 2017. *Autonomie: Ein Versuch über das Gelungene Leben [Autonomy—An Essay on the Life Well-Lived]*. Berlin: Suhrkamp.

Schensul, Stephen L., Jean J. Schensul, and Margaret D. LeCompte. 1999. *Essential Ethnographic Methods: Observations, Interviews, and Questionnaires*. Walnut Creek: AltaMira Press.

Schnurr, Stefan. 2017. Child removal proceedings in Switzerland. In *Child Welfare Removals by the State: A Cross-Country Analysis of Decision-Making Systems*. Edited by Kenneth Burns, Tarja Pösö and Marit Skivenes. International Policy Exchange. Oxford and New York: Oxford University Press, pp. 117–45.

Schnyder, Bernhard, Martin Stettler, and Christoph Häfeli. 1995. *Zur Revision des Schweizerischen Vormundschaftsrechts. Bericht der vom Bundesamt für Justiz im Hinblick auf die Revision des Vormundschaftsrechts Eingesetzten Expertengruppe vom Juli 1995 [Revision of the Swiss Guardianship Law: Report of July 1995 by the Expert Group Commissioned by the Federal Office of Justice with a View to Revising Guardianship Law]*. Bern: Bundesamt für Justiz, July 19.

Schoch, Aline, and Brigitte Müller. 2020. *Eingriffe in Familien früher und Heute: Historische Beispiele von Kindswegnahmen und Einblicke in ein Laufendes Forschungsprojekt zur Aktuellen Kinderschutzpraxis in der Schweiz [State Interventions in Families in the Past and Present: Historical Examples of Placements and Insights into an Ongoing Research Project on Current Child Protection Practices in Switzerland]*. Working paper, Sommerhochschule Kindesschutz Bremen, Schriftenreihe Bremer Schriften zur Sozialen Arbeit, City University of Applied Sciences. Bremen: Staats- und Universitätsbibliothek.

Seglias, Loretta. 2013. Heimerziehung—Eine historische Perspektive [Residential care—A historical perspective]. In *Hinter Mauern [Behind Walls]*. Edited by Markus Ries and Valentin Beck. Zürich: Theologischer Verlag Zürich, pp. 19–80.

Spradley, James P. 1980. *Participant Observation*. New York: Holt, Rinehart and Winston.

Steinmann, Gerold. 2014. Anspruch auf rechtliches Gehör (Abs. 2) [The right to be heard]. In *Die schweizerische Bundesverfassung. St. Galler Kommentar [The Swiss Federal Constitution. St. Gallen Comment]*, 2nd ed. Edited by Bernhard Ehrenzeller, Rainer J. Schweizer, Benjamin Schindler and Klaus A. Vallender. Zürich: DIKE, pp. 660–71.

Svevo-Cianci, Kimberly A., Maria Herczog, Lothar Krappmann, and Philip Cook. 2011. The new UN CRC General Comment 13: The right of the child to freedom from all forms of violence—Changing how the world conceptualizes child protection. *Child Abuse & Neglect* 35: 979–89. [CrossRef]

Swiss National Science Foundation (SNSF). 2020. *The NRP*. Available online: http://www.nfp76.ch/en/the-nrp (accessed on 9 March 2020).

Thieme, Nina. 2013. *Kategorisierung in der Kinder- und Jugendhilfe. Zur Theoretischen und Empirischen Erklärung Eines Schlüsselbegriffs Professionellen Handelns [Categorization in Child and Youth Welfare. A Theoretical and Empirical Explanation of a Key Term of Professional Action]*. Weinheim: Juventa.

Tisdall, E. Kay M. 2016. Subjects with agency? Children's participation in family law proceedings. *Journal of Social Welfare and Family Law* 38: 362–79. [CrossRef]

Willumsen, Elisabeth, and Marit Skivenes. 2005. Collaboration between service users and professionals: Legitimate decisions in child protection—A Norwegian model. *Child & Family Social Work* 10: 197–206. [CrossRef]

Wohlwend, Lotty, and Arthur Honegger. 2004. *Gestohlene Seelen: Verdingkinder in der Schweiz [Stolen Souls: Indentured Child Laborers in Switzerland]*. Frauenfeld: Huber.

Wolff, Reinhard, Uwe Flick, Timo Ackermann, Kay Biesel, Felix Brandhorst, Stefan Heinitz, Mareike Patschke, and Pierrine Robin. 2016. *Children in Child Protection. On the Participation of Children and Adolescents in the Helping Process: An Exploratory Study. 2. Contributions to Quality Development in Child Protection*. Köln: National Centre on Early Prevention in Childhood (NZFH) within the Federal Centre for Health Educa-tion (BZgA).

MDPI

St. Alban-Anlage 66

4052 Basel

Switzerland

Tel. +41 61 683 77 34

Fax +41 61 302 89 18

www.mdpi.com

Social Sciences Editorial Office

E-mail: socsci@mdpi.com

www.mdpi.com/journal/socsci

www.ingramcontent.com/pod-product-compliance
Lightning Source LLC
Chambersburg PA
CBHW041609260326
41914CB00012B/1431